Management of Sports Development

Management of Sports Development

Edited by

Vassil Girginov

School of Sport Education, Brunel University

ELSEVIER

Amsterdam • Boston • Heidelberg • London • New York • Oxford
Paris • San Diego • San Francisco • Singapore • Sydney • Tokyo

Butterworth-Heinemann is an imprint of Elsevier

Butterworth-Heinemann is an imprint of Elsevier
Linacre House, Jordan Hill, Oxford OX2 8DP, UK
30 Corporate Drive, Suite 400, Burlington, MA 01803, USA

First edition 2008

Notice
No responsibility is assumed by the publisher for any injury and/or damage to persons
or property as a matter of products liability, negligence or otherwise, or from any use or
operation of any methods, products, instructions or ideas contained in the material herein.

British Library Cataloguing in Publication Data
A catalogue record for this book is available from the British Library

Library of Congress Cataloging-in-Publication Data
A catalog record for this book is available from the Library of Congress

ISBN: 978-0-7506-8562-7

For information on all Butterworth-Heinemann publications
visit our web site at www.elsevierdirect.com

Printed and bound in Italy
08 09 10   10 9 8 7 6 5 4 3 2 1

For Rosi and Katerina for their love and support and for
reasons sometimes they don't understand

Contents

Part Four   Sports Development Delivery   201

List of Tables and Figures

Tables

Figures

Sports development has been enjoying a growing interest in academic, professional and policy circles worldwide. Recently, the social, political and economic importance of sport has been recognized by two major international declarations sponsored by the United Nations (FOSM, Magglingen, 2003 and 2005), whilst the 2006 World Economic Forum in Davos gave prominence to the theme 'The impact of sport in the world'. There is a burgeoning body of literature, academic and vocational courses, and many cities vying to host major events which would go out their way to demonstrate their commitment to sustainable sports development. All this would suggest that the field is undergoing a healthy process of invigoration. Upon closer scrutiny, however, we discover that a range of conceptual and practical uncertainties persist, which create a number of challenges for the management of sports development as an academic subject and a profession.

Writing a text on the management of sports development is a humbling process, yet such a text seems necessary for several reasons. First, most sport development texts have been written from a narrow sport perspective and little attention has been given to the nature of the development enterprise, at the heart of which are the people and not objects or targets. Less still has been said about the management of sports development. Second, a focus on management transcends the established dichotomy of development *through* sport with its emphasis on social objectives and as a tool for human development, and development *of* sport, where sport is valued as an experience for its own sake. It allows examining sports development as a social construct, a set of visions promoted through the policies of various agencies, locally, nationally and internationally; as a process of intended state practice; as a form of relationship between developers and developed; as a specific language with its meaning-generating capacity; and as a set of functions performed by managers. Third, twinning sports development with management helps promote similar studies beyond national boundaries as sports development is as much a local as it is a global issue. Finally, the management of sports development as an academic discipline implies an expressed concern with generating applied knowledge in the form of development policies and implementations. In pursuing those reasons then, the book interrogates the management of sports development as a process of simultaneous destruction of old forms of organization and experiences and the creation of new conditions and opportunities for personal and social improvement. The underlying aim of this book is to extend our knowledge about a relatively under-conceptualized and complex field. It was not conceived as an alternative to existing sport management texts. The book builds on years of experience with the management of development both in the 'developed' North and 'underdeveloped' South, as well as authors' own experiences and intellectual endeavours. These have taught us that main-stream management techniques are not and may be cannot produce the desired developmental outcomes, partly because of the prescribed behavioural patterns they promote and their neglect of local cultures and indigenous knowledge production.

This book advances three key contemporary meanings of sports develop-ment as a *vision* (a desirable end state), process of *social change* and *delivery process* expressed in the deliberate efforts for improvement of human condi-tions. The book recognizes the conceptual and practical complexities of sports development, and in order to respond to its changing interpretations and their implications for management, the 14 original contributions as well as the book's dedicated website (www.sportsdevelopmentbook.com) critically interrogate the interplay between visions setting, social change and sports development practices and offer food for thought for further explorations of the topics. This is achieved with the help of a number of additional resources (e.g., case studies, conference presentations, web links, policy documents and reports and online forums) made available on the book website.

The authors would be grateful if they have succeeded in stimulating further discussions and would equally welcome any critical comments. Nothing could be more rewarding than the thought that this text could help students of sports development and practitioners advance their understanding and perfor-mance in the pursuit of enhancing peoples' lives. I hope you will enjoy turning the pages.

Vassil Girginov
4 December 2007

Acknowledgements

Writing and publishing a book involves a number of people and ideas. First, an acknowledgement is in order of a number of people who I never met but whose ideas and expertise have shaped this book. Secondly, and more importantly, however, is to acknowledge the contribution of those individuals without whom this book would not have been possible. I would like to thank Aaron, Andy, Barrie, Christine, Cora, Emma, Iain, Ian, Kevin, Laura, Mick, Milena, Mike, Nicola, Peter and Roger for their trust in this project and passion about sports development; Ian Campbell for ensuring the support of the School of Sport & Education at Brunel University. In particular, my appreciative thanks are extended to Francesca Ford, acquisitions editor, for her fantastic help and encouragement. Last but not least I would like to thank Rosi for her unpaid editorial assistance.

PART ONE

Management of Sports Development: Visions, Change, Delivery

CHAPTER 1

Management of Sports Development as an Emerging Field and Profession

Vassil Girginov

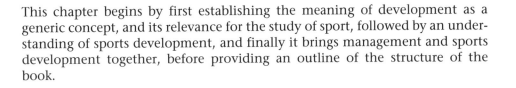

This chapter begins by first establishing the meaning of development as a generic concept, and its relevance for the study of sport, followed by an understanding of sports development, and finally it brings management and sports development together, before providing an outline of the structure of the book.

Development: Origins, Meaning and Paradoxes

Definitions of development abound in the literature, and it is customary for any text on the subject to offer one. However, most writers tend to agree that it is impossible to pin down this concept in a neat definition. It is not the intent of this text to contribute to the existing list of definitions, but rather to conceptualize the meaning of development that would later help establish an understanding of the related concept of sports development.

Development, as Esteva's (1997) elegant analysis demonstrated, is a concept whose historical–political meaning has evolved in the course of 250 years. Various perceptions, events and power relations have shaped it, and as the *Encyclopedia of All Systems of Teaching and Education* published in Germany in 1860 indicated about development 'this concept is applied to almost all that man has and knows' (Esteva, 1997, p. 9). As early as 1878 Eucken noted that the word 'has become almost useless for science, except in certain areas' (cited in Esteva, 1997, p. 9). Eucken's remark is informative here as it expressed a realization that intellectuals', economists' and politicians' preoccupations with development had created conceptual and practical confusion. But what caused the 'uselessness' of this word at the end of the nineteenth century? The answer to this question is critical for understanding the meaning of development.

The first half of the nineteenth century saw the growth of industrial capitalism originally in Great Britain, which then spread throughout Europe, the USA and the rest of the world. This was a process of capitalist expansion and accumulation of wealth and natural resources. It was also a process of social change on a mass scale which built on itself and which was largely responsible for creating new forms of livelihood and aspirations. This social change, which

Cowen and Shenton (1996) termed *immanent* progress, 'implied continual improvement reaching higher and higher levels perhaps without limit' (Thomas, 2000a, p. 25). Immanent progress is spontaneous and associated with development from within – 'a society tendency to change its form' (Barnett, 1988, p. 8), and also entails destruction of old forms of livelihood in order to achieve the new ones.

Industrial progress and growth became a subject of the theory of economic development which established itself in Britain around 1650 and was hugely influenced by the works of Hume (1748), Steuart (1767) and Adam Smith's *The Wealth of Nations* (1776). The main purpose of these writings, as Lewis (2002, p. 28) pointed out, was 'to reconcile modern economic life and institutions (especially trading, interests, profit-making, and the right to hold private property) with ethics and religion, and their method was to quote from the Bible and the writings of the early Church'. Indeed, religious teachings were amongst the first precursors of the doctrine of development, which was the opposite of the idea of progress epitomized by the drive for capital accumulation.

From a materialist and theological point of view, development, as Cowen and Shenton (1995, p. 29) eloquently put it, 'emerged to ameliorate the perceived chaos caused by progress'. Development was shaped as a problem 'grounded in the European experience of governability, disorder and disjuncture' (Crush, 1995, p. 8). It was in the European context that development was first conceived as a state practice and as 'one means to construct the positive alternative to the disorder and underdevelopment of capitalism' (Cowen and Shenton, 1996, p. 57). The nineteenth century marked the beginning of *intentional* development concerned with the deliberate policy and actions of the state and other agencies, which were expressed in various developmental doctrines. The visions promoted by these doctrines were rooted in the normalizing practices of the modern state and its efforts to produce disciplined citizens, soldiers, leaders and governable subjects. History reveals that sport has played and continues to play a major part in those state-building activities, not only in Europe but throughout the world (Black and Nauright, 1998; Mangan, 2000, 2002).

A cultural perspective on development locates it within the broader notion of modernity. This is a world view representing a break from the bonds of the traditional social order, and which challenged the main pillars of the old regime including the authority of the Church and the absolute power of kings. Modernity challenged deeply rooted cultural values and beliefs. Inglehart (1997, p. 24) noted that 'the essential core of Modernization is a syndrome of changes closely linked with industrialization: this syndrome includes urbanization, the application of science and technology, rapid increasing occupational specialization, rising bureaucratization, and rising educational levels. It also includes one more thing, which was the motivating force behind the whole process: industrialization was a way to get rich.' The eighteenth-century Enlightenment movement gave rise to the belief in human progress and that the social conditions of people can be improved through application of reason and science. The philosophers of Enlightenment, as Perry (1992, p. 161) wrote in *An Intellectual History of Modern Europe*, 'sought to emancipate the mind from the bonds of ignorance and superstition and to rescue people from intolerance, cruelty and oppression'. Indeed, the motto of the Enlightenment, *sapere aude!* (dare to know!), deeply permeates our modern way of thinking. The Enlightenment, however, should not be seen only as an intellectual triumph, but as an ideology and particular policies as well. For instance, it assumes that since reason is common to all peoples, state institutions, morality, education and other systems of thought could be based on common principles and applied to all peoples regardless of their cultures and histories. It demonstrated the dialectics between philosophy and ideology in that, while philosophy involves the organization of ideas and values, the purpose of ideology, usually expressed in doctrines, is to shape beliefs that incite people to action. The Enlightenment project was premised on a number of central ideas which have great relevance for the way we perceive sports development today, and which will be elaborated in the next section. These include reason, empiricism (all knowledge is based on empirical facts), science, universalism (reason and science produce general principles and laws which can be applied to all situations), progress, individualism, secularism (secular knowledge and structures replacing traditional religious authority), uniformity of human nature and freedom. However, Inglehart (1997, p. 23) also saw industrialization and Modernization as an 'attractive package' but which carried a high cost. He argued that modernization 'dismantles a traditional world in which the meaning of life is clear; warm, personal communal ties gives way to an impersonal competitive society geared to individual achievement'.

For the first time the ideas of Enlightenment allowed humans to conceive of development as an intention and people came to see history as a linear trajectory containing a promise of a better future. The concept of development in its modern form emerged as a corollary of the notion of progress and the capitalist accumulation of wealth. Developmental ideas reflected two conflicting approaches – one which saw development as closely linked to progress (Inglehart, 1997) and the other which perceived development radiating from the limitations of progress (Cowen and Shenton, 1996). Despite a multiplicity of definitions of development, most commentators agree there are three main interrelated contemporary meanings of the term. Those meanings, according to Thomas' (2000b) and Schech and Haggis' (2000) comprehensive analyses include (i) a vision, description or measure of the state of being of a desirable society; (ii) a historical process of social change implying a progressive movement from backwardness to forwardness; and (iii) deliberate efforts on the part of various agencies aimed at improvement.

When considered as a *vision*, as Schech and Haggis (2000, p. 15) observed, 'whether capitalist or Marxist, development theorist and policy makers have identified development with material progress and improved living standards'. This seemingly universal striving for better living should not conceal the fact that different political ideologies have different visions of what ideals should be pursued by society. For example, how should social and economic development be achieved? Shall we leave development to the market or should the state assume a leading role? Who should be the main beneficiaries of development? How should development be measured? These are all important questions to which different political ideologies provide competing answers.

As Seers (1979, p. 10) noted, 'development is inevitably a normative concept, almost a synonym for improvement. To pretend otherwise is just to hide one's value judgements.'

A book on the management of sports development cannot do justice to these various doctrines. What follows instead sketches briefly the gist of four contemporary views on development, namely, Neoliberalism, Structuralism, Interventionism and People-Centred Development, and their relevance to how we think about sports development. The first three views represent what is regarded in development circles as mainstream doctrines, while the fourth is an alternative view of development which has recently been gaining momentum. These views do not represent coherent theories as they draw on diverse schools of thought such as Marxism, Modernization, Dependency, Feminism, Critical Theory and Alternative Development. Table 1.1 summarizes these four visions of development. Apart from the obvious differences in their basic assumptions, they share a lack of specific prescriptions of how their proclaimed

Table 1.1 Main views of development.

Vision	Neoliberalism	Interventionism	Structuralism	People-centred development
	Liberal capitalism (modern industrial society and liberal democracy)	(plus achieving basic social/ environmental goals)		
Theory of social change	Internal dynamics of capitalism	Need to remove 'barriers' to modernization (change can be deliberately directed)	Struggle between classes (and other interests)	(not clear)
Role of 'development'	Immanent process within capitalism	To 'ameliorate the distorted faults of (capitalist) progress'	Comprehensive planning/ transformation of society	Process of individual and group empowerment
Agents of development	Individual entrepreneurs	Development agencies or 'trustees' of development (states, NGOs, international organizations)	Collective action (generally through the state)	Individuals, social movements

Source: Adopted from Thomas (2000a, p. 43)

goals are to be achieved. Thorbecke (2000) offered a comprehensive review of the history of these doctrines and their relationships with policies, development models and systems for performance measurement from their inception in the 1950s through to 2000.

Modern developmental doctrines formulated after the Second World War drew on the economic and social theories from the seventeenth and nineteenth centuries, and the instructive colonial experiences in Africa, Asia and Latin America. They all possess two main properties – analytical, explaining how development occurs, and normative, suggesting how it should occur. What, therefore, these doctrines share in common are two things: (i) an interpretation of development, which, as Cowen and Shenton (1996, pp. 444–5) posited, 'in both its classical and modern expression, includes processes of decay, decomposition and destruction as well as growth, expansion and improvement', and (ii) the intent to develop. Where they differ is on matters of principles, ends and means, so questions such as how development was to be achieved, what values should underpin it and what the outcomes should be became central to any vision of development and its management.

The Neoliberal school had its roots in the classical economics of Adam Smith and viewed the process of capitalist development as inevitably leading to the outcome of modernization by increasing the economic and political capabilities of society. The modernization perspective, first elaborated in the work of Rostow (1960), envisaged five stages in the development of capitalism. This kind of modernization was a highly desirable end state, because as Inglehart (1997, p. 5) observed 'it enables a society to move from being poor to being rich'. Analytically, neoliberalism favoured industrialization as the only realistic way to the economic growth required to ensure development in terms of improved living standards. Normatively, it proposed that development will occur as a result of the materialist motivation of individuals and the invisible hand of the free market without the need for any intentional development. In fact, actions taken in the name of development were considered as likely to create obstacles to the proper working of the market. Neoliberalism attributes the lack of development to three such obstacles – tradition, monopoly and state regulation (cf. Thomas, 2000a, p. 43).

The structuralist school insists on development which involves changes in underlying social and economic structures. Its main representatives are Marxism and the dependency theory (Frank, 1969). Similar to the neoliberal stance, analytically structuralists also favour industrialization as the main driver of economic growth, but they disagree on the role of individuals and groups in this process. In contrast to the neoliberal vision of history as a sum of individuals' actions and those of individual governments, structuralists interpret history as political and economic struggles between large social groups and classes in particular. Social change is to be a planned process guided by the state as the supreme power capable of ensuring social justice and equal development for all. Normatively, the opposition between individual and collective action is represented as market versus state or profit versus planning. Henry's (2001) work on *The Politics of Leisure Policy* examined in great detail the tension between various political ideologies and their implications for leisure policies. However, the above tension is partly misleading as it does not capture the complexities of development which go beyond ensuring the conditions of market competition and include a whole range of non-economic considerations, and the role of national and international agencies. As Thomas (2000b, p. 781) pointed out, 'the main area of debate in what may be called "mainstream" development circles is no longer "market versus state" but about the form and degree of intervention'.

The interventionist school admits the structural inequalities and contradictions of capitalism, but instead of insisting on replacing the market, normatively it suggests combining the market and state. The state is seen here as one of many agencies with a role to play in intervention. Historically, there have been four main rationales for intervention which broadly reflected the different stages of capitalist accumulation and growth. These include restoring the balance between supply and demand by state spending in creating employment, protectionism of new industries through tax concessions, welfarism through planning and creation of jobs, welfare payments and eradicating poverty and environmentalism through international agreements. Each rationale serves different purposes but all are indicative of the need to combine the working of the market with well-considered state measures by simultaneously addressing social goals directly, and by strictly regulating the market in order to achieve development. Recently there has been a growing realization of the need for coordinated international and corresponding state interventions in promoting development. Sports development is not exempt from this process, as it is expected to contribute to meeting the Millennium Development Goals (MDGs) established by the United Nations (UN) in 2000 (UN, 2005).

However, neoliberalism, structuralism and the interventionist schools, as macro-level theories, have been largely discredited as they failed to deliver development not only in the industrialized North but also in the 'underdeveloped' South. This failure gave rise to a number of alternative views of development. A recent change of priority in development from production (economic factor) to human needs (social factor) resulted in a greater attention to a more people-centred vision. Human-needs-centred development (Sen, 1999) means combating poverty and restoring basic human capabilities and freedoms simultaneously. Normatively, these are often expressed in terms of enhancing people's participation in the control of their lives and empowerment. Empowerment represents a means for accomplishing individual and community development tasks. Zippay (1995, p. 264) argued that it 'can be conceptualized as involving two key elements: giving community members the authority to make decisions and choices and facilitating the development of the knowledge and resources necessary to exercise these choices'. Although some commentators criticized this doctrine as being populist and utopian (Kitching, 1982), currently, empowerment constitutes a desirable objective and outcome of various development and sport programmes in particular.

As the doctrines of modernity are being gradually contested by post-modernity (Inglehart, 1997) with its insistence on greater tolerance, new values and lifestyles, a final critical point of alternative development concerning cultural diversity deserves consideration here. Indeed, if we insist that development serves to empower people and communities, it follows that they will do so in culturally different ways representing their attitudes to time, history, people and nature. Most of us live in multicultural societies which renders universalist models of development of limited use. Schech and Haggis's (2000) insightful critical introduction to culture and development amply illustrates this interplay and suggests that anthropological approaches to development can make a major contribution to understanding this phenomenon by 'turning the anthropological gaze on development institutions and professionals' (p. 54).

The second meaning of development is concerned with the *process of social change*. This is a complex process which reflects the internal dynamics of capitalist economic growth as the driver of development, and the political struggle over whether this development should be occurring in a self-regulating market society or be regulated by governments. Social change unfolds over long periods of time and does not necessarily conform to the visions of development outlined above. Indeed, not all development projects succeed and when failures happen, we talk about underdevelopment. Sometimes, the reasons for underdevelopment stem from the very process of development which may leave behind environmental disasters, poverty and greater dependency. The 1992 Winter Olympic Games in Albertville will remain in history both as an environmental disaster, because of the damage which building Olympic infrastructure had caused to a whole region in the French Alps, and as a catalyst for the International Olympic Committee (IOC) formulating an environmental policy, Agenda 21 (Cantelon and Letters, 2000). Commentators agree that development is explicitly defined, and cannot be conceived of without a notion of its opposite of underdevelopment. This implies that 'development' is not only a social construction but equally serves as a constructor because it can create its opposite of underdevelopment, and so it carries specific power. The point is, as Esteva (1997, p. 10) eloquently put it, that 'for two-thirds of the people on earth, this positive meaning of the world "development" – profoundly rooted after two centuries of its social construction – is a reminder of *what they are not*. It is a reminder of an undesirable, undignified condition. To escape from it, they need to be enslaved to others' experiences and dreams (emphasis in original).' Thus, development inevitably involves overcoming a perception or a position of what one is not in order to become something new.

Thomas (2000b, p. 778) suggested that to fully comprehend development as a social change we have to consider three points: (i) 'development implies an all-encompassing change, not just improvement in one aspect; (ii) development is not just a question of a once-off process of change to something better, but implies a process which builds on itself, where change is continuous and where improvements build on previous improvements; and (iii) development is a matter of changes occurring at all levels of society and at the level of the individual human being at one and the same time'. Clammer (2005, p. 109) echoed this view by further pointing out that 'all social change involves a reconstruction of subjectivity – new conceptions of the self, of identity, of the person's relationship to nature, to God, to others in general and to the other gender in particular'. What follows is that change happening as a result of development is to be understood as affecting equally both structures and personal behaviour.

The internal dynamics of the process of capitalist development also suggest that concentrating only on the drive for achievement and individualist motivation for personal gain is not sufficient to secure its sustainability. This is because, as Granovetter's seminal contribution argued, 'all economic action was inherently enmeshed in social relations of one configuration or another, and that development essentially brought about a change in the kind, not degree, of embeddedness' (cited in Woolcock, 1998, p. 162). Therefore, it is necessary to transform personal gain into productive investment for the benefit of the whole society. A similar logic implies that we have to go beyond the notion of capital as accumulated material resource and pay attention to another form of it – social capital. Social capital is a much contested concept, the intellectual history of which can be traced back to the Scottish Enlightenment. Social capital concerns the knowledge and skills of human beings and their ability to associate. Coleman's (1988, p. 5108) much-cited definition of the concept makes this point explicit – 'the ability of people to work together for common purposes in groups and organizations'.

The third meaning of development draws attention to *what is done* in the name of development by various state and non-governmental agencies. It urges us to look not so much to the fundamental economic and social activities seeking to ensure capitalist growth, but to the work of a myriad of organizations including those involved with sport in tackling poverty, social exclusion, education, health and environmental problems. Two important management questions arise here – of power, i.e., what gives those agencies the mandate to do development and do they have the capacity for that; and legitimacy, i.e., whose visions of development they promote. Cowen and Shenton's (1996) insightful work on *Doctrines of Development* helps us to link the intent to develop (visions) with agency through the notion of trusteeship. As they (1996, pp. ix–x) argued, 'development doctrine rested upon the intent to develop through the exercise of trusteeship over society. Trusteeship is the intent which is expressed, by one source of agency, to develop the capacities of another. It is what binds the process of development to the intent of development.'

Whilst during the eighteenth and nineteenth centuries trusteeship was predominantly exercised by the state on behalf of society, gradually and particularly after the decolonization of Africa, Asia and Latin America in the late 1960s, more national and international agencies started to assume trusteeship over the development of others. Since the Labour government came into power in the UK in 1997 there has been a tendency for encouraging non-governmental sport organizations, Local Authorities (LAs) and Regional Development Authorities (RDAs) to claim trusteeship to promote a wide range of social policy agendas through sport. The Sport Action Zone initiative (DCMS, 2002) is a prime example for the use of sport in tackling social exclusion in deprived areas. The field of global sports development provides another instructive example. The Sport and Development International Platform website lists 154 development programmes (www.sportanddev.org, 2007) offered by various international consortia, multilateral partnerships and forums representing six main groups of developers – international organizations, government agencies, sports federations, NGOs, research institutes and consultancies and the sporting goods industry. The intent and process of sports development has been manifested in terms of establishing a set of legal and policy instruments (the rules of the game) and formal organizations (structures). Table 1.2 shows those instruments

Table 1.2 Legal/policy instruments supporting sport designed by major international agencies.

ILO	ILO Convention 182 on the Worst Forms of Child Labour (1999): see especially articles 3(a), 3(d), 7(2b) and 7(2c) and 8
	Recommendation R 190 (1999) on elimination of the worst forms of child labour: see especially article 2(b)
	ILO Convention 138 on Minimum Age (1973): see especially article 7(§§1–4)
	Declaration on Fundamental principles and Rights at Work (1998)
UNESCO	International Charter on Physical Education and Sport (1978); see especially article 1, which states 'The practice of physical education and sport is a fundamental right of all'
	Recommendations from the International Conference of Ministers and Senior Officials for Physical Education and Sport (MINEPS) meeting: see especially the most recent Declaration of Punta del Este (1999) from MINEPS III
WHO	World Health Assembly resolution WHA55.23 (2002) on diet, physical activity and health: see especially articles 2, 3(1) and 3(5)
	World Health Day 2002, 'Move for Health'
	Framework Convention on Tobacco Control (2003)
UNEP	UNEP Governing Council Decision (2003) on long-term strategy on sport and the environment: see especially the section of using spot to promote environmental awareness
UNICEF	Convention on the Rights of the Child (1990): see especially article 31, which states: 'The practice of physical education and sport is a fundamental right of all'
	Declaration on the Rights of the Child (1959): see especially principle 7, which states: 'The child shall have full opportunity for play and recreation, which should be directed to the same purposes as education, society and the public authorities shall endeavour to promote the enjoyment of this right'
	'A World Fit for Children', outcome document from the special session on children (2002): see especially paragraphs 37 (19) and 40 (17)
UN General Assembly	Resolution 48/10 of 25 September 1993: International Year of Sport and of the Olympic Ideal, which proclaimed 1994 as the International Year
	Resolution 50/13 of 7 November 1995: The Olympic Ideal
	Resolution 52/21 of 25 November 1997: Building a peaceful and better world through sport
	Resolution 54/34 of 24 November 1999: Building a peaceful and better world through sport
	Resolution 55/2 of 8 September 2000: Building a peaceful and better world through sport

(Continued)

Table 1.2 Continued

Other United Nations instruments	Convention on the Elimination of All Forms of Discrimination against Women (1979): see especially articles 10(g) and 13(c)
	Platform for Action adopted at the UN World Conference on Women in Beijing (1995): see especially paragraphs 85(m), 107(f) and 280(d)
European Commission Council of Europe	The European Model of Sport (1998)
	European Sports Charter (1992)
	European Sport for All Charter (1976)
Other relevant instruments	Geneva Convention (1949): see especially GC III, article 38 the right of prisoners of war to ('physical exercise, sports and games, and for being out of the doors'), and GC IV, article 94 (regarding children's right to 'outdoor sports and games' during times of war)
	The Olympic Charter of the International Olympic Committee: see especially article 8, which states: 'The practice of sport is a human right'

Source: United Nations (2003, pp. 27–8) and own sources

designed by major international agencies. As a result, a number of new international trusteeships such as the Sport and Development International Platform (SDIP), Right to Play and Sport for Development and Peace International Working Group (SDPIWG) have emerged. These organizations not only share a space traditionally dominated by major sports-governing bodies such as the IOC and the Federation Internationale de Football Associations (FIFA), but have become integrated in the networks of international organizations to form a part of an emerging system of global sports development governance (Girginov, 2008). Van Eekeren (2006) documented in some detail the history and current state of actors and networks in global sports development. These are part of the transnational community of NGOs, as described by Townsend et al. (2002). Those trusteeships have assumed the responsibility for representing global constituencies (e.g. athletes, clubs and national associations) and have been actively involved in the process of implementing their intent to develop sport with the immanent process of sports development.

A final aspect of the meaning of development, as something managers and agencies do, which also helps link it with visions, concerns the power-generating capacities of the development discourse. As Clammer (2005, p. 107) explained: '"development" does not float above or outside discourse: it is a specific language game that, like, say, theological language, has attempted to define its specific discursive strategies as privileged, while in fact being as much subject to deconstruction as any other world view'. Sachs (1997, p. 4) echoed this view arguing that the development discourse is made up of a web of concepts: 'it is impossible to talk about development without referring to concepts such as poverty, production, the notion of state or equality'.

In summary, development is a multifaceted concept which has been associated with progress and capitalist accumulation and represents a unity of destruction and creation. It was conceptualized as immanent and intentional, reflecting the notion of spontaneous progress and state and other agencies' development practices, respectively. Development is a normative concept which became associated also with three universalizing powers of the state, market and science. There are three contemporary meanings of development including vision, a process of social change and practice. Four main development doctrines, namely, neoliberal, structuralist, interventionist and people-centred, have been favoured over the past 60 years. Each of these visions of development has had an impact on development policies, strategies and management practices. Development as a process of social change emphasizes the importance of subjectivity and the reconstruction of identities. A focus on what is done in the name of development brings to the fore the notion of trusteeship and how various development agencies operate. There has been a growing realization about the importance of the cultural meaning of development and that it represents a specific language with power-generating capacities.

Sports Development – Towards an Understanding

The development of modern sport both mirrored and facilitated the process of capitalist growth and accumulation, and rightfully has been associated with commercialism (Andrews, 2004; Slack, 2005). The industrialization and urbanization of societies was responsible for creating a new social class and organized competitive sports emerged as a private domain of this class. The early years of modern sport closely resembled the immanent development of capitalism. However, this was not the case with gymnastics. As Riordan and Kruger (2003, p. 1) argued, 'the various schools of physical exercise – associated with Jahn in Germany, Nachtegall in Denmark, Ling in Sweden, Lesgaft in Russia – developed as pedagogical, political and military instruments for building a national identity. And that involved everybody: man and woman, squire and peasant, factory owner and worker. To learn to put one's body at the service of the nation emanated from a policy of acculturation of the common people in the same way as learning one's national language.' It follows that gymnastics represented an intentional and state-sanctioned development activity, the main purpose of which was nation building. This is not surprising, given that Europe in 1500 was composed of 1500 independent political units, which by 1900 were reduced to some 25. As Crampton (1994, p. 7) observed, 'of all the new states born in Europe between 1815 and 1914 only two, Belgium and Norway, had appeared without war'. Sports and gymnastics, of course, competed for influence and resources, and this nineteenth-century European phenomenon was largely responsible for establishing the dichotomy between Sport for All and elite sport, which pervades much of contemporary thinking and sports development practices.

The interplay between immanent and intended development of sport was embedded in the social and political fabrics of society. Much of the current visions of sports development have actually been designed to compensate the negative propensities of capitalism through the reconstruction of social order by tackling class, poverty, gender and age inequalities. What originally emerged as immanent sports development in the form of private sport practices was gradually transformed by the state and its institutions into intended development. In Victorian and Edwardian Britain, this was achieved through the idea of athleticism in public schools (Mangan, 1981), as the model of dominant groups to be diffused downwards through class and gender. This model was based on the logic of exclusion (Gruneau, 1997), and as Tranter (1998, p. 41) put it, 'the reality is that the Victorian and Edwardian sporting "revolution" was a phenomenon of class division, not conciliation and, between as well as within sports, of widening rather narrowing division'. Clearly, sport favoured particular forms of development that offered benefits to a limited number of members within a well-protected network of independent voluntary clubs and associations. Traditionally, those clubs have been mostly smaller entities serving a single sport and as in Britain today numbering some 150,000 with an average size of British clubs of 43 (Collins, 2002). Apart from their members, they did not seek legitimation to act on others' behalf. The state's intention to develop sport, however, was about to change this. The evolution of modern sport attests to the dual role of development as a destructor and a creator of meaning, structures and practices.

The concept of sports development has also been shaped by the growth of international sport at the end of the nineteenth century. At present, major international sports-governing bodies such as the IOC and FIFA exercise significant power over the course of sports development nationally. The first major international sports development project can be attributed safely to the founder of the Olympic movement, Pierre de Coubertin. It emerged as a reaction to Coubertin's and his associates' dissatisfaction with the process of capitalist accumulation and the poor fitness of youth. Pierre de Coubertin was disillusioned with the emerging internationalization of life with its emphasis on material culture and proposed an educational doctrine aimed at countering this negative trend. It was promoted through the Olympic Games, and similar to athleticism, Olympism was also a model of downward diffusion. As Brown (1996, p. 126) commented, 'Coubertin's broader mission was, after all, to train the lower classes to be modern sport spectators'. Olympism is a prime example of intended development at the international level in which the newly established IOC (1894) entrusted itself and its constituencies, the National Olympic Committees (NOCs), with the role of spreading the educational mission of sport for the betterment of the world.

Sports development in the UK is widely considered as a post-Second World War phenomenon. Its history has been well documented by a number of commentators from historical (MacIntosh and Charlton, 1985), political (Houlihan and White, 2002; Wolfenden, 1960), social (Collins, 2002; Hylton et al., 2001, 2007), practical (Collins, 1993, 2008; Eady, 1993) and system's (Green, 2005; Green and Houlihan, 2005) perspectives. What emerges from various interpretations is a chequered picture which defines sports development as a process, policy domain, activity/practice and discourse. Houlihan and White (2002, pp. 3–4) neatly captured this variety: 'sports development has been conceptualized as an activity preoccupied with service inputs (facility provision) and the creation of opportunities, but it has also been conceptualized as an activity whose proper focus is on service outcomes and the maximization of benefits'.

However, with a few noticeable exceptions (Houlihan and White, 2002; Lawson, 2005), sports development has been predominantly concerned with practice, and there has been little or no attention to its management. Reducing sports development to practice ignores the meaning of development as a vision and process of social change (Thomas, 2000a). Recently, the tendency of associating sports development with practice has been reinforced by two high-profile international conferences held by the UN in Magglingen in 2003 and 2005, which stressed the contribution sport could make to meet the MDGs (FOSM, 2005). The significance of the 2005 Magglingen Declaration to sports development is three-fold. First, it calls for a move from theory and pilot projects to implementation and scaling-up activities on the ground, thus largely reducing sports development to mean sport practice. Second, it implicitly asserts the logic behind the five guiding principles for the governance of global capitalism developed by the World Bank and International Monetary Fund (Kohler and Wolfensohn, 2000). Cammack (2003) referred to these principles as the 'manifesto' of the governance of global capitalism, which sees development as (i) a comprehensive approach (recognizing the multi-dimensional nature of development); (ii) equitable pursuits (barriers related to gender, ethnicity or social status needing to be overcome); (iii) national ownership (which is paramount, with nations accepting responsibility for their own development); (iv) financial support (which should be linked to level of performance); and (v) transparency (to ensure clarity and accountability around roles, responsibilities and outcomes). Third, it urges us to consider sports development practice as an important source of theory building.

Sports Development as Vision

As a *vision*, sports development in the twenty-first century takes on a whole new meaning. It has been conceptualized within the broader philosophy of sustainable development, which embraces a variety of social, political and economic objectives. These include improving people's quality of life, tackling social exclusion, widening access and the pursuit of excellence, greater efficiency and effectiveness of services, involvement of local people, recognition of voluntary work and citizenship, lifelong learning, removing organizational barriers and preserving the environment (Sport England, 1999). A representative UK survey with community sports development workers presented them with a list of 21 rationales and missions, including social justice, sustainable communities, community development, community safety, crime reduction, equitable practice, health promotion, social inclusion, social control, empowerment, success in sport, personal/career development, rehabilitation, self-help, devolution, self-determination, inclusion in a specific faith or community agenda, ethical practice, working and learning together, collective action and social education. The survey found that 'the majority were unable to identify a clear underpinning rationale for their work. Instead, participants claimed to be pursuing an agenda which covered many, and in some cases all, of these themes ... This lack of clarity can be attributed to the fact the sector is increasingly pursuing a wide range of funding streams in order to secure and develop their work, forcing them to engage with new and challenging social and welfare agendas' (Millar, 2005, p. 8).

As the above list evidences, the doctrine of sports development has been evoked to compensate what has been lost in the pursuit of capital growth and accumulation. It has been used to arrest a number of pressing problems concerning the current obesity epidemic in Western countries which costs the taxpayer in the UK some £500 million (Fox, 2004) and up to $5.7 billion per year in Canada (Starky, 2005); social exclusion (Collins, 2003); the need to enhance national identity and cohesion; and economic regeneration of cities and regions (Gratton and Henry, 2001). Lentell's (1993, p. 141) observation demonstrates that this is not a new issue: 'sports development has been a microcosm of the forces affecting leisure policy and illuminates the consequences of particular policy outcomes'. Currently in the UK those policy outcomes are representative of the New Labour government's new social policy agenda. Four important points deserve consideration here. First, those themes represent a combination of internal and external goals, which all developers face. For example, while addressing crime reduction and devolution could be seen as two internal goals for local authorities, these sit outside the remit of a sports club or a national sport-governing body (NGB). Conversely, if the pursuit of excellence is what chiefly justifies the existence of a NGB, it appears as an external goal for local authorities. This implies that sports development has to be located in the wider social and economic milieu, and cannot be considered only from the point of view of a single agency. It is context-specific and requires transcending institutional barriers in order to enable various developers to achieve a synergy between their agendas. As Houlihan (2000, p. 180, in quoting Majone, 1989) contended in relation to the growing number of public policies on sports development, 'one important implication of the increased density packed policy space is that "as the population of policies grows relative to the size of the policy space, individual policies necessarily become more interdependent. The consequences produced by one policy are increasingly likely to interfere with the working of other policies".' Second, NGBs have increasingly been 'disciplined' by governments (Green and Houlihan, 2006), which is indicative of the formation of new state–voluntary sector relationships of dependency. Third, the delivery of intentional sports development is no longer tied to a few earmarked funds. Instead, sports development officers are expected to be able to tap into a range of funding opportunities linked to those wider social, economic and political objectives. Fourth, attention needs to be paid to the issue of consistency and the fit between external and internal goals, and their impact on delivering a sustainable sports development for sport's sake.

Sports Development as Social Change

Considered as *social change*, sports development entails giving proper attention to the relationship between visions of development and people's subjective perceptions of it. Whilst change at the community level has received some treatment (Hylton et al., 2007), the impact of sports development on the reconstruction of subjectivity is a key aspect which has been largely absent from its various interpretations and strategies. Even the most comprehensive Internet-based academic and professional sports development portal in English language hardly acknowledges the importance of subjectivity by considering only the structural side of sports development (see Chapter 10). It defines sports development 'as an equivocally contested term. It can mean the development of sport for sports sake, and equally the use of sport and physical activity opportunities for the development of society – sport as a social instrument' (www.sportdevelopment.org.uk, 2007).

Powell (1995, p. 200) distinguished clearly between change and development. He argued that 'Change can be positive or negative. Development is supposed to equal progress, to lead to improvements. Improvement is a subjective concept, and subjectivity is determined by identity and culture.' Powell stressed the inadequacy of the position advocated by NGOs when determining change and wider developmental effects and doubted whether it would be conceivable to talk of any sustainable development which depends only on the approval of outsider agencies. Thomas (2000b) also pointed out that development implies a process of an all-encompassing change, which builds on itself and occurs simultaneously at the social and individual level of change. Houlihan's (2000) analysis of schools and sports development demonstrated that change could be interpreted very differently by educators, NGBs and community workers, which leads to fragmented results. The implications for sports development are that we need to comprehend change not simply as a one-dimensional process or a move from one destination to another, but as a process involving objective conditions and subjective perceptions of those affected by development. Hence, Powell's (1995, p. 201) conclusion – 'whatever the self-definition of the supporting agencies, if "development" is not imbued with acceptable and comprehensible cultural values, it will not work'. Powell's criticism bears particular relevance to the developmental work undertaken by NGBs, as in many cases this has to be approved by governmental or international agencies.

Sports development encompasses visions of change promoted by a multiplicity of agencies (see Table 1.1). Those visions do not enjoy equal popularity, and it seems that the current dominant perception of change has been of something 'tangible'. It has been reinforced by the 'Best Value – The Value of Sport' (Sport England, 1999, p. 1), one of the most influential policy documents in the field, which stated that 'sport needs to demonstrate *tangible* benefits to individuals, communities and the nation as a whole, if it is to compete with many other worthy causes for a share of limited resources'. The Enlightenment (positivist) belief in scientific rationality is clearly evident from the thinking behind this logic of change. It tends to present sports development as a positive-sum game where 'increasing physical activity by 10% could save 6000 lives, and £500 million per year' (Sport England, 2004, p. 29). It follows that the obvious thing for sports development managers is to focus on increasing participation. Furthermore, the document envisaged drawing 'on the best scientific evidence available, combined with local examples of good practice, to demonstrate that sport can make a difference to people's lives and to the communities in which they live' (Sport England, 1999, p. 1).

Whilst remaining conscious of the need for an approach to sports development grounded in current political and economic realities, managers may also have to ask the fundamental question 'what constitutes development and who determines it?'

A commitment to 'tangible' benefits pushes us into the realm of statistics and evidence-based policy which largely ignores the real object of development. It is informative to quote in full Dorfman's eloquent comment on this matter:

> The real advance consists in having made some people feel more human. How do you measure that? How do you measure the amount of dignity that people accumulate? How do you quantify the disappearance of apathy? With what machines do you evaluate someone's rediscovered identity, the power that they now feel to set their own goals and not merely take what others are willing to hand down? With what graphs would you chart the curves of increased memory, increased self-reliance, increased group solidarity, increased critical awareness
>
> (quoted in Staudt, 1991, p. 27).

Not one of *The Framework for Sport in England: Vision 2020* (Sport England, 2004) seven main outcomes of change is concerned with the 'intangibles' of sports development suggested by Dorfman. The problem of uncritically accepting performance targets as indicative of successful sports development is two-fold. First, targets are inherently unidimensional and cannot capture the richness of human experiences and the complexities of change occurring within sports development. Second, the application of management techniques to achieve such targets tends to simplify theory to the idea that large-scale social change may be achieved by deliberate actions. The fact that years of concerted efforts in boosting participation rates failed to produce the desired outcomes supports this conclusion. Harvey (2002, p. 161) observed that 'despite more than 20 years of promotional campaigns on the importance of exercise, Canadians have become less active'. Rowe et al. (2004, p. 12) echoed this view from an English perspective: 'sports participation rates in England remained broadly unchanged over the last two decades or so and that sport in England has continued to be characterized by considerable social inequalities. The 1980s and 1990s saw the development of the recreation management profession, an increase in sports development officers, an expansion of local authority leisure departments, a number of national campaigns, a national junior sports development programme, improved support and training for volunteers and a number of coaching initiatives. And still participation rates did not go up or inequalities become narrowed.' Two recent authoritative international studies on leisure and sport participation (Cushman et al., 2005; Van Bottenburg et al., 2005) largely confirmed this trend for many Western societies. Sports development professionals know all too well that they alone cannot make people more physically active, but they continue to play the targets game because of political and economic pressures. The British government's document *A Sporting Future for All* amply illustrates the point that 'the success or failure in achieving milestone targets in performance plans will be an important factor in deciding future levels of funding' (DCMS, 2002, p. 44).

Sports Development as Delivery

Considering sports development as a delivery urges us to focus our attention on *who does what* and *how in the name of development.* As visions of sports development tend to change over time, so do the range and role of various providers. Currently, the local, national and international sports development scene is cluttered with agencies, some of which operate at all three levels, while others specialize in one. The six main groups of developers identified earlier include international organizations (e.g. UN, European Community, IOC), government agencies (e.g. DCMS, Sports Councils), sports federations (e.g. FIFA, British Gymnastics), NGOs (e.g. Youth Sport Trust, Youth Active, Right to Play), research institutes (e.g. North American Youth Sport Institute, NAYSI, Institute of Youth Sport, UK, Institute for Sport, Parks and Leisure, ISPAL) and consultancies (e.g. PMP) and sporting goods industry (e.g. Sporting Goods Manufacturers Association, SGMA). Table 1.3 provides a summary of the main categories of sports developers and their visions and management approaches. In addition to this multiplicity of developers, there is another *ad hoc* hybrid category involving

Table 1.3 Main categories of sports developers.

Level of development	Local	National	International
Agents of development 'trustees'	Schools, Sport clubs, Local Authorities, RDA	NSGBs, DCMS, DE, Sport Councils, ISPAL, YST	UN, EU, IOC, FIFA, Right to Play, SCORE
Vision/ desirable outcome	Personal development, physical education, talent identification, reducing anti-social behaviour	Active citizens, performance targets, professional standards, good governance	Promote democracy, group solidarity, equality, achieving MDGs, good governance
Drivers of change	Utilizing education, levels of investments	Ageing population, well-being and obesity, levels of investment, utilizing education, variations in access, volunteers and professionals	Political pressure, environmental concerns, MDGs, international agreements
Role of development	Tackling obesity and crime, process of individual and community empowerment	Promote government social agenda, talent identification, nation building, compensate for the faults of capitalism	Tackle poverty and poor health, capacity building, immanent process within capitalism
Management approach	Active communities, partnerships and projects	NPM, demonstrative projects	Aid, Tool kits, Standard manuals, Mega sport events

many of the above agencies and formed around the hosts of major sporting events such as the Olympic Games. The 2012 London Olympics are a case in point as they served as a catalyst for bringing together a wide range of governmental, non-governmental and private agencies in order to deliver sustainable developments not only in sport but also in the fields of vocational training, employment, regeneration and environmental protection.

The three interrelated meanings of sports development entail that it cannot and should not be seen only as a means of empowering people and organizations and improving the well-being of societies. What is done in the name of sports development could be equally destructive, as for example, the promotion of certain sports is achieved to the detriment of others, while building sporting infrastructure often upsets local people's way of life (or even displaces them as in Olympic host cities such as Moscow, Sydney and Beijing) and the environment. The case study 'Plymouth-Banjul Challenge' on the book website also illustrates this point. The above observations suggest that the concept of sports development is a social construct, a perception and a collective endeavour, which reflects specific visions about the purpose of human life, time, progress and social change, which can be appropriated by various parties to suit their purposes. Sports development is rarely a positive-sum game as it reflects managers' and policy makers' thinking which is always positing alternative priorities between performance and participation development; talent identification and lifelong learning; economic impact and community needs; and long-term investments and short-term solutions. In this context visions of desirable end states are closely intertwined with an ever expanding institutional apparatus of sports development.

Sports development is also a specific language game which uses a wide range of labels to indicate which sports and in what parts of the world are 'developed' or 'underdeveloped'. One of the most successful labels has been to divide sports into Olympic and non-Olympic. This is reflected in the categorization of sports in Britain into groups of 10 UK Sport priority sports and in England 10 priority and 12 development sports (Sport England, 2004). A similar categorization is in place in Chinese sports (Hong et al., 2005), as indeed elsewhere. Another label applied equally nationally and internationally has been to divide sports organizations around the world into 'rich' and 'poor'. The IOC Olympic Solidarity (IOC, 2005, p. 4) mission is to 'provide support to the poorest NOCs to fulfill the ideals of the Olympic Movement'. Similarly, FIFA's Goal project (FIFA, 2004, p. 3) promises to 'provide a comprehensive approach to football development including its social, educational and cultural values by offering tailor-made solutions to specific needs of the member associations and in particular those in the underprivileged countries'. The point is that those categorizations have massive implications for the public standing, promotion and funding of NGBs, the course of sports development and people's experiences.

Management of Sports Development

In exploring the world of the 'cynical manager' Cutler (2000, pp. 310–11) contended that 'the *most* fundamental challenge facing managers in the new millennium is not how profitable or competitive their company is, but how management can, and will, affect the kind of world in which we all have to live and work'. This statement concerns not only the 'developed' North, to which Cutler was referring, but equally the 'underdeveloped' South. Ross and Bouwmeesters'(1972, p. 10) comprehensive field survey of management in 46 developing countries demonstrated that 'far from being mere administrators of a number of existing undertakings, managers must be in the forefront of a surprisingly broad social change'. These comments are instructive for understanding the management of sports development, as in addition to the substantive aspects of management (e.g. what managers do and how) they urge us to consider it as a socially responsible conceptual and practical tool, which impacts directly on people's lives.

The term 'management of sports development' is somehow misleading as it suggests that the subject of management is the various interventions or what is done in the name of sports development. Therefore, a conceptual clarification is in order as the literature abounds with studies on development management (Wallace, 2000) and management development (Robinson et al., 2000; Woodall and Winstanley, 1998). Esman (1972) made a useful distinction between these two concepts. The former focuses on the development of managerial capabilities and institutions, while the latter emphasizes the management of concrete practical development activities, and maintains that this type of management must concentrate on performance aimed at delivering the goods, meeting needs and providing tangible benefits. Esman (1972, p. 20) also offered an approach which combines the two interpretations and defined development management as 'comprising both the strengthening of managerial capabilities that can sustain complex activities through time and changing circumstances and the ongoing management of development programmes'. However, as argued above, sports development is more than a practice and development of individuals through sport. In order to understand the meaning of the management of sports development, it would seem appropriate to return to our conceptualization of the term. Sports development was conceptualized as a social construct, a perception of what a person or an object is and the strive to become something new, and a collective endeavour, which revolves around three interrelated meanings of vision, process of social change and practice. The cultural relevance of sports development and its meaning-producing capacities were also stressed. Indeed, as Staudt (1991, p. 35) maintained in her study of the management of development, 'understanding culture is a starting point for learning the meaning of development, the values that guide people's actions, and the behaviour of administrators'.

Those three meanings provide useful devices for bringing management and sports development together, as they correspond to a widely accepted conceptualization of management operating at macro, meso and micro levels. Building on Thomas' (1996, 1999) work, the role of management of sports development at each level is further unpacked. Thomas (1999, p. 10) contended that development management is 'management undertaken with a developmental orientation, rather than management in the context of the development process or the management of development interventions or tasks'. For him, it is a particular kind of orientation and a style. This point is critical for understanding the management of sports development, as it entails that not only the proclaimed management goals, but every management function has to have a developmental orientation. Coalter (2006, pp. 150–1) clearly illustrated this point in relation to one such function, monitoring and evaluation of sports development programmes: 'in the context of sport-in-development, it is essential that M&E play a *developmental role*', and that '*people* (or "responsible citizens") are a major outcome of such organisations (in traditional sports development programmes these are usually regarded simply as *inputs*), one that precedes the programmes whose impacts are often the subject of evaluation'.

As established earlier, the focus of intended sports development is the people and not objects and targets. Its main concerns are with eliminating poverty, ensuring rights and improving lives. This implies that, as a vision (macro level), the focus of management will be *for* sports development aimed at progressive and sustainable change. Many otherwise excellent sports programmes fall short of delivering developmental outcomes because of their short-term orientation and failure to build on what has been achieved, and to offer clear progression pathways. The main function of management is of setting policy visions about the role of sport in society, focusing on establishing frameworks and policy instruments in the field to be promoted locally, nationally or internationally. Various developers and the alliances they form are concerned with making the right policy choices that determine how the many and diverse public, voluntary and private actors will behave. Considered as a social change the role of management is realized *in* the context of a sports development process. Of particular importance here is to understand the framing of change, which always unfolds simultaneously at social, community and individual levels, and that there is a complex interplay between them. Management at this level (meso) concerns the engineering strategies for using sport to affect wider changes in society. The process of development is manifested in concrete policies and programmes through which sports development alliances provide services and promote and regulate certain forms of political and social behaviour. Sports development management involves managing resources provided by individual or group actors. When conceived as practice, management becomes *of* sports development, and is concerned with the planning and outcomes of various interventions. The practice of development at this level (micro) consists of operations and individual associations (communities, clubs, leisure/sport centres or teams) and directly affects the daily lives of people. Houlihan and White's (2002) analysis of the politics of sports development offered further support for a similar interpretation and suggested that the meaning of sports development has constantly changed in line with dominant political visions, interests of stakeholders and social values of British society. Table 1.4 shows the relationship between sports development, the main management functions and the core skills needed by managers.

A similar conceptualization of the management of sports development presents a number of theoretical and practical challenges and opportunities concerning three key issues – values (i.e. what is regarded as sports development), trusteeship (by whom) and management approaches (how), which are briefly explored below together with the management skills required to successfully

Table 1.4 Relationship between sports development, management functions and management skills.

Sports development	Main management functions	Core skills required
Vision (management *for*)	Setting policies, designing instruments and frameworks, coordinating between trustees, management of inter-organizational relationships	Negotiating and brokering, policy analysis, fund raising, convergence, inter-organizational learning
Change (management *in*)	Framing change at social, community and individual level, engineering change strategies, developing practical policies and programmes, managing resources from multiple sources	Personal and social psychology, planning and forecasting, personal and mass communications, grant writing, data base development (IT)
Practice (management *of*)	Planning the outcomes of various interventions, capacity building, personal and community empowering, operational management, monitoring and evaluation of interventions	Observation, research and writing, personal and organizational learning, individual and group communications, sports sessions planning and delivery, conflict and financial management

deal with them. First, as demonstrated above, sports development may be undertaken in the name of diverse social, political, economic and sport agendas. The variety of sports developers operating across the field entails considerable variations in their visions and practices as well. These may range from tackling personal development to crime reduction, city regeneration and devolution, and often represent external social or economic goals rather than internal sport organizations' goals. This implies that the agencies involved in a particular sports development project will have different expectations based on their values. As values represent differences it is likely that when these collide they will produce conflicts between participants. This tension is further compounded by the interplay between global and local visions of sports development. Recently, Mintzberg (2006, p. 4) opened his thought-provoking article with the words 'we develop leaders. And we develop countries. So we believe. We also believe that we develop countries by developing leaders. Perhaps we need to develop our thinking.' He described globalization as an antithesis of local development and the importation of techniques, controls and beliefs from outside agencies and experts as the very problem of development. Mintzberg (2006, p. 8) further argued that 'there is nothing in globalisation that responds to host-country conditions, save cosmetic modifications to the products and the ideology for local consumption' and proposed a model of indigenous development. This model, which is an 'inside-up' form of development, builds on the strengths of local communities, leaders and enterprises. It exists alongside the dominant 'outside-in' global model and the 'top-down' planned development. The above observations define the management of sports development as a contested policy field with a great deal of interdependence of polices at macro, meso and micro levels. From this perspective, development management, as Wallace (1999, p. 19) persuasively argued, 'seeks to accommodate the idea of complex negotiations between a range of social actors'. What is more, as Robinson et al. (2000, p. 3) wrote, 'the process of negotiation over development lies at the heart of the idea of "public action" '. They continued by citing Dreze and Sen (1989), 'public action is not … just a question of public delivery and state initiative. It is also a matter of participation by the public in a process of social change', and concluded that the management of interactions between different organizations 'can fairly be seen as the essence of how development takes place'.

However, the multiple ownership of various sports development projects implies not only tensions but also new possibilities for inter-organizational learning, knowledge building and funding. Sports development managers, therefore, have to develop conceptual and practical skills concerned with negotiation and brokering, policy analysis, personal and organizational learning, grant writing and database development, monitoring and evaluation of the likely impact of proposed interventions and conflict management. Managers will have to learn to discern between fashionable ideas promoted by international organizations and culturally meaningful local sports development visions as well. A series of policy documents and research reports into the working practice and training needs in the sports development sector specifically highlighted the constraining role of tendencies towards 'model-driven managerialist' interventions and the limited understanding of parallel, 'converging' welfare agendas (Boutall, 2003; Collins, 1995; Community Development Foundation, 2004; SPRITO, 2001) on the success of various projects.

Second, sports developers intervene on behalf of others, which raises the question of the legitimacy of their claimed trusteeship (Cowen and Shenton, 1996), or who is in control of development. In particular, what rights do those agencies have to develop others, and how accountable are they to those they are developing? Here the picture is very mixed and complex as there are three main categories of agencies, each drawing on one or a combination of three key resources – political authority (public sector), financial capital (commercial sector) and self-motivation (voluntary sector). The problem arises because sports development concerns issues which are in the public domain, but various developers may lack the power of political enforcement (NGBs), the financial capital (LAs) or the political legitimacy (private businesses) to undertake it. The strategic goal of increasing participation in sport is a classic example in this respect. NBGs know well what constitutes regular physical activity but cannot enforce it in the lives of different groups; local authorities understand that the key to participation is removing social and economic barriers, but don't have the resources to do that; while a similar goal lies outside the legitimate remit of many private businesses. Thus, managing in the multi-actor sports development contexts, as Robinson et al. (2000, p. 4) asserted, involves '(i) considering when and how to choose between various possible inter-organisational strategies, such as collaboration, advocacy, direct opposition, or organizational growth in order to achieve developmental ends, and (ii) developing the practical skills for working with competitive, co-ordinated, or co-operative strategies for dealing with inter-organisational relationships'.

From a management of development point of view the diffusion of various sports development visions creates institutional difficulties by breaking down the symmetry between decision makers (the development community of trustees) and decision takers (communities and people subject to development). This results in neglecting the equivalence principle, which at its simplest suggests that 'those who are significantly affected by a global good or bad should have say in its provision and regulation' (Kaul, cited in Held, 2006, p. 166). This principle bears important implications for matching circles of stakeholders and decision makers in sports development, for systematizing the financing of global public goods delivered by sport and for spanning borders and group of actors in establishing the ownership of and promoting the management of the strategic issues of sports development. Hence, the importance of the issue of power relations between trustees and developed. As demonstrated, NGBs in the UK have increasingly been put in a dependent position in relation to government. Abbott et al.'s (2007) analysis of 62 MBA dissertations by active development managers across various fields supported this conclusion and suggested that in some cases the whole process of development management was regarded as 'generating skewed power relations' (p. 198). To paraphrase Banuri (1990, p. 96), if development means 'what "we" can do for "them"' then it is just a 'licence' for administrative intervention, and largely ignores the importance of the process of change.

The expansion of trustees' models of sports development creates another management challenge concerning the cost of compliance with this model. The Labour government's 'Modernisation Agenda', as well as the policies of the IOC and FIFA, requires beneficiaries to commit themselves to certain management standards (e.g. performance management, logical frameworks, effectiveness) including a culture of reporting and good governance. This implies that they have to divert attention and resources from what they do to a process of accounting for what they do. In the language of managerialism this spending is referred to as compliance cost and is routinely monitored by its promoters. This situation confers sanctioning and monitoring capacities to the NGBs and other national and international agencies, which in turn produces reciprocal relationships in that group. These can later turn into an obstacle for promoting sports development at different levels because of their prescriptive behaviour routes, reciprocity and cultural inadequacy. Sports development managers, therefore, have to coordinate resources from multiple sources, to learn not only to use those resources to meet their goals, but how to influence and intervene in social processes by paying attention to both objective conditions and subjective perceptions.

Finally, it is important to consider how visions of sports development are implemented on the ground, which brings up the issue of management approaches used in the field. A broad examination of the literature produced by the community of six providers identified earlier offers ample evidence for a growing homogenization of management approaches or what could be called the meta-language of sports development (see Table 1.3). Drawing from Townsend et al. (2002) it is contended that this meta-language represents a limited and culturally embedded view of sports development. Indeed, increasingly sports development has been couched in terms uncritically borrowed from the tenets of the New Public Management (NPM) school of thought that emerged in Western Europe and America in the 1980s. Contrary to the belief that the NPM represents a neutral and technical set of activities, performed by neutral technical experts, as Flynn (1997, p. 41) argued, 'management techniques and styles are themselves political', and that they form the core of 'managerialism' as an ideology. Brikenhoff and Coston (1999, p. 350) also explicitly defined development management as a 'value-laden endeavor'. Clarke et al. (2000, p. 9) contended that 'managerialism...defines a set of expectations, values and beliefs. It is a normative system concerning what counts as valuable knowledge, who knows it, and who is empowered to act in what ways as a consequence'.

Conceptualizing NPM as a meta-language highlights the constructive powers of the sports development discourse. The tenets of the NPM pervade the current thinking of sports development. For example, the *Government Plan for Sport* (DCMS, 2002) urged NGBs to improve the quality of their management and the use of modern business practices, such as strategic planning, target-setting and monitoring and evaluation. The Skills Active Research Report also encouraged sports development workers to polish their business management skills (Millar, 2005). Similarly, Thibault et al. (2002) demonstrated how the rise of the NPM ideology in local sport and recreation departments in Canada was partly responsible for a managerial discourse that rationalizes the withdrawal of government provision of services under the guise of community development. Whilst there is nothing wrong with sports development managers acquiring business skills to be deployed when dealing with complex issues, it should be remembered that sports development is not a business enterprise, but a social process of change, which involves real lives. As one community sports worker put it eloquently, 'no, I am not a manager. My job is about empowering communities. I don't manage, in the way you are describing, it wouldn't be appropriate' (Millar, 2005, p. 11).

Mintzberg et al. (2002) proposed an alternative notion of 'engaging management' and compared it to heroic management taught in the West. They described the former as 'to manage is to bring out the energy that exists naturally within people. Managing thus means inspiring and engaging', and the latter as 'to manage is to make decisions and allocate resources-including "human" resources. Managing means analyzing, often calculating' (p. 71). Mintzberg et al.'s (2002) argument challenges the logic of managerialism in sport, which is premised on the management of finite resources in a fragmented policy area. As established, sports development is a much broader and complex field of work, which is not confined to the narrow realm of physical activity. Engaging or creative management (Abbott et al., 2007) implies reconsidering the traditional models of targets setting, monitoring and eva-luation of sports development projects. It sensitizes managers that corporate writings produced by sports development agencies often locate 'development and poverty problems, ideas and policies not in social and political space but as a house ideology, presented however as beyond ideology, and therefore unquestionable' (Apthorpe, 1999, p. 540). Sports development workers have to engage with those they try to develop and generate indigenous information and knowledge as a basis for action.

Equally important, however, is another set of skills urged by globalization that managers need to master.

Edwards et al. (1999, p. 130) drew attention to the shift in the management of development from 'development-as-delivery to development-as-leverage'. The important point here is how the costs and benefits of global sports development are distributed. Major international organizations such as the EU, IOC and FIFA channel considerable financial and material resources, which have significant implications for sports development locally. Sports development managers have to learn how to better raise and utilize those resources and to relate to those providing them. The tension between global and local sports development influences the different skills required, and confuses organizations and managers about their identity. They have to be partly market-oriented by providing a cost-effective service in a highly competitive and politically regulated sports development field, and partly agents of fundamental social change concerned with transforming individual, community and organizational lives. Skills Active's (Millar, 2005, p. 5) representative survey identified some 30 relevant job titles pertinent to what might conveniently be called 'sports development managers', who performed several main functions, including 'practical coaching, teaching, leadership, face-to-face outreach work, advisor or councillor, facilitator or co-ordinator, manager, strategist or planner, senior or chief officer, hybrid and other'.

Thus, the management of sports development could be seen as distinctive and counter to the notion of the universal principles of management rooted in the belief in the universalizing power of the market, state and science. This is because the roles of the market, state and science varies enormously across countries. The same applies to their role in sport, as a recent British government policy document acknowledged the multiplicity of sport models in Western democracies based on differing philosophies, structures and delivery systems (DCMS, 2002, p. 84). Those models have evolved over many years and, as demonstrated by Collins (2003) and Houlihan and White (2002), are still far from producing an egalitarian vision of sports development that would benefit all members of society. Linstead's (1997, p. 88) social anthropology of management provided further support for its distinctiveness by suggesting that 'management is differentially defined at the operational level. This implies the need to study management closely in the field with sensitivity to both actions performed and the inter-subjective meaning given by the actors to those actions.'

In summary, the management of sports development could be described as possessing three interrelated aspects: (i) normative (for), which reflects various ideals of development; (ii) analytical (of) dealing with how the specific tasks involved in different interventions have to be managed; and (iii) process-oriented (in), which sets it 'not simply as a set of tasks to be performed but an ongoing set of relations, changing and emerging, affected by communication, perception, behavioural problems and styles, which need to be nurtured, developed or changed on a continuing basis' (Linstead, 1997, p. 88). It is value-laden and differs from the 'mainstream' management in its orientation and starting point.

Sports Development as an area of academic study

What does this mean for the study of management of sports development? Bernstein (2006, p. 53) argued that 'what justifies development studies as a specialism in its own right is the presumption that it is dedicated and *equipped* to generate *applied* knowledge in the formulation and implementation of development policies and interventions' (emphasis in original). Virtually all academic writings dedicated to sports development have centred on three sets of issues: (i) how to use sport for personal development; (ii) participation in sport and how to increase it; and (iii) inequality and how to overcome it through sport. In a comprehensive study of the social work of sport, Lawson (2005, p. 155) provided support for this conclusion, noting that sport, exercise and physical education professionals strive to achieve three interrelated aims concerned with improving the well-being of people, of places and government policies. Thus, the management of sports development as an academic discipline implies an expressed concern with generating applied knowledge in the form of development policies and implementations. The definition of the management of sports development employed by this book locates it in the realm of political, social and historical as well as management and organizational sciences. Hence, as an academic subject it has to contain both an applied and a non-applied theoretical aspect, ranging from policy analysis to social and personal change and managing organizational relationships and practical interventions.

The UK academic landscape of sports development studies is very diverse. At the time of writing there are some 246 courses with 'sports development' in their titles offered by 46 universities in combination with English literature, journalism, biological sciences and midwifery, to name but a few (UCAS, 2007). If the management of sports development is to establish itself as a credible academic discipline it has to adopt a clear developmental orientation and methods of enquiry that can generate indigenous and culturally relevant applied knowledge. A similar task amounts to reconsidering the epistemiological and ontological premises on which much of our understanding of mainstream management is built, and echoes the call for a management-with-development orientation. Recently, there has been a growing awareness among sport commentators for the need of such reconsideration. Maguire (2006, p. 114) addressed a fundamental tension between the technocratic and humanistic models in sports science, and argued for reconfiguring sports sciences: 'Sports science practice is guided and shaped by a technological discourse which focuses attention on talent identification, optimal training regimes, goal-setting and attention styles. Not all sports scientists embrace this focus. The humanist tradition was once an integral part of PE and found expression in areas, such as history, philosophy and pedagogy: at its best, it was concerned with themes and issues such as morality, equity, participation, learning, cooperation and the intrinsic properties of play and games. Humanists, at least in the context of Sport Exercise Science Departments, are in danger of becoming extinct.'

Amis and Silk's (2005, p. 363) discussion on critical and innovative approaches to the study of sport management advocated 'rethinking of the traditional criteria of validity, generalizability, credibility, and believability of our research – as assessed by the academy, our communities, and our participants – as we consider how we serve the interests of those who are researched, and how those research participants have more of a say at all points of the project'. Similarly, Frisby's (2005) critical sport management research raised a number of important issues concerning the epistemological and ontological premises of sport management as well as its constructive and deconstructive powers. Coalter (2006) also challenged the value of dominant outcome-driven sports development monitoring and evaluation manuals. The need for specific sports development management training and learning has been supported by evidence from staff working in various interventions settings, and is informative for the design of academic curricula. Table 1.5 shows the training needs of community sports development workers in six main clusters of work. Those needs may differ from the skills required from sports development officers in NGBs or local authorities, and further reinforce the point that sports development is a unique and complex field where the application of management tool kits is not unproblematic and where finding solutions to real life problems is what really matters.

Table 1.5 Training priorities of community sports development workers.

Clusters of workers	Training priorities (percent respondents)
Neighbourhood workers	Funding (46)
	Managing challenging behaviour (40)
	Sport session delivery (39)
	Sustainability (28)
Inner city	Funding (47)
	Managing challenging behaviour (38)
	Sustainability (33)
Coaching and leadership	Sport session delivery (45)
	Managing challenging behaviour (43)
	Funding (37)
Facilitators	Funding (48)
	Financial/budget management (29)
	Managing challenging behaviour (27)
	Sustainability (26)
Managers	Convergence training (42)
	Strategy, policy, development (42)
	Funding (37)
Workers under 24 years of age	Funding (59)
	Budget/financial management (38)
	Career development planning (31)

Source: Adopted from SkillsActive (Millar, 2005, p. 16)

Structure of the Book

This book offers a systematic and balanced approach to the study of the theory and practice of management of sports development. It is structured into five interrelated parts organized around the three contemporary core meanings of sports development as a *Vision, Social Change* and *Delivery Process*. The purpose of the introductory part is to provide an understanding of the meaning of the management of sports development, and to create an argument justifying it as an emerging academic field and profession. It uses those three interpretations of sports development as a guide to the content to the book. The first interpretation of sports development implies that we have to examine it as a *Vision*, as expressed in discourses promoted by various public, non-governmental and international agencies. The second suggests focusing on it as a *Historical Process of Social Change*, thus requiring an understanding of organizational behaviour and subjectivity. Finally, an interpretation of sports development as a deliberate effort on the part of various agencies aimed at the improvement of personal and social conditions entails dealing with the *Delivery* end. Contributions are explicitly concerned with identifying the key management issues that sports development workers have to be aware of and the skills they need to successfully tackle the challenges posed by those issues. The concluding part reflects back on the lessons from different chapters and draws some conclusions about the management of sports development and its study.

The purpose of Part Two, *Visions of Sports Development*, is to develop an understanding of sports development as a set of desirable end states, as expressed in the visions and practical policies of various public, voluntary and international organizations. The four chapters in this part seek to explain how visions of sports development come about, what are the key contributing factors shaping those visions and how they inform the practice of sports development. In *Models of Sports Development*, Kevin Hylton and Peter Bramham offer an overview of various conceptions about sports development, the key values they promote and the philosophical anthropology and political ideology that underpins them. It provides an interpretation of the relationship between visions (conceptions) of sports development and practical policies. The chapter on *Public Policies on Sports Development* by Mike Collins concentrates on current UK public policies on grass roots and elite sports development and analyses what visions of citizenship and organization of sport they envisage. A number of appropriate comparisons with other European countries and Australia are made. The third chapter on *Non-governmental Organisations in Sports Development* by Mick Green examines the role of non-profit developers in promoting the sports development agenda. Examples are drawn from a range of voluntary sport providers, and the Central Council for Physical Recreation and Youth Trust in particular, and the key management challenges they face including their relationships with the public sector are highlighted. Finally, Aaron Beacom and Roger Levermore's chapter on *International Policies and Sport-in-Development* interrogates the role which international agencies such as the UN, the IOC and the FIFA play in shaping the course of global sports development. The sports development policies designed by these organizations have significant implications for national and grass-roots sport associations, and this chapter addresses those issues by looking into the management tensions and opportunities which the global–local nexus creates.

Part Three of the book scrutinizes sports development as a *Process of Change* by establishing it within the wider social process of change, which concerns both organizations and individuals. In particular, the four contributions discuss the role of sport as an agent of social and personal change, as promoted through social institutions such as sport organizations, cities and the media and how people make sense of and experience it in different locations and cultural environments.

In *Sport as an Agent for Social and Personal Change*, Christine Green explores the potential of sport to affect organizational and personal changes. More specifically, she discusses how certain visions of sports development (e.g. as inclusion, diversion and 'hook') translate into changes on the ground and affect the culture, structures and modes of operations of sport organizations as well as the perceptions and experiences of different categories of participants. The chapter on *Mega Sporting Events and Sports Development* by Milena Parent examines a relatively little understood area which is the relationship between mega sporting events and sports development. It focuses on the connection between mega events and sports development policies and programmes both in Canada and the UK. The chapter provides evidence for three levels of change including policy, facilities and human resources and identifies managerial approaches for planning and utilizing this connection. The chapter on *Culture and Sports Development* by Laura Hills interrogates change at a personal level by looking at the link between subjectivity and sports development. This is achieved by examining how youth culture and gender construct young people's identities and perceptions about what constitutes improvement through sport and shapes their involvement in various initiatives. It provides managers with valuable insights into the role of culture in getting people involved in decision making, delivery and participation in sport. *Geographies of Sports Development: Understanding the Role of Space and Place* by Emma Wainwright and Nicola Ansell interprets sports development as an encounter between people and places that takes place in and through space. This is a central topic which affects the success of sports development policies and practice. Spaces of sports development are discussed as absolute, material and concrete but also as metaphorical and imaginative. Thus sports development is used to shape space and give meaning to place. The chapter reinforces the notion of sports development as a process of change that takes place through space involving negotiations over the meaning of place and who belongs in it, and offers valuable insights to sports development managers.

Part Four deals with sports development as *Delivery*. It concentrates on the building of organizational and management capacities needed to deliver the goods of sports development (development management) and on the practical activities aimed at meeting the needs and providing the tangible benefits of sports development to various constituencies (management of development). Andy Adams sets the scene in *Building Organisational and Management Capacity for the Delivery of Sports Development* by demonstrating how visions and policies on sports development are translated into concrete practical activities on the ground. In particular the chapter attempts to answer multifaceted questions such as what is capacity building and why is it important for sports development? What is civil society and why is it important to develop our understanding of the capacity-building enterprise for sports development? What is social capital and what is the relationship between this concept, civil society and the need or desire to build organizational and management capacity for sports development? It identifies core management competencies and skills needed by sport organizations at grass-roots and national levels in order to be able to implement and sustain the visions of development. In *Networks and Partnerships in Sports Development*, Barrie Houlihan and Iain Lindsey continue the theme of capacity building by focusing on the delivery of sports development through the combined efforts and resources of various agencies. The chapter discusses the process of developing three specific forms of partnerships between public, voluntary and private organizations – County Sport Partnership, New Opportunities for Physical Education and Sport Programmes and School Sport Partnership – concerned with the delivery of sports development and highlights the advantages and challenges involved in this process as well as the core management skills needed. *Funding Sports Development Activities* by Ian Jones explores the funding of sports development initiatives, focusing particularly on the issues related to the actual processes by which funding is gained, and the key concerns affecting both funding bodies and those seeking funding. A range of public, private and mixed (international) sources are discussed within the wider policy funding context in the UK and useful approaches and techniques are offered for sports development managers. Cora Burnnett's *Accounting for Sports Development (Progress Monitoring and Evaluation)* explores the controversial nature of the sports development monitoring and evaluation process. It advocates a bottom-up approach with clear guidelines on how co-ownership could be negotiated and could function for monitoring, evaluation and impact assessments of sports development programmes and interventions. The chapter suggests a practical tool for managing, monitoring, evaluation and impact assessments that may enhance comparative research and implementation of sports development.

The final chapter of the book *Managing Visions, Changes and Delivery in Sports Development: Summary and Prospects* by Vassil Girginov offers a summary of the three main interpretations of the management of sports development as a vision, process of organizational and personal change and related practices. It builds on the lessons from all previous chapters by providing a definition of the management of sports development and a conceptualization of the key issues and practical skills needed by sports development workers. The chapter concludes with some suggestions for future research and teaching and training agendas.

References

Abbott, D., Brown, S., and Wilson, G. (2007). Development management as reflective practice. *Journal of International Development*, **19**, 187–203.

Amis, J. and Silk, M. (2005). Rupture: Promoting critical and innovative approaches to the study of sport management. *Journal of Sport Management*, **19**, 355–66.

Andrews, D. (2004). Speaking the 'universal language of entertainment': News corporation, culture and the global sport media economy. In *Critical Readings: Sport, Culture and the Media* (D. Rowe, ed.). Maidenhead: Open University Press, pp. 99–129.

Apthorpe, R. (1999). Development studies and policy studies: In the short run we are all dead. *Journal of International Development*, **11**, 535–46.

Banuri, T. (1990). Modernization and its discontents: A cultural perspective on the theories of development. In *Dominating Knowledge* (F. Marglin and S. Marglin, eds). Oxford: Claredon Press.

Barnett, T. (1988). *Sociology and Development*. London: Hutchinson.

Bernstein, H. (2006). Studying development/Development studies. *African Studies*, **65**(1), 45–62.

Black, D. and Nauright, J. (1998). *Rugby and the South African Nation*. Glasgow: Manchester University Press.

Boutall, T. (2003). *Competences for Sport Workers in Community Cohesion*. Report prepared on behalf of Positive Futures and CCU.

Brikenhoff, D. and Coston, J. (1999). International development management in a globalized world. *Public Administration Review*, **59**(4), 346–61.

Brown, D. (1996). Pierre de Coubertin's Olympic exploration of modernism, 1894–1914: Aesthetics, ideology and the spectacle. *Research Quarterly for Exercise and Sport*, **67**(2), 118–39.

Cammack, P. (2003). The governance of global capitalism: A new materialist perspective. *Historical Materialism*, **11**(2), 37–59.

Cantelon, H. and Letters (2000). The making of the IOC environmental policy as the third dimension of the Olympic movement. *International Review of the Sociology of Sport*, **35**(3), 294–308.

Clammer, J. (2005). Culture, development, and social theory: On cultural studies and the place of culture in development. *The Asia Pacific Journal of Anthropology*, **6**(2), 100–19.

Clarke, J., Gewirtz, S., and McLaughlin, E. (eds). (2000). *New Managerialism, New Welfare?* Maidenhead: The Open University Press.

Coalter, F. (2006). Sport-in-development: Process evaluation and organisational development. In *Sport and Development* (Y. Vanden Auweele, C. Malcolm, and B. Meulders, eds). Leuven: LannooCampus, pp. 149–63.

Coleman, J. (1988). Social capital in the creation of human capital. *American Journal of Sociology*, **94**(supplement), 5095–120.

Collins, M. (1993). *Research on Sports Development*, mimeo, Loughborough: University of Loughborough.

Collins, M. (1995). *Sports Development Locally and Regionally*. Reading: Institute of Leisure and Amenity Management.

Collins, M. (2002). England: Sport for all as a multifaceted product of domestic and international influences. In *Worldwide Experiences and Trends in Sport for All* (L. Da Costa and A. Miragaya, eds). Aachen: Mayer & Meyer, pp. 493–523.

Collins, M. (2003). *Sport and Social Exclusion*. London: Routledge.

Collins, M. (2008). *Examining Sports Development*. London: Routledge.

Community Development Foundation (2004). *Survey of Community Development Workers in the UK*. A report on paid and unpaid community workers.

Cowen, M. and Shenton, R. (1995). The invention of development. In *Power of Development* (J. Crush, ed.). London: Routledge, Ch. 1, pp. 27–44.

Cowen, M. and Shenton, R. (1996). *Doctrines of Development*. New York: Routledge.

Crampton, R. (1994). *Eastern Europe in the Twentieth Century*. London: Routledge.

Crush, J. (1995). Introduction: Imagining development. In *Power of Development* (J. Crush, ed.). London: Routledge.

Cushman, G., Veal, A., and Zuzanek, J. (eds). (2005). *Free Time and Leisure Participation: International Perspectives.* Wallingford: CABI Publishing.

Cutler, I. (2000). The cynical manager. *Management Learning,* **31**(3), 295–312.

DCMS (Department of Culture, Media Sport) (2002). *Game Plan.* London: DCMS.

Eady, J. (1993). *Practical Sports Development.* London: Hodder & Stoughton.

Edwards, M., Hulme, D., and Wallace, T. (1999). NGOs in a global future: Marrying local delivery to worldwide leverage. *Public Administration and Development,* **19**, 117–36.

Esman, M. (1972). *Management Dimensions of Development.* West Hartford: Kumarian Press.

Esteva, G. (1997). Development. In *The Development Dictionary* (W. Sachs, ed.). London: Zed Books.

Federal Office of Sport Magglingen (2005). The Magglingen Call for Action 2003 and 2005 (available at www.magglingen2005.org, accessed on 18 July 2007).

FIFA (2004). *FIFA World Report on Football Development,* Vol. 1. Zurich: FIFA.

Flynn, N. (1997). *Public Sector Management.* Hemel Hempstead: Prentice-Hall/Harvester.

Fox, K.R. (2004). Tackling obesity in children through physical activity: A perspective from the United Kingdom. *Quest,* **56**, 28–40.

Frank, A.G. (1969). *Latin America: Underdevelopment or Revolution.* New York: Monthly Review.

Frisby, W. (2005). The Good, the Bad, and the Ugly: Critical Sport Management Research. *Journal of Sport Management,* **19**, 1–12.

Girginov, V. (2008). Management challenges to global sports development governance. *Sport Management Review* (forthcoming).

Gratton, C. and Henry, I. (eds). (2001). *Sport in the City.* London: Routledge.

Green, C. (2005). Building sport programs to optimize athlete recruitment, retention, and transition: Toward a normative theory of sport development. *Journal of Sport Management,* **19**, 233–53.

Green, M. and Houlihan, B. (2005). *Elite Sport Development.* London: Routledge.

Green, M. and Houlihan, B. (2006). Governmentality, modernization, and the 'disciplining' of national sporting organizations: Athletics in Australia and the United Kingdom. *Sociology of Sport Journal,* **23**, 47–71.

Gruneau, R. (1997). The politics and ideology of active living in historical perspective. In *Physical Activity in Human Experience. Interdisciplinary Perspective* (J. Curtis and S. Russell, eds). Champaign, IL: Human Kinetics.

Harvey, J. (2002). Sport and citizenship policy: A shift toward a new normative framework for evaluating sport policy in Canada. *Printemps,* Spring, 160–5.

Held, D. (2006). Reframing global governance: Apocalypse soon or reform! *The New Political Economy,* **11**(2), 157–76.

Henry, I. (2001). *The Politics of Leisure Policy,* 2nd edn. Basingstoke: Palgrave.

Hong, F., Wu, P., and Xiong, H. (2005). Beijing ambitions: An analysis of the Chinese elite sport system and its Olympic strategy for the 2008 Olympic games. *The International Journal of the History of Sport,* **22**(4), 510–29.

Houlihan, B. (2000). Sporting excellence, schools and sports development: The politics of crowded policy spaces. *European Physical Education Review,* **6**(2), 171–93.

Houlihan, B. and White, A. (2002). *The Politics of Sports Development: Development of Sport or Development Through Sport?* London: Routledge.

Hume, D. (1748). *Essays Moral and Political* (edited by Eugene Rotwein; London: Nelson, 1955).

Hylton, K., Bramham, P., Jackson, D., and Nesti, M. (2001). *Sports Development: Policy, Process and Practice.* London: Routledge.

Hylton, K., Bramham, P., Jackson, D., and Nesti, M. (2007). *Sports Development: Policy, Process and Practice*, 2nd edn. London: Routledge.

Inglehart, R. (1997). *Moderenization and Postmodernization: Cultural, Economic and Political Change in 43 Societies*. Princenton: Princenton University Press.

International Olympic Committee (2005). *Unity of Strength, 2005-2008 Quadrennial Plan*. Lausanne: IOC.

Kitching, G. (1982). *Class and Economic Change in Kenya*. New Haven: Yale University Press.

Kohler, H. and Wolfensohn, J. (2000). The IMF and the World Bank Group: An Enhanced Partnership for Sustainable Growth and Poverty Reduction, Statement issued 5 September, Washington DC.

Lawson, H. (2005). Empowering people, facilitating community development, and contributing to sustainable development: The social work of sport, exercise, and physical education programs. *Sport, Education, Society*, **10**, 135–60.

Lentell, B. (1993). Sports development: Good buy to community recreation? In *Body Matters: Leisure Images and Lifestyles* (C. Brackenridge, ed.). Hove: LSA Publication, No. 7, pp. 141–50.

Lewis, A. (2002). The roots of development theory. In *Handbook of Development Economics*, Vol. 1 (H. Chenery and T.N. Srinivasan, eds). London: Elsevier, Ch. 2, pp. 28–37.

Linstead, S. (1997). The social anthropolgy of management. *British Journal of Management*, **8**, 85–98.

MacIntosh, P. and Charlton, V. (1985). *The Impact of the Sport for All Policy*. London: Sports Council.

Maguire, J. (2006). Development through sports science and sports industrial complex: The case of human development in sports and exercise sciences. In *Sport and Development* (Y. Vanden Auweele, C. Malcolm, and B. Meulders, eds). Leuven: LannooCampus.

Mangan, A. (1981). *Athleticism in the Victorian and Edwardian Public School: The Emergence and Consolidation of an Educational Ideology*. Cambridge: Cambridge University Press.

Mangan, A. (ed.). (2000). Making European masculinities: Sport, Europe, gender. *The European Sports History Review*, Vol. 2. London: Frank Cass.

Mangan, A. (ed.). (2002). Reformers, sport, modernizers: Middle class revolutionaries. *The European Sports History Review*, Vol. 4. London: Frank Cass.

Millar, T. (2005). *Community and Sport Development Research Project Report*. London: SkillsActive.

Mintzberg, H. (2006). Developing leaders? Developing countries? *Development in Practice*, **16**(1), 4–14.

Mintzberg, H., Simons, R., and Basu, K. (2002). Beyond selfishness. *MIT Sloan Management Review*, Fall, **44**(1), 67–74.

Perry, M. (1992). *An Intellectual History of Modern Europe*. Boston, MA: Houghton Mifflin.

Powell, M. (1995). Culture: Intervention or solidarity. *Development in Practice*, **5**(3), 196–206.

Riordan, J. and Kruger, A. (2003). Introduction. In *European Cultures of Sport: Examining the Nations and Regions* , (J. Riordan and A. Kruger, eds). Bristol: Intellect.

Robinson, D., Hewitt, T., and Harris, J. (2000). Why inter-organizational relations matter. In *Managing Development. Understanding Inter-Organizational Relationships* (D. Robinson, T. Hewitt, and J. Harris, eds). London: Sage.

Ross, H. and Bouwmeesters, J. (eds). (1972). *Management in the Developing Countries: A Field Survey*. Geneva: UN Research Institute for Social Development.

Rostow, W. (1960). *The Stages of Economic Growth: A Non-communist Manifesto*, 2nd edn. Cambridge: Cambridge University Press.

Rowe, N., Adams, R., and Beasley, N. (2004). Driving up participation in sport: The social context, the trends, the prospects and the challenges. Cited in Sport England (2004) *Driving up participation: The challenge for sport*. London: Sport England.

Sachs, W. (ed.). (1997). *The Development Dictionary*. London: Zed Books.

Schech, S. and Haggis, J. (2000). *Culture and Development*. Oxford: Blackwell.

Seers, D. (1979). The meaning of development. In *Development Theory: Four Critical Studies* (D. Lehmann, ed.). London: Frank Cass, pp. 9–32.

Sen, A. (1999). *Development as Freedom*. Oxford: Oxford University Press.

Slack, T. (ed.). (2005). *The Commercialisation of Sport*. London: Routledge.

Smith, A. (1776). *An Inquiry into the Nature and Causes of the Wealth of Nations*. Reprinted; edited by R.H. Campbell and A.S. Skinner. Oxford: Clarendon Press (1976).

Sport and Development International Platform (2007). www.sportanddev.org.

Sportdevelopment.org.uk (2007). www.sportdevelopment.org.uk, accessed 28 February 2007.

Sport England (1999). *Best Value – The Value of Sport*. London: Sport England.

Sport England (2004). *The Framework for Sport in England: Vision 2020*. London: Sport England.

SPRITO (2001). *Social Exclusion and Sport: The Role of Training and Learning*. London: SPRITO.

Starky, S. (2005). Obesity Epidemic in Canada. Ottawa: Parliamentary Information and Research Services (available at http://www.parl.gc.ca/information/library/PRBpubs/prb0511-e.htm, accessed 18 July 2006).

Staudt, K. (1991). *Managing Development: State, Society, and International Contexts*. London: Sage.

Steuart, J. (1767). *Enquiry into the Principles of Political Economy* (edited by A. Skinner; London: Oliver & Boyd, 1966).

Thibault, L., Kikulis, L., and Frisby, W. (2002). Partnerships between local government sport and leisure departments and the commercial sector: Changes, complexities, and consequences. In *The Commercialisation of Sport* (T. Slack, ed.). London: Fran Cass, pp. 119–40.

Thomas, A. (1996). What is development management? *Journal of International Development*, **8**(1), 95–110.

Thomas, A. (1999). What makes good development management? *Development in Practice*, **9**(1&2), 9–17.

Thomas, A. (2000a). Meanings and views of development. In *Poverty and Development into the 21st Century* (T. Allen and A. Thomas, eds). Oxford: Oxford University Press, pp. 23–51.

Thomas, A. (2000b). Development as practice in a liberal capitalist world. *Journal of International Development*, **12**(6), 773–87.

Thorbecke, E. (2000). The evolution of the development doctrine and the role of foreign aid, 1950–2000. In *Foreign Aid and Development: Lessons Learnt and Directions for the Future* (F. Tarp and P. Hjertholm, eds). London: Routledge.

Townsend, J., Porter, G., and Mawdsley, E. (2002). The role of transnational community of non-government organisations: Governance or poverty reduction? *Journal of International Development*, **14**, 29–39.

Tranter, N. (1998). *Sport, Economy and Society in Britain 1750–1914*. Cambridge: Cambridge University Press, p. 41.

UCAS (2007). UCAS web site www.ucas.ac.uk, assessed 5 September 2007.

United Nations (2003). *Sport for Development and Peace: Towards Achieving the Millennium Development Goals*. Report from the UN Inter-Agency Task Force on Sport for Development and Peace: New York.

United Nations (2005). *Millennium Development Goals* (available at http://www.un.org/millenniumgoals/, accessed 18 June 2007).

Van Bottenburg, M., Rijnen, B., and van Sterkenburg, J. (2005). *Sports Participation in the European Union: Trends and Differences*. Nieuwegein: W.J.H. Mulier Institute and Arko Sports Media.

Van Eekeren, F. (2006). Sport and development: Challenges in a new arena. In *Sport and Development* (Y. Vanden Auweele, C. Malcolm, and B. Meulders, eds). Leuven: LannooCampus.

Wallace, T. (2000). Development management and the aid chain: The case of NGOs. *In Development and Management: Experiences in Values-based Conflict* (Deborah Eade, Tom Hewitt, and Hazel Johnson, eds). Oxford: Oxfam GB, 18–38.

Wolfenden Report (1960). *Sport in the Community: The Wolfenden Committee on Sport 1960* (chairman: Sir John Wolfenden), London: CCPR.

Woodall, J. and Winstanley, D. (1998). *Management Development: Strategy and Practice.* Oxford: Blackwell.

Woolcock, M. (1998). Social capital and economic development: Toward a theoretical synthesis and policy framework. *Theory and Society*, **27**, 151–208.

Zippay, A. (1995). The politics of empowerment. *Social Work*, **40**(2), 263–7.

PART TWO

Visions of Sports Development

CHAPTER 2

Models of Sports Development

Kevin Hylton and Peter Bramham

A vision without action is just a dream,
Action without vision passes the time
A vision with action can change the world.

Nelson Mandela (cited by Gordon Brown,
UK Chancellor of the Exchequer, 2006)

Introduction

This chapter examines the protean nature of sports development as its policy
and practice are viewed through three distinctive lenses: political ideology,
functionalist social theory and community development. Sports development
in the United Kingdom mirrors its instrumental and global use as an expressed
panacea for many social ills. Sport policy and practice are often driven by
potential benefits that may accrue to social groups, whether they be local,
national or transnational, elite performers or the more marginal disaggregated
and unhealthy individuals suffering various forms of social exclusion. This
chapter emphasises different political roots of sporting discourses and in particular aligns mainstream sports development with functionalist arguments
that emphasise sport's role in sustaining diverse externalities. The chapter will
further problematise some of the conservative domain assumptions of func-
tionalism as they apply to power relations, ideas of community and diverse
practices of sports development.

Drawing on policy analysis and community development perspectives, the
chapter explores the relationship between different political ideologies and
sports development models as they conflate mass and elite sports development. It will be argued that the development of sport requires a different
infrastructure to one for developing local communities because different skills,
knowledge and resources are necessary to maintain conditions for success in
each case. Competing discourses in the development of sport and the development of community emphasise the inadequacy of traditional approaches to
sports policy, persisting institutional arrangements and established coaching

practices. This is emphasised in the persistence of traditional models of sports development that simplify pathways to success from foundation level skills development to excellence (see Hylton and Bramham, 2008, pp. 5–6). In addition, periodic strategic visions of sports development supplement these traditional conceptions as they emphasise the potential for success in achieving current agendas.

John Major's Raising the Game (DNH, 1995) initiatives in the mid-1990s for school sport and excellence, and New Labour's Joint–Working for Neighbourhood Renewal Strategies (ODPM, 2004) are examples of how inconsistent stresses are placed upon sports development. These recurring challenges place the onus on those in sports development to envision new versions of sports development that are both proactive in tackling contemporary problems and able to satisfy emerging issues. These visions of sports development must also take into consideration the dynamics of

- the political economy of sectors and levels of sports development (Hylton and Totten, 2008);
- the plethora of cross-sectoral stakeholders;
- the complex cross-sectoral funding arrangements;
- changing demographic patterns.

Indeed, one task of policy advocacy is to outline strategies which map out distinctive models of sports development. Such models offer new visions and policy opportunities for both established sports institutions and new sports organisations. They are generated in response to challenges, either from new governments driven by distinctive political ideologies or from policy communities keen to find solutions to recalcitrant problems with respect to mass participation and sport performance. Policy brokers offer models of sports development that address current political discourses with new prescriptions for partnerships and management practice. We must be certain that sports development is situated and understood in relation to its history, its present context and its often uncertain future. Sports development is a complex maelstrom of processes, practices and policies that generate both continuities and change and as such must be treated with some caution.

In the second edition of *Sports Development* (Hylton and Bramham, 2008) we emphasise these conceptual and practical anomalies by adopting a pragmatic approach to how we consider the field. We conclude that as an academic arena sports development is ostensibly a multidisciplinary one that draws critique about its constituent elements. Sport *policies, processes and practices* make up the sports development triad, which together enable policymakers, practitioners and academics to forge a coherent picture of this thing labelled *sports development* (Hylton and Bramham, 2008, p. 2). It is not the aim of this chapter or even this book to resolve the problematics presented here but to continue debates and illuminate discussions. But how we label and identify something affects the way others see it and the way we theorise conceptualisations affects the behaviours of others in ways that we cannot fully appreciate as we put pen to paper. So as we now write about sports development do not conclude that it is

- an uncontested concept;
- clearly defined in political discourse;
- historically or geographically fixed;
- a coherent profession;
- recognised across professions.

Such caveats hint at the delicate setting that those writing about and planning for sports development find themselves. The plethora of bodies with some responsibility for the development of sport results in difficult questions about how we can establish coherent sports development policies. The who, where, how and why of sports development have constantly been questions framed without sustained critical evaluation and it is a sign of the times that it is only in this last decade that sports development has been considered a serious proposition for academic and professional debates.

We contend that the elite–grassroots sport dichotomy has exercised the minds of sports professionals and policymakers with few instances of sustained critical analysis (Houlihan and White, 2002; Hylton and Bramham, 2008, and indeed this book – see the introductory chapter). Conceptualisations of the sports development process and programmes have often revolved around simple models of the way things ought to happen in the development of sport. More recently notions of delivery systems for sport using the concepts of community sport networks have supplemented traditional sports development continua and frameworks advocated by quangos like Sport England. However, what we detect is not development in the way key stakeholders think about sports development but conceptual inflation as new ideas on 'the way forward' become reinvented so that those who see themselves as part of the sports development profession have to manage disparate ideas to ensure good practice.

Policies and underpinning ideologies often lead to how we approach the development of sport and there are many examples over history of the quality of sport today being the result of policy developments from yesterday. What the team behind the London 2012 Olympics and key stakeholders in sport achieve in the next few years will have a direct impact on elite developments in relation to Olympic Games as well as foundation level grassroots sport.

Sports Development as Intended Policy

One key argument of this chapter is that sports development is not only a contested field of policy and professional practice but it is also championed as a contemporary solution to past problems and failures. It is therefore essential to provide some historical backdrop to our analysis in order to highlight tensions in sports policies. One must also identify the UK context which privileges an ideological space for sports development to be championed by some as the rational solution to previous contradictions and unresolved problems. This is in keeping with the view that sports development must be seen as a *process* rather than a secure and steady state of institutionalised professional practice.

So what are the acknowledged and unacknowledged tensions in sport and how do they find their expression within sports policy? One obvious way to trace the history of sport and sport policy is to offer a detailed account of how sporting experiences are delivered and realised by the major institutions of modernity – market, society and the nation state. Ken Roberts (2004) has clearly pointed out that modern leisure is made up in both fact and values by three leisure sectors – commercial, voluntary and public institutions, each driven metaphorically by different 'engines'. One could then offer a descriptive account of each sector and detail the functional division of labour to emerge. Each period of UK sports history can be characterised by the hegemonic leadership provided by one sector or secured by negotiated alliances between them. These three sport sectors function as tectonic plates that offer both stability and change in the everyday lives of individuals, routines of organisations and key institutional structures. At critical times they can grind together and generate contradictions, which sometimes undermine the best-laid plans of human agency. Participation or recreational sport has been nurtured by local enthusiasms of the voluntary sector, whereas performance or elite sport has been driven globally by commercial companies, particularly transnational media conglomerates. However, post Second World War the nation state itself has intervened, often 'at arm's length', in order to coordinate, to regulate and, at times, to provide directly through the local state.

But Roberts' seminal ideas are more complex. His arguments and evidence can be stated briefly here – the commercial sector is economic and is driven forwards by the capitalist quest for profit and accumulation. The voluntary sector is social and is forged in enthusiasms, thereby nurturing bedrock relations of neighbourhood, community and social capital in civil society. Discourses on business management and professionalisation mean very different things for the diverse sectors, and have different implications for managers. Roberts examines the voluntary base to sporting organisations and maps out factors that have led to the growing commercialisation and mediatisation of elite national and international sport (see also Horne, 2006).

By way of contrast, the public sector is political and must continually search for political ideas to legitimate state regulation, taxation and policy provision. Whereas the commercial and voluntary sectors are in their different ways self-referencing, self-contained and self-sustaining, the public sector is more open to changing discourses, shifting rationales in order to justify the distinctive function of the state and its precise relationship with the other two leisure providers. In contrast, the public sector presents much more of a paradox, as it is all about politics and ideological justification. Consequently, policymakers are open to intellectual debate, drawing upon a variety of justifications and evidence to authorise interventions and perhaps unsurprisingly, these can shift over time. Roberts is quite clear in his own mind about the scope of public policy in sport and leisure,

> It will be argued that redressing economic disadvantages (reaching out to the poor) spreading virtue, and enabling people to fulfil their own leisure ambitions, fall into the former (unrealisable) group. The genuine capabilities which are special to public provisions are investing in loss leaders in order to trigger an economic multiplier, extending citizenship, enhancing national (or local or regional) prestige and identities, and setting standards
>
> (Roberts, 2004, p. 39).

So one direct challenge to sport policy is to come to terms with complexity of the three diverse sectors. Political ideologies can prescribe favoured relations between the commercial and voluntary sectors as well as map distinctive political externalities that sports may aim for and realise in practice. But, as is often the case with public policies, governments do have to deal with institutional inertia, enthusiasms and resistances of established 'insider' policy communities, as well as new demands from 'outsider' social movements. There is also the corrosive nature of the policy cycle – policy initiation, policy strategy and implementation and not least strident media and electorate demands for research and evidence of promised policy outcomes. Are sports policies value for money? Do sports policies achieve stated outcomes and are they grounded in realistic timescales? Sports development managers may feel the need to be firm advocates for their programmes, pilot schemes and fund-winning initiatives but politicians and policymakers feel for the safe grounds of pragmatism. In sport it seems so much better to settle for incrementalist policies than embark on major structural reform of traditional institutions, policy networks and organisations.

Policy making is a risky business. But nevertheless governments are often forced reluctantly into sports policy arenas or they demand that sports policies contribute to wider cultural, social and economic goals. Even within the narrower sphere of sports policy there are a myriad of reactive policies necessary to sort out existing 'bad' practices. Do all sports deal with discrimination on the grounds of disability, class, 'race' and gender? Should talent and gifted policies specialise or focus on multi-skills development? Do sports initiatives and extra-curricular activities reach and develop intended targets? Can such programmes in specialist sports schools raise generic education standards and attainments? Are child protection policies sufficiently robust and transparent to deal with sexual, physical and verbal abuse against child athletes? Are coaching styles safe in avoiding sports injuries and player burnout? Are volunteer coaches sufficiently competent in knowledge transfer, training regimes, personal and management skills and so on? Are there clear coaching pathways to develop young athletes in order to build bridges between school, sports clubs and local wider communities? Do individual sports have adequate long-term athlete development plans in place? What happens to elite athletes once sporting careers are over? These may be major concerns for sports policy wonks but media coverage on sport focuses on more controversial 'newsworthy' issues – success and failure, drug use and abuse, violence and cheating in professional sports. Sports reporters forensically explore the private lives of sports stars, those shifting class, racial and sexual identities of global heroes and heroines. With growing commodification and commercialisation of sport in the form of media sponsorship, merchandising and image rights, gambling and corruption on sporting outcomes become more viable.

Political Traditions, Policy and Sports Development Models

As we have recently argued (Hylton and Bramham, 2008), major political ideologies of conservatism, liberalism and social reformism offer different prescriptions for public policy; they define the preferred relationship between nation state, civil society and markets. Political traditions direct public policy as well as map out contours of key institutions which define and empower stakeholders in the policy process. In post-war UK, policy has been shaped by social reformism in the domain of sport, leisure and culture. Conservative and Labour governments gradually set up quangos such as the Arts Council, the Sports Council and the Countryside Commission, to plan and develop facilities and opportunities. In 1994 the Department of Heritage empowered agencies to distribute National Lottery funds. Despite changes in governments, this 'arm's length' approach to policy has been both politically and ideologically expedient by providing institutional continuity. Governments provide subsidy and appoint quango personnel but are not directly accountable in parliament for policy decisions and outcomes. This is in no way to suggest that sports policy is an ideologically battle-free zone. Sports policy cannot avoid moral panics in the media mentioned earlier with regard to national elite sports performance, alcohol and drug abuse, football hooliganism, racism and sexism, childhood obesity and so on. The sports policy universe is inevitably drawn into each government's political ideology and policy agenda therein sabotaging concerted attempts to make any sports development more coherent.

Detailed histories of the development of UK sports policy are already well established. Establishment of the Sports Council in 1972 was a response to successful lobbying by voluntary governing bodies organising sport (NGBs), orchestrated by the Central Council for Physical Recreation (CCPR), but was also a clear expression of conservative beliefs in the intrinsic value of sport. Sport and recreation were also seen as means to deal with disaffected British youth. National culture had to be preserved within the next generation as the 1960s witnessed growing moral panic about the corrosive impact of American media and consumer culture. The 'expressive' revolution of sex, drugs and rock-n-roll diluted traditional authority of the family, school and community. Equally, black youth were scapegoated as the cause of inner-city problems rather than victims, as news media amplified 'mugging' into a symptom of a violent racially divided society (Hall et al., 1978). Youth work and sport were therefore seen as crucial ingredients to divert youth, particularly those unemployed and living in inner-city working class neighbourhoods away from crime and delinquency and into sport and active lifestyles. Effectively this policy provided one of the first examples of sport crossing boundaries and joining up thinking using a targeted community development approach (DoE, 1989).

Youth sport, whether organised by physical education teachers, youth development workers, coaches and sports *animateurs* or the police, was and still is defined as a crucial setting to re-establish moral values, healthy lifestyles and so rebuild fragmenting communities and avoid social exclusion. These themes have been popularised by Robert Putnam's (2000) idea of 'social capital'; US bowling leagues had acted as social glue, binding together healthy community networks. High-achieving schools, excellent health and care services, high rates of employment and sporting opportunities all served to build local relations of trust; good neighbouring suppressed high rates of family breakdown, of crime, delinquency and social disorder. Around this time, Conservatism defined performance of national teams in international sport as an important indicator of successful sports policy. Conservatism valued the voluntary sector in sports organisations (see Roberts, 2004), particularly traditional male 'English' team games, such as cricket, rugby and football. Failures in World and Olympic Games were read as significant historical indicators of decline in UK culture and competitiveness. Consequently, tension between national elite performance and local community participation, albeit often focused in targeted populations, has been the hallmark of post-war UK sports policy.

Discourses around sports development have filled an ideological space in order to address some inherent contradictions between elite sport performance and mass participation. Sports development has been articulated as a model or framework to build bridges or pathways between elite sport performance and sport as mass sport participation. As we shall see later, it provides a functionalist account of an integrated system of sport that works organically and systemically. It performs the ideological repair work of justifying the status quo, ignoring contradictions and silencing systemic inequalities. Perhaps unsurprisingly these shifting priorities in sports policies have been conflated and reconfigured in the Sports Council's sporting pyramid, a continuum from foundation, to participation, performance and on to elite excellence (see Hylton and Bramham, 2008, pp. 5–6). A broad base of mass participation and talent identification of young athletes was perceived as essential for excellence in elite performance. It is stridently reiterated that sports development should increase sports participation, whilst simultaneously provide sporting and coaching pathways to elite performance.

If the Conservative government was attracted to sport mainly because of intrinsic benefits, during the 1970s a social reformist Labour government was keen to promote sporting opportunities as an integrated part of a comprehensive welfare state. Such an inclusive approach was heralded in the 'Sport for All' campaign (Sports Council, 1982). One important physical expression of this policy appeared in the planning, management and development of sports facilities. Local authorities, encouraged by Regional Sports Councils, invested heavily in both large-scale and community-based facilities. As with other aspects of state welfare provision, there developed a growing professionalism within the public sector around marketing and delivery of leisure services. At the same time, there was growing dissatisfaction with social reformism, mounted by New Right ideas around public choice. Sports policy was now felt to be dominated by local government. The nature of sports provision was seen to be inefficient, ineffective and unnecessary.

New Right ideology argued that government subsidy in sport was inappropriate (Henry, 2001). Individuals should be free to meet their sporting wants through the commercial or voluntary sectors rather than having their sporting needs defined by distant quangos or central or local government. Olympic elites and national governing bodies should look to business sponsorship for support rather than rely on welfare subsidies from a 'nanny state'. However, faced by inner-city riots, the New Right Thatcherite government was not completely deaf to extrinsic benefits of sports provision for troublesome youth. During the 1980s, unemployed and black minorities were drawn into a variety of community-based sports leadership schemes, financed by urban aid programmes. This was the emergence of what came to be seen as the new profession of sports development through the 'Action Sport' programme (Rigg, 1986).

Another paradox of New Right policies at this time was the growth of diverse government quangos to bypass the power of local authorities and to weaken the collective professional base and trade union rights of public sector producers. The Thatcher hegemonic neo-liberal project vaunted a minimalist state yet simultaneously presided over expansion of a wide range of government agencies and quangos. Traditional government bureaucracies and civil servants were viewed by the New Right as self-serving inefficient bureaucrats and the Sports Council itself was subjected to numerous reviews which raised severe doubts about its future policy direction and possible continuation of the sports development model it promoted.

During the mid-1990s the Major government pragmatically breathed new life into the Sports Council through National Lottery Funding and with its commitment to the UK Sports Institute to secure excellence. The government reasserted the intrinsic benefits of team sports and introduced a raft of policy initiatives in *Sport: Raising the Game* (1995) to strengthen sporting opportunities within the PE curriculum and within extra-curricular activities. Emergence of the Youth Sports Trust provided new pathways for youth sport through TOP initiatives in combination with the National Coaching Foundation's Champion Coaching scheme. Some commentators argued that media panic about loss of school playing fields and sports opportunities has overstated the crisis in youth sport (Roberts, 1996). Conservative emphasis on traditional team sports (and their local playing field infrastructure) fails to acknowledge emerging choices for more individualised lifestyle sports, physical conditioning and exercise regimes. Healthy lifestyles are more likely to be realised indoor inside the gym and leisure centre than outside on grass or artificial pitches. Roberts argues that school sport is not so much in decline but rather that pupils are adopting a more personalised individualised approach.

New Labour and a New Role for Sport

During the past decade New Labour has pursued similar sports objectives as a New Right administration. But it is a complicated narrative. Discourses on social exclusion have become increasingly central to New Labour political ideology and policies. However, tensions continue to exist in current policies between Fordist and post-Fordist regimes of regulation, between collectivist and individualist ideologies, between social exclusion and inclusion. Such tensions find their expressions not only in academic literature but also in national policy documents. With these debates unresolved it is hardly surprising that local managers and front-line practitioners are confused or take a pragmatic response in using presumed extrinsic benefits in their justification for funding for sports and cultural projects.

In the 2000s, New Labour's 'Third Way' has tentatively reaffirmed a more holistic approach to public policy in rhetoric only with its demand for more 'joined-up thinking' in policy planning as well as through an increased emphasis on partnerships for policy delivery (ODPM, 2004). Sports development has not been immune from this shift in policy; indeed, it is a response to it. But as Stuart Hall (2003) has rightly pointed out, New Labour has simply continued the neo-liberal project. Whereas Thatcher's 'odd couple' were the ideologies of conservatism and liberalism to form the New Right, Blair has synthesised neo-liberalism with a much weaker social reformism. New Labour stresses the importance of 'governance' of deploying partnerships with the private and the voluntary sector so that state institutions dissolve into civil society. But it is still committed to a centralised 'contract culture' where local authorities have to meet centrally defined and determined policy indicators which bypass democratic local politics, interest groups and community networks. It is through this contract culture and partnership that New Labour demands hard evidence that projects meet its agenda for tackling social exclusion.

Because sport and culture are seen to be public goods, there is a presumption that they can be set to the task of addressing social inclusion. Indeed, the report of Policy Action Team 10 (arts and sport) to the government's Social Exclusion Unit (PAT 10, 1999, pp. 5–6), suggested just that: 'Arts and sport are inclusive and can contribute to neighbourhood renewal. Arts and sports bodies should acknowledge that social inclusion is part of their business. Arts and sport are not just an add-on to regeneration work.'

These beliefs were further reflected in the foreword by Chris Smith (then Secretary of State for the Department for Culture Media and Sport – DCMS), who wrote:

'The report shows that art and sport can not only make a valuable contribution to delivering key outcomes of lower long-term unemployment, less crime, better health and better qualifications, but can also help to develop the individual pride, community spirit and capacity for responsibility that enable communities to run regeneration programmes themselves' (DCMS, 1999, p. 2).

However, the authors of the PAT 10 report went on to note that there is little substantive evidence to support the claims for social benefits that might advance inclusion. These presumptions, despite the lack of evidence, are exacerbated by

the unproblematic treatment of social inclusion in academic and policy literature. With New Labour encouraging a distinctive modernising policy discourse
about sports and cultural projects and social exclusion, a real challenge is posed
for local, regional and national sports and cultural projects claiming social
inclusion to appear transparent in their accounting for such things (see Girginov's introductory chapter). Government now demands hard evidence to
measure policy outcomes on performance indicators such as education, employment, crime and health. However, community-based sports development
workers are hard pressed to collect valid and reliable data that evaluate
projects against clear criteria for social inclusion (Long and Sanderson, 2001).
Considerable energy is required to form new alliances and sports partnerships to
resolve the dilemmas posed by a confused policy discourse and by fragile funding
streams. To make matters worse local authorities now compete against others to
win resources from such initiatives as City Challenge and Spaces for Arts and
Sport. Rather than collective welfare provision, New Labour governance is 'hol-
lowed out' into pragmatic local and regional partnerships and projects. However,
Local Public Service Agreements and Local Area Agreements ensure that the local
state functions as an agent rather than a partner to central government policies
(see Long and Bramham, 2006).

During the first years of this century, government departments such as the
Department of Culture Media and Sport and the Social Exclusion Unit in the
Cabinet Office have therefore put increasing pressure on Sport England, NGBs
and local authorities to demonstrate how sporting outcomes contribute to its
wider policy agenda related to social exclusion (Collins and Kay, 2003). With
its Physical Education School Club Link initiatives, the Labour government has
also funded education and sporting partnerships between Specialist Sports
Colleges and NGBs to increase both mass participation and to identify talent
and gifted young athletes. Deep-seated contradictions between intrinsic and
extrinsic rationales for sport abound and are glossed over in sports policy
discourse. For example, the presentation bid, strongly supported by New
Labour, to host the 2012 Olympics in London illustrated sport's complex
position in relation to a broader government agenda of social, economic and
cultural policies (London 2012 Website, 2007). A multi-racial group of inner-
city school children were taken along to help Lord Coe justify the British bid,
as if they were to be the main beneficiaries of the Olympic sporting facilities. It
is this capacity of sport to offer governments help in achieving wider policy
goals which explains continuity in support for sports policies, albeit from
governments working from different ideological scripts.

Mainstream and Radical Perspectives of Sports Development: Functionalism and Community Development

A key imperative underpinning sport policy is its function as a tool for social
good. Sport is traditionally promoted as a method of building character and
community, discipline, morality and ethical behaviour, reducing exclusion,

increasing cohesion, reducing illness, improving well-being and quality of life. Major social divisions of 'race', class, gender and disability are also legitimate targets for sports development and sports capabilities to effect positive and sustained change for policymakers and practitioners. Those emphasising what could be deemed a functionalist view of society reiterate a view of social order which is fundamentally consensual and harmonious. Here social groups negotiate their different needs for the greater good of the community to ensure harmony and stability are maintained. Implicit confidence among those making such bold statements on sports efficacy as in the previous statement by Chris Smith in the PAT 10 report is underpinned by a series of presumptions:

Presumption 1: Society is a simple system of structures and agents to be kept in balance to function smoothly.
Presumption 2: Sport is manifestly good for you.
Presumption 3: Sport has a part to play as a cultural product to maintain this equilibrium.
Presumption 4: Sport participation provides sufficient conditions for social goods to be achieved.

Jarvie (2006, p. 24) goes further to identify sport's potential functions as enhancing adaptability, goal orientation, integration, political order and social mobility; sport projects for alleviating dysfunction are well documented (Jarvie, 2006; Jarvie and Maguire, 1994; Sugden and Tomlinson, 2002):

- Social–emotional function: sport's contribution to social–psychological stability

- Socialisation function: sport's contribution to the reinforcement of cultural norms and mores

- Integrative function: sport's contribution to the integration of individuals and groups in society

- Political function: sport's use as a political tool for ideological purposes

- Social mobility function: sport's potential to increase social improvement through enhanced prospects

As hinted earlier, sport's functional capacity is often illustrated in its deployment as a tool for social engineering of some form. Social control is a process of social engineering popular amongst policymakers and those managing its implementation using a variety of tools. Sport and the arts have been regularly used as vehicles for change, to the point that, in many circumstances, their deployment in public policy is rarely challenged or is their potential for success refuted. The Policy Action Team (PAT 10, 1999) did not so much question the claims of sports professionals but demand proof of the functionalist ideals of sport and the arts integrative capacity in relation to reducing social exclusion, neighbourhood renewal and social cohesion.

In political terms, a reading of Prime Minister Gordon Brown's attendance at the Rugby World Cup Final in 2007 can be seen as an opportunity for him to affirm his place as the (unelected) leader of the government and also to position his brand of 'Third Way politics by association' with elite sporting success. Although the England defeat may have stymied him and his party's strategic use of the RWC final, it is still believed that high-profile patronage of elite sport and its development makes governments vicariously successful. The London 2012 Olympic Games and high-level political and financial support for the Football World Cup reinforce the notion of sport as a medium to celebrate national identity and sporting heritage. However, sport functions as a metaphor for how we should conduct our lives. Good grace and humility, at least expected of our political leaders and celebrity sports people, at these times reinforce the standards and expectations of UK citizens who are managing adversity and challenges of other kinds in wider society. The hegemony of cultural norms and mores become crystallised at times of high-profile sports competition. For policymakers and practitioners, these events become self-serving opportunities to reinforce what sport can offer society, whilst also leading the people by example without a hard political intervention but with a more subtle 'soft touch'.

Sport is a prime example of a cultural product that can be both leisure and work. Sport and sports development clearly offer many opportunities for us to participate as players or sports workers at any level of whatever sports development model one wishes to use. Sport appears to offer as much to those in the lowest socio-economic groups as it does to those at the top. However, on closer inspection of functionalist ideals and prescriptions, we get a sense of the empty promises implicit in sports development and related policies over many decades. What we rarely see in the public domain is a challenge to these optimistic claims of smooth, systemic, sporting pathways to success. When we become critical of functionalist accounts of sports development we are close to 'mentioning the unmentionable' that 'the emperor is wearing no clothes'! Indeed, when adopting a functionalist approach how can we explain the inequalities in a harmonious 'sport for all' culture, especially where sport serves some better than others? How can we explain the tensions and contradictions of sport policy across the sectors and levels of sports development? How can we explain sport's role in *serving* dysfunction within its subcultures as we witness controversies from illegal betting, violence, bigotry to doping?

The dangers of viewing sport in such a positive but uncritical way leads us to argue that a functionalist approach to sports development would conclude that,

> Sports Development polices gaps in provision and participation. It distributes social justice in the face of market trends. It circumvents barriers to participation. It spreads the benefits of sport. It presides over competing plural interests. It advocates on behalf of marginalised interests. It applies the glue to bind diverse strands into an integrated whole
> (Hylton and Totten, 2008, p. 65).

Hylton and Totten's (2008) assessment of a functionalist view of sports development is not uncommon in sports development discourses and any simplistic premise to such complex issues is likely to go unrewarded for those who invoke it. Sports development remains the umbrella term for a plethora of political, processual and practice issues with regard to sport that requires deconstruction. Some of the mainstream approaches typified by these functionalist themes have been criticised as unrealistic and unsuccessful in developing sport in its broadest sense for social groups traditionally excluded from core facilities and coaching provision. Community sports development (CSD) arose as a response to these concerns about equity and participation. CSD is more than *just sport in the community* and is also a form of provision which addresses social and political concerns about the nature and extent of inequality, especially as its professional management and practice emerged at the same time and in the spirit of *'Sport for All'* in the early 1970s. CSD interventions include those in sports development intent on developing *sport in the community* as well as those focused on developing *community through sport.* In both cases participation is the starting point, yet that is where the philosophical similarities end. Hylton and Totten (2001, 2008) are clear that under the umbrella of CSD there is a continuum that could be utilised to illustrate these philosophical differences between interventions that could be deemed CSD. However, one form adopts a conventional sports development model (CSD-SD) and ostensibly utilises a grassroots/community setting for such activities; for example, football in the community officers. At the other end of the continuum is a community development model (CSD-CD) that is unsurprisingly focused on social groups and their development using sport as the medium. Hylton and Totten (2008, p. 80) utilise a community sports development continuum to illustrate the relationship between these two forms of community sports development (Figure 2.1). As they argue:

> At one extreme is pure 'sport' development, or 'sport in the community', where the practice of sport is an end in itself. Here practice does not stray beyond the primary focus of participation in sport as sports development beyond participation is best catered for by other mainstream agencies. At the other extreme is sport as 'community development' where sport is simply a means to human development
>
> (Hylton and Totten, 2008, p. 80).

CSD was initially seen as a challenge to traditional ways of approaching provision for disadvantaged groups; it was almost a progressive counter culture. This emphasis on community practice in public services creates a paradox as the turn to community approaches is often a tactic to address failures of mainstream provision (see Haywood, 1994). When policy systems

---

Sports development ⇐ ⇒ Participation ⇐ ⇒ Community development

Figure 2.1 Community sports development continuum.

are dysfunctional in some way, it becomes necessary to offer remedial treatment. Indeed, this is precisely what one would expect from a functionalist analysis. In a way community sports development is a side-effect or 'by-product' of sports development (which supports the conceptualisation of sports development as a simultaneous process or construction and destruction established in the introductory chapter). The change in emphasis from facility-based sport to community sport and recreation has proved effective. In the past this shift persuaded many to 'take on board' ideas by 'mainstreaming' projects, and/or project philosophy into more established units. Consequently, in recent times demarcations between established and what were emergent ways of providing sport and recreation opportunities for most priority groups in society have become much less obvious. In reality, the current use of the term 'community sports' is almost as ubiquitous as the term 'community' in other areas of policy provision. It invokes positive images of considerate client-oriented practice. Further, when Sport Scotland reviewed sport they considered both community recreation, which they see as the 'informal world of sport', and sports development which is part of the 'more formal world of sport' (Scottish Sports Council, 1998). The validity of both forms of provision are now unquestioned and they are characterised as 'co-dependent' which is both pragmatic and redolent of the way community sport and community recreation are practiced today.

Returning to the topic of conceptualising sports development, the term *community*, as in community sports development, is contested and can be interpreted to have multiple meanings. Community implies some notion of collectivity, commonality, a sense of belonging or of something shared. A community can be self-determined by its members, or it can be a label externally constructed and defined by some statutory agency. The Standing Conference for Community Development posits that community development interventions occur in communities of place, identity and interest (SCCD, 2001). However, community can be imagined as much as it can be realised. It can be inhabited, as place, a specific locality or a geographical area. It can be an experience, through a gathering, an interest or affiliation to a social, leisure or sports activity. It can also be experienced as a shared identity, history or nostalgia, or as an action when engaged in some form of interactive process. It can be 'protective' of a way of being, or 'expansive' in terms of some aspiration (Brent, 2004; Fremeaux, 2005).

Hylton and Totten (2008, p. 81) argue that community as place or locality is diminishing as social relationships and society transcend locality due to increased personal mobility and new technologies such as mobile phones, the Internet and their synthesis in iPhones. But this narrow model traditionally courts more favour from sport policymakers (trustees) and is in greater evidence in working practice. In this approach the nation state and its agents have traditionally taken a leading role in identifying disadvantaged communities and in targeting groups of disenfranchised people. This links with notions of community as shared identity. This deterministic concept of community has connotations of working-class status, shared experiences and living in the inner city, thus reinforcing the notion that our practice emerges from our understanding of concepts, issues or 'problems'. Pragmatically, Brent

(2004) suggests that community remains an 'absent presence' due to our continual aspiration for it when we can never actually complete the process; hence community development workers' penchant for long-term community development processes.

In the interests of transparency and ensuring that community development was indeed taking place, the PAT 10 report on Sport and the Arts (DCMS, 1999, p. 41) devised a test for sports organisations that purported to be involved in community development. Many mainstream providers, governing bodies and voluntary groups perpetuate sporting inequalities because they are insensitive to some or all of the key principles that underpin working with marginalised or excluded communities. The PAT 10 test included ascertaining if the following are taking place: Valuing Diversity; Embedding Local Control; Supporting Local Commitment: Promoting Equitable Partnerships; Working with Change; Securing Sustainability; Pursuing Quality; Connecting with the Mainstream. Recent instances of CD practice in sport include the Active Communities Projects (Sport England, 2002; Sport England, 2005) whose underpinning ideals are concerned with the community development ideals of encouraging empowerment, devolution, self-determination, active citizenship and neighbourhood renewal. As a result of recognition from policymakers and practitioners, community sport is recognised as a valuable tool to pursue community or socio-cultural development (DCMS, 1999; Sport England, 2005). The Community Development Foundation (CDF, 2001) offers the following definition:

> Community Development is about building active and sustainable communities based on social justice and mutual respect. It is about changing power structures to remove the barriers that prevent people from participating in the issues that affect their lives
>
> (CDF, 2001, p. 3).

So, where popular mainstream functionalist-underpinned ideologies emphasise a logical harmony in society, community development approaches recognise the complexities of living in a dynamic, fragmented society, which necessitates social transformation and anti-discriminatory action against broader social inequality (see Table 2.1). Elite sports development is not exempt from these processes either, and sports development does not exist in an objectified and rose-tinted 'sports bubble' as it requires an engagement with social justice in addition to clear systems of development. One consequence of practitioners and policymakers ignoring community development principles was outlined by Ledwith (2005) who describes the pitfalls of 'thoughtless action' and 'actionless thought'. 'Thoughtless action' would include attempts at sports development which failed to engage with underlying political issues and power processes. 'Actionless thought' would be recognition of social issues but with no plan for change. Clearly, when it comes to CD, sports development must represent a form of 'thoughtful action'! Thoughtful action is clearly energised when SD is planned in a holistic way that incorporates the needs of all parties without recourse to short-term gains.

Table 2.1 Mainstream and community development models to sports development and society.

Model of sports development	Functionalist	Community development
Political ideology	Society reflects a system that can be kept in balance (homeostasis) through social and cultural arrangements. Any social breakdown (dysfunction) occurs where these arrangements fail. Inequalities in society are inevitable; however, state and citizen plural interests ensure that needs are met	Communities are disparate, unequal and fragmented but can be essential social units to develop empowered active citizens and social capital. Communities can link social agents in many ways, e.g. geography, interests, identity, affiliation or 'imagined'. 'Community' can *identify* and be used as *identification*
Core values	Society is based on broad agreement (consensus) that ensures a smooth and harmonious functioning social system	Community development ensures a long-term inclusive and sustainable infrastructure to meet 'community' needs
Role of sports development	Sports development polices gaps in provision and participation. It presides over plural interests. It applies the 'glue' to bind society into an integrated whole. Sport is central to any development work	A community focus is utilised where traditional sports development has failed. CD offers alternative, sometimes radical, techniques to transform established sports development approaches. Sport, in its broadest sense, is used as a means to an end
Agents of development	Identified sports development professionals and stakeholders, policymakers, commercial interests, voluntary groups. Some cross-boundary working	'Community' interests, trans-professional working that includes sport. Ultimately self-sustaining developments
Key processes	Participation, coaching, funding, initiatives, social control, social welfare, structures, 'top-down' management	Inclusivity, empowerment, self-expression, agency, 'bottom-up' management

Political approaches fundamentally inform stakeholders and have significant effects on how sport is developed and viewed by others. Table 2.1 presents an overview of the political roots and domain assumptions of both a functionalist and community development approach. For sports development to sustain emancipatory practice and sports-specific goals, people must be open to the benefits of competing critical approaches and be prepared for how they may present alternative knowledge, skill and resource-based challenges for open-minded stakeholders. To quote Nelson Mandela again,

A vision without action is just a dream,
Action without vision passes the time,
A vision with action can change the world

References

Brent, J. (2004). The desire for community: Illusion, confusion and paradox. *Community Development Journal*, July, **39**(3), 213–23.

Brown, G. (2006). Speech by the Rt. Hon Gordon Brown MP at the Financing for Development Conference, Abuja, Nigeria, http://www.hm-treasury.gov.uk/news-room_and_speeches/speeches/chancellorexchequer/speech_chx_220506.cfm (accessed 18 November 2007)**.**

Collins, M. and Kay, T. (2003). *Sport and Social Exclusion*. London and New York: Routledge.

Community Development Foundation (CDF) (2001). The Strategic Framework for Community Development, http://www.cdx.org.uk/resources/library/docs/sframeword.doc (accessed 5 July 2006).

DCMS (Department of Culture Media and Sport) (1999). *Policy Action Team 10*. A report to the social exclusion unit. London: DCMS.

Department of the Environment (1989). *Sport and Active Recreation Provision in Inner Cities*. London: Crown Publications.

Department of National Heritage (1995). *Sport: Raising the Game*. London: HMSO.

Fremeaux, I. (2005). New labour's appropriation of the concept of community: A critique. *Community Development Journal*, July, **40**(3), 265–74.

Hall, S. (2003). New labour has picked up where Thatcherism left off. *The Guardian*, 6 August.

Hall, S., Critcher, C., Jefferson, T. and Clarke, J. (1978). *Policing the Crisis: Mugging, the State and Law and Order*. London: Hutchinson.

Haywood, L. (1994). *Community Recreation: Theory and Practice*. Oxford: Butterworth Heinemann.

Henry, I. (2001). *The Politics of Leisure Policy*. Basingstoke: Palgrave Macmillan.

Horne, J. (2006). *Sport in Consumer Culture*. Basingstoke: Palgrave Macmillan.

Houlihan, B. and White, A. (2002). *The Politics of Sport Development*. London: Routledge.

Hylton, K. and Bramham, P. (2008). *Sports Development: Policy, Process and Practice*. London and New York: Routledge.

Hylton, K. and Totten, M. (2001). Community Sports Development. In *Sports Development: Policy, Process and Practice* (K. Hylton et al., eds). London: Routledge, pp. 66–98.

Hylton, K. and Totten, M. (2008). Community Sports Development. In *Sports Development: Policy, Process and Practice* (K. Hylton and P. Bramham, eds). London and New York: Routledge.

Jarvie, G. (2006). *Sport, Culture and Society: An Introduction*. London: Routledge.

Jarvie, G. and Maguire, J. (1994). *Sport and Leisure in Social Thought*. London: Routledge.

Ledwith, M. (2005). *Community Development: A Critical Approach*. Bristol: Policy Press.

London 2012 Website (2007). http://www.london2012.com/about/about-the-2012-games/london-s-winning-bid.php.

Long, J. and Bramham, P. (2006). The changing role of the local state in UK leisure provision. *DOZ, Journal of Leisure Studies*, **30**, 43–54.

Long, J. and Sanderson, I. (2001). The social benefits of Sport – Where's the proof? In *Sport in the City* (C. Gratton and I. Henry, eds). London: Routledge, pp. 187–203.

Office of the Deputy Prime Minister (2004). *Joint-Working in Sport and Neighbourhood Renewal*. Wetherby: ODPM.

Putnam, R. (2000). *Bowling Alone: The Collapse and Revival of American Community*. New York: Simon & Schuster.

Rigg, M. (1986). *Action Sport: An Evaluation*. London: Sports Council.

Roberts, K. (1996). Young people, schools, sport and government policies. *Sport, Education and Society,* **1**(1), 47–58.

Roberts, K. (2004). *The Leisure Industries*. London: Palgrave Macmillan.

SCCD/Community Development Foundation (CDF) (2001). The Strategic Framework for Community Development, available from http://www.cdx.org.uk/resources (accessed 5 July 2006).

Scottish Sports Council (1998). *Sport 21: Nothing Left to Chance*. Edinburgh: Scottish Sports Council.

Sports Council (1982). *Sport in the Community: The Next Ten Years*. London: Ashdown Press.

Sport England (2002). Active Communities experimental Projects, sportengland.org/active_communities/acf/active_communities_projects.htm (London, Sport England).

Sport England (2005). *Sport: Playing its Part*. London: Sport England.

Sugden, J. and Tomlinson, A. (eds). (2002). *Power Games: A Critical Sociology of Sport*. London: Routledge.

CHAPTER 3

Public Policies on Sports Development: Can Mass and Elite Sport Hold Together?

Mike Collins

Introduction: The Many Strands in British Sport

This chapter concentrates on two matters: first, the development of sports policy since 1960. It will cover this as a series of snapshots, because much has been written elsewhere. Secondly, it will focus specifically on the uneasy and changing balances between grass roots and elite sports development. Where appropriate, comparisons with other countries are made.

Sport in Britain developed, as in other countries, variously from exercises to toughen up soldiers and folk games, and from groups in pubs, companies and churches (Lupson, 2006 described how one in three Premier League soccer clubs originated in churches). The Church, however, was never quite the pillar of sports organisation it became in France, Netherlands and Germany, and nor were companies; on the continent company sport became part of the social contract (Kruger and Riordan, 1996), whereas outside the coal and rail industries and the civil service, British trades unions were interested only in wages, working hours and conditions and holidays.

In the nineteenth century, however, Britain codified more than 25% of modern sports, and between the 1880s and the 1930s formalised 67 national governing bodies (NGBs) which set the rules, ethos and discipline, supervised the organisation of competition, and as the latter developed, trained the national teams (Interestingly there was another burst of NGB formation in the 1960s, and despite Sports Council attempts to reduce the numbers from over 470 for 103 sports by merger or forming an overarching body (as for lawn bowls), devolution of government to Wales and Scotland may lead to yet more splitting of GB/UK bodies. Subsequently, NGBs took on coach training, handling sponsorship and the media. The British model was adopted world wide with modifications. The confederation of sports, the Central Council of Physical Recreation (CCPR) was formed late, in 1935, and has been a forum and lobbyist for sport, but never became the agent of government and power found in other countries (Evans, 1974). Perhaps the most potent is the Deutsches Sportbund, with 22 m of Germany's 80 m citizens in membership (more than any political party), a regular levy which supports among much else, the German Sports University in Berlin, and which is consulted by the Federal government on every bill that comes before it; compare the CCPR which depends substantially on a grant from Sport England and has no levy on its member NGBs, which enrol only 6m citizens. Green examines the NGBs and their relationship to the state in Chapter 4.

Commerce has been growing in sport world wide, most ubiquitously through sponsorship and TV fees which go mainly to a few televisual sports (75% to only 15 sports in Britain) and to world class performers, clubs and teams. In Britain it started in sports that could charge higher prices for higher quality services that above average income groups could afford, like golf, shooting, horseracing and sailing: these were joined by more popular activities like spectating in soccer/rugby/cricket/motor sport, and dancing and ice skating. TV franchises and greater affluence supported the growth of commercial sport (Slack, 2004) and in the late twentieth century the fitness industry has boomed worldwide, with the UK a leader in Europe; there are some chains in sports goods retailing and in contract management of public facilities, but the majority of firms are small, even micro (with fewer than 10 workers – Collins and Randolph, 1993; Viallon et al., 2003) making it difficult to deal with the commercial sector; Business in Sport and Leisure only represents some of the larger firms. The reservoirs of commercial water authorities provide important sites for water sports (Collins, 2000b; Sports Council, 1992).

The state came later: after 1888 with public baths and swimming pools, initially for hygiene and then for swimming safety and enjoyment; with the current cost of building and running pools, swimming is perhaps the sport most dependent on local authority and education building policy. Then came public parks and playing fields, boosted by job-creation schemes in the 1930s and planning legislation from 1947 onwards: local authorities provide 28% of England's playing field sites. At that same date Physical Education (PE) became compulsory in the state school curriculum, and schools provide 44% of team game sites. These figures compare to 11% by clubs, so many clubs without their own sites are tenants of municipalities and schools (Sports Council, 1994a).

Universities are growing as a force in sport, not only for producing young elite sports people – in England already exceeding Sir Roger Bannister's forecast that they would yield a third of the nation's performers, but increasingly they offer facilities and programmes to local communities (Collins, 2004; Collins and Kennett, 1996) and a selected few will host British and overseas squads training for London 2012.

State agencies are relatively minor providers: Sport England provides five national multi-sports centres for regional and national squads, but from the 1990s national training centres for individual sports have been grant aided, usually attached to university or local authority sites. National Parks and the Forestry Commission's woodlands and privatised Regional Water Authority reservoirs provide large areas for outdoor sports (Collins, 2000b).

Phases of English/British Sports Policy Development

This section will provide only a summary, since Collins (2002a) and others have dealt with policies or aspect of them in greater detail elsewhere (e.g. Bergsgard et al., 2007; Coalter, 2007; Coghlan, 1990; Green and Houlihan, 2005; Houlihan, 1991, 1997, 2002; Houlihan and White, 2002; Hylton and Bramham, 2008).

Developing the Facilities Base and Facility Management (1960s–1982)

The CCPR had administered Department of Education grants to NGBs, and their coaches and sports development officers focussed on informal processes for identifying talented youth and 'creaming them off' from schools and club teams to feed national squads. To its credit, the CCPR identified that Britain's youth and its sports teams had poorer sports opportunities than its main competitors and facility provision for the whole population was poorer; the report produced by Sir John Wolfenden (1960) called for a national Sport Development Council. Such a development was anathema to many conservatives in and out of government who saw sport as private, pastime, something government should steer clear of, including the CCPR's patron, the Duke of Edinburgh. An Advisory Council was set up in 1965, serviced by the CCPR's staff. Then, after much debate and political haggling, in 1972 an executive Sports Council was born under a Royal Charter, a mechanism much less open to political manipulation than an act of parliament. The idea was that it should be an advisor to government, operate through specialists, 'at arms length' from government. Green and Houlihan (2005, p. 53) saw it as a 'buffer' between government and he lobbying of the hundred or so NGBs.

The CCPR lost control of the national centres and was seen as a forum for the NGBs and advisor to the Council, with a core grant whose size and purpose was never specified, giving ground for much contention over the next 20 years. The Royal Charter empowered the Council to

1. encourage participation 'in the interests of social welfare and the enjoyment of leisure among the public at large;

2. encourage others to provide facilities;

3. support the development of high level performers; and

4. do or get done research.

It supported the Council of Europe's span of activities including recreations and physical activities like dancing and its interpretation of Sport for All covered the whole range from novice and informal playing to the most specialised, professional elite competitors, unlike many countries where that was either left to local government and clubs, or to a separate organisational stream (as in Canada, where Sport Canada and Recreation Canada co-existed from 1970 to 1980 (Green and Houlihan, 2005)). The Council was responsible for international performance for Britain and the UK, while Sports Councils responsible for domestic policy were set up in Scotland, Wales and Northern Ireland. With representation from the regions, the other three parts of the UK and governing bodies made the Council large and its debates and lobbying tangled.

The new Council set about assessing the facility needs across the country (Table 3.1). Much of this was done through Regional Councils for Sport which gave direct links and representation to local authorities and local education

Table 3.1 Sports policy, phase 1: Developing the facilities base and facility management (1960s–1982).

Policy and institutional developments	Major reports
SC assesses needs for facilities in town and country	• basic community provision (sports halls, swimming pools, golf course (SC, 1971))
	• specialist facilities (Collins, 1973)
1972 Regional Councils for Sport; 1975 RCSRs formed	
SC promotes community use of schools	• White Paper, *A Chance to Share* (DfE, 1964)
White Paper gives social role to sport	• White Paper, *Sport and Recreation* (DoE, 1975)

authorities (again making membership large, usually over a hundred); these also advised on priorities for local grants, a device which effectively decentralised some power (though over modest resources) and created a line of trust and policy support that other cultural agencies lacked. This line was reinforced by the Council being under the aegis of the Ministry of Housing and Local Government from 1974, and later the Departments of Environment (DoE) from 1990 (responsible for local government) and National Heritage (DNH) from 1992 until the formation of the Department of Culture Media and Sport (DCMS). To improve regional links, in 1975 Minister Denis Howell extended the Regional Councils' remit and membership to include countryside recreation, reflected in 'and Recreation' added to their titles (RCSRs), and a new wave of reviews and policies (Collins, 1985).

The weakness of this arrangement was that there was no political or policy link with education and schools, the most common organisational arrangement of government across the world. Indeed, until the 1990s the Council was expressly told not to be involved in such matters, the closest it achieved being a White Paper *A Chance to Share* in 1964 to encourage community use of schools physical sports resources, a policy which only one in three LEAs formally adopted, though its benefits were admired internationally (Collins, 1980).

Local government reorganisation in 1974 created many more Departments of Leisure in bigger authorities. These sought to exploit a buoyant economy, and local authority spending found a favourable response, and the targets for sports halls was 81% met by 1981, that for pools exceeded and a new wave of public and private golf courses built. This engendered new postgraduate and later undergraduate courses for managers, and employment in sport grew by 42% (Sports Council, 1982). At this stage there was growing demand for sport with an increase in participation of more than 1% pa (Gratton and Tice, 1994). Sports Minister Denis Howell averred in a 1975 White Paper that sport 'was part of the fabric of the social services' and that it was a means for youth of 'reducing boredom and urban frustration' (DoE, 1975, pp. 1–2), and sport was included in the Urban Programme from 1976. Denis Howell (responsible also for water policy) found £1 m a year for three years from underspend in building dams, and offered it for new youth sports work. Thus was born Action Sport, the first co-ordinated sports development programme putting credible young officers on the street in deprived communities (Rigg, 1982). This lead Coalter (1998) to describe this phase of policy as 'recreation as welfare', catering for those missing out on sport.

In this period, support for elite sport was a second priority, though chairman Sir Roger Bannister drove vigorously the first drug abuse research and testing programme; sprinter Sebastian Coe, appointed vice chairman, complained that this funding was inadequate in the wake of disappointing Olympic results.

A Strategy of Targeting and the Evolution of Sports Development (1982–91)

By the early 1980s under Mrs Thatcher, Ministers started taking a much closer eye on the performance of the many Non-Departmental Public Bodies under their aegis; not only did they approve appointments, they had to produce strategies, action plans and zero-based budgets (where each policy and its associated spending had to be justified each time). Failure to do so was likely to lead to losing out in bidding for resources. Accordingly, the Sports Council was no exception and produced its first review and 10-year strategy *Sport in the Community* in 1982. This continued demands for new local and national sports facilities, but for the first time identified low participant groups (housewives, semi and unskilled workers, non-car owners, lower income groups, including older people – an analysis supported by six of the nine RCSRs); to these the Council thought to add unemployed and disabled people, but lacked the justifying data. For the first time a target for increasing participation was set – 1.2 m more people in both indoor and outdoor sport, the majority women. Because resources were insufficient to meet all needs, target groups were chosen at two points of change in lifestyle when it was thought policy might impact effectively (leaving school and starting college/work at age 13–24 and pre-retirement at 45–59). The strategy also identified the need for improved coaching and administration in 20 sports to help develop performers (Table 3.2).

In implementation, the success of Action Sport led to National Demonstration Projects using outreach workers, now called Sports Development Officers (SDOs). This extended work from cities to rural areas and embodied the three

Table 3.2 Sports policy, phase 2: Targeting and early sports development nationally and regionally (1982–91).

Policy and institutional developments	Major reports
Targets and target groups for participation	• *Sport in the Community: The Next 10 Years* (SC, 1982) and *Into the 90s* (SC, 1987)
Improved coaching and administration, sport medicine – NCF, NCSM formed 1983, 1993	
Market testing of local government sports services	• Audit Commission (1989) *Sport for Whom?*

Table 3.3   Target groups/priorities for sport for all in England.

Priority	Year
Youth/School leavers	1982, 1987, 1989, 1993 onwards
Older people	1975
Women	1976, 1982, 1987, 1989, 1993
Disabled people	1980, 1989, 1994 onwards
Ethnic minorities	1982, 1984 onwards
Joint provision with schools	1968, 1982, 1987, 1989
Inner cities/areas of special need	1978, 1987
Exercise and health	1977, 1981

principles of going to potential customers rather than expecting them to come to new facilities; to use other available community facilities (like working men's clubs, women's groups like the Women's Institute (WI), health centres and pubs); and to involve new partner organisations in health, crime and regeneration. An evaluation confirmed the success of these moves (Tungatt and MacDonald, 1992), but also some challenges – for instance, the success of one and a half women sport promoters in Cambridgeshire could not be cloned for all counties because the WI could not shoulder the responsibility of employing four times their current workforce. The success of SDOs became evident; by the early 1990s they numbered over 2000 compared to 8–10 000 in facility management (Collins, 1995) and have possibly doubled since (Pitchford and Collins, forthcoming 2008). Particular features have been that they showed relative youth and gender equity, compared to other areas of sport employment like facility management, administration and coaching.

Also, the sport for all policy was reflected in a number of campaigns or programme priorities, as shown in Table 3.3 These were modest, with insufficient funds for the TV coverage necessary to reach mass markets. *50+ and All to Play For* was a little guide to attracting older people to sport and physical activity, reprinted several times; already population projections demonstrated the ageing trends, but unlike several European countries, to the present day there has been no major campaign aimed at this older group who would show the greatest gains in mobility and coping with life's demands and some of the greatest savings in NHS spending.

The review of the strategy after five years (Sports Council, 1987) clearly showed three things, that

1. by comparison, insufficient resources had been available to make up the facility shortfalls and increasing obsolescence of cheaply built, hard-used 1970s buildings inefficient in increasingly costly energy use;

2. income inequality had grown greatly under the Tories and posed stark challenges for sports policy in meeting the needs of deprived people – 'a market where the commercial sector has had relatively little impact,

and the voluntary sports club only a modest one . . . . the need for a strong public sector will be vital' (1987, pp. 1, 24); and that

3. more and better specialist facilities and support services in coaching and sports medicine were needed.

During this period, government became convinced that public services were inefficient and needed to adopt structures and methods tried and tested in commerce: smaller more streamlined management hierarchies, more directors from business, cutting waste and becoming more productive; and market testing by competition for certain services. The Sports Council was reduced in size and more members appointed from a commercial background. Capping on local authority spending led to reduced new investment. Perhaps beguiled by the facts that marketing of priced services was a feature of local sport programmes (Collins and Glyptis, 1992) and that some private management contractors had appeared, HMG decided that it should put its work out to competitive tender by compulsion (CCT). It may have been persuaded by a report by its spending watchdog that during the 1980s local sports services had not widened their appeal much, and users should pay a greater proportion of costs and local taxpayers who formed the majority of non-users less (Audit Commission, 1989). This led to a decade of price increases above inflation, and countermanded Chairman Peter Yarranton's desire (*Annual Report*, 1989, p. 2) that a primary Sports Council aim be that 'access to sport should be readily available and affordable'.

In contrast, the longstanding neglect of school sport was recognised: a predilection in some labour-controlled LEAs to reduce the emphasis on traditional games and competition was reversed in reviews of the national PE curriculum (Penney and Evans, 1999): a programme to invest in new school, including sports facilities was identified. Another area in which the Sports Council had been working away for a decade was to improve the data on the links with health, and in 1992 published the *Allied Dunbar National Fitness Survey* (Department of Health/Sports Council and others, 1992) which showed that only a minority were active enough in undertaking moderate exercise that brought physiological benefits sufficient to combat ischaemic heart disease, strokes, type 2 diabetes and other ill-effects of growing obesity, while many men and women were deluding themselves about how active they were. Sadly the DNH failed to put in a share of ADNFS' financing.

Regarding elite sport, this period saw the establishment of the National Coaching Foundation refusing to support either the World Student Games in Sheffield or Birmingham's bid to host the Olympics.

Shifting Priorities to Performance and Excellence (1992–7)

Given the surrounding uncertainties, it was not surprising that the Sports Council's (1993a) Strategy *New Horizons* was more a vision/manifesto, seeing the agency as an advocate for the sector, a promoter of activities by partners, including training and education of their workforces; no targets for provision or spending here. With John Major replacing Mrs Thatcher, the UK had its first

Prime Minister to voice his interest in sport; this led to active support for Manchester to bid successfully for the Commonwealth Games. But yet another review of the Sports Council's role and resources was underway, against continuing desire to slim down central bodies. So for the first time the Gordian knot was cut, and an English Sports Council (ESC) was formed to deliver domestic policies like its Celtic counterparts, and a UK Sports Council (UKSC) to deliver international competitive success including grant aid to NGBs, to handle international affairs like representation on international bodies, hosting international events and dealing with drug abuse testing. However, the new tension being created was that aiding NGB strategies and funding for specialist facilities to support performance athletes had to be handled by the four domestic Councils from the bottom up and by the UK Sports Council top down; how these became reconciled in the middle was more a matter of argument and power games than an outcome of an overall strategy, and all four domestic agencies were jealous of their own turf (Pickup, 1996).

In 1995 the government produced its first broad White Paper for 20 years – *Sport: Raising the Game.* This demonstrated a renewed interest in school curricular and extra-curricular sport and school – club links, and a stronger focus on elite sport (Table 3.4). At the same time, the Prime Minister (and the ESC) backed the

---

Table 3.4   *Sport Raising the Game: Main proposals, 1995.*

Sport in schools

- Two hours a week of high quality sport and PE
- extend extra-curricular sport; four hours for Sportmark sites; teachers paid?
- Sportsmark recognition for primary and secondary sites
- Reports to OFSTED/school governors
- New in-service teacher training
- More coaching courses
- Volunteers to support coaches

Extending the sporting culture

- ESC challenge fund for clubs to develop school links
- Links mandatory for ESC grants to clubs
- ESC to become a mandatory consultee on planning applications affecting playing fields
- Lottery money for facilities especially in poor areas

Further and Higher Education

- FE and HE funding bodies to review provision (see Collins and Kennett, 1996)
- Bannister working group on scholarships (DNH, 1996)

Development of excellence

- British Academy of Sport to produce medal winners, plus regional network
- Mandatory targets for talent in NGB plans
- Continued doping control and ethical education for young performers

introduction of a National Lottery, seeking a non-government source of funding for sport and other good causes which had proved lucrative to sport and the state in many countries, and recognising in an increasingly liberal climate that growing public interest in gambling as leisure might divert to European lotteries. These two acts constituted what Kingdon (1984) called 'a focussing event', changing operating conditions. The early years of the Lottery produced income well above expectations, with over £200 m a year for sport, distributed under the agency of the four domestic sports councils. In the light of the international Brighton Declaration on women and sport, the ESC produced policy statements on increasing inclusion in sport for them, young and disabled people (Sports Council, 1993b,c,d) and people from ethnic minorities (Sports Council, 1994b). As a first shot at a policy for strengthening volunteering, the Council also published research on its scale and nature, suggesting 1.5 m people spending 183 m hours, worth £1.5 bn, a contribution the system could not replace or afford to pay for (Gratton et al., 1997).

In terms of mass participation, another short-lived sports minister, now Ian Sproat, brought changes:

■ Seeking to transfer all responsibility for health matters from ESC – 'I am keen to help the Department of Health, but I think this is work that should be done by them' (interview with J. Gilling, *Leisure Management* 14.10) – this only two years after the Sports Council with the advice of eminent epidemiologist Professor Jerry Morris and physiologist Professor Peter Fentem had driven the first national fitness survey (DoH/Sports Council et al., 1992);

■ Reducing the emphasis on sport for all (a term that now disappeared from policy discourse) which he regarded as vague, expensive and difficult to demonstrate, in favour of targeted equity policies;

■ After a review, removing the 19 years-old link provided by the RCSRs which he regarded as 'unwieldy...[and] led to confusion as to who was responsible for policy, encouraged the Regional Directors of the Sports Council to become more concerned with local sports politics and less concerned with getting sport on the agenda in the region's schools and clubs' (speech to CCPR 25th annual conference 26 November 1996, 1998), he replaced them with small discussion forums with no resources to produce new regional strategies. In 2004, independent, more potent Regional Sports Boards were appointed.

From her international vantage point in the NCF, Sue Campbell could see the need for an agency to bolster the skills of both primary and secondary school teachers, especially those without specialist training (which meant all primary teachers, unlike many countries). She obtained funding from Sir John Beckwith, who had made money in fitness clubs and moved to found and head the Youth Sport Trust which rapidly developed packs and courses for teachers of various age groups from 18 months to 15 years. Their huge popularity soon attracted funding from the Lottery, Department of Education and Science (DfES) and commercial sponsors. Another innovation in junior sport had been Champion Coaching, a series of coaching sessions in a number of sports seeking to get schools and clubs working together to filter talent for 10–14, which spread to one in three LEAs. Though never evaluated by Sports Council/ESC, there is evidence that it did provide some groundwork for later SDO and coach development (Bell, forthcoming 2008). However, it failed to get wholehearted teacher support and struggled to get response in deprived areas (Collins and Buller, 2000).

Pressures were building to give elite sport more priority and resources: the medal haul from the 1996 Atlanta Games needed to improve and prominent athletes and NGBs were pressing; the Australian Institute of Sport's success in supporting that country's athletes was acclaimed as a model, and the complexity of needs and interests needed was ever more evident. David Pickup (1996, pp. 172–3), reviewing his years 1988–93 as Director-General, argued that it was time to co-ordinate the expensive and scarce human and scientific resources needed to nurture top talent; under his direction in the five financial years 1989–90 and 1993–4 spending on coaching increased by 58%, on sports science and medicine 279% and on doping control by 66% (Pickup, 1996, p. 213).

The twists and turns of forming the British Academy/UK Sports Institute is told elsewhere (Theodoraki, 1999), with Loughborough University and Sheffield city whittled down from a longer list of bidders to host a centralised site; then under a new Labour administration, lessons from Australia that athletes wanted to spend less time a long way from home led to the decision to form a UK network, mainly based on University sites, with a small central administration in UK Sport.

At the end of this period, the ESC produced another vision, *England: The Sporting Nation* (ESC, 1996), showing already a closer reflection of government policy in elaborating on themes in *Raising the Game.* The author criticised it (Collins, 1997) for setting over-ambitious targets for participation (e.g. 20% more adults regularly active by 2001, 20% more girls and 10% more adults in clubs) and improvements in performance (10% more having coaching) and excellence (champions in five sports by 2003–5 from current positions ranging from 2nd to 12th) (Table 3.5).

Table 3.5   Sports policy, phase 3: Shifting priorities to performance and excellence (1992–7).

Policy and institutional developments	Major reports
New national strategy – stepping back from specialist advice	• *New Horizons* (SC, 1993a)
White Paper focusing on school/youth and elite sport	• *Raising the Game* (DNH, 1995)
SC targets groups for equity	• Reports on women, young people, ethnic groups, disabled (SC, 1993b,c,d; 1994b)
ESC reviews volunteering	• *Valuing Volunteers* (Gratton et al., 1997)
Youth Sport Trust set up – TOPs programmes	• See www.yst.org.uk
English Sports Council new vision	• *England: A Sporting Nation* (ESE, 1996)

Social Inclusion and More Medals (1997–Date): 'Sport for Good'

At the end of 20 years of Tory rule, New Labour under Tony Blair swept in with promises of widespread major changes. One of the strongest was to combat social inequality – or as they termed it social exclusion – with a dedicated Cabinet Office Unit which described a nexus of problems in the 330 worst estates (SEU, 1997). Those classed as poor had grown from 9% of adults in 1979 to 24% in 1994, together with 30% of children; a major policy plank was to eradicate the latter by 2020, and major changes were made to a range of welfare policies. A review of effects in sport and recreation was commissioned (Collins et al., 1999), which showed sport reflected society-wide inequalities, and a Policy Action Team 10 reported on attempts to increase inclusion in sport (DCMS, 1999) but virtually no mention of sport and recreation appeared in the SEU's overview or updates. Collins and Kay (2003) updated and expanded this review, looking at exclusion as it affected young and disabled people, women, older people, ethnic minorities, disaffected youth and urban and rural dwellers.

While stressing the importance of success in international competition, time and time again, HMG stressed the gains sport could make to the national cross-cutting 'wicked' issues, through

1. helping to improve mental and physical health;

2. providing jobs and income as part of economic regeneration especially in towns and also in the countryside;

3. contributing to lifelong learning;

4. increasing social cohesion between different cultural and social groups;

5. reducing youth disaffection and crime.

This expectation of societal and communal benefits which started with 'character-building' in Victorian times and was continued with helping disaffected youth in the 1975 White Paper, Coalter (2007) described as 'sport for good', involving active citizens in improving their own society. These issues became outcomes in SE's next strategic framework (see below). The government also now emphasised evidence-based policy, which is a weakness for social science generally, but especially in new areas like sport, with a lack of longitudinal data and inadequate focus on what works in what circumstances and for whom.

The evidence on health benefits rests on physiological, psychological and epidemiological evidence cumulated worldwide over 50 years; reviewing that led the Chief Medical Officer (2004) to support the benefits of sport and advocate five half-hour sessions a week; some comes from work-based labour, bicycle/pedestrian commuting and household chores, but Sport England (2004) took responsibility for promoting three of these five sessions, including a new programme promoting sport in workplaces.

SE employed Coalter to review emerging research and evidence for its Value of Sport Monitor database; from this informed stance he has produced an overview of issues 2–5 above (Coalter, 2007). For all of these, he came to the conclusion of 'not proven' for lack of evidence on intermediate outcomes and mechanisms. Regarding intervening in youth crime, despite many heartening stories, Nichols (2007) would agree after riots in Oldham, Burnley and Bradford in 2001, where Cantle spoke of communities leading 'parallel lives', that there has been policy pressure for new programmes in schools workplaces and communities, including sport (ICC, 2006; SE and others, 2004). NGBs have been required to produce and embody Equality Standards and plans regarding gender, race and disability (SE, 2002), but while these have been approved nationally, it is more difficult to get grass roots clubs to take implementation seriously.

Reports continued to flow out. In 2000 DCMS produced *A Sporting Future for All* (Table 3.6), perhaps to demonstrate that sports policy was still on the table; as the author wrote (Collins, 2000a), much of it gathered together previous policy and resource announcements, a PR device popular with the Blair governments. Its new idea was to provide multi-sport clubs which might also accrete other community functions (like libraries, pharmacies, post offices). The problem is that outside the coal industry and the civil service, England has no tradition of such clubs, unlike some European states. Two years later *Game Plan* (DCMS, 2002a) appeared and shaped parts of SE's agenda (Table 3.7 and 3.8). The link with health seemed to have run into the sand, but following the evidence-based theme, the large Active Places database and the first Active People survey were in place.

By this stage, Sport England was effectively an agency of HMG, and the Royal Charter no longer conveyed the degree of independence conveyed in 1972. In 2000, shortly after taking office, then Sports Minister Richard Caborn, made it 'clear to Department for Culture Media and Sport officials that he wanted a fresh start at Sport England and that he felt it essential that a new Chief Executive should be appointed to drive the changes he regarded as necessary' (Bourne, 2000, p. 1). Derek Casey, CEO of six years' standing with the Sports Council and then Sport England left two years before the end of his contract with a pension enhancement of £494 000.

In working out its new programme, SE (2004) took another look at is new context, identifying seven key drivers of change and five settings, of which homes, workplaces and FE/HE were substantial new work areas It identified six policy areas with priorities, summarised in Table 3.9. The Active People survey provided a base for regional and local authority analysis, for relating to the index of deprivation, and recent analysis describes 19 segments of society to help local authorities and their partners to more accurately target their promotion.

HMG also reviewed CCT; in sport it had undoubtedly cut costs (which also meant cutting staff), and the above-inflation price increases already mentioned almost certainly had acted regressively against poorer people (Nichols and Taylor, 1995). In common with other services CCT had not improved quality and was judged to have 'provided a poor deal for employees, employers, and local people' (DETR, 1999, p. 6). So it was made voluntary within a broader and more demanding regime called Best Value, in which local authorities had to justify their modes of provision (direct, contracted or trusts), demonstrate efficiency

Table 3.6 *A Sporting Future for All*, 2000.

	Collins' (2000a) comments
Sport in education – increasing youth participation	
• £150 m for sports and arts facilities in school (50% exchequer, 50% Sports Lottery Fund), targeted	Already announced 1999
• 110 Specialist Sports Colleges by 2003 – to link to UK Sports Institute regional centres	43 already announced
• Out of hours support £160 m New Opportunities Fund, £80 m Dept for Education, focused on areas of need	Already announced
• 600 school sport co-ordinators by Sport England, to link with 3000 primary schools	Already announced
• school visits by elite performers as champions	Happening *ad hoc*
Sport in the community – lifelong participation	
• ensuring playing pitch losses are justified/replaced; £125 m for open space from New Opportunities Lotterry Fund	Regulations in place; lottery money announced 1999
• Sport Direct inquiry phone line	Already provided by On Line in London
• Hub and satellite sports clubs to overcome fragmentation	Right problem – clumsy solution?
• Professional sports clubs support e.g. Dept for Education Playing for Success schemes for maths/ English and football sessions evenings and weekends at pro soccer clubs	P for S first year show real gains in learning, self-esteem of under-achievers
• Junior section accreditation by Sport England	Codifying practice
Sporting excellence	
• Performance plans for sports governing bodies, more openly appraised by Sport England	A variant on what they produce for Sport England and Lottery?
• Fast track to train world performers as elite coaches	
Modernising	
• Governing body partnerships, in return for objectives on excellence and inclusion	More standoff role for Sport England?
• 5% or preferably 10% of TV income for grassroots, including Football Foundation	Long overdue
Implementation	
• Oversight groups for education, community, excellence	

Source: Adapted from Collins (2000a).

Table 3.7 Sports policy, phase 4: Social inclusion and more medals (1997–date): 'sport for good'.

Policy and institutional developments	Major reports
HMG identifies social exclusion as major issue, including in sport; reviews of progress	• SEU, (1997), Collins et al. (1999), PAT 10 (DCMS, 1999)
New government strategy for sport	• *Game Plan* (DCMS, 2002a)
DCMS reviews coaching provision, and subsequent plan	• Report of Coaching Task Force (DCMS, 2002b); Plan for coaching (ScUK, 2006)
Sport England policy framework – new context, Marketing/advocacy impetus	• *Framework for Sport in England* (SE, 2004)
Sport England establishes Equality Standard	• *Equality Standard* (SE, 2004)
Research review, and new policy on activity and health	• *At Least 5 a Week* (CMO, 2004), *Choosing Health* (DoH, 2004)
Lord Carter reviews policy and resources for HMG; Independent Sport Review ineffectual	• Carter (2005), ISR (2005)
Riots in northern cities call attention to social cohesion, and Cantle identifies role of sport	• ICC (2006)
UK Sport strategy for hosting mega-events; London bid wins 2012	• UKSport (1999, 2005)

through Performance Indicators (PIs) and consult with and report to their residents. The Audit Commission watchdog produced a new Comprehensive Performance Assessment system in which there was less inspection and more self-regulation; after much wrangling, the sports part of the Culture Block could only agree three PIs and may lay itself open to inadequate demonstration of performance, since in such regimes what cannot be measured may not be valued (Collins, 2005b). SE joined with the Improvement and Development Agency (2006a) to formulate a new performance assessment tool, *Towards an Excellent Service,* whose value was soon recognised and extended from sport to the wider culture block and to parks and open spaces (IdeA, 2006b, 2007; a version was also developed for and piloted with NGBs and CSPs).

Community Sports Development had grown and changed; Pitchford undertook an Internet survey in 2005 and compared results with Collins (1995). His survey showed slightly fewer female SDOs (41% cf. 50%); a reasonable representation of ethnic minorities (8%) but less so disabled groups (4%); three-quarters were graduates and 22% postgraduates (cf. 35% and 2%); a quarter had reached managerial positions. Of the groups they were mandated to serve, youth still predominated, but unemployed and older people had virtually disappeared from the agenda (Pitchford and Collins, forthcoming 2008).

With Sue Campbell's advice, the DfES (2003) had been developing a series of substantial programmes for schools and their links with clubs – the PESSCL Strategy. Since these also involved sports agencies, it is not surprising that

Table 3.8 *Game Plan* (DCMS 2002a).

Topics and recommendation	Progress to 2006–7
Increasing mass participation in sport and physical activity	
4.1 Sport & PA Board with DoH and others to co-ordinate	• renamed PACT – strategy for regional delivery 2004 but no public announcement
4.2 Better evidence on facilities, participation	• Active Places set up
	• Active People survey with 364 000 sample, undertaken repeated 07–08, with LAs sharing costs?
Improving success in popular sports	
5.1 financial rewards for success?	• All projects to including evaluation and penalties for failure – ASA loses £300K for poor results in Sydney 2004
5.2 improve Talent Identification	• Long Term Athlete Development model adopted
5.3 Simplify funding UK vs devolved Councils; focusing input one-stop planning for NGBs	• negotiated; 20 priority sports for funding
	• whole sport plans produced
Improving the approach to hosting mega-events	
6.1 urged caution in hosting – via Cabinet committee	• UKSport committee
Simplifying the fragmented funding arrangements	
Reforming the organisational framework	
7.1 DCMS Director of Sport	• appointed, no visible effect
7.2 SE/UKS to be primarily fund distributors	• already much reduced technical input
7.4 Best Value PIs for sport and PA Sector Skills Council action plan for key worker training	• all but 3 rejected by District Councils
	• strategy developed by SkillsActive

Houlihan (2000) described youth sport as a 'crowded policy space'. School Sports Partnerships drew a family of primary and secondary sites around a Specialist Sports College with extra resources for staff and equipment, expected to form club and community links and use coaches in schools. These were supported by YST *TOPs* programmes for teachers and *Step into Sport* to help youngsters to get into the habit of volunteering.

Table 3.9 *The Framework for Sport in England,* 2004 – priorities for action.

	Progress
Promotion and marketing	
• social marketing campaign	• Everyday Sport budget of £60 m? via regions, no national impact
• making the case	• Value of Sport Monitor; research into barriers and motivations
Legislative/Regulatory change	
• New Public Service Agreements	• in 2006
• Tax incentives for clubs, and for employers to allow staff to volunteer	• no action on latter?
Quality accreditation and improvement	
• *Towards an Excellent Service-Sport*	• IdEA (2006a) extended from LAs to NGBs, County Sports Partnerships, to Culture (2006b) and parks and open spaces, 2007
• Include PA in agenda of Primary Health Care Trusts	• nothing happened?
• Performance-related grant aid for clubs, public facilities	• No action?
Structures and partnerships	
• PESSCL target 75% of children with two hours of PE by 2006	• - % by 2006 n/a
• Better co-ordination of outdoor recreation	• no action?
Innovation and delivery	
• Active England £100 m in line with PAT10	• Through ~RSBs and CSPs?
• Family oriented, multi-sport 'hub clubs'	• being developed via RSBs
• Workforce development	• SkillsActive Plan
• Widen community use of schools	• DfES Extended Schools, wider version of 1964 policy
• Qualified PE teacher in each primary school	• ? not mandatory
Strategic planning and evidence	
• Integrate sport with other planning processes	• rhetoric?
• Develop Value of Sport monitor	• co-operation with Australia
• Economic model of benefits of sport and PA	• any action?
• Research into motivations/barriers re non-participation	• commissioned 20 years after first suggested
• New facilities database	• Active Places launched 2005

HMG and SE both continued to stress the importance of the voluntary sector, and an update of the 1997 survey with a more sophisticated sample showed 5.8 m volunteers (15% of England's population), supporting 106 000 clubs, and contributing the equivalent of 720 000 fulltime workers valued at over £14bn. It confirmed national studies of volunteering that sport constituted 26% of all volunteering (Taylor et al., 2003). DCMS encouraged LAs to use rebate on community charges developmentally with voluntary clubs, and Lottery grants continued to flow; but given the small average size and modest budget and human resources of British clubs relative, say, to those in Germany, there has been no direct help to strengthen the system while calls on its volunteers have increased for both mass and elite purposes – the latest being to try to get 10 000 volunteer community coaches in the 70 most deprived areas of England (the least likely to have such resources) to offer three hours a week for input of only £5 m (DCMS *Press Release* 25 September 2007). DCMS has promoted community sports volunteering and is helping SportscoachUK to professionalise higher level coaching but much training is left for individuals to fund themselves.

Another current buzzwords is 'partnership', and the government is trying to promote these at every level and in every direction (ODPM and others, 2004) The most significant of these is Strategic Local Partnerships which affect resource distribution to local authorities; Sport England had promoted County Sport Partnerships to bring together LAs, LEAs and regional/county NGBs and their clubs (e.g. Charlton, forthcoming 2008), the Department of Education instituted School Sport Partnerships (SSPs) clustering primary schools around a Specialist Sport College and providing a base for School Sport Co-ordinators (SSCos). CSPs have an agenda to

- ensure the implementation of PESSCL;
- nourish club development;
- encourage LAs and NGBs in their workforce development; and
- help sport to contribute to the wider social agenda.

But old regional tensions arose for them, of serving SE priorities against a wider sport agenda.

By pooling resources and influence and accessing sources one partner has no route to partnerships that can be fruitful (Robson, chapter 7 in Hylton and Bramham, 2008). Some examples are that SSPs widen the range of activities available, especially to older primary children, and enable professional development for PE teachers (Loughborough Partnership, 2005). But they have transaction costs, can be cumbersome if partners are numerous and can be drawn by the priorities and cultures of major players (Collins and Kay, 2003, pp. 226–7; Houlihan and White, 2002, p. 225). When the funding for PESSCL finishes in 2008–9, there will be a major financial hole in CSP budgets. Houlihan and Lindsey explore partnership issues in Chapter 11.

At elite level UK Sport under the chairmanship of Sue Campbell, also chair of the YST, has encouraged for NGBs the development of Whole Sport Plans;

the reshaping of administrations under the modernisation programme (very analogous to programmes in Canada and Australia (Green and Houlihan, 2005)); and supporting Sportscoach UK in its professionalisation policy. This has involved introducing the National Coaching Certificate and encouraging the 1.2 m UK coaches to upgrade their skills; only 38% in 2004 had an NGB qualification (MORI, 2004), but already 50% by 2007 (Townend and North, 2007). Lyle (2008, p. 231) saw coaches as 'service agents', but argued that the very different demands on and skills needed by community as opposed to high level coaches means that in the longer term, 'it may not be helpful in terms of recruitment, education and professional development to conceive of a coherent, integrated continuum of coaching roles' perhaps calling into question how the new National Certificate should be designed and delivered.

The Talented Athlete Scholarship Scheme (TASS) was introduced with £3000 to help 18–25 year olds in 32 sports and 15 disability sports to prepare themselves for competition, though course run by Higher Education Institutions in each region; in 2005 £1000 bursaries were introduced to help younger people to prepare with 2012 in mind. These moneys were in addition to the larger sums available for World Class athletes through Lottery funding.

In this period, offering British expertise overseas was positively encouraged. In the 1970s, despite promoting and selling expertise in transport technology and the planning of new towns, the Sports Council was told it was a domestic agency and to go no further, while its European neighbours did so vigorously. UK Sport offered advice for using-sport-in-development, as Coalter (2007) put it; translating advice culled from Britain in co-operation with people from Africa and India (Coalter, 2006). The Youth Sport Trust developed its partnerships, services and grants overseas including Dreams and Teams (www.yst.org.uk). The winning of the bid for the 2012 Games has put a huge direct pressure on governing bodies and athletes to do well in Beijing 2008 and the run-up to London, and indirectly on UK Sport and its strategy. If the hopes are not reasonably fulfilled, then inquests will be as severe as in Canada after Seoul 1988 and the Ben Johnson doping scandal (Green and Houlihan, 2005), and again in Canada and New Zealand after disappointing results in 2000 (Knight et al., 2005).

Before the end of this period, other reports appeared; Patrick Carter had saved the government's face over the handling of the rebuilding of Wembley and the cancellation of the Lee Valley athletic centre, was ennobled and became chair of Sports England. In 1995 he undertook a wide-ranging review of structures, resources and policies (Carter, 2005 – Table 3.10). Some ideas were short lived, like the commercially co-sponsored revenue fund; others became part of SE policy.

1. The single sports system, with a 'delivery chain' from Whitehall to village green. This seems an over-optimistic simplistic view of a pluralist set-up. But it does contain the concept of Community Sports Networks, a wider-reaching version of a successful form of networking in the 1970s – Local Advisory Sports Councils, which have died in England but continue to flourish in Scotland.

Table 3.10 Carter Report 2005 policy-delivery recommendations.

Recommendation	Collins (2005a) comment
1. Robust measurement and evidence	
(a) establish national/local participation surveys	• excellent; but we must wait and see whether, outside metropolitans and unitaries, LAs will buy into parallel samples of 1000
(b) develop/publish benchmarks	• including PIs in culture bock for CPA *very* important, but public facilities are only a part of the system
(c) evaluation of investment and research 'knowledge gaps'	• fine; need to know more about personal and organisation processes and outcomes. *Value of Sport* monitor is an excellent start
(d) systems for continuous improvement (e.g. TAES)	• essential; Quest system will need radical updating to cope with health agenda and new partnerships
2. Sustained promotion and marketing	
(a) Create long-term social marketing campaign	• excellent, if government will fund at £30 m a year, like anti-smoking and safe driving
	• Everyday Sport launched
3. Renewed infrastructure and local delivery	
(a) single system for community sport	• great ideal, *but* not convinced if this simplification is achievable or that CSPs can carry the expected burden of being *the* link – it presumes not only a sharing of aims but a subsuming of autonomy
(b) work with ODPM on local planning guidelines	• limitation exaggerated; public investment is a *much* greater issue
(c) ensure VAT is no obstacle to community use of schools	• newly uncovered bureaucratic Treasury hurdle *must* be remedied, *but* given undue coverage
(d) Government support existing investment streams	• OK, *but* is a new NIF needed to lever in private money? No acceptance of need for *new* Exchequer and LA money equal to the *Game Plan* target – indeed this might be seen as side-stepping this
4. Single brand and streamlined 'back office'	
(a) cross Department Sports Cabinet committee	• Good to cover sport and PA, *but* no evidence this alone will promote salience of sport
(b) single access point and national brand	• e-systems will help access, *but* will private commercial/ voluntary sector gain in their terms from signing up to a single brand?
(c) explore common back offices and services	• Danger of incorporation and 'MacDonaldisation' of sporting bodies, as has happened in welfare

(Continued)

Table 3.10 Continued

Recommendation	Collins (2005a) comment
5. *Targeted incentives and commercial assistance*	
(a) create a large, capped co-sponsorship NS revenue Fund for grass roots incl. facilities	• gearing 2:1, *but* why yet another fund? Not convinced
(b) NSF help NGBs approach sponsors, offer training credits	• CCPR already offers matchmaker function; commercial insights helpful for NGBs, *but* this can be done more simple via Sport E
(c) HMG guides for 'socially responsible' sponsorship	• OK – Corporate SR is a rising issue, and this could be helpful and avoid a repetition of the smoking sponsorship issue
(d) communicate all tax-deductible opportunities	• Good idea

Source: Adapted from Collins (2005a).

2. For social marketing as outlined in Game Plan, Carter gathered more than the £30 m he sought to emulate safe driving and anti-smoking campaigns. The Everyday Sport campaign was rolled out regionally, but has made no visible impact on the national scene.

In the same year, two former sports ministers unlikely yoked, Conservatives' Colin Moynihan (soon to become CCPR chair) and Labour's Kate Hooey led a team sponsored by five major corporations, producing what they called the first independent review since Wolfenden in 1960 (ISR, 2005). Sadly it produced no clear, broad-minded sweep, having no-one with the brain of Wolfenden, and it was a mishmash, overestimating the importance of NGBs and the voluntary sector.

Balancing the Needs of the Large Mass and the Small Elite

This is a policy dilemma for all sports systems; under communist regimes, apart from some dynamo clubs and some sport for all days, the poverty of facility and human resources for mass participation reductions in participation have been shown in the post-1989 period (DaCosta and Miragaya, 2002; Girginov and Collins, 2004). The scale of provision, the span of time needed and other favourable contextual policies to provoke major lifestyle and participation changes are huge, challenging and beyond the sport policy community, which is usually marginal.

Already by 1989 in a 15-nation review, Kamphorst and Roberts (1989) perceived a developing focus in national policies on elite sport and winning medals; rubbing shoulders with personalities is attractive to politicians, but more importantly even if at a high unit cost, funding the training travel and competition, medical and science support for elite athletes was a much more manageable task than supporting nation-wide mass participation with its many partners, sponsors and interests.

In the UK, after a period of some 20 years where Sport for All dominated, the pendulum shifted; Lentell (1993, p. 147) suggested that 'the [Sports] Council is ending its "dangerous liaison" with the world of "community" to rejoin the more comfortable world of "sport" '. The Lottery funding which broke the forty-year long shunning of what had been called 'broken time' payments for amateur elite athletes, and the emergence of the internationally focused UK Sport, and a lead body for coaching produced a separate policy community/advocacy coalition separate from those for school and community sport (Green and Houlihan, 2005; Houlihan and White, 2002).

In this same period, school sport received funding for new physical and human resources, training and organisation – School Sport partnerships, School Sport Co-ordinators, Space for Sport and the PE School Sport and Club Links Strategy, the work of the Youth Sport Trust. So, with funding from the Lottery and Department of Education and Science and support also from the School Sports Alliance, there was a policy community/advocacy coalition for performance and elite sport (Houlihan and White, 2002). These two coalitions left the participation level supported by Sport England and local authorities, increasingly marginalised by government in policy and funding terms, despite the recognition of the County Sports Partnerships (Table 3.11). As a foundation for participation, the national curriculum and school practices still advantage boys over girls and competitive over recreational sports.

How does this compare with other countries? Australia is reputed to be sport mad, but has the same problems as the UK with static participation only a few percent above that in Britain; its system is fragmented and pluralist – being federal with three tiers, and a similar relationship between the Sports Commission and the Federal ministry as Sport England and UK Sport, with similar tensions. It started earlier on support for youth through Aussie Sport, and excellence though its Institute; its programme and budget were increased markedly to ensure success in the Sydney Games, but has only recently begun to grapple with doping, tobacco sponsorship and free-to-air TV coverage. There is a stronger link with health issues, but politics makes a difference concerning mass sport, with more interest from Labour administrations (Stewart et al., 2004). Both Australia and Canada have had similar demands from NGBs for plans, with a very formal quadrennial process in Canada.

The voluntary–state partnership is very strong in Scandinavia, with the state trusting voluntary sport to take the lead; in Germany there is partnership at all three levels of the federation and every Chancellor since the Second World War has made a major speech on sports policy. Willy Brandt was typical: 'we in government wish to remain partners of sport . . . . . . thus [German] sport can reckon on [a] kind of subsidiary partnership and expect the state's co-operation' (Geisler, 1978, p. 72).

Table 3.11   PE School Sport and Club Links Strategy.

DfES (2003) elements	Developments
• PSA target 75% of children having two hours high quality PE and sport a week by 2006	
• 400 Specialist Sport Colleges (SSCs) by 2005	DfES say exam results improved; still struggle between PA, competitive and lifelong recreation; help raise the floor rather than raising the ceiling (Houlihan and Wong, 2005)
• 400 School Sport Partnerships (SSPs)	Do develop networks; help teacher development and focus on neglected primary PE (Loughborough Partnership, 2005)
3200 School Sport co-ordinators (SSCos) by 2006, linked to 18 000 primary teachers	
• increase proportion entering clubs	
• gifted and talented development programmes including camps	
• Step into Sport to encourage youth volunteering in 200 SSPs	SSCs helping interest in leadership

Public Policies on Sports Development: Lessons for Managers

Hylton and Totten (2008) suggest there has been a failure to realise Sport for All, and their analysis argues that this in part a failure to appreciate the wider UK social context; but this author would say that there is a wider reason still – a failure to realise what sort of society the UK is compared to those ministers and senior public servants have chosen as models – Australia, Canada and Finland in particular.

What can be concluded from the tangled story this chapter has told? At least six things are suggested:

1. Sport England faces the same challenge in trying to raise participation as other developed states. The difficulty of persuading people to give up enough time to undertake the 1.5 hours a week of moderate intensity exercise is clear – especially since it involves giving up something else as enjoyable and less hard work, especially watching TV.

2. HMG's comparison with Finland is inappropriate, setting Sport England and others up for failure; compared to England, Finland has a more equal society regarding income inequality and welfare and the status of women; a longstanding higher commitment to sports investment and healthy activity; a better diet across the nation; and a simpler sports delivery system with one strong sport confederation and local authorities backed by the government.

3. It is clear that while most people do not do enough exercise to keep fit, many delude themselves that they do, especially women (Future Foundation, 2007). Despite the advocacy of the Chief Medical Officer and productive partnerships between CSPs and some Primary Care Teams, neither the Department of Health nor the NHS Executive has espoused physical activity.

4. Investment in updating major public sports facilities for adults rather than schoolchildren has kept pace with neither inflation nor obsolescence. In any case it can be estimated that these major facilities have capacity for at most 14% of the population. Ministers have glibly pointed to a few successful Public–Private Partnership schemes and (steadily reducing) Lottery funding as adequate to stop the gap, when patently they cannot (Collins, 2002b).

5. Promotion of sport for health requires more officers on the streets and in the lanes, like SDOs, but with better public health knowledge and training; there is a major growth in sports development and physical activity degrees but generally without the degree of crossover knowledge required (Pitchford and Collins, forthcoming 2008).

HMG has consistently argued that winning the London 2012 summer Games can be a major boost to sport for all and a springboard to 'fighting the flab' – the effect of 'Olympic stardust', as Minister for Olympic delivery Tessa Jowell called it (CCPR conference, 9 May 2007). First, there is not a shred of evidence that any of the two-week Olympic spectacles has had, or can have, this effect (Coalter, 2004). Second, the division of the Lottery funding was raided to help pay rising Games costs to the tune of £65 m, reducing that for mass sport, and causing newly appointed chair of Sport England, Derek Mapp, to complain mightily about a 'cut too far'. The diversion represented an 8% budget cut, but because Sport England levers in £3 for every £1, 'what that really means is that £1.6 bn is not going to community sport; that would buy the same number of coaches that there are in the whole of France', or 186 000 fewer participants from his target of two million'. (quoted by A. Culf, *Guardian*, 22 March 2007).

So, it is not a harsh comment to say that British sports ministers have failed to see the policy challenge in a broad enough frame and have consistently underfunded both the Sports Councils and local government in the sphere of mass participation, relative to the real growth in the last decade of resources and strong policy communities for school and elite sport. Despite internally moving and renaming some of the deckchairs, what Pickup said in 1996 (pp. 218–19) of government policy is even more true:

at a time when sport has more money flowing in its direction than ever we are perversely in danger of allowing that vision to fade because of our failure to overcome administrative, regional and bureaucratic divisions....and implications of political dogma.

At the time of finishing this chapter this uncertain see-saw of policy priorities in British sport has taken another unpredictable and apparently crazy swing. Mapp had been spending his first year in office accepting that Sport England would take responsibility for encouraging people to take three of the five half-hour activity sessions required, and that some would take the form of informal activities and exercise rather than formal sport ('Engaging the Nation', speech to CCPR conference 9 May 2007). Newly appointed Secretary of State James Purnell, whose background was in broadcasting rather than sport, seemed to take exception to Mapp's criticisms, asked Sport England to focus on more traditional sports to free up money for developing a world class legacy to the Olympics and besought the Department of Health to take responsibility for such activities as jogging and walking.

When Mapp warned Purnell to be careful about this turn, he was asked to resign. He accurately commented 'I accept that the DoH should be getting people fitter but their contribution over recent years has been very little' (www.politics.co.uk), and 'I am bound to say I think it's unfair. I was mandated to produce an agenda which I was delivering on but now that has been changed and I have been dumped on' (D. Bond, *Daily Telegraph*, 30 November 2007). He also said 'Purnell is an arrogant young man who doesn't reflect what I thought this Government was trying to do' (A. Hubbard, *The Independent*, 2 December 2007). An interim chair will be appointed, and former Executive Chair of the Rugby Football League, Richard Lewis, was asked to review SE's spending priorities in time to influence the next three-year public spending settlement.

The governing bodies in English sport command only some 6 m members, not all playing. Without exception they argue they need more volunteers to cope with the growing roles the government expects them to play; they struggle with working out the expressed aims of equality, of increasing involvement of more women, ethnic minorities, disabled people and other hard-to-reach groups. The Secretary of State's action will almost certainly slow down the already uncertain progress of increasing mass participation. This clearly shows politicians' continuing wedding to elite over community sport. Politicians' rhetoric reinforces the mythopoeic (myth-making) qualities of sport as character building and foundational to society. Tessa Jowell said in her preface to *Game Plan* (DCMS, 2002):

> Sport defines us as a nation. It teaches us about life. We learn self discipline and team work from it. We learn how to win with grace and lose with dignity. It gets us fit. It keeps us healthy (p. 6) and then 'those of us who carry [this blueprint] out must take our responsibilities seriously. But we should always remember that sport should be fun'. (p. 11)

That was as near as she got to a statement of belief in the intrinsic value of sport. She had made an explicit statement about the intrinsic value of culture in 2004. James Purnell's act shows a different face. So, in the next policy phase it seems likely that school and elite sport will continue to thrive and mass sport will struggle with local authorities and clubs low in priority and funding.

What lessons does this have for sports development managers?

1. if your focus is on youth/school, competitive or elite sport, the policy and funding tides are with you, though you still have to bid for resources;

2. if your focus is on mass/sport for all, then you have to wait for the next swing of the policy pendulum, and you will need all projects to have a link to one or two of the cross cutting issues;

3. the current bidding culture rewards ability to bid rather than need, so you need to target projects closely on groups and areas, and be very clear about which intermediate outcomes you seek to produce (Coalter, 2007);

4. do not set yourself up for failure by promising more than you can deliver; over-achievement equals extra success;

5. if you want to be 'ahead of the game' for that policy swing, the policy area where great health, socialisation and social capital gains are to be had is in sport for older people.

References

Audit Commission (1989). *Sport for Whom?* London: Audit Commission.

Bell, B. (forthcoming 2008). Building a legacy for youth and coaching – champion coaching on merseyside. In *Examining Sports Development* (M.F. Collins ed.). London: Routledge.

Bergsgard, N.A., Houlihan, B., Mangset, P., Nodland, S.I., and Rommetvedt, H. (2007). *Sport Policy: A Comparative Analysis of Stability and Change.* Oxford: Butterworth Heinemann.

Bourne, J. (2000). *Report of Auditor and Comptroller General to Parliament on the Departure of Mr Derek Casey, former CEO of Sport England.* London: National Audit Office.

Carter, P. (Lord) (2005). *Review of National Sport Effort and Resources.* London: DCMS.

Charlton, A. (forthcoming 2008). A new active sports partnership – Lancashire sport. In *Examining Sports Development* (M.F. Collins, ed.). London: Routledge.

Chief Medical Officer (2004). *At Least Five a Week: Evidence of the Impact of Physical Activity and its Relationship to Health.* London: HMSO.

Coalter, F. (1998). Leisure studies, leisure policy and social citizenship: The failure of welfare or the limits of welfare. *Leisure Studies*, **17**, 21–36.

Coalter, F. (2004). Stuck in the blocks? A sustainable sporting legacy? In *After the Gold Rush: The London Olympics.* London: Institute for Public Policy Research/DEMOS.

Coalter, F. (2006). *Sport in Development: A Monitoring and Evaluation Manual.* London: UKSport.

Coalter, F. (2007). *A Wider Role for Sport: Who's Keeping the Score?* London: Routledge.

Coghlan, J. (1990). *Sport and British Politics Since 1960.* London: Falmer Press.

Collins, M.F. (ed.). (1973). *Provision for Sport Vol II Specialist Facilities.* London: Sports Council.

Collins, M.F. (ed. and contributor). (1980). *Integrated Facilities.* Strasbourg: Council of Europe.

Collins, M.F. (1985). Regional strategies for sport and recreation: Coherence or confusion? In *Sport in the Community, the Next Ten Years: Problems and Issues* (L. Haywood, ed.). Leisure Studies Newsletter Supplement.

Collins, M.F. (1995). *Sports Development Regionally and Locally*. Reading: Institute of Leisure and Amenity Management.

Collins, M.F. (1997). Sporting Nation. *Leisure Management*, **17**(12), Sports management section 16–18.

Collins, M.F. (2000a). Sporting future [review of DCMS strategy]. *Sports Management*, July 6–8.

Collins, M.F. (2000b). Riding on a wave? Water recreation on privatized and public inland resources in England. In *Leisure Planning in Transitory Societies Publication 58* (M.F. Collins, ed.). EastBourne: Leisure Studies Association, pp. 69–84.

Collins, M.F. (2002a). England: Sport for all as a multifaceted product of domestic and international influences. In *Worldwide Experiences and Trends in Sport for All* (L. DaCosta and A. Miragaya, eds). Oxford: Meyer and Meyer Sport, pp. 493–522.

Collins, M.F. (2002b). *Sport for all in the UK: Between Social Exclusion, Facility Obsolescence, and Priorities for Elite Sport?* Paper to 9th Sport for All Congress. Arnhem, 27–30 October.

Collins, M.F. (2005a). Sport report [review of Carter report]. *Sports Management*, **2**, 18–20.

Collins, M.F. (2005b). Where next with CPA? *Recreation*, **64**(12), 14.

Collins, M.F. and Buller, J.R. (2000). Bridging the post-school institutional gap in sport: Evaluating champion coaching in Nottinghamshire. *Managing Leisure*, **5**, 200–21.

Collins, M.F. and Glyptis, S.A. (1992). Marketing public leisure services in the UK. *Library Management*, **13**(4), 33–42.

Collins, M.F. and Kay, T. (2003). *Sport and Social Exclusion*. London: Routledge.

Collins, M.F. (ed.). (2004). *Participating & Performing: Sport in HE in the UK*. London: Universities UK.

Collins, M.F. and Kennett, C. (1996). *Sport and Community Use in Higher Education in the UK*. London: Committee of Vice Chancellors and Principals.

Collins, M.F. and Randolph, L. (1993). Business or hobby, small firms in sport and recreation. In *Leisure and Tourism: Social and Environmental Change* (A. Veal et al., eds). Sydney: University of Technology, pp. 433–8.

Collins, M.F., Henry, I., Houlihan, B., and Kennett, C. (1999). *Research Review: Sport and Social Exclusion*. London: Department of Media Culture and Sport.

DaCosta, L. and Miragaya, A. (eds). (2002). *Worldwide Experiences and Trends in Sport for All*. Oxford: Meyer and Meyer Sport, pp. 493–522.

Department for Education & Skills (2003). *Learning through PE and sport; A guide to the Physical Education, School Sport and Club Links Strategy*. London: DfES.

Department for Education and Science (1964). A chance to share. London: HMSO.

Department of Culture Media and Sport (1999). *Report on Sport and Arts*, to Policy Action Team 10 Social Exclusion Unit. London: The Department.

Department of Culture Media and Sport (2000). *A Sporting Future for All*. London: The Department.

Department of Culture Media and Sport (2002a). *Game Plan: A Strategy for Delivering the Government's Sport and Physical Activity Objectives*. London: The Department.

Department of Culture Media and Sport (2002b). *The Coaching Task Force: Final Report*. London: The Department.

Department of the Environment (1975). *Sport and Recreation White Paper*. London: HMSO.

Department of the Environment, Transport and Regions (1999). *Modernising Local Government: Improving Local Services Through Best Value*. London: HMSO.

Department of Health (2004). *Choosing Health: Making Healthy Choices Easier*. London: DoH.

Department of Health/Sports Council and others (1992). *Allied DunbarNational Fitness Survey*. London: Sports Council.

Department of National Heritage (1995). *Sport: Raising the Game*. London: The Department.

Department of National Heritage (1996). *Report of the Working Group on University Sport Scholarships*. London: The Department.

England, The Sporting Nation (1997). *England: The Sporting Nation*. London: The Council.

English Sports Council (1996). *Valuing Volunteers in UK Sport*. London: The Council.

Evans, H.J. (1974). *Service to Sport: the Story of the CCPR 1935–72*. London: Pelham Books.

Future Foundation (2007). *It's Time: Future Forecasts for Women's Participation in Sport and Exercise*. London: Women's Sport Foundation.

Geisler, K. (ed.). (1978). *Sport in derBundesrepublik Deutscheland*. Frankfurt: Deutsche Sportbund.

Girginov, V. and Collins, M.F. (eds). (2004). Sport in Eastern Europe. *International Journal of the History of Sport*, **21**(5), Special issue.

Gratton, C. and Tice, A. (1994). Trends in sports participation in Britain 1977–87. *Leisure Studies*, **13**, 49–66.

Gratton, C., Taylor, P., Nichols, G., and Kokolakakis, T. (1997). *Valuing Volunteers in UK Sport*. London: Sports Council.

Green, M. and Houlihan, B. (2005). *Elite Sport Development: Policy Learning and Political Priorities*. London: Routledge.

Houlihan, B. (1991). *The Government and Politics of Sport*. London: Routledge.

Houlihan, B. (1997). *Sport, Policy and Politics*. London: Routledge.

Houlihan, B. (2000). Sporting excellence, schools and sports development: The politics of crowded policy spaces. *European P E Review*, **6**, 73–92.

Houlihan, B. (2002). *The Politics of Sports Development: Development of Sport or Development through Sport?* London: Routledge.

Houlihan, B. and White, A. (2002). *The Politics of Sports Development: Development of Sport or Development through Sport*. London: Routledge.

Houlihan, B. and Wong, C. (2005). *Report on 2004 Survey of Specialist Sports Colleges*. Loughborough: Institute of Youth Sport, Loughborough University.

Hylton, K. and Bramham, P. (eds). (2008). *Sports Development: Policy, Process and Practice*, 2nd edn. London: Routledge.

Improvement and Development Agency (2007). *Towards an Excellent Servioie: A Performance Management Framework for parks and open spaces*. London: IDeA.

Improvement and Development Agency (2006a). *Towards an Excellent Service: A Performance Management Framework for Sport and Recreation Services in Local Government*. London: IdeA.

Improvement and Development Agency (2006b). *Towards an Excellent Service: A Performance Management Framework for Cultural Services in Local Government*. London: IdeA.

Independent Sports Review (2005). *Raising the Bar*. London: ISR Office.

Institute for Community Cohesion (2006). *The Power of Sport*. Coventry: Coventry University for SE.

Kamphorst, T. and Roberts, K. (eds). (1989). *Trends in Sports: A Multinational Perspective*. Culembourg: Giordano Bruno.

Kingdon, J.W. (1984). *Agendas, Alternatives and Public Policy*. Boston: Little, Brown.

Knight, G., MacNeill, M., and Donnelly, P. (2005). The disappointment games: Narratives of Olympic failure in Canada and New Zealand. *International Review for Sociology of Sport*, **40**(1), 25–51.

Kruger, A. and Riordan, J. (1996). *The Story of Workers Sport*. Champaign, IL: Human Kinetics.

Lentell, R. (1993). Sports Development: Goodbye to community recreation. In *Body matters: Leisure time and lifestyle Leisure Studies Association publication* (C. Brackenridge, 9 ed). 47 Eastbourne: Brigton Univeristy.

Loughborough Partnership (2005). *School Sports Partnerships: Annual Monitoring and Evaluation Report.* Loughborough University: Institute of Youth Sport.

Lupson, P. (2006). *Thank God forFootball!* London: Azure-SPCK.

Lyle, J. (2008). Sports development and sports coaching. In *Sports Development: Policy, Process, Practice,* 2nd edn. (K. Hylton and P. Bramham, eds). London: Routledge, pp. 214–35.

MORI (2004). *Sports Coaching in the UK.* Leeds: SportscoachUK.

Nichols, G. (2007). *Sport and Crime Reduction: The Role of Sports in Tackling Youth Crime.* London: Routledge.

Nichols, G. and Taylor, P. (1995). The impact on local authority leisure of CCT, financial cuts and changing attitudes. *Local Government Studies,* **21**(4), 607–22.

Office of the Deputy Prime Minister and others (2004). *Teaming Up: How Joint Working Between Sport and Neighbourhood Renewal Practitioners can Help Improve Deprived Areas.* London: ODPM.

Penney, D. and Evans, J. (1999). *Politics, Policy and Practice in Physical Education.* London: E&F Spon.

Pickup, D. (1996). *Not Another Messiah: An Account of the Sports Council 1988–93.* Edinburgh: Pentland Press.

Pitchford, A. and Collins, M.F. (forthcoming 2008). Sports development as a job, a career and training. In *Examining Sports Development* (M.F. Collins, ed.). London: Routledge.

Rigg, J. (1982). *Action Sport: An Evaluation.* London: Sports Council.

Slack, T. (ed.). (2004). *The Commercialization of Sport.* London: Routledge.

Social Exclusion Unit (1997). *Bringing Britain Together.* London: SEU, Cabinet Office.

Sport England (2002). *The Equality Standard.* London: Sport England.

Sport England (2004). *Framework for Sport in England: Making England an Active and Successful Sporting Nation: A Vision for 2020.* London: Sport England.

Sport England and others (2004). *Bringing Communities Together Thorough Sport and Culture.* London: Sport England.

SportscoachUK (2006). *UK Action Plan for Coaching.* Leeds: SportscoachUK.

Sports Council (1971). *Sport in the Seventies; Making Good the Deficiencies.* London: The Council.

Sports Council (1982). *Sport in the Community: The Next Ten Years.* London: The Council.

Sports Council (1987). *Sport in Community: Into the 90s.* London: The Council.

Sports Council (1992). *A Countryside for Sport.* London: the Council

Sports Council (1993a). *New Horizons Sport in the Nineties.* London: The Council.

Sports Council (1993b). *Young People and Sport: Policies and Frameworks for Action.* London: The Council.

Sports Council (1993c). *Women and Sport: Policy and Frameworks for Action.* London: The Council.

Sports Council (1993d). *People with Disabilities and Sport: Policy and Current/Planned Actions.* London: The Council.

Sports Council (1994a). *Playing Fields Count.* Mimeo. London: The Council.

Sports Council (1994b). *Black and Ethnic Minorities in Sport: Policy and Objectives.* London: The Council.

Stewart, R., Nicholson, M., Smith, A., and Westerbeek, H. (2004). *Australian Sport: Better by Design. The Evolution of Australian Sport Policy.* London: Routledge.

Taylor, P., Nichols, G., Holmes, K., James, Gratton, C., Garrett, R., Kokolakakis, T., Mulder, C., and King, L. (2003). *Sports Volunteering in England.* London: Sport England.

Theodoraki, E. (1999). The making of the UK sports institute. *Managing Leisure,* **4**(4), 187–200.

Townend, R. and North, J. (2007). *Sports Coaching in the UK II.* Leeds: SportscoachUK.

Tungatt, M. and MacDonald, D. (1992). *National Demonstration Projects; Major Lessons and Issues for Sports Development.* London: Sports Council.

UKSport (1999). *Major Events: The Economics of Measuring Success.* London: UKSport.

UKSport (2005). *Major Events: The Guide* (2nd edn). London: UKSport.

Viallon, R., Camy, J., and Collins, M.F. (2003). The European integration of a new occupation, the strategies of national professional organisations: The case of the fitness sector in France and the UK. *Managing Leisure: An International Journal,* **8**(2), 85–96.

Wolfenden, J. (Sir, later Lord) (1960). *Sport and the Community.* London: Central Council for Physical Recreation.

CHAPTER 4

Non-Governmental Organisations in Sports Development

Mick Green

Introduction

This chapter explores the role of non-governmental organisations in promoting a sports development agenda in the UK. In drawing examples from significant voluntary sport providers some of the key contemporary challenges for sport management professionals are identified and interrogated, and the (inter)relationships with key public sector sporting organisations examined. At the outset it should be recognised that one of the defining characteristics of what is usually termed the 'voluntary sector', within which non-governmental organisations for sport operate, is its size, complexity, and diversity. As Hoye and Cuskelly (2007, pp. 7–8) note, 'It is somewhat difficult to ascertain how many nonprofit [or voluntary] sport organisations there are within the sporting system of any individual country'. The size of the sector is highlighted by The Leisure Industries and Research Centre (LIRC). Research by the LIRC in 2003 estimates that there are some 106 000 volunteer-run sports clubs in England in addition to regional and national governing bodies of sport (quoted in Hoye and Cuskelly, 2007, p. 8). Therefore, the usual caveats apply here in as much as that it is not possible to provide an exhaustive consideration of all the different types of non-governmental organisations involved in the sports development field.

A further contextual factor to bear in mind in any discussion of non-governmental organisations in sport is the ambiguity surrounding the meaning of the term, 'sports development'. In terms of scope, Houlihan and White (2002, p. 3) suggest that sports development refers not only to those currently involved in sport as well as those already physically active but also to the general or mass participant and the aspiring high performance athlete. Moreover, as Girginov notes in Chapter 1 sports development can not only be viewed as an activity concerned with service inputs (e.g. facility provision) and the creation of opportunities, but also as an activity that focuses on service outcomes and the maximisation of benefit.

In addition, at different times, the emphasis in sports development in the UK has varied between reactive and proactive strategies (cf. Green, 2006,

2007), and between participation and high performance objectives (cf. Green, 2004). In other words, today, non-governmental organisations involved in the management of sports development opportunities are faced with a number of complex challenges. On the one hand, these organisations have to satisfy the end-user of services, programmes, and activities provided. On the other hand, they increasingly face the need to meet objectives set by, or in some cases agreed in collaboration with, public and private sector bodies that provide much needed funding and sponsorship money for operational purposes.

Significant Non-Governmental Organisations

National Governing Bodies of Sport

The primary focus for us in this chapter concerns the management and operations of national governing bodies of sport (NGBs). There are more than 100 sports recognised by the Sports Councils in the UK and they in turn are affiliated to some 400 national governing bodies of sport and recreation (Independent Sports Review, 2005): NGBs therefore play a prominent role in supporting sports development in the UK. Most NGBs were established as voluntary organisations in the nineteenth century in order to regulate and administer their respective sports. They were primarily concerned with drawing up the rules of their sport, organising domestic competitions and selecting national teams to play against other countries. However, as sport has developed over the past century or so, so has the role and remit of NGBs changed. The focus on NGBs is useful because it allows an interrogation of some of the key contemporary challenges facing non-governmental sporting organisations. On the one hand, NGBs are now grappling with an increasing array of government-related objectives in respect of sports development (often performance sport-related) opportunities. On the other hand, NGBs are also required to meet other government objectives related to social welfare polices in areas such as community development, social cohesion, and health (Sport England, 2006).

At this point, it is worth noting Fishel's (2003, quoted in Hoye and Cuskelly, 2007, p. 9) description of some of the distinctive characteristics of non-governmental sporting organisations, all of which, to a greater or lesser degree, have some bearing on the ensuing discussion and analysis of NGBs. Fishel suggests that non-governmental (usually nonprofit) sporting organisations display the following characteristics:

- these organisations are not driven solely by financial motives and may have imprecise objectives, consequently making it more difficult to monitor performance than commercial organisations;

- they are accountable to many stakeholders including their members, users, government, sponsors, volunteers, and staff;

- organisational structures can be complex, especially if they have adopted a federated or representative model to facilitate the involvement of a wide range of diverse stakeholders;

■ these organisations rely heavily on the input of volunteers for both service delivery and governance roles;

■ they are created and maintained on the basis of a set of values or beliefs about the service or opportunities the organisation provides; conflict over direction or priorities can arise through differing interpretations of these values, making it difficult to govern;

■ the relationship between the board and paid staff is potentially difficult if there remains uncertainty over who is in control of the organisation.

It is clear then that, today, NGBs operate within a complex and complicated environment mediated by different motivations, standards, challenges, and practices. These organisations have to work with, and manage through, 'a definable membership or user base, a set of relationships with key funding agencies, contractual obligations to government, a set of business contracts with other commercial, nonprofit or public sector organisations and a volunteer base' (Hoye and Cuskelly, 2007, p. 9; see also Anheier, 2005).

In the early years of their development, government policy had little influence on the operations and management of NGBs: In the early twenty-first century there are few that can afford to ignore it in the UK. Exceptions to this assumption, perhaps, are the wealthier NGBs, such as the Football Association, Lawn Tennis Association and the England and Wales Cricket Board. For most NGBs, however, government funding, and thus government expectations, are now commonplace. And of course, as Houlihan and White (2002, p. 164) note, 'Public funding is available to governing bodies to help them run and develop their sport, but it comes with strings attached'.

The relationship between NGBs and government is not direct; the five Sports Councils in the UK play a mediating role in that they collaborate with NGBs regarding the ways in which government's sports development objectives might be realised as well as being the distributing organisations for government funds to NGBs. Since the introduction of the National Lottery in 1994, NGBs (and sport in general) have enjoyed enormous increases in their levels of funding in respect of World Class Performance funding for the development and support of their elite performers (cf. Green, 2004). These increases have been accompanied, however, by performance targets and demands for a sea-change in the ways in which NGBs would be managed and governed in the future. In relation to this, sport has not been immune from changes in the wider political context and, in this respect, the government's far-reaching 'modernisation' project (cf. Finlayson, 2003) is important. As part of New Labour's drive to improve the efficiency, effectiveness, and accountability of organisations in receipt of public funding (cf. Newman, 2001), there has been a far greater emphasis on improved corporate governance and financial management as NGBs have been 'encouraged' to modernise (Deloitte and Touche, 2003).

New Labour's sport policy strategy, *A Sporting Future for All* (Department for Culture, Media and Sport [DCMS], 2000), was a clear statement of intent with regard to the nature of future relationships between government and NGBs. For all governing bodies, the requirement was modernisation and professionalisation. In particular, the government would only devolve greater responsibility for the use of public funds by non-governmental bodies such as NGBs, if they had a clear strategy for sports development activities related to 'participation and excellence; and commit themselves to putting fairness and social inclusion at the heart of everything they do' (DCMS, 2000, p. 20). Thus, not only are NGBs now expected to identify, support, and develop talented athletes towards the goal of medals and trophies on the international stage, they are also expected to commit to the government's goals for social welfare policy objectives. And New Labour has set a number of demanding sport development-related targets that NGBs are now expected to meet:

- developing sport in schools and the community, especially in areas of deprivation;

- providing appropriately trained coaches to support teachers in primary and secondary schools;

- improving the opportunities for ethnic minorities, people with disabilities, and for girls and women to participate, lead, coach, and officiate;

- have strong talent development plans to enable those with the wish and ability to reach the top levels of competition to do so; and

- having robust management, planning, and monitoring of all their activities (DCMS, 2000, p. 20).

In sum, in recent years, NGBs have emerged as key 'delivery partners' in and for the implementation of a number of government sport (and broader social welfare-related) policy objectives. Although NGBs currently enjoy far greater funding allocations than ever before, this has to be tempered by the increasingly 'demarcated freedom' that characterises contemporary relationships between governing bodies of sport and government sports agencies. Some of the key ramifications of, and challenges raised by, these changing relationships are explored in a later section of the chapter, following a brief review of two of other significant non-governmental organisations for sport in the UK.

As noted, aside from NGBs, there are also many other sporting organisations operating independently from government. Two national organisations, in particular, warrant attention given their significance in sports development activities; namely the Central Council of Physical Recreation (CCPR) and the Youth Sport Trust (YST). We deal with each of these organisations in turn.

Central Council of Physical Recreation

The CCPR maintains that it acts as the 'independent voice' for sport in the UK and, as such, is involved in sport in the following ways:

- acts as the umbrella organisation for the national governing and representative bodies of sport and recreation in the UK;

- speaks and acts to promote, protect, and develop the interests of sport and physical recreation at all levels;

■ is at the forefront of sports politics, providing support and services to those who participate in and administer sport and recreation;

■ is completely independent of any form of Government control;

■ has no responsibility for allocating funds;

■ is strictly non-party and will support or oppose proposed measures only on the basis of their perceived value to sport and recreation (CCPR, 2007).

Despite the CCPR's claims for autonomy from government, in reality it too is constrained to a large degree in the ways in which it might actively promote an 'independent' agenda for sport. The CCPR's restricted room for manoeuvre is clearly signalled in *Game Plan*, the government's latest sport policy strategy (DCMS/Strategy Unit, 2002). Here, it is acknowledged that government has little control over the CCPR 'but it does have one crucial tool – its funding. Where possible it should use this to drive modernisation and wider partnership working with the voluntary and private sectors' (2002, p. 180). Again we not only have reference to the government's modernisation project but also to another significant plank underpinning much of New Labour thinking: partnerships (cf. Newman, 2001). Yet, despite the encouragement by government for partnership working, an emerging tension in British sport is the relative lack of autonomy enjoyed by organisations such as the CCPR, and its primary constituents, the national governing bodies of sport. *Raising the Bar*, a report by the Independent Sports Review (2005, p. 87) (commissioned by two former Ministers of Sport, Kate Hoey and Colin Moynihan) highlights some of the key aspects of this debate:

> There is a need for a new partnership between government and sport. The government's role should be to provide funding to national governing bodies against agreed outcomes. The governing bodies should be free to deliver these objectives with the Government monitoring their effectiveness as partners, *not as subsidiaries* (emphasis added).

Moreover, *Raising the Bar* also maintained that 'Governing bodies must retain democratic accountability to their members and promote representation from all sections of the sport' (2005, p. 87). This, however, is increasingly difficult for NGBs to achieve in the current political and policy climate where funding for grassroots sports development opportunities is being clawed back in order to provide further support for the country's elite athletes. On this issue, the Chair of Sport England, Derek Mapp, stated that:

> Our commitment for the 2012 [Olympic] Games is unquestioned and we know the Government has had to make tough choices. However, the decision to divert a further £55.9 million of Sport England's share of lottery income between 2009 and 2012 to fund the 2012 Olympic/ Paralympic Games is a cut too far and seriously endangers the creation of a sporting legacy from the 2012 Games

> (quoted in Sport England, 2007).

At the heart of the 2012 bid was the promise to build a legacy from the Games by increasing participation in sport and boosting community sport across the country. Yet, as Derek Mapp goes on to argue, quite how such a significant reduction in funding for sports development activities 'can be squared with the clear commitments the Government has already made about the wider benefits the Games will bring' is not altogether clear. Thus, at least one of the major roles for the CCPR within the current policy climate will be to maintain pressure on, and collaborate with, government, the Sports Councils and local authority leisure/culture services in order that sports development opportunities for all are not subsumed within the inexorable drive for Olympic glory. In this respect, the CCPR might also work with another increasingly important organisation for sports development: the Youth Sport Trust.

Youth Sport Trust

The Youth Sport Trust (YST) is a charitable organisation set up in 1994 to develop and implement, in partnership with other organisations, PE, and sport programmes for young people up to 18 years old in schools and their communities. A prominent part of the organisation's work is the TOP programmes which form a sporting pathway along which young people can progress according to age and development. Key features of the programmes are resource cards, child-friendly equipment, and quality training and support for teachers and deliverers. Following a reorganisation of national sporting structures/responsibilities in the UK during 2006, the YST now has the major responsibility for school sport and PE and thus plays a considerable role in promoting and supporting sports development opportunities at this level.

The YST plays a central role, for example, in supporting the government's national strategy for PE, School Sport and Club Links (PESSCL) which aims to increase sport and physical activity levels among 5 to 16 year olds (Department for Education and Skills [DfES]/DCMS, 2003). Working with the DfES[1] and the DCMS, the YST aims to increase the percentage of school children who spend a minimum of two hours per week on high quality PE and school sport within and beyond the curriculum to around 85% by 2008. The significance of the YST's work was signalled in December 2004 when the Prime Minister Tony Blair announced a new ambition to offer all children at least four hours of sport every week – at least two hours curriculum PE and an additional two to three hours beyond the school day. Government interest in maintaining a high profile for school sport and PE does not appear to be on the wane. In July 2007, the new Prime Minister, Gordon Brown, announced a £100 million campaign to give every child the chance of five hours of sport every week (including extra-curricular time) through the provision of: a new National School Sport Week; a network of 225 competition managers; more coaches in schools and the community; and, with the help of organisations such as the

---

[1] In June 2007, following Gordon Brown's succession to Tony Blair as leader of the Labour party and Prime Minister, and a major reorganisation of central government departments, the DfES was restructured as two separate departments: the Department for Children, Schools and Families and the Department for Innovation, Universities and Skills.

YST, to encourage sporting bodies to develop modern school sport competitions (Department for Children, Schools and Families, 2007).

As part of the PESSCL strategy, again in partnership with the DfES (Department for Children, Schools and Families from June 2007) and DCMS, the YST supports the development of Specialist Sports Colleges and School Sport Partnerships. In addition, the YST supports the following three strands of the PESSCL strategy: Step into Sport – a programme which focuses on young people aged 14 to 19 giving them a chance to become involved in sports leadership and volunteering; Gifted and Talented – a programme designed to help elite young athletes realise their potential; and The National Competition Framework – which aims to build a world-class system of competitive sport for young people.

The YST's rapid emergence over the past decade or so as a key non-governmental organisation that supports, promotes, and provides sports development opportunities for children and young people in the UK is striking. However, such a rapid rise in prominence has perhaps inevitably led to a number of, as yet unresolved, tensions as the organisation seeks to embed its position as a key provider and supporter of sports development-related programmes (Phillpots, 2007). For example, the YST's role in helping to deliver the government's PESSCL objectives is reliant upon partnership working with other groups, notably the professional association for PE: the Association for Physical Education (AfPE).

Although partnership working is key to the successful delivery of the outcomes for the School Sport Partnership programme, the YST made a clear delineation between its role in the management and implementation of school sport partnerships and the role and responsibilities of the AfPE. For the YST, having a strong subject association helped to support its work, but it was made clear that it was not the role of the YST to galvanise, motivate, and support the professional workforce leading the subject in a local authority context. For a senior manager at the YST, the role of the AfPE was to support the subject in schools, and especially in primary schools: 'Part of the role of the Youth Sport Trust is to ensure that the way we work with AfPE through the school sport coordinator education training programme is towards a bigger vision for primary PE which we support whilst they lead it' (quoted in Phillpots, 2007).

A senior AfPE official questioned the involvement and role of the YST, however, as the perception of the Trust is that it is a sports development agency managing an educational infrastructure of specialist schools. Although it was acknowledged that the YST was outstanding in their advocacy and communications, there was a clear tension between its role as a sports charity and its involvement in education and PE. The concern expressed by one senior official at the AfPE was that there was

> a popular misconception out there that PE has had a lot of money through the PESSCL strategy. The only money physical education had out of £469 million is £18 million and that's for CPD [continuing professional development]. All the rest of the money went into infrastructure posts to support the work of sports colleges, School Sport Partnerships, PDMs [partnership development managers] and the PLTs [primary link teachers]
> (quoted in Phillpots, 2007).

Clearly, in the crowded space that characterises the broader sport policy environment, the demands by government on its non-governmental delivery agents (e.g. NGBs, YST, and the CCPR) require a commitment to partnership working that embraces the inter-relationships between sports development, school sport, PE, sporting excellence, and health-enhancing physical activity. In order to explore some of the key contemporary challenges faced by non-governmental organisations involved in sports development, the next section provides an in-depth examination of a major Olympic sport (athletics) and in particular, UK Athletics, the NGB for the sport – for a similar analysis of Athletics Australia, see the case study, available at the book website which reveals the degree of commonality of issues not only between Australia and the UK but also between the two NGBs.

Changing Relationships Between Government and NGBs

Before the 1970s, a piecemeal and reactive approach characterised the government's attitude to sport and recreation in the UK. The establishment of an Advisory Sports Council in 1965, however, was the first serious indication of a shift towards proactive and strategic government involvement in sport. For example, the receipt of grant aid now depended on the ability of the various organisations to comply with criteria formulated by the Council. As Coalter et al. (1988, p. 58) note, 'via the use of economic power, the ASC [Advisory Sports Council] was directly involved in rationalising the elite [sport development] sector'. The extent of direction provided by the Council was constrained by a degree of deference towards voluntary sports organisations and the persistence of a view within a number of NGBs that they had an entitlement to public funding (Houlihan, 1991). Deference from a government-sponsored agency towards NGBs can be set against 'a more general mood in Britain' at this time that coalesced around 'numerous critiques of the habits of deference to authority, elitism and the secrecy in Whitehall' (Finlayson, 2003, p. 71).

Increasing Government Influence

In the UK, it is only since the mid-1990s that government involvement in sport has strengthened to the extent seen in Australia, for example. Government intervention was limited until the establishment of the executive Sports Councils in the early 1970s, a decision that signalled an emerging interest in improving the organisational and administrative structure of sport and recreation, primarily through the building of facilities and the adoption of a Sport for All programme. Throughout the 1980s, government involvement increased, largely through programmes delivered by its arm's length agencies, the Sports Councils (Green and Houlihan, 2005). It was the publication of *Sport: Raising the Game* (Department of National Heritage, 1995), a Conservative government sport policy statement, which signalled a sharp increase in the salience of sport at central government level. *Sport: Raising the Game* focused primarily on the reinvigoration of school sport and physical education, support for elite performers and an elite sport academy/institute, the development of the role of higher education institutions in the fostering of elite athletes and the funding allocations to governing bodies, which would now be conditional on the explicit support for government objectives (cf. Houlihan, 1997).

Arguably, for the first time in its relatively short history, 'sport' was considered a discrete domain for government intervention, with a particular emphasis on supporting an organisational, administrative, and funding framework at the elite level. The introduction of a National Lottery in 1994 also had a profound effect on sports development in general, with over £2 billion of Lottery money awarded to sports projects in England since 1995 (The National Lottery, 2007). The five Sports Councils in the UK receive grant-in-aid funding from government and are the distributing bodies for the Lottery Sports Fund. The National Lottery also funds the World Class Performance programmes of NGBs and the development of the UK Sports Institute – a UK-wide network of specialist facilities and services for elite performers.

Against this background, the Labour government (elected in 1997) published its own strategy for sport, *A Sporting Future for All* (DCMS, 2000). Although the Labour strategy and *Sport: Raising the Game* are from different sides of the political spectrum, they demonstrated a striking note of unity on the twin emphases of school (youth) sport and elite development. Although sport in general has clearly benefited from political and financial support over the past 5 to 10 years, such support has not emerged without a requirement for NGBs to adhere much more closely to government objectives. For example, in respect of the development of elite athletes, *A Sporting Future for All* emphasised the importance of target-setting and warned, 'The success or failure in achieving milestone targets in performance plans will be an important factor in deciding future levels of funding' (DCMS, 2000, p. 44).

Government interest in sport was further entrenched in 2002 with the publication of *Game Plan*, a report described by the Secretary of State for Culture, Media and Sport as a comprehensive 'blueprint for the structure of sport' (quoted in DCMS/Strategy Unit, 2002, p. 11). It is indicative of the increasing salience of sport to government that the Strategy Unit (which reports directly to the Cabinet Office and the Prime Minister) was asked to report on, and set priorities for, a wide range of aspects of sporting activity including participation rates, elite sport development, the hosting of major events, and, notably, the overly bureaucratic nature of sports administration in the UK. Since the publication of *Game Plan*, the sport of athletics (and thus its NGB) has clearly been singled out as one that is not meeting government's policy objectives. In 2004 a UK Sport and Sport England commissioned report into the need for change in athletics in the UK found that the sport manifested 'destructive hostility between individuals and organisations, backbiting, prejudice and blindness to the facts, resistance to change [and] self interest' (Foster, 2004, p. 11).

Part of the explanation for such divisiveness, as in the Australian context (see the case study available at the book website), is the apparent inability of UK Athletics to balance the needs of its elite performers with club members, volunteers, and officials at the grassroots level of the sport (British Athletic Federation, 1995). From a broader perspective, this raises questions in respect of the ways in which government programmes, strategies and techniques for the 'conduct of conduct' (Rose, 2000, p. 322) of NGBs have set prescriptive limits on the autonomy of UK Athletics and thus its capacity to balance these seemingly irreconcilable demands from its various stakeholders. In the next section (and in the related case study of Athletics Australia), our focus narrows to an exploration of the NGBs for athletics in an attempt to discern the extent to which, and the means by which, government retains the capacity to significantly shape and direct policy in the area of sport development.

Athletics in the UK (and Australia)

The experiences of the NGBs for athletics in the UK and Australia provide us with a particularly rich vein of material to investigate the relationship between government, NGBs, and sports development (cf. Green and Houlihan, 2005). UK Athletics and Athletics Australia have remits for a number of athletics disciplines, as well as being the lead coordinating bodies for other vested interests in the sport. Their administrative and organisational responsibilities are therefore both complex and diverse. Despite both NGBs being in receipt of large amounts of public funding (cf. Australian Sports Commission, 2004; UK Sport, 2005), the two NGBs have also suffered from financial problems, failed to raise participation rates at grassroots levels in line with government targets, presided over crumbling club structures, failed to perform consistently well at the elite level, and therefore, might be considered to have generally failed to manage their sports with the degree of efficiency and effectiveness expected by government (Commonwealth of Australia, 1999; DCMS/Strategy Unit, 2002). Thus both NGBs have been subject to performance reviews instigated by government and their key sports agencies. The nature of, and conditions within which, such government intervention has occurred in the UK is our primary interest here and for a similar analysis of Athletics Australia see the case study material available at the book website.

UK Athletics

UK Athletics is the NSO for the six athletics disciplines of track and field, cross-country, fell and hill running, race walking, road running, and tug-of-war. Thus the breadth of UK Athletics' remit shapes the conditions of action within which the organisation and administration of athletics in the UK has developed. In this respect, Ward (2002b, p. 23) argues that 'There is no more diverse sport than athletics and the problems of diversity have been and are compounded by the Byzantine committee structures that have come about over the past century which have become sacred cows to so many'. Thus, much of the history of the administration of athletics in the UK has been an attempt to cope with and reconcile the tensions among disciplines and between Home Countries and English regions (cf. Foster, 2004; Green and Houlihan, 2005).

Indeed, UK Athletics' predecessors – the British Amateur Athletic Board and the British Athletic Federation – struggled to overcome the jurisdictional tensions pervading the sport.

The formation of the British Athletic Federation (BAF) in 1991 as successor to the British Amateur Athletic Board was seen as a major step forward, the principal aim of which was to unite the various organisations charged with administering the sport. The intention was that the BAF would provide a single autonomous body and also one that would give greater accountability to grassroots athletics; clubs, of which there were 1500, would have a vote at the Federation's annual meeting and, in so doing, 'dodge the masonic order of the old constitution' (Ward, quoted in Gillingham, 1991, p. 3). The BAF's short history, however, was plagued by a series of damaging events, including power struggles between the various English regions and Home Country Associations, financial squabbles regarding payments to elite athletes, and the drug abuse case against the athlete Diane Modahl. In short, the BAF was an organisation struggling to come to terms with a sport that had attracted increasingly large amounts of television and sponsorship monies throughout the 1980s, a trend, moreover, that led towards professionalisation of management and an elite group of 'professional athletes' (Mackay, 1997, p. 9).

The upshot was insolvency for the BAF, which went into administration in 1997 with debts of over £1 million. The Amateur Athletics Association of England was called upon to provide financial aid for a body called UK Athletics 98, which managed the sport until January 1999, when the organisation now known as UK Athletics was formed. The organisational complexity evident in the case study of Australian athletics is mirrored in the UK context. What is also very apparent is central government's increasing emphasis on elite athlete achievement and the creation of performance pathways from the school playing field to the Olympic podium (cf. Green, 2004; UK Sport, 2002).

The emphasis on elite achievement is clear in *Sport: Raising the Game*, *A Sporting Future for All*, and *Game Plan*. Drawing on MacKinnon's (2000, p. 296) comments in relation to general programmes of government, these three sport policy statements 'specify intended outcomes consistent with the principles of the underlying political rationalities', in this case, those associated with international sporting success. One of the key mechanisms, or 'technologies for governing' (Rose and Miller, 1992, p. 173), through which such programmes are operationalised is the requirement for NGBs to produce planning documents (notably, World Class Performance and Whole Sport plans) in order to elicit National Lottery funding and the consequent auditing of agreed targets. These processes of data collection and reflexive monitoring rely upon technologies of inscription and calculation. The effect is to render the domain for which NGBs are responsible 'susceptible to evaluation, calculation and intervention' (Rose and Miller, 1992, p. 185). Through specific forms of inscription and representation (for example, World Class Performance plans and Olympic medal tables), NGBs are actively constructed as domains which can be programmed, evaluated, and managed. According to McDonald (2000, p. 84), however, this represents 'a qualitative shift in the sports-participation culture away from the egalitarian and empowering aspirations of community-based sporting activity to an hierarchical and alienating culture of high-performance sport'. McDonald's analysis draws attention to the type of concerns raised by a former high-ranking official at the BAF, who suggested that:

> The way athletics and sport generally, is going, [what] we're all trying to do is find talent and hothouse it to the top. We don't believe that any experience is, in a sense, intrinsically worthwhile anymore. Anything is only worthwhile if there is a big pay-off at the end.
>
> (Interview, 28 May 2002)

In the UK sport policy sector, then, we can see evidence of Foucault's notion of 'the "governmentalisation of the state"', referring to the tendency for state power to be exercised and realised through a heterogeneous array of regulatory practices and technologies' (MacKinnon, 2000, p. 297). These leave little room, however, for alternative voices within the wider sporting community. For example, according to Ward (2002a, p. 50), competition structures in athletics are 'geared to those few … who carry the flag at major championships. About [0.]001 per cent of the athletic population at a reasonable guess'. Indeed, a former public relations officer at the BAF argued that 'The sport's competition structure is about the drive for medals. That's what the government wants … That's not the way a sport should be judged, but it is unfortunately' (Interview, 30 April 2002). It is argued that the sport policy sector in the UK (and in Australia) is/has been strongly conditioned by the mechanisms and devices operating according to a disciplinary logic set by government. As Rose (1999, p. 147) argues, 'Through such techniques … strategies of governing seek to attack immediate enclaves of power'. Within athletics in the UK, these enclaves of power were viewed as those organisations and individuals seeking to hold on to notions of amateurism, voluntarism, and personal and organisational fiefdoms of the past (cf. British Athletic Federation, 1995; Foster, 2004).

UK Athletics thus emerged as a prime candidate for 'modernisation'. As the UK Sport and Sport England commissioned report into the need for change in athletics in the UK stated, 'As a modern enterprise in a modern world, it [athletics] requires a modern approach to organisation and management' (Foster, 2004, p. 11). The report into UK Sport's own modernisation programme for NGBs states that modernisation is 'The process of continuing development for an NGB towards greater effectiveness, efficiency and independence' (Deloitte and Touche, 2003, p. 2). Once again we are drawn to the conclusion that modern sport management is commercial management; the key building blocks upon which NGBs can achieve modernisation, argue Deloitte and Touche, are those of professional and commercial values, 'strategy setting', 'prioritisation', and the use of 'accountability' systems (2003, p. 2). Of note is that the 'independence' promised in the Deloitte and Touche report is tightly constrained by the internalisation of commercial values and business practices. Therefore, picking up on Girginov's observations in Chapter 1, in the current political climate of 'new managerialism' NGB managers/officials do not now 'have an unfettered "right to manage", free from political interference' (Newman, 2001, p. 31).The past 'anti-modern' world of athletics was one in which the values and practices of the commercial sector, in particular those regarding strategy development and leadership, were patently absent. Indeed, Foster (2004, p. 11) argues that:

> The world of athletics is run by individual people and organisations without a strong sense of common purpose, team membership, or partnership, and with an inclination to compete for dominance. This militates against unified leadership .... One interviewee memorably described athletics as an archipelago not a landmass.

Three points are important here. First, the policy environment within which UK Athletics operates has clearly favoured the imperatives of elite athletes over the past 5 to 10 years (cf. Green, 2004, 2007; Green and Houlihan, 2005). Although the UK's Olympic athletes have outperformed their Australian counterparts, the sport has struggled to meet government expectations on this priority objective over the past five Olympic Games, winning just seven gold medals. A recent example illustrates the disciplinary nature of the contemporary rationalities of government in this respect. At the 2004 Athens Olympic Games, UK athletes won three gold medals and one bronze. The sport's target, agreed to by UK Sport, was five to seven medals. The response to this 'poor' performance was both punitive in nature and potentially crippling for future outcomes: UK Athletics not only faced a reduction in funding of some £1 100 000 for the development of its elite athletes for the period 2005–2009, it also faced funding cuts by Sport England for developmental programmes – from £2 million to £1.35 million for 2005–2006. Under the present conditions of organisational 'self-reform' in the UK, UK Athletics has clearly failed. This 'failure' is evident in comments by the chair of UK Sport on the athletics outcomes in Athens: 'if we are to continue to make progress we have to sharpen our focus and invest in those sports and individuals who demonstrate they have what it takes to deliver on the biggest stage' (quoted in MacKay, 2005, p. 30). Second, the athletics community has been characterised as divisive and self-interested at least since the creation of the British Amateur Athletic Board in the 1930s. Third, the sport's leadership is itself fragile, with three changes of administration since the early 1990s.

The unsurprising corollary is that UK Athletics, with its funding skewed towards elite objectives (UK Athletics, 2001, 2003), has struggled to meet the requirements of a modern, strategically oriented NGB, as advocated by UK Sport (Deloitte and Touche, 2003). Although it is recognised that large amounts of public funding have been allocated to school sport, physical education, and physical activity initiatives more broadly (Houlihan and Green, 2006), there is little evidence to suggest that UK Athletics has had the capacity to (autonomously) invite collaboration on policy outcomes for the sport within the broader confines of the environment within which it operates. There is evidence here of Rose's (2000, p. 323) argument that contemporary strategies for the conduct of government do not seek 'to crush and eliminate the capacities for action of those persons and forces they act upon ... [but] seek to foster and shape such capacities such that they are enacted in ways that are broadly consistent with particular objectives'. In recent years, the 'particular objectives' for the sport of athletics have closely mirrored the importance placed upon elite success set out in the Lottery Strategy 2002–2005, which stated that 'winning medals is just as important as getting people to take part in sport' (UK Sport, 2002, p. 8).

In summary, the rubric of UK Sport's modernisation programme has clear aims to autonomise NGBs and enhance service responses to those now constituted as their customers or stakeholders, for example, individual athletes, coaches, officials, volunteers, regular spectators, and club administrators. At the same time, however, the modernisation programme can be seen as a disciplinary practice, putting in place 'new techniques of control, strengthening the powers of the centres of calculation who set the budgetary regimes, the output targets . . . [and] reinstating the state in the collective body in a new way and limiting the forms and possibilities of resistance' (Rose, 1999, p. 147). Therefore, recalling the example of funding reductions post-Athens 2004, the government's message to UK Athletics essentially mirrors that given to local authorities in a non-sporting context: 'organise yourself to deliver what government wants and you will be rewarded; fail to deliver what the government wants and your days will be numbered' (quoted in Wilson, 2003, p. 331).

Sports Development Visions and National Governing Bodies: Conclusions

What is very clear both from the general overview of significant non-governmental organisations involved in sports development and the more detailed analyses of the two athletics NGBs (in this chapter and in the associated case study) is not only an indication of the complexity of the policy area, but more importantly a signalling of the intensification of government interest over the past 10 to 15 years. Along with this intensification of interest has come innovation in the forms of intervention in sport policy. Following the early establishment of elite success in athletics as a key government policy priority, governments in both the UK and Australia have sought to refashion the NGBs in a way that reinforces that policy priority first, by insulating the respective NGB from internal frictions and second, by designing and maintaining a supportive culture and set of day-to-day business practices.

The then Prime Minister's (Tony Blair) concern to 'challenge every part of our country to modernise [because] without modernisation, adaptability, creativity, we will fail to fulfil our lives' (quoted in HMSO, 1998, p. 9) has become the conventional wisdom with surprisingly little challenge. Modernisation, in Australia, but especially in the UK, has been the dominant programme since the late 1990s. Over the past 15 years both athletics NGBs have been subject to a barrage of technologies designed to achieve first, the recognition of the applicability of the modernisation programme to them and second, the absorption of values and day-to-day practices typical of the commercial business sphere. These technologies have included subjection to a series of performance reviews chaired by sporting or business 'grandees'; requirements to undertake business strategy development, annual audits, and reviews by governmental funding bodies; and target-setting. Where acculturation has been slow or problematic, discipline has been enforced by 'naming and shaming' and the threat of cuts in public sector grant. Linking public shaming and funding to compliance and performance creates a pseudomarket which accelerates the acceptance of neo-liberal imperatives.

Today, what is particularly striking about relationships between NGBs and government generally, and the modernisation strategy in particular, is how the focus is not on sport, as a set of organisations with a broadly common set of interests, but on individual sports and NGBs. A key element of the modernisation programme is the individualisation of relationships with government and the atomisation of policy sectors. Modernising is about 'responsibilising' and individualising, the antithesis of which is collective solidarity and community. On the one hand, the decentralist rhetoric of the modernisation reforms aimed to constitute NGBs as self-regulating organisations charged with the responsibility of solving their own problems. On the other hand, this illusion of agency was masked by an intensification of centralised technologies for governing, such as the setting and enforcing of performance standards, the introduction of auditing procedures, and the imposition of government-led inspection and sanctions if NGBs failed to meet agreed targets.

What is notable by its absence from the discussion of UK Athletics (and Athletics Australia) is a strong defence of their pre-modernisation arrangements. In part this might be because in neither the UK nor Australia is there an effective independent 'voice for sport' (despite claims from the CCPR in the UK, for example), but it is also because there was a general recognition within the two NGBs that they had serious organisational deficiencies which hampered their capacity to achieve key objectives (however and by whomever they might be defined). Indeed it is hard to have much sympathy with organisations that have lurched from one crisis to another for much of their recent history. Mere organisational eccentricity and even inefficiency and ineffectiveness should not in themselves be sufficient reasons for government intervention. However, once government recognises a sector or organisation as significant for the achievement of its own objectives and particularly once that organisation accepts public funding it is difficult to object too strongly when government sets expectations for its new 'partner'.

Despite the difficulty in generating much sympathy for UK Athletics (and Athletics Australia) it is important to acknowledge the serious implications for them arising from their modernisation. The range of centralised technologies for governing noted above produce particular forms of calculation and control, and also prioritise particular forms of judgement and action. Of significance in this regard for the two NGBs in particular as well as for non-governmental sports organisations more generally is the profound shift in the pattern of accountability away from traditional stakeholders (clubs, members, volunteers, officials, coaching bodies, area associations, and so forth) and towards government and its agencies and commercial sponsors.

Modernisation marginalises some stakeholders and creates a democratic deficit. Lines of accountability for both UK Athletics and Athletics Australia are more firmly drawn upwards to government and outwards to commercial sponsors than downwards to members. The use of audit creates a calculable space within which experts from the centre can pronounce on the health of an organisation, but audit often provides little useful information for other stake-holders on which they can base judgements about the merits and impact of NGB activity at member and club levels. Crucial to the resultant power relations that emerge from such an analysis are the capacities and liberties of NGBs to act in ways that might diverge from the 'desired directions' of government. The analysis in this chapter and in the associated case study has revealed little room for such divergence on the part of the two athletics NGBs in the UK and Australia.

It is also important, however, not to lose sight of the political and social interests that support the deployment of the modernisation programme and the various associated technologies. Governments in both countries have a history of viewing sport in an instrumental manner and both countries have strong sports-related industries, especially in the media, which are keen to develop robust sports brands and products. Non-governmental sports organisations (and NGBs in particular) that have modernised along neo-liberal lines and willingly conform to commercial values and practices are much more suitable partners for both government and business. That willingness to conform is only slowly developing and, in relation to UK Athletics (and Athletics Australia), clearly has some way to go before we can talk of them having earned their autonomy by enabling government to govern '*through* freedom' (Dean, 2002, p. 38).

From the evidence presented above it is clear that, in the early twenty-first century, NGBs operate in a complicated and complex policy environment. At a strategic (visionary) level, managers/officials concerned with management *for* sports development opportunities face a number of challenges and on different levels. On the one hand, for many NGB personnel the vestiges of amateurism and Corinthian ideals remain important cornerstones of what 'sport' is (or at least should be) all about. Yet, as discussed throughout, on the other hand, NGB managers now work in an environment where government increasingly 'calls the tune', primarily in relation to increased funding (to be welcomed) but where, inevitably, such funding comes with a requirement to modernise and professionalise operating procedures. A similar argument might be made with other NGB 'partners', notably commercial sponsors. Thus at this visionary level an important ongoing task for NGB sports development staff will be to encourage and maintain grassroots allegiance amongst club members while at the same time not losing sight of the requirements from important external stakeholders.

We can point to three 'tensions' to be managed in this respect. The first tension is between elite development and club development. That is, the need to address the apparent incompatibility between the needs of the elite athlete for a concentration of expertise, financial resources, and management time and their requirement for non-transferable resources (e.g. specialist competitions and sports science support), and the needs of the club infrastructure and the grassroots participant for access to adequate facilities, a competition calendar that reinforces the value of club membership and provides a supportive pattern to the club member's season. The second tension overlaps substantially with the first and is that between the highly individual needs of the elite athlete, the value placed on individual achievement, and the progressive isolation of the elite athlete from her/his club origins on the one hand, and the collective needs of club members, the value placed on sport as a socially valuable undertaking, and sports participation as a social activity on the other. The third tension concerns aspirations towards a professional/rational–bureaucratic model of management and the voluntaristic and more sectional/political model of decision-making found in many sports. In the former, success is more likely to be equated with change or modernisation (and driven by government objectives), while in the latter success is more likely to be measured in terms of stability, continuity, and longevity.

Such a conclusion inevitably casts considerable doubt on aspirations for an integrated and multidimensional approach to sports development as conceived in the late 1980s by the GB Sports Council around the sports development continuum of four tightly integrated elements: foundation, participation, performance, and excellence. In short, any requirement for a base level of mass participants from which talented performers will eventually emerge is becoming ever more obsolete. Today, young athletes are increasingly 'subjected' to talent identification procedures and 'hot-housed' into elite institute environments where they enjoy state-of-the-art facilities, sophisticated sports science and sports medicine support, and world-class coaching. With the London 2012 Olympic Games just five years away it is hard to imagine a scenario where this elite emphasis will diminish. Under these conditions, NGBs' sports development staff will need to manage the apparent tension between the wish for authoritative action from government on the one hand (which is dependent on the compliance and actions of staff 'on the ground') and their own professional concerns to act in ways in which they see fit and which may not meet all government guidelines and targets.

References

Anheier, H.K. (2005). *Nonprofit Organisations: Theory, Management, Policy*. London: Routledge.

Australian Sports Commission (2004). *Annual Report*. Canberra: Australian Sports Commission.

British Athletic Federation (1995). *Athletics 21: Strategic Planning for British Athletics in the 21st Century*. Birmingham: BAF.

Central Council of Physical Recreation (2007). Representing sport and recreation (available online: http://www.ccpr.org.uk/aboutus.cfm, accessed 5 July 2007).

Coalter, F., Long, J., and Duffield, B. (1988). *Recreational Welfare*. Aldershot: Gower.

Commonwealth of Australia (1999). *Shaping Up: A Review of Commonwealth Involvement in Sport and Recreation in Australia (Sport 2000 Task Force)*. Canberra: Commonwealth of Australia.

Dean, M. (2002). Liberal government and authoritarianism. *Economy and Society*, **31**(1), 37–61.

Deloitte and Touche (2003). *Investing in Change – High Level Review of the Modernisation Programme for Governing Bodies of Sport*. London: UK Sport.

Department for Children, Schools and Families (2007). Five hours of sport a week for every child (available online: http://www.dfes.gov.uk/pns/DisplayPN.cgi?pn_id=2007_0128, accessed 27 September 2007).

Department for Culture, Media and Sport (2000). *A Sporting Future for All*. London: DCMS.

Department for Culture, Media and Sport/Strategy Unit (2002). *Game Plan: A Strategy for Delivering Government's Sport and Physical Activity Objectives*. London: DCMS/Strategy Unit.

Department for Education and Skills/Department for Culture, Media and Sport (2003). *Learning Through PE and Sport: A Guide to the Physical Education, School Sport and Club Links Strategy*. London: DfES/DCMS.

Department of National Heritage (1995). *Sport: Raising the Game*. London: DNH.

Finlayson, A. (2003). *Making Sense of New Labour*. London: Lawrence and Wishart.

Foster, A. (2004). *Moving On: A Review of the Need for Change in Athletics in the UK*. London: UK Sport/Sport England.

Gillingham, M. (1991). Long wait is over as the BAF is born. *Athletics Weekly*, 20 March, p. 3.

Green, M. (2004). Changing policy priorities for sport in England: The emergence of elite sport development as a key policy concern. *Leisure Studies*, **23**(4), 365–85.

Green, M. (2006). From 'sport for all' to not about 'sport' at all? Interrogating sport policy interventions in the United Kingdom. *European Sport Management Quarterly*, **6**(3), 217–38.

Green, M. (2007). Olympic glory or grassroots development?: Sport policy priorities in Australia, Canada and the United Kingdom, 1960–2006. *The International Journal of the History of Sport*, **24**(7), 921–53.

Green, M. and Houlihan, B. (2005). *Elite Sport Development: Policy Learning and Political Priorities*. London: Routledge.

HMSO (1998). *The Government Annual Report (Cmnd. 3969)*. London: HMSO.

Houlihan, B. (1991). *The Government and Politics of Sport*. London: Routledge.

Houlihan, B. (1997). *Sport, Policy and Politics: A Comparative Analysis*. London: Routledge.

Houlihan, B. and Green, M. (2006). The changing status of school sport and physical education: Explaining policy change. *Sport, Education and Society*, **11**(1), 73–92.

Houlihan, B. and White, A. (2002). *The Politics of Sport Development: Development of Sport or Development Through Sport*. London: Routledge.

Hoye, R. and Cuskelly, G. (2007). *Sport Governance*. Oxford: Butterworth Heinemann/Elsevier.

Independent Sports Review (2005). *Raising the Bar*. London: Independent Sports Review.

Mackay, D. (1997). Brave new world beckons Moorcroft after bedlam. *Observer*, 9 November, p. 9.

Mackay, D. (2005). Athletics pays a heavy price in Athens backlash. *Guardian*, 3 February, p. 30.

MacKinnon, D. (2000). Managerialism, governmentality and the state: A neo-Foucauldian approach to local economic governance. *Political Geography*, **19**(3), 293–314.

McDonald, I. (2000). Expedience and excellence? Olympism, power and contemporary sports policy in England. In *Issues and Values in Sport and Leisure Cultures* (M. Keech and G. McFee, eds). Oxford: Meyer and Meyer, pp. 83–100.

The National Lottery (2007). Lottery funding: Sport England (available online: http://www.lotteryfunding.org.uk/uk/sport-england, accessed 15 August 2007).

Newman, J. (2001). *Modernising Governance: New Labour, Policy and Society*. London: Sage.

Phillpots, L. (2007). An Analysis of the Policy Process for Selected Elements of the PESSCL Strategy in England. Unpublished PhD Thesis. Loughborough: Loughborough University.

Rose, N. (1999). *Powers of Freedom: Reframing Political Thought*. Cambridge: Cambridge University Press.

Rose, N. (2000). Government and control. *British Journal of Criminology*, **40**(2), 321–39.

Rose, N. and Miller, P. (1992). Political power beyond the state: Problematics of government. *British Journal of Sociology*, **43**(2), 172–205.

Sport England (2006). *Sport Playing its Part: Executive Summary*. London: Sport England.

Sport England (2007). Setback to community legacy (available online: http://www.sportengland.org/news/press_releases/setback_to_community_sport_legacy.htm, accessed 20 March 2007).

UK Athletics (2001). *UK Athletics News: Annual Review*. Birmingham: UK Athletics.

UK Athletics (2003). *UK Athletics News: Annual Review*. Birmingham: UK Athletics.

UK Sport (2002). *UK Sport Lottery Strategy 2002–2005*. London: UK Sport.

UK Sport (2005). World Class Performance Programme: Summer Olympic Investment 2005–2009. London: UK Sport.

Ward, T. (2002a). Follow the sun. *Athletics Weekly*, 15 May, p. 50.

Ward, T. (2002b). Unfinished odyssey. *Athletics Weekly*, 9 January, pp. 20–3.

Wilson, D. (2003). Unravelling control freakery: Redefining central-local government relations. *British Journal of Politics and International Relations*, **5**(3), 317–46.

CHAPTER 5

International Policy and Sport-in-Development

Aaron Beacom and Roger Levermore

Introduction

The increasing prominence of sport in the public policy agenda of advanced industrial countries is a characteristic of late twentieth-century politics. The idea of sport-in-development, initially linked to the domestic policy arena, has increasingly been drawn into wider visions of international development. A number of high profile statements including the Magglingen Recommendations of 2003 and 2005, and United Nations (UN) Resolution 58/5 have further increased already high expectations concerning the capacity of sport to deliver a range of development goals. Sport-in-development initiatives range from individual projects that are moulded to specific problems (such as addressing the integration of child soldiers into particular post-conflict societies) to broader programmes that have a wider remit or geographical spread (for instance, HIV/Aids awareness education across continents and a vague awareness that sport can promote economic development).

Such prominence and heightened expectations of capacity to deliver have not been matched by a systematic analysis of the dynamics of international policy as it relates to the so-called 'sport-in-development' agenda. None of the seminal international development texts or journals includes even a cursory mention of this relationship. A search of the last 15 years of *International Development Abstracts* (articles from 720 development-oriented journals) obtained only 12 references to sport. Of these, none really critically examine the growing use of sport for (international) development.

The International Working Group that was charged with the task to promote the use of sport-in-development lists eight ways in which sport contributes to development, namely, individual development (improves health, social skills and organisational ability); health promotion and disease prevention; promotion of gender equality; social integration and development of social capital; peace building and conflict prevention or resolution; post-disaster trauma relief and normalisation of life; economic development; and finally, communication and social mobilisation (Sport for Development and Peace, International Working Group, 2006).

Despite widespread promotion of sport to further development from some specialist development agencies, such as the UN and World Health Organisation (WHO), the same enthusiasm is not repeated regularly by many traditional/ mainstream development agencies. This is particularly so with international financial institutions, whose often formal approach to development is probably a reason for its occasional failure to reach out or appeal to communities in need, particularly youth audiences. This lack of engagement is recognised by a range of commentators including the International Labour Organisation (ILO), World Bank and the UN. The ILO (2005), for instance, states that, 'in most cases development leaders perceive sports as a recreational tool rather than value-based engine for social changes'. Similarly, it is suspected that some traditional non-governmental organisations (NGOs) regard sport in much the same manner, viewing sporting projects (for development) as amateurish and distracting from the important/main realities and solutions for which funding is required.

The chapter traces key aspects of the sport-in-development policy and provides a frame of reference for further analysis of the challenges faced by practitioners as they pursue development visions through a range of sport-centred initiatives. It begins by identifying the origins and changing focus of the sport-for-development movement and assesses international sport-in-development policy in the context of policy theory. From there, it investigates the types of actors who have become involved in the sport-in-development frame, considering their relative influence on the international policy process. The interaction of these actors and the imperative for partnerships to secure delivery emerges as a particular focus. Challenges faced by the sport-in-development community in the rapidly changing global political environment are considered from the perspective of both the policy maker and the participant. While ongoing case studies are monitored through the book website, the chapter concludes by outlining the terms of reference for those studies and how they relate to the arguments presented here.

Finally, as discussed in the introductory chapter, the authors consider as unhelpful, the traditional distinction made between the so called development *of* sport and development *through* sport. From the perspective of international development, it may be argued that such categories are not mutually exclusive. When considering factors that motivate engagement in the process, there are fundamental characteristics common to both aspects of development. It is recognised that many sport development programmes may aspire to the development of sporting excellence, while at the same time contributing to broader development objectives through the sporting activity. Indeed programmes designed to assist the development of sport, may contribute to the pursuit of wider political and diplomatic objectives of a donor in terms of their relationship with the recipient. For that reason, the term 'sport-in-development' has been used throughout the chapter, to convey both aspects of the development frame.

Sport in International Development: Emergence of a Vision

The introductory chapter has presented a number of scenarios regarding the idea and the substance of development. The relationship between development and ideas about progress, modernity, growth and change has been

discussed. The argument that sport can provide a vehicle for achieving immanent progress is central to the ideal of sport-in-development.

The long history of belief in the capacity of sport to contribute to the
development process is articulated through attempts to replace barbaric local
customs with the 'civilising' influence of particular sporting forms. Mangan
(2006) explores this vision in the context of the so-called muscular Christian
ideology that underpinned the exporting of modern sporting forms. This
vision in the capacity of sport to enhance the human condition is clearly
articulated in historical literature relating to the domestic development and
subsequent 'diffusion' of a range of sporting forms. The civilisational analysis
of historical sociologists Elias and Dunning (1986), typically reflects the idea of
the progressive refinement and increasing sophistication of sporting forms as
contributing to the so-called civilising process initially in the societies that
gave rise to those sports and subsequently within societies into which the
sports were exported. Much has been written around this central thesis in
the intervening years (Dunning et al., 1993).

While there is ongoing debate as to the contribution of this early exporting
of sport to the enhancement of the human condition, there is much to
support the argument that it constituted, albeit at an incremental level, a
deliberate effort by 'donors' to engage the development process. In this sense,
literature relating to international diffusion of modern sporting forms provides a valuable resource when investigating the visions underpinning contemporary sport-in-development initiatives. Indeed rationales relating to
such initiatives would suggest that they remain within the frame of reference
established during the period when modern sporting forms were going
through the process of international transmission and translation. This
frame of reference presumes that sport is a priori a force for good, that it
can provide a catalyst for instilling the qualities of discipline, team work,
respect for authority and commitment to hard work, that underpin the very
concept of modernity.

Evidence of engagement in deliberate policy making at international level,
while emerging somewhat later, has a history dating back to the inter-war
years. The response of the Olympic Movement to the process of decolonisation
and the challenge to its legitimacy as an organisation representing the interests
of all member states, established and emerging, was to begin developing a
strategy aimed at supporting the enhancement of the sporting infrastructure
in those developing states. This resulted in particular, to the creation of Olympic Solidarity (in 1962) whose objective, according to the Olympic Charter, is
to 'organise assistance to NOCs, in particular those who have the greatest need'
(Olympic Solidarity report, 2006, p. 1).

By 1978, sport had moved up the international political agenda sufficiently
for it to be declared as a basic human right by the United Nations Educational,
Scientific and Cultural Organisation (UNESCO). In so doing it was moving
gradually towards the centre of the international development frame. The
rationale for sport to appear in subsequent development policies, including
its link to delivery of the Millennium Goals, was already in place.

In relation to analysis of contemporary international sport-in-development
initiatives, attention will focus on the recent emergence of a number of

programmes aimed at achieving a range of social, educational and health-related objectives. These projects can be traced to deliberate policy by international organisations often in collaboration with NGOs, governments, business and sports organisations, to respond to perceived lack of success in orthodox approaches to development. The UN, in particular, extended development activity beyond traditional development assistance initiatives, largely in an attempt to close the development gap. Recent commitments set out in the form of the UN Millennium Development Goals (MDGs) have increased the pressure to deliver. At the same time, recent narratives underpinning domestic policy in many donor states and the development strategies of a range of private actors are constructed around the idea of sport as having the capacity to deliver a wide range of social, educational and health-related benefits. This is articulated in a range of strategic planning and policy documents such as the International Business Leaders Forum (IBLF) report on promoting sport and business partnerships (May and Phelan, 2005).

The general perception that sport is a useful vehicle for achieving a range of social and economic objectives is increasingly evident in official public policy discourse. For example, the Australian Sports Commission in a press release following the 2002 Commonwealth Games, argued that, 'the manner in which sport can be used to address social issues adds to its value to the Commonwealth, beyond its capacity to bring nations of the Commonwealth together' (Australian Sports Commission, 2002). Similar sentiments are noted by many governments in the industrialised world, whereas some emerging economies have gone further by clearly linking sport to national development strategies (such as Angola and Zambia). Initially such sentiments emerged on the basis of conjecture, with little empirical evidence to support them. Increasingly, however, efforts are being made to apply a set of criteria that will enable the impact of such programmes to be gauged. This has proved to be a particular challenge for the sport development community and is perhaps one area where lessons learned in the wider development community will have some resonance.

Aside from such development goals, there continues to be an increasing politicisation of development assistance. The more overt political dimension to development assistance through sport is brought into sharp relief when viewed in the context of a recent initiative in the USA where the Bureau of Educational and Cultural Affairs, provided support for the development of sport in Iraq in the wake of the invasion by American and British troops. Part of the assistance package included transporting the Iraqi delegation to compete in the international 'Titan Games' in Atlanta in June 2004. The visit also included the opportunity to train with American athletes and enjoy the hospitality of families of the USOC staff. The political message linked to the visit was reflected in the statement by Assistant State Secretary Patricia Harrison, who at one press conference remarked that, 'liberty is the key word. Our programme will be an important resource to Iraqi men and women as they construct a civil society and as they take their place in leadership roles and as communities rebuild'. It is noteworthy that support for the Iraqi athletes led, ironically, to the Iraqi athletic team being one of the best resourced athletics teams taking part in the 2004 Pan Arab Games in Algeria.

The International Policy Framework

Literature relating to international sport generally develops from a set of assumptions about what constitutes policy. A consideration of wider discourse concerning what is meant by policy should provide a clearer insight into the international policy as it relates to sport-in-development.

In dealing with the conceptual challenge of what constitutes policy, most writers present the term as in some way relating to a 'process'. Hill (2005) cites a range of writers who variously focus on policy as a course of action (Helco, 1972) and a set of inter-related decisions (Jenkins, 1978). Recent debate on the nature of the policy process, however, highlights the limitations inherent in presenting it as constituting a sequence of events moving from initiation to outcome. Interpretations emerging from research into a number of policy scenarios have highlighted the extent to which policy constitutes a series of simultaneous activities all contributing in a variety of ways to outcomes (Dorey, 2005). Certainly an assessment of international policy, as it relates to sport-in-development, would support the need for a more interpretive approach to understanding the dynamics of the policy process. Interpretation of 'policy positions' in a range of culturally diverse development settings can and does lead to a reworking of objectives by practitioners as situations unfold. At the same time, agencies involved in agenda setting and policy initiation are simultaneously interpreting policy outcomes and are subject to a range of influences from various interest groups. This is evident for instance, in the working relationships developed by the International Development department of the agency UK Sport, with a range of sport-in-development organisations.

As with any area of policy, when assessing international policy connected with sport-in-development, the fundamental issue of power relations and how they influence the policy frame is of particular significance. Theories of power relations concern identification of how power and authority is attributed in society and how actors seek to use that power to achieve their objectives. Dahl and other pluralist thinkers during the 1950s developed theories concerning power relations and decision making, that focused on the increasing diversification of organised interest groups characteristic of modern democracies. The strongly prescriptive strand in such writing focused on pluralism as an ideal synonymous with modernity in advanced industrial democracies. In this context, the policy process was open to the influence of a wide range of actors with a rejection of the idea that any one held a monopoly of power.

Interpreting this in the context of international development, the emphasis for development becomes the need to 'modernise' the structures, institutions and decision-making culture within developing states, so ensuring enhanced governance within a more open 'democratic' society. Such a perspective is open to criticism on the basis of its capacity to appreciate the dynamics of underlying power inequality. Nevertheless, it remains as a useful starting point in the attempt to develop an appreciation of the dynamics of the policy process.

The primacy of the state in relation to the development of policy would suggest that private actors are required to operate within the terms of reference created by public policy. There is for instance considerable evidence to support the view that foreign, defence and economic policies create parameters within which trade and development activity of private actors will be required to operate. Within development policy specifically, so-called 'aid-diplomacy' developed by USAID and operated under the auspices of the US State Department has, for example, created a range of policy priorities linked to wider foreign policy considerations. The delivery of programmes by private operators, conducive to those wider considerations is then supported through carefully targeted grant aid. This includes programmes relating to sport-for-development. In this context, the most prominent of the current operators is the Detlef Schrempf Foundation that has been involved in a range of 'Basketball Diplomacy' initiatives in the Middle East. One example is the 'Understand the Game' initiative – a basketball diplomacy exchange programme that is designed to promote positive aspects of American culture around the world. Understand the Game's mission is to 'utilise basketball as a catalyst to open dialogue with a younger and broader audience, demonstrate the positive messages of sports diplomacy and personally communicate American culture'. Using grassroots sport development strategies and partnering the Fédération Royale Marocaine de Basket-Ball, it hoped to 'reach as many Moroccan citizens as possible'. The initiative was funded by the U.S. Department of State's Bureau of Educational and Cultural Affairs and is one of a succession of activities implemented by this particularly active NGO.

Finally in relation to the policy framework, it should be noted that no policy develops in a vacuum. It is important to recognise both the historical and political frame of reference and the inter-relationship between apparently separate policy areas. Hill (2005, p. 35) usefully suggests that, even when policy appears 'new' it will be taking shape in an 'already crowded policy space'. This is particularly significant when considering policy relating to sport-in-development where assumptions about the capacity of sport to affect change are rooted in domestic social policy and is increasingly factored into public health and education policy. In this sense, policy networks relating to sport-in-development are gradually expanding across a number of policy communities. On the outer limits of this process, the linking of sport-in-development with foreign policy considerations opens up another dimension in the policy process.

Actors and Visions in the Sport-in-Development Policy Frame

The complexity of the international policy process has already been identified. In relation to policy and planning for international development assistance, there have been an increasing number of stakeholders seeking to influence the process and this has increased its complexity. This phenomenon has been discussed extensively in development literature including Hulme and Edwards (1997), Killick (1998) and Smillie (1999). While states continue to play a pivotal role in international relations, international policy is the result of complex interactions between states, private organisations and NGOs, often through interfacing, formally and informally, within international organisations such as the UN. This is evident when assessing policy as it relates to the sport-in-development process. It is now necessary to consider in more detail the characteristics of these actors and their visions and how they relate to the wider sport-in-development policy process. While for the purposes of analysis actors are presented in separate categories, it should be noted that the blurring of distinctions between sectors and the imperative for partnership arrangements are prominent features of the contemporary development community (see Table 5.1).

NGOs and Sport-in-Development

Chapter 3 of the book has explored a range of non-governmental organisations that are engaged in the sport development process such as the CCPR and the Youth Sport Trust. Given their central role in the sport development matrix, it is not surprising that a number of these have also been referred to elsewhere in the book. While not wishing to replicate those discussions, it is important to consider the central and evolving role of particular forms of NGOs in relation to international sport-in-development activity.

The term non-governmental organisation (NGO) is used in reference to a wide number of organisational forms, an issue that creates problems when attempting to identify their key features. Willetts (2006, p. 2) notes that, 'at the UN virtually all types of private bodies can be recognised as NGOs...they only have to be independent from government control, not seeking to challenge governments as a political party, non-profit-making and non-criminal'. Arguably, given the decay of traditional demarcation lines between public, private and third sector domains, the term can be as much a 'flag of convenience' as an accurate summary of the characteristics of an organisation. Nevertheless, essential elements, in particular relative autonomy from state institutions, provide a rationale for considering this diverse range of organisations collectively.

Listings of NGOs typically include a wide range advocacy groups, voluntary and not-for-profit (as well as, in some cases, for-profit) organisations and institutions with global reach. They can emerge and operate at national, transnational and international level (Baylis and Smith, 1997). The World Bank (1989) helpfully differentiates between 'operational' (engaged in implementation of development-related projects) and 'advocacy' (defending or promoting a particular cause) NGOs, in both cases, underlining the important development role of such organisations. Examples of organisations engaged in sport-in-development activity can be found in all of these categories. For instance, the disabled advocacy group Landmine Supporter's Network has over the past five years increasingly embraced sport programmes as an essential element of rehabilitation and re-skilling of landmine victims in developing states, most notably perhaps, Cambodia and Bosnia. Large international organisations such as UNESCO and the WHO have already been referred to in the context of attempts to integrate sport development into the wider development process in their efforts to achieve a range of development goals.

Key sports NGOs, national and international, have also been referred to in terms of their engagement in sport-in-development. At international level, the

Table 5.1 Key actors engaged with sport-in-development and their declared visions.

Actors	Classification	Visions	Programmes
UN	International organisation	Sport and delivery of MDGs Magglingen Declaration General Assembly Declaration 58/6 (2003)	Co-ordination and strategic leadership role Partnership – e.g. with IOC (promote Olympic Truce) Global Health Leadership Summit
WHO	International organisation	Physical activity and diet – key factors in enhancing public health Developed 'Global Strategy on Physical Activity and Health'	International partnerships with UN/EU/FAO WHO Europe: 'A European Framework to Promote Physical Activity & Health'
UK Sport	Quasi-governmental	Promoting power of sport as a tool for human and social development Intergovernmental alliances to share best practice	Strategic development partnerships (part funding range of NGOs through Int. Dev. Ass. Programme) Int. Sport Development Fund Int. Conf and Networking
DFID	Governmental (UK government department)	Stated commitment to support delivery of MDGs Working with non-profit delivery orgs. To enhance quality of life	Links with British Overseas NGOs for Dev. (BOND) Case study – DFID funding support for 'Promoting Healthy Life Choices among Young People in Zambia'
FIFA	Non-governmental (sport centred)	Improvement of football infrastructure and general development goals	The GOAL programme and hosting 2010 World Cup in South Africa
Right to Play	Non-governmental (development centred)	Co-ordinating sport and play programmes to improve health, build life skills and foster peace for children and communities affected by war, poverty and disease Membership of SDPIWG	Country based Right to Play progress: 'Sport and Play as Effective & Innovative Learning Tools (S & W Africa)' Collaboration with range of international and indigenous partners (funding, etc.)
NIKE	Private (sports manufacturer)	The power of sport in human development. 'Innovate for a Better World: Nike FY05-06 Corporate Responsibility Report'	Minority Enterprise Business Awards Ninemillion.org: partnership with Right to Play to enhance quality of life of children in Refugee Camps
BP	Private	Integration of children into post-conflict society in Colombia	Football For Peace, run by UNICEF

Federation International Football Association (FIFA) and the International Cricket Council (ICC) have been particularly active recently, while it is noteworthy that national sports federations such as the Rugby Football Union (RFU) and the Football Association (FA) have also been engaged in a range development initiatives linked to their longer term strategic objectives. Finally, a wide variety of small development NGOs are currently partnering with agencies such as UK Sport through their World Wide Impact programme, in an effort to secure funding and logistical support and to develop a more coherent strategy for delivery of health, education and inclusion-related programmes. In relation to this chapter, the latter two groupings are of particular significance and will be reflected in the ongoing case studies on the book website designed to track the dynamics of contemporary sport-in-development thinking.

Concerning the engagement of international federations in sport-in-development programmes, the link to organisational objectives is as noteworthy as in the case of international and transnational corporations. For example, the challenge for the International Rugby Board (IRB) has for a number of years, been to provide development assistance sufficient to enable 'weaker' participants to improve performance to a level appropriate to international competition. This challenge still remains and was brought into sharp relief in the wake of what were reported as 'disastrous' results in the Fiji versus New Zealand (0–91) and Samoa versus Australia (7–74) matches in June 2005. The difficulties faced by world rugby as a result of this disparity have continued to draw the attention of the world sporting press. Mairs (2005) referred to the announcement by the IRB of a 'whopping' £30m investment programme in a 'welcome bid' to improve the competitiveness of 'second tier' countries.

In addition to the diversity of sports federations engaged with the sport-in-development process and their contrasting rationales for such involvement, the form that development interventions take can also differ significantly depending upon the context within which they take place. In the period after the 2004 Tsunami in South East Asia, the momentum to secure emergency relief aid drew in many private organisations and agencies that were not generally considered as part of the overseas development assistance community. The call for help received a response from, among others, the ICC and FIFA. While the ICC engaged in a series of fund-raising events, with money passed directly to mainstream aid organisations, FIFA mobilised their technical, logistical and medical expertise, which became subsumed within the general aid effort. As the initial emergency receded, sports organisations and agencies joined the increasing numbers of longer-term development assistance initiatives.

Governmental and Quasi-Governmental Organisations (UK)

Despite reduction of the state as provider, the primacy of public policy in the wider policy frame results in particular attention being focused on the engagement of governmental organisations in the sport-in-development process. While development assistance requires both donors and recipients and the notion of partnership increasingly reflects the aspirations of the development community, the asymmetry inherent in such power relations results in a primary focus on such organisations within donor countries.

Within the UK government, inclusion of sport within the development agenda has resulted in a range of cross-departmental interests and activities, in particular involving collaboration between the Department for International Development (DFID), the Department for Culture Media and Sport (DCMS) and the Foreign and Commonwealth Office (FCO). This is reflected in high profile development assistance projects that have been resourced by all three departments. For instance, cross-departmental support for post-Tsunami (2004) relief projects that included a range of sport and recreational activities can be considered in this context.

At agency level, UK Sport operates as a point of reference for cross-departmental activity relating to international development policy. Moving beyond its core remit: to work in partnership to lead sport in the UK to world-class success (UK Sport, 2007), the organisation is engaging in an ambitious range of international development assistance activities. This has included the launch of the International Development Assistance programme where the agency partners indigenous and international NGOs to deliver targeted sport-in-development projects. In addition, the initiation of its charitable arm, International Development Through Sport (IDS) has provided further modest support opportunities for programmes aiming to deliver health and education development targets through sport. In this and in view of its own limited resources, it is again dependent upon effective partnership with a range of governmental and non-governmental organisations. From a reciprocal perspective such increasing engagement in international projects contributes to the UK Sport objective of enhancing the influence of British sports organisations and agencies in the international arena while providing the framework for sharing best practice with other overseas agencies.

Private Actors

Hamann (2006, p. 176) classifies three important roles played by private interest corporations within development in general. These are (i) Social investment/philanthropic activities; (ii) Via core business activities/competencies (in other words going about their normal business practices); and (iii) Entering into 'public policy dialogue and advocacy'.

Private interest involvement with sport-in-development has influenced development policy dialogue but this has yet to be empirically tested and it is too early in the research process to conclude how far sport-in-development programmes have shaped public policy in the realm of development. However, there are many examples of private interests' involvement with sport/development in terms of social investment (the focus here) and core business competencies.

In the context of the sports manufacturing sector, there are a number of well-documented examples of multinational companies engaging in the development process through corporate social responsibility programmes. Perhaps the most prominent is the case of NIKE. As with key sports agencies and governmental organisations, NIKE do not present themselves as providers of assistance but as enablers, engaging in support of a range of NGOs and other partners who design and deliver programmes on the ground. Their initiatives, particularly through the NIKE Foundation, relate more directly to the general ODA agenda. In this, the focus is on support for programmes relating to either emergency relief or longer-term community development programmes. With a mission to 'contribute to poverty alleviation through improving the overall well-being of the world's most disadvantaged girls, in the developing world' (Nike Foundation, 2007), the Foundation works through a number of partnership arrangements to support education and leadership initiatives aimed at assisting the empowering of girls and young women who can subsequently engage in the organisation and development of their communities. The initiatives supported by them emerged against the backdrop of ongoing difficulties with the corporate image of the company, which has since 1997 been under attack on a range of issues, most notably working conditions in contract factories (Connor, 2001). The corporate responsibility strategy should be considered at least in part as a response to that.

Assessing the Benefits and Limitations of Sport-in-Development

The fundamental indicators of enhanced quality of life as it is determined by access to material resources, improved health and education and fundamental human rights remain key considerations when attempting to assess the benefits of sport-in-development. In this respect, initiatives designed to deliver such benefits through sport face similar challenges as other economic and social development programmes, when attempting to quantify their impact. Jones and Burnett discuss in detail the challenge of developing and operationalising performance indicators elsewhere in the book. This chapter is concerned with presenting the general criticisms of the sport-in-development movement as a counterbalance to key assumptions concerning its capacity to deliver benefits.

A comprehensive range of benefits are commonly believed to generate from sport-in-development initiatives in lesser-developed regions of the world. These have been alluded to in the previous sections to this chapter, especially in illustrating the use of such programmes in furthering the eight aspects of development.

Moreover, it is important to recognise here the mutual compatibility that sport have to support/supplant the heavily criticised state in attempts to deliver neo-liberal and modernisation-inspired ideas of development. Of interest are the many sport-in-development initiatives that promote principles of good governance. One example is the 'Supersports agreement' whereby the University of Witwatersrand in Johannesburg helps improve the skills and micro governance of sports administrators in Southern Africa. Within most of these schemes and general linkage of sport-in-development, there appears to be an implicit understanding that the increased use of sport to promote dimensions of international development is an overwhelmingly positive one.

Many in-house reports by those who utilise sport-in-development initiatives demonstrate this (May and Phelan, 2005).

However, there are increasing concerns over use of sport to promote international development. The first relates to fears that sport has helped the hijacking of altruistic developmental creeds. This is seen especially through a contradiction in motives by those involved in sport-in-development programmes; whilst some are involved in supporting development/sport projects they are simultaneously involved in actions that are detrimental to development. For instance, as noted above, a growing level of sport-in-development projects are supported by sports merchandising companies like Nike and Adidas. They (logically) provide these projects with equipment but do so at the expense of indigenous (or NGO) suppliers, who use local supplies and labour. Closely associated to this is the way in which some companies use sport (and sport-in-development) as a vehicle by which to further the brand and purchasing power of supporting companies without delivering or improving the standard of living that they claim to. This is particularly the case for marketing to children (Hawkes, 1998).

Therefore, partly because of private interest involvement, some sport-in-development projects are often perceived to be driven more by the needs of the donor, rather than the needs of the community for which the development programme is tailored to.

Furthermore, one of the perceived major benefits of sport-in-development is the improvements it can offer to the physical and psychological well-being of individuals as well as the general welfare of communities. For instance, the WHO (2003, p. 1) claims that participation in sport 'improves diets, discourages the use of tobacco, alcohol and drugs, helps reduce violence, enhances functional capacity and promotes social interaction and integration'. However, many of the corporations involved in sport/development are large fast food, soft drinks or tobacco companies. Some of these have been criticised for supporting sport-in-development initiatives whilst simultaneously plying its customers with unhealthy products. For instance, tobacco companies continue to sponsor many sporting events around the world, especially in lesser-developed regions, which can have laxer rules on advertising and sponsorship. Top football clubs and federations in particular have been condemned for being sponsored by the likes of McDonald's, Pepsi and Coca Cola, whilst also promoting healthy eating initiatives. The Food Commission (2003) notes a particularly embarrassing example where the English Football Association's Medical Education Centre distributed health education packs to parents and football academies. This carried an endorsement by Mars Snickers bars. Therefore, sport federations have faced criticism concerning their eagerness to attract sponsorship, without reminding their partners of social responsibility.

These criticisms will come as no surprise to those who view development through dependency/post-colonial perspectives. They can point to private interest in sport, especially European professional football, perpetuating unequal political/economic relations between the south and north by extracting far more from lesser-developed regions than is given back. The fact that the value of leading sport franchises can exceed the GDP of many developing countries demonstrates this (Nauright, 2004). Some write of a new type of slave trade, where young athletes are enticed to richer Western European leagues (Bale, 2004; Bale and Cronin, 2003; Bale and Maguire, 1994). The few that become successful generate considerable income for their club, without much trickling back to where they originated. Those that do not can be trapped in poverty in the countries which they migrated to.

Furthermore, those controlling sport-in-development schemes tend to be Northern-dominated, thus reflecting another post-colonial concern with development initiatives. Darby (2002, p. 168) views football's governing body, FIFA in such a way, noting that 'FIFA is not uncommonly regarded as an instrument of neo-colonial domination by African and other non-European football associations and that ties between Africa and FIFA are often characterised by ambivalence and wariness on the part of Africans'. This mirrors Bendell's (2005) concern that development is driven by Western aims, objectives and what is seen as feasible – this marginalises/excludes Southern alternative approaches. What is more, Southern NGOs are also criticised as being excessively influenced by those Northern bodies that fund them.

Learning From Experience: Challenges in the International Sport Environment

The accumulation of experience of practitioners seeking to deliver sport-in-development programmes in a wide variety of international contexts over the past decade provides a valuable resource for those currently involved throughout the sport-in-development policy process. Through examining the role of a number of actors in this process, the chapter has already drawn from those experiences. This last section highlights one key area of concern that requires careful consideration in future policy developments. This is subsequently articulated in the two ongoing case studies that are developed through the book website.

The Area of Concern

Despite growing challenges to the power and authority of the state there remains a considerable body of evidence to support the claim that the state as a set of institutions, retains superordinate authority over activity in territory within its jurisdiction. The capacity of the state to maintain this authority is discussed in the works of Weiss (1998) and Vogel (1996). Hill (2005) discusses the implications of such superordinate authority for the policy process. As such, policy initiated and developed by the state – so-called 'public policy' – is usually attributed primacy within the wider policy frame. At the same time, Hill (2005) draws attention to the increasing role of private operators within public life and the implications of this for the policy process. The inability to separate out implementation of policy by a wide range of private operators, from the wider policy process, calls into question the whole notion of so called 'public' policy.

This has far-reaching implications for discussion concerning policy relating to sport-in-development. The advent of sport-in-development policy lies within the public sphere yet those delivering programmes and initiatives are almost exclusively from the private sphere. The key issue then becomes, how effectively are the concerns of practitioners incorporated into the policy process? Concern relating to this articulates itself in two ways.

Firstly, as the chapter has already indicated, many of the key actors engaged with sport-in-development are operating on a comparatively small scale. Where such small-scale operators are dependent upon obtaining funding from governments and other public bodies, the process by which this can be achieved can become an area of considerable controversy. Mechanisms for monitoring the effectiveness of delivery, upon which further evidence based funding is linked, may create significant obstacles for practitioners who lack the administrative frameworks to respond effectively to requests for information. Recent efforts by UK Sport to develop more 'user friendly' monitoring frameworks reflect their commitment to attempt to address this dilemma. Nevertheless, the significant difference in organisational cultures does present challenges for those involved with the management of the sport-in-development process.

The first case study related to this chapter and developed through the website addresses such challenges faced by a small development NGO and suggests how they might be addressed in order to facilitate more effective engagement in the policy process. The chosen case study is the organisation entitled 'The Great Football Giveaway'. This development NGO is a UK-based registered charity that identifies its core charitable objects (The Great Football Giveaway, 2006, p. 2) as

- To provide and assist in providing equipment for sport, recreation and other leisure time occupation for such persons who have need of such by reasons of their youth, age, poverty or social and economic circumstances with the object of improving their condition of life.

- To advance the education of children and young people through the provision of sports equipment.

In order to achieve these objectives, the key activity of the organisation is the supply and distribution of footballs, paid for by individuals and businesses, direct to schools, established centres and community organisations in developing states, most recently Angola. Related to this, the organisation is beginning to engage in coach education initiatives and has developed a partnership arrangement with the sports manufacturer Puma. It's key challenges, however, remain to identify and secure a wider range of funding streams, to secure its activities as an element of wider development assistance strategy and to establish the organisation and gain recognition within the sport-in-development community. The study reflects the ongoing tension between the needs of practitioners engaged in delivery on the ground and those engaged in the initiation of policy. Responses to this challenge will be monitored on an ongoing basis through the book website.

The second area of concern regarding private operators and the policy process is capacity to affect sufficient co-ordination in the policy process to ensure the activities of the range of actors involved in sport-in-development are complementary and relate to wider development goals rather than to act in an unconvincing manner to further organisational aims over altruistic development goals. This is particularly the case given the marked increase in the number of private actors and the role of public organisations and agencies in the policy process. The second case study addresses this issue through an analysis of the evolving role of FIFA in sport-in-development activity. Specifically, FIFA has a number of initiatives that aim to promote development, the most relevant being its 'Football for Hope movement', which sees FIFA partner a number of NGOs around the world that focus on the range of development initiatives outlined in the introduction to this chapter, notably, building capacity in post-conflict societies, empowering children, promoting health and environmental protection (FIFA, 2005). However, FIFA has been accused of displaying contradictory motives in its pursuit of development, especially in using development funding (including the 'GOAL programme') to allegedly help re-elect Sepp Blatter, the current President of FIFA (Jennings, 2007).

Considerations for the Management of Sport Development

Changes in the policy process have enabled those engaged with sport-in-development to gradually move towards the centre stage within development policy. Partly, this may have resulted from changes in perceptions towards sport, particularly by some of those who are in positions of power. Those who might have regarded sport suspiciously or dismissed the seriousness of its potential for 'social good' in the past are occasionally replaced by a generation who see sport in a more positive light. This climate of sport being 'in vogue' is a trend fuelled by its often mutually interdependent relationship with the media and by the financial and quasi-political power/influence that sport – and certain sports federations – now possess.

At the same time, there is a clear perception that sports organisations are able to bring their unique contribution to the development process. Whether the objective is health and community improvements or the opportunity to maximise sporting performance, intervention through sport has demonstrated its potential to enhance life chances of the recipient. With their record of development assistance in, often difficult, domestic settings and their potential to provide a forum for education and development that is both popular and accessible, they continue to consolidate their position as contributors to the development process.

Difficulties have, however, arisen in terms of the gap between expectations as to what can be achieved through sport-in-development initiatives and evidence from programme outcomes. In addition, the problem of effectively engaging the wide range of stakeholders in the policy process to ensure the best use of existing funding and to co-ordinate programme delivery provides an ongoing challenge.

An appreciation of the diversity of organisational cultures and the contrasting motives underpinning engagement with sport-in-development is crucial if sport-in-development policy is to be enhanced.

The capacity of public sector organisations and agencies who have traditionally initiated development policy to relate to private sector organisations who are increasingly at the sharp end of delivery presents a particular challenge for all engaged in the policy process. From concerns with brand and product development to commitment to consolidate the international reach of sports, organisational objectives ultimately inform decisions to engage in development interventions. Tensions exist between those factors motivating engagement on the one hand and the needs of the recipients on the other. Whether seeking organisational growth, consolidation or brand development, reconciling the capacity to balance these objectives against the needs of recipients requires an appreciation as to what constitutes those needs, how they might be best served and how outcomes can be assessed. While superficial engagement in a range of development initiatives may assist in enhancing the international status of a sports organisation, it may not necessarily provide the most effective method of maximising the impact of development assistance within the recipient states. As a relative 'newcomer', those sports organisations engaging in the process have much to learn from the wider debates currently taking place within the development community, from identifying need to monitoring the impact of programmes as the basis for strategic planning and investment.

The tendency to treat domestic sport development and sport as an aspect of international development assistance programmes and as discreet and separate areas of competence is damaging to both the domestic and international development portfolios. While sharply different cultural contexts mitigate against the simplistic transference of sport-in-development ideas, many of the problems and solutions identified in one situation are applicable to others. One example is how best to develop a response to the gap between expectations on what sport can deliver and available evidence supporting those expectations. This has implications for both the domestic and international development environments. Various attempts are being made to quantify the value of sport, for example, the development of the joint agency (Sport England and UK Sport) 'Value of Sport Monitor'. By extension, as discussed by Burnett in this volume, instituting a strategy for effective performance evaluation of international sport-in-development initiatives that in turn provides evidence for resource applications is currently attracting much attention from the ODA community. Yet to date, there is little evidence of dialogue between the domestic and international sport development communities regarding such key concerns.

Another particular challenge to the management of sport-in-development is the general lack of understanding of what motivates engagement by a range of organisations in the development process. Contending perceptions of what motivates private operators has already been discussed as a potential challenge to the process. In this respect, it is important that those, particularly from the public and the voluntary sectors, who are engaged in the management of sport-in-development engage in an open dialogue with private sector operators. Only in this way can potentially competing motivations be reconciled within the development frame.

Finally, from the perspective of those managing the sport development process, there is a pressing need to engage more effectively with the wider development community. This concerns strengthening linkages with the development community at the level of policy networks as well as becoming conversant with the responses of development practitioners to logistic and operational challenges faced in delivery. Through such engagement, those managing the sport-in-development process can become better equipped to respond to the demands of securing appropriate resources and delivering effective programmes that are ultimately about the enhancement of the human condition.

References

Australian Sports Commission (2002). Congratulations Manchester, http://wwwausport. gov.au/fulltext/2002/ascmedia/20020804 a.asp (accessed 20 February 2006).

Bale, J. (2004). Three geographies of African footballer migration: Patterns, problems and postcoloniality. In *Football in Africa: Conflict, Conciliation and Community* (G. Armstrong and R. Giulianotti, eds). Basingstoke and New York: Palgrave Macmillan, pp. 229–46.

Bale, J. and Cronin, M. (2003). *Sport and Postcolonialism.* London: Frank Cass.

Bale, J. and Maguire, J. (1994). *The Global Sports Arena: Athletic Talent Migration in an Interdependent World.* London: Frank Cass.

Baylis, J. and Smith, S. (eds). (1997). *The Globalization of World Politics.* Oxford: Oxford University Press.

Bendell, J. (2005). In whose name? The accountability of corporate social responsibility. *Development in Practice,* **15**(3&4), 362–74.

Connor, T. (2001). *Still Waiting for Nike to do it: Nike's Labour Practices in the Three Years Since COE Phil Knight's Speech to the National Press Club.* San Francisco: Global Exchange.

Darby, P. (2002). *Africa, Football and FIFA: Politics, Colonialism and Resistance.* London: Frank Cass Publishers.

Dorey, P. (2005). *Policy Making in Britain.* London: Sage.

Dunning, E., Maguire, J., and Pearton, R. (eds). (1993). *The Sports Process: A Comparative & Developmental Approach.* Champaign, IL: Human Kinetics.

Elias, N. and Dunning, E. (1986). *Quest for Excitement: Sport and Leisure in the Civilizing Process.* Oxford: Basil Blackwell.

FIFA (2005). *FIFA World Report on Football Development.* Zurich: FIFA.

The Food Commission (2003). Football sells out to junk food brands. *Food Magazine,* **9**(2), 27 January, n.p.

The Great Football Giveaway (2006). *Organisational Plan 2006–2010.* February.

Hamann, R. (2006). Can business make decisive contributions to development? Toward a research agenda on corporate citizenship and beyond. *Development Southern Africa,* **23**(2), 175–95.

Hawkes, T. (1998). Scoring an own goal? Ethical issues in the UK professional soccer business. *Business Ethics: A European Review,* **7**(1), 37–47.

Helco, H. (1972). Review Article: Policy Analysis. *British Journal of Political Science,* **2**, 63–104.

Hill, M. (2005). *The Policy Process.* Harlow: Longman.

Hulme, D. and Edwards, M. (eds). (1997). *NGOs, States and Donors: Too Close For Comfort?* Basingstoke: MacMillan Press.

International Labour Organisation (2005). *ILO's Youth Sport Programme and Common Framework on Sport and Development. Socio and Economic Insertion and Jobs Opportunities for the Youth.*

Jenkins, W. (1978). *Policy Analysis*. London: Martin Robertson.

Jennings, A. (2007). *Foul!: The Secret World of FIFA: Bribes, Vote Rigging and Ticket Scandals*. London: Harper Collins.

Killick, T. (1998). *Aid and the Political Economy of Policy Change*. London: Routledge.

Mairs (2005). IRB unveil £30m cash boost for minor nations. In *Belfast Telegraph*, 4 August, p. 32.

Mangan, J. (2006). Christ and the Imperial Playing Fields: Thomas Hughe's Ideological Heirs in Empire. *The International Journal of the History of Sport*, **23**(5) August, 777–804.

May, G. and Phelan, J. (2005). *Shared Goals: Sport and Business in Partnerships for Development*. London: IBLF, p. 16.

Nauright, J. (2004). Global games: Culture, political economy and sport in the globalised world of the 21st century. *Third World Quarterly*, **25**(7), 1325–36.

Nike Foundation (2007). *She's an Economic Powerhouse: Economic Empowerment for Girls*. October.

Olympic Solidarity (2006). *Balancing Our Strengths*. IOC, 2006 Report.

Smillie, I. (eds). (1999). Stakeholders: Government-NGO partnerships for International Development. London: Earthscan.

Sport and Development first International Conference (2003). *The Magglingen Declaration and Recommendations*. UN (Sport for Development and Peace)/Swiss Academy for Development.

Sport and Development second International Conference (2005). *The Magglingen Call for Action*. UN (Sport for Development and Peace)/Swiss Academy for Development.

Sport for Development and Peace, International Working Group (June 2006). *Sport for Development and Peace: From Practice to Policy*. Toronto: UNDP.

UK Sport (2007). *Mission 2012*. UK Sport publication.

UN (2003). Sport as a Means to Promote Education, Health, Development and Peace (Resolution 58/5). United Nations General Assembly.

Vogel, S. (1996). Freer Markets, More Rules: Regulatory Reform in Advanced Industrial Countries. Cornell: Cornell University Press.

Weiss, L. (1998). The Myth of the Powerless State: Governing the Economy in a Global Era. Cambridge: Policy Press.

Willetts, P. (2006). *UNESCO Encyclopaedia of Life Support Systems, Section 1*. Institutional and Infrastructure Resource Issues, Article 1.44.3.7, NGOs. UNESCO.

World Bank (1989). Operational Directive 14.70: Non-governmental Organizations in World Bank-Supported Activities.

World Health Organisation (2003). Health and Development Through Physical Activity and Sport. Geneva: World Health Organisation.

CHAPTER 6

Sport as an Agent for Social and Personal Change

B. Christine Green

Introduction

Sport has long been considered a tool for social change. In fact, Coubertin drew on classic Western traditions to envision the modern Olympics as a tool for peace and understanding. Coubertin's vision for the Olympic Games is also grounded in the values evident in the British Public Schools during 1800s, that sport competitions are a way to build character (MacAloon, 1981). By the late nineteenth century, it was believed that sport changed boys into civilized gentlemen embodying the ideals of unselfishness, fearlessness, teamwork, and self-control. Coubertin also felt sport to be a vehicle for social and personal change. For him, sport served three objectives: (1) to develop aesthetic appreciation through participants' experience of the body during sport; (2) to use international sport as a tool with which to establish peace and cross-national understanding; and (3) to teach participants to strive for and to respect excellence wherever it occurred (Chalip, 1992). The idea that sport can act as an agent for social and personal change has been with us for centuries and is still salient today.

Sport has become a significant component of the United Nations development goals, in particular, the Millennium Development Goals (United Nations, n.d.). The UN is partnering with non-governmental organizations at the local, national, and international levels to organize and promote development, health, human rights, and peace through sporting events. Acknowledging growing perceptions of the importance of sport for development, the Secretary-General appointed Adolf Ogi to the post of Special Adviser on Sport for Development and Peace in 2001. The UN sees what it calls, 'the fundamental principles of sport – respect for opponents and for rules, teamwork and fair play' as consistent with its own principles as laid out in the United Nations Charter (United Nations, 2004). The potential 'convening power' of sport (i.e. sport's ability to bring people together) is claimed by the UN to contribute to economic and social development, improved health, and a culture of peace and tolerance. As Adolf Ogi puts it:

> Sport, with its joys and triumphs, its pains and defeats, its emotions and challenges, is an unrivalled medium for the promotion of education, health, development and peace. Sport helps us demonstrate, in our pursuit of the betterment of humanity, that there is more that unites than divides us.
>
> (United Nations, n.d., p. 2)

Why Sport and Social Change?

There is a long history of belief that sport can foster social change. Social change is defined as shifts in social phenomena at various levels, ranging from the individual or personal level to that of society as a whole (Lauer, 1982). Although social change can be either positive or negative, Coubertin, the UN Secretary-General, and others (e.g. Holt, 1989; Labour Party, 1997; Wilson, 1994) have viewed sport as a tool for positive social change. But what underlies the commonly held belief that sport is inherently beneficial?

Perceptions of sport as a tool for positive social and personal change are grounded in the belief that sport is an effective and positive socializing agent (e.g. Grove and Dodder, 1982; Spreitzer and Snyder, 1975). Sport participation is commonly believed to develop positive character traits, to assist young people to become better citizens and more successful adults, to reduce delinquency rates and risky behaviours, to assist with moral development including a sense of fair play, and to instil a strong achievement orientation. In short, sport is expected to teach basic rules of social behaviour and to inculcate fundamental societal values such as hard work, competitiveness, and sacrifice. While these intended outcomes are expected to accrue to the participants, there is an underlying assumption that personal change (i.e. the socialization outcomes of sport participation) benefits the broader society by curbing deviant behaviour while creating individuals accepting of the norms and values of society. That is, sport is believed to provide a form of salubrious socialization resulting in 'better' societies.

Although there is general popular agreement about the values of sport as a tool for socialization, there is not always general agreement about what it is that sport provides. For example, Watson (1977) showed that parents from different social classes agreed that sport taught important values to their children, but they disagreed about what those values are. Working class parents felt that sport teaches teamwork and obedience to authority, while parents in white collar occupations felt that sport teaches individual achievement and leadership. The difference rests in the projection of values that are important to the observer into sport. In other words, we believe that sport does what we want it to, but what we want it to do may, in fact, differ.

This is important because the empirical evidence demonstrates that sport can have a variety of different effects, some of which policymakers would decry. For example, sport can enflame existing political, religious, or cultural conflicts (Semyonov and Farbstein, 1989). The emotional attachment of many competitors and fans can result in offensive and sometimes violent behaviours against opponents and fans of opponents (Gaunt et al., 2005). Sport contexts can socialize participants into subcultures of violence, substance abuse, eating disorders, and dependence (Heffner et al., 2003; Martens et al., 2006; Visek and Watson, 2005). One experimental study of youth sport demonstrated that organized sport experience can retard the moral development of participants (Kleiber and Roberts, 1981).

This is not to say that sport is universally bad for people; it is merely to point out that it is sometimes bad for people. There is also evidence that sport can do many of the things we claim for it (e.g. Larson, 2000; Poinsett, 1996). It is not sport per se that is responsible for particular outcomes; it is the ways that sport is implemented. In other words, it is the specific socializing experiences that particular sport settings provide (or do not provide) that result in particular outcomes (McCormack and Chalip, 1988). A similar interpretation of the change potential of sport echoes the view that sports development is a perception and a social construct as discussed by Girginov in Chapter 1.

Sport Development Programmes for Social Change

Since the 1990s sport has increasingly been considered a panacea for what Pitter and Andrews (1997) call the 'social problems industry'. A veritable smorgasbord of sporting schemes has been developed to address a wide range of social problems. These programmes can be categorized by their objectives. There are three broad categories of programme objective, those that seek to: (1) bring sport to underserved or at-risk populations; (2) replace or divert deviant behaviours with socially desirable behaviours; and/or (3) use sport to attract deviant or at-risk populations in order to provide other social welfare services. At first glance, only one type seems to be the purview of sport development officers – programmes designed to bring sport to the underserved. But all three programme types can help sport development officers meet their objectives. Each increases participation, particularly in underserved populations. A perhaps unintended but valuable consequence of designing sport programmes to meet social inclusion needs is the potential to enhance sport funding via grants from other funding sources. These sources may be government initiatives (e.g. Youth Justice Board in the UK), voluntary sector charities (e.g. West Yorkshire Sports Counselling in the UK), community groups (e.g. Community Action Resource Team in the US) or schools. In practice, the most sustainable programmes are those that represent partnerships between sport or recreation and other organizations (Sandford et al., 2006).

Consequently, all programme types assist sports development officers to enhance the pool of sport participants while also meeting social inclusion objectives. Further, the three programme types are nested. Programmes with diversion objectives also share the belief that sport is an appropriate context for re-socializing programme participants into more socially acceptable values and behaviours. If this were not the case, programmes would use other forms of leisure to attract participants. Yes, sport is attractive to the target populations, but not uniquely. Music, dance, art, and technology may be equally attractive. Yet it is sport that forms the core of these programmes.

Similarly, programmes that use sport as a hook to attract participants to a site where other services are provided are still providing sport opportunities. While it is unclear whether these programmes embrace sport as an intervention per se, these programmes have, in fact, selected sport as their hook. In fact, the most successful programmes of this type fully integrate the sport into the intervention. For example, the San Fernando Valley Child Guidance Clinic (SFVCGC), a delinquency treatment programme in the US, found that at-risk youth did not make use of their services (Fleisher and Avelar, 1995). However, these youth were very interested in the martial arts. The SFVCGC decided to offer a judo programme to attract at-risk youth in their community. The programme consisted of judo instruction, tutoring, and bi-monthly parent training sessions. The judo instruction itself incorporated a segment in which the class discussed issues concerning judo's impact on one's lifestyle. The tutoring sessions were linked to concepts of respect and honour, core traditions of judo. Parents were taught to monitor and chart their child's behaviour and to understand and reward behaviours representing values espoused by the programme. The elements of the intervention were thus intertwined, providing consistency and relevance for participants.

Each of the three types of programmes has the capacity to serve as an agent of social and personal change. Yet, evaluations of programmes in all categories show conflicting results. While it is impossible to conclude that sport does or does not affect social change, we can examine the programme types, and their successes and failures to begin to identify programme elements common to successful programmes.

Sport for Social Inclusion

Programmes designed to reach specific populations (variously termed 'underserved', 'at-risk', 'disaffected', 'disengaged') serve the purpose of sport development by increasing the number of individuals participating in sport, and by increasing the diversity of participants. This also contributes to issues of equity and distributive justice by providing sport and the benefits claimed for sport to individuals who, for one reason or another, have not been provided the same sport participation opportunities as others. Equitable provision of social goods, such as sport, is an important issue for government-funded programmes. Programmes in this category are built on the belief that:

> Sport can be crucial to the social and personal development of young people. By participating in sporting activities they can learn to differentiate between good and bad behaviour.
>
> (Labour Party, 1997, p. 8) [cited in Crabbe, 2000, p. 381]

The belief that sport builds character is so ingrained that neither providers nor participants feel it necessary to do anything more than provide opportunities. The benefits are thought to accrue to participants merely as a function of the opportunity. Consequently, we have research showing that sport builds values and enhances life skills (e.g. Eccles et al., 2003; Eitle and Eitle, 2002; Fleisher and Avelar, 1995; Long and Sanderson, 2001; Nichols, 2004; Petitpas et al., 2004; Sandford et al., 2006), whereas others have argued that sport-based programmes fail to show positive outcomes (e.g. Howell, 1995; Morris et al., 2003). Still other research shows that sport impedes moral development and facilitates anti-social behaviours (e.g. Begg et al., 1996; Kleiber and Roberts, 1981) and can even reinforce deviant behaviours by providing a gathering place for at-risk youth (Dishion et al., 1999; Jacob and Lefgren, 2003) or by 'exacerbating the social and racial divisions responsible for the very conditions the initiatives are trying to improve' (Pitter and Andrews, 1997, p. 93).

Even researchers reporting positive social outcomes from sport-based programmes qualify their findings by suggesting that specific aspects of the programme studied are responsible for positive outcomes. Essentially, programme elements that provided participants with close human relationships with peers and adults, with opportunities for problem solving and decision-making, and that enhanced participants' self-worth were seen to produce the outcomes sought (cf. Carnegie Council, 1995; Witt and Crompton, 1996, 1997). In short, the programmes that seem to be the most effective are those that do not look like traditional sport programmes.

Women were early beneficiaries of programmes intended to reach underserved populations, but are no longer the main thrust of these programmes. Increasingly, programmes are targeted at economically disadvantaged youth, mainly in urban areas. Often these participants are labelled 'at risk' and consist of ethnic minorities, recent immigrants, and other marginalized groups. Sport is often seen as a way to socialize participants into the majority values and norms of a society (Coakley, 1993). Often termed 'integration programmes', they are intended to reach minority populations with the goal of acculturating them to the principles and values of the sports culture – one based on the cult of performance, rules, and a sense of fair play, while instilling a strong sense of the social order (Arnaud, 2002). Arnaud describes a sport initiative in Lyon, France intended to promote the integration of immigrant populations this way:

> Here, sport is a favoured tool to 'bring children, adolescents and young adults together around an ambitious project in which they can learn a regulated, collective way of life, aiming to resocialize them' (Ville de Lyon, 1991, p. 82).... By minimizing differences in order to impose a legitimate way of attaining better performance, sport structures – or even creates – an identical model for relating to things and to people and thus contributes to lack of differentiation between populations. (p. 577)

Notice that the emphasis is on the benefits (e.g. acceptance of multi-ethnic groups/contexts) that are obtained as a by-product of sport participation. The case of *Belfast United* on the book website describes a football (soccer) initiative designed to bring Irish Catholic and Protestant youth together to form a football club which toured the US. This initiative brings youth together initially with a superordinate goal of winning, but ultimately requires them to participate in integrated activities to minimize the hostilities between the two groups. In embracing the performance ethos of the competitive sport culture, participants are no longer focused on ethnic differences. The superordinate goal of winning supercedes their original biases. Programmes, like this one, that provide sport participation opportunities with the expectation that the setting itself will impart valued benefits are numerous. Yet, the outcomes of these programmes vary in terms of their efficacy.

Winning or striving to win can and does bring team mates together for a common purpose. But critics note that an overemphasis on winning and other extrinsic goals has been shown to decrease enjoyment and interest in sport for many participants (Kohn, 1986). Enjoyment is a key indicator of sport commitment (Scanlan et al., 1993). As sport development is concerned to retain participants, a focus on winning may provide only a short-term benefit for participants. If there are no other programme elements to enhance participants' enjoyment of the experience, the programme is not likely to sustain itself.

Individuals' experience of any programme is likely to vary from participant to participant. Sport programmes focused on winning are also likely to provide more playing time, instruction, and attention to more highly skilled players. Consequently, highly skilled players will have a very different experience of the programme than will less skilled players who do not feel that they contribute to the team's success (Hill and Green, 2008).

Winning is not the fundamental goal of social inclusion programmes, but it provides a good illustration of the double edged nature of benefits. It is certainly possible to forge a team that seeks to win, while also ensuring equal contributions (at least in terms of playing time) by all team members. A team that learns to value each member for their unique contribution on the field and off can translate into individuals who are more tolerant of differences and more likely to see beyond stereotypes. Yet these outcomes are entirely dependent on one's experience of the programme, including the values of coaches, administrators, and other programme personnel.

Sport as Diversion

Midnight basketball (see Hartmann, 2001 for a review) is widely acknowledged as one of the earliest and best-known examples of a sport-based programme developed in response to a social problem (Schultz et al., 1995). It was originally developed to reduce criminal activity and its main mechanism of intervention is its ability to divert people from criminal behaviours during peak crime hours (generally, evenings between 10 p.m. and 2 a.m.) and into a more pro-social activity valued by the intended participants – basketball. Although there is little scientific evidence that midnight basketball programmes have the intended diversion effect, the concept was quickly adopted in urban environments throughout the United States (Hartmann and Depro, 2006).

Basketball was the sport of choice for reaching inner-city, African-American males in the US, but similar programmes (using different sports) were implemented to reach other populations. The case of *Midnight Sport* on the book website compares and contrasts midnight sport programmes in several countries including the Midnight Golf in the US, Midnight Basketball in Australia, and Midnight Ping-pong in Hungary.

The *Kirklees Splash* programme is one example from the UK. Splash is an open access sports activity programme using fields, parks, and areas near leisure centres. Participation is free and sports and games are led by professionals. Loxley et al. (2002) report that Splash programmes are put into high crime areas and occur, like midnight basketball programmes, at times when most youth crimes occur. These programmes, while avowedly sport-based, are not intended to develop elite athletes or even long-term participation in sport. In fact, many of these types of programmes have their genesis outside of sport and recreation and often do not provide high-quality sport experiences because their goals are not about sport. Their objective is to reduce crime and other anti-social behaviours. Diversion programmes require an activity that is attractive enough to divert participants from anti-social behaviours. Sport is popular enough to do this. Diversion programmes have met with some success. Although actual impacts do not measure up to claimed decreases in crime, cities identified as 'early adopters' of midnight basketball programmes show greater declines in crime rates than do those cities that lacked midnight basketball leagues (Hartmann and Depro, 2006). However, even advocates of these programmes admit that the relatively small numbers of young people active in midnight basketball leagues cannot, in and of themselves, account for the significant decreases in property crime. Two indirect effects of these programmes have been suggested (1) bundling of crime initiatives; and (2) publicity effects. In other words, midnight basketball leagues tend to be part of a whole package of crime prevention programmes. Therefore, it is difficult to attribute changes to any one programme. Also, media coverage of these programmes, along with the community attention resulting from that coverage may deter would-be criminals. On a more positive note, media attention may build trust among community members in response to the pro-active nature of the programme. What is noteworthy about these indirect impacts is the implications for programme design. Providing diversion programmes may be useful, but they do not seem to be sufficient by themselves. At least for crime prevention, sport programmes need to be incorporated into a wider array of initiatives and their success may be, at least in part, dependent on positive media attention.

Sport as a Hook

The third category of programme consists of programmes that use sport to attract participants, and then provide core services such as tutoring, counselling, and other social services. Midnight basketball programmes, although originally designed as a diversionary intervention, evolved to include mentoring, tutoring, and advising workshops (Hartmann, 2001). The Positive Futures programme, a joint partnership of Sport England, the Youth Justice Board, and the UK Anti-Drugs Coordination Unit uses sport, recreation, and other educational activities to 'reduce anti-social behaviour, crime and drug use among 10–16 year olds' (Sport England, 2002, p. 1). The programme uses sport to attract teens, but is ultimately intended to help participants form relationships with other participants and with adult programme leaders. One of the most successful programmes in the US has been Larry Hawkins' Institute for Athletics and Education (Hartmann, 2003). Hawkins, originally a teacher and coach, draws participants to his programmes with sport and turns them into serious, committed students. Like the Positive Futures Programme, IAE programmes are built on the value of relationships, particularly between coach/tutor and participant, and highlight the interrelationship of academics and athletics. For example, one programme was structured so that boys practiced two days a week and participated in supervised tutoring sessions on the other days. Girls alternated tutoring and sport practice with the boys. Students could not practice if they had not participated in the tutoring session the previous day. Further, coaches also did the tutoring and brought educational lessons into the coaching sessions. In this way, athletics and academics were part of a common educational process.

Numerous programmes have been developed to satisfy a plethora of social ills. These include crime (Geoff, 2004; Nichols and Crow, 2004), violence (Hellison et al., 1996), anger management (Stevenson, 2002), gang membership (Thurman et al., 2001), drug use (Crabbe, 2000; Eitle et al., 2003), teen sex (Eitle and Eitle, 2002), lack of educational achievement (Hartmann, 2003), intolerance (Wilson and White, 2001), and other forms of disengagement (Gray and Seddon, 2005). Programmes claim to develop an endless array of beneficial skills such as life skills (Petitpas et al., 2004), decision making and problem solving skills (Newton et al., 2001), responsible behaviours (Hellison and Walsh, 2002), and healthy lifestyle changes (Boon and Clydesdale, 2005), among others. Yet, the evidence that sport-based programmes actually produce social and personal change is scant (cf. Collins and Kay, 2003; Smith and Waddington, 2004). While there is a paucity of rigorous scientific evaluation of sport programmes designed to enhance social and personal change, there is a more fundamental reason that research on the efficacy of such programmes has been inconclusive at best and contradictory at worst.

Change Implementation Matters

Sport has been treated as if it were a unitary experience. That is, all sport is seen as the same; it is assumed to provide the same benefits to all participants no matter the programme or context. Yet we know that sports vary dramatically. Even traditional programmes offering the same sport differ as a function of their rewards and expectations. Seemingly simple things can make a substantial difference in the impacts that the sport experience can have. For example, McCormack and Chalip (1988) found that athletes are more likely to take lessons away from sport if their coach seems to enjoy coaching than if he or she treats coaching merely as a job. In other words, something as subtle as the coach's demeanour moderates the effect that a sport experience has on the attitudes and values of participants. Thus, it is not sport, per se, that causes change. It is the experience as a function of implementation and an individual's interpretation of that experience which makes the difference. We do not yet know enough about the full range of factors that determine the effects that sport can have, but it is clear that the effects of sport depend on the experiences that it provides, and those experiences depend on variations in the ways that sport is implemented. In other words, the effects of sport are not inherent in sport, but are due to what sport enables or hampers. These outcomes are directly related to programme elements.

Elements of Successful Sports Development Programmes

A number of researchers (e.g. Eccles and Gootman, 2002; Hellison and Walsh, 2002; Petitpas et al., 2004; Sandford et al., 2006; Smith and Waddington, 2004) have studied youth sport and recreation settings purported to promote positive development. Although the programmes vary in terms of their goals, participants, sport activities, and political and geographic contexts, programmes that have had success as change agents share two common features: (1) an emphasis on relationships and relationship building; and (2) a positive experience. These elements are present in successful programmes of all kinds – sport for social inclusion, sport as diversion, and sport as a hook. However, the way that each of these elements is provided varies dramatically and must be tailored to the programme's goals and targeted participants to have a clear developmental orientation.

Relationships and Relationship Building

Relationships are at the core of participants' experience of the sport programme. Participants come into contact with adult programme leaders, coaches, mentors, and other specialists as part of their programme experience. When participants characterize their relationship with adults associated with the programme in terms of support and trust, the relationships facilitate positive outcomes for participants (Petitpas et al., 2004). Further, adults must be perceived to have relevant knowledge and expertise without being seen as an authority figure (Smith and Waddington, 2004). In fact, the most powerful adult–participant relationships are those in which the adult is able to empower the participant to take ownership of the programme, embracing the intended goals and processes of the programme. This is the biggest challenge for many adult programme leaders. It requires adults to support participants in planning and decision making without imposing their own views.

Chalip et al. (1996) describe one such programme in New Zealand. Adolescents were invited to form a committee to plan, organize, and administer the local recreation club. Thirty to forty teens served on the committee at any one time. Seven adults also served on the committee. The adults provided guidance and expertise to the group, but left the teens to determine the programming, policies, and other managerial issues. Adults helped teens to learn the requisite skills to effectively manage their own programme. The programme was a huge success; the community gained a programme that was attractive to teens, especially teens not well-served by more traditional sport clubs and did so at very low cost since the teens supplied the labour. The authors supplied five recommendations to adult programme administrators hoping to develop positive relationships with teens: (1) be willing to share power with teens; (2) maximize opportunities for participants to take on meaningful, adult-like roles and responsibilities; (3) design programmes to be congruent with teens' reasons for participating; (4) have realistic expectations; and (5) show confidence in participants' ability to succeed. These suggestions are far from revolutionary, but result in a programme that looks very different from traditional adult-centred sport programmes with their well-prescribed outcomes.

Indeed most sport programmes are coach/manager-centred. Coaches do the planning, make the decisions, and tend to be rather authoritarian in their administrative style (Penman et al., 1974). It has been argued that authoritarian settings can actually inhibit the social and moral development of participants (Theodoulides and Armour, 2001), largely because participants do not build two-way relationships with coaches or programme leaders. Rather, they are socialized to 'do what the coach says' and never fully engage with any problem solving, decision making, or social responsibility. The coach, then, is a pivotal element in sport programmes, particularly sport for social inclusion programmes in which participants' relationships with adults are largely limited to player–coach relationships.

Diversion programmes do not necessarily have the same focus on sport performance as do programmes reliant entirely on sport. Remember, the key objective of diversion programmes is to divert participants from a time or place when they would be engaged in risky or socially deviant behaviours such as drug use, teen sex, and criminal activity. The relationships that participants develop with adult programme leaders in diversionary programmes are critical to the success of these programmes. Like coaches, effective programme leaders should have a high degree of relevant knowledge and skill, but should not be seen as authority figures (Smith and Waddington, 2004). Often, however, adults are volunteers who are drawn to the mission of the programme. They do not necessarily have the appropriate expertise. Davis and Dawson (1996) conclude that programme leaders need more than a quick education about the social concerns of participants; programme leaders should be specialists able to handle the issues with confidence. Participants in diversion programmes interact and build relationships with a variety of adults in the programme, not just a coach. Adults may take on different roles within the programme (e.g. mentor, coach, teacher, counsellor). Regardless of role, it is important that adults are supportive and respectful of participants and that they are a consistent presence for participants. Adults must invest in one-on-one relationships with participants. After all, trust does not come quickly to the disaffected youth expected to participate in diversion programmes.

The same is true for programmes that use sport to attract participants in order to provide more active interventions – developing life skills, conflict management skills, emotional maturity, etc. It is easy for adults to fall into the trap of explicitly attempting to create better people, but participants sense this as judgement rather than support. Instead, programme personnel should be focused on assisting participants to learn the skills necessary to make more healthy choices, not by telling them (this is a key complaint about school teachers made by disaffected youth), but by providing them a warm, close, caring relationship. The relationship provides a safe context for participants to discuss issues and seek guidance that is available, appropriate, and predictable (Mahoney et al., 2004). For many disaffected and at-risk youth, this may be their first supportive, caring relationship with an adult (Sandford et al., 2006). As important as adult relationships are to facilitating personal development and change, participants have many more interactions with other participants than they do with adult programme leaders. Positive relationships with adults are necessary, but without supportive peer relationships, they are not sufficient to create sustainable change.

Peer groups exert tremendous influence on youth, particularly during adolescence (Kiesner et al., 2002; Lee, 2007). At-risk, disaffected, and underserved youth are no exception. However, in many instances, peer relationships support their anti-social behaviours. The most obvious example is gang membership. Gang members have strong relationships with in-group members, yet the norms and values of the group do not support the personal growth and social development of individual gang members. Rather, gang members instead support violence, vandalism, and other criminal behaviours. At the same time, gangs provide a sense of belonging, status, and a valued identity (Petitpas et al., 2004). Sport-based interventions can also provide belonging, status, and a valued identity (McPherson et al., 1989). The values, beliefs, and behaviours of peers (and adults) in the programme will ultimately determine the norms and values that are salient aspects of the setting. So, the challenge for programme providers is to create and support a culture of positive norms and values, and to do it in a way that creates buy-in by participants. Sport programmes that provide more than sport training seem to be best suited to the task. For example, The First Tee of Greater Austin uses golf to attract at-risk students to its programme. Once there, participants work with a mentor and a small peer group to learn golf and life skills. Course etiquette such as introducing oneself to an opponent, shaking hands, and self-monitoring are taught as part of the game of golf. However, these behaviours also help to structure the ways that participants interact with one another, facilitating respectful and supportive relationships (see www.firstteeaustin.org).

Diversionary programmes must be particularly attentive to peer support of anti-social behaviours among programme participants. Providing a space and time for participants to meet without working to develop a positive group climate based on supportive peer relationships can facilitate the very anti-social behaviours the programme is intended to curtail. Midnight basketball programmes, for example, were designed to reduce crime by attracting potential criminals to play basketball peak crime hours. Before programmes expanded by offering other social services and training, the basketball gym became a place to meet (and perhaps partner with) like others to plan more criminal activity (Hartmann and Depro, 2006). For this reason, programmes that embed character building, life skills, education, or other activities to build social capital, are more effective at facilitating change. Programmes that lack structure, opportunities to build skill, and guidance from caring adults seem to attract youth with social adjustment problems and facilitate the further development of anti-social behaviours (Mahoney et al., 2004).

In summary, caring and supportive relationships with adult programme leaders and peers are common elements to successful programmes. The specific processes for developing these relationships should be tailored to fit the needs of participants and the mission of the programme. However, these relationships are built over time and require the development of a positive and supportive environment to flourish. Consequently, the relationships participants develop within the programme are embedded in the broader organizational culture and will colour their overall experience of the programme.

Experience of the Programme

Interactions with programme leaders, participants, and others within the programme are core to one's experience of the programme. However, the structure and activities of a programme form the context in which relationships are built and maintained. Programme features as diverse as the sport or activity selected, the amount of structured versus unstructured time available, the diversity of programme participants, and the amount and type of adult supervision engender very different contexts for interaction and relationship building. Consider the interactions which might occur in a standard competitive volleyball programme with adult coaches, referees, and league administrators. Coaches and athletes have multiple opportunities to interact formally at practices and matches, and informally before and after programme activities, and while waiting for the next match. Officials interact with participants in a very formal context and their interactions are often negative. Team mates may support one another against an opponent, but compete with one another to earn playing time and the coach's attention. Now consider the same volleyball programme which uses the sport education model (Siedentop, 1994). Participants coach one another, officiate, keep score, and administer the league. In this context, adults' roles are to support and guide participants as necessary. Then consider a league that provides volleyball because it is a popular sport. Matches are scheduled to alternate with career planning sessions. Mentors help participants to translate situations and lessons faced on the court to those faced in everyday life. What interactions would be engendered in this model? Clearly, participants would experience each of these settings very differently. All are built around the core activity of volleyball, but each would engender different subjective experiences and outcomes, including different relationships. Is one better than another? Not necessarily. The key is to consider the outcomes valued by the organization and its participants. Then, determine the interactions necessary to achieve those outcomes. Finally, design and implement programme elements that engender the requisite interactions.

Change Potential of Sports Development Programmes: Management Implications

It is clear that sport is not unique in its ability to capture the attention of participants in order to facilitate positive social development (cf. McCormack and Chalip, 1988). However, sport's appeal across a wide range of groups and cultures, the strong emotional attachments developed through sport, and its strength as a context of identity formation position it as a potentially powerful tool for social and personal change. Programmes of all types have been successful when they are designed to meet the needs of participants, engender positive relationships among participants, peers, and programme leaders, and implement activities that facilitate appropriate interactions. In combination, these elements create a culture which values and supports positive social norms. Table 6.1 summarizes the key aims and change potential of the three main types of sports development programmes and their implications for managers.

Table 6.1 Types of sports development programmes, potential for personal–social change, and management focus.

Sports development programme aims	Social–personal change potential	Management focus
Inclusion programmes		
• bring the benefits of sport participation to traditionally underserved populations • socialize participants into the norms and values of society through sport participation	• enhance sense of belonging • enhance or detract from perceived self-worth • increase respect for authority • acculturation • increase tolerance and respect for diversity or inflame existing ethnic tensions • enhance or impede moral development	• identify underserved populations • conduct needs assessments • design programmes which are inclusive and meet the needs of specific populations • train coaches to deliver the intended benefits
Diversion programmes		
• use sport as a substitute activity to replace anti-social behaviours • provide sport at a time and place which disrupts usual patterns of anti-social behaviours • often used to divert participants from anti-social behaviours such as gang activities, property crime, violent crime, drug use, and sexual risk-taking	• reduce property crime • reduce violent crime • reduce gang activity • provide alternative community of belongingness • provide positive role models • create opportunities for positive activities and relationships • can provide a meeting place for deviant or delinquent participants to gather • can provide a space for socializing individuals into anti-social values and behaviours	• partner with other community agencies to integrate sport programmes with other initiatives (e.g. crime prevention, drug education, health promotion campaigns • structure programmes to keep participants involved in the sport activity • monitor informal interactions to prohibit anti-social group behaviours • train programme leaders to empower participants to take ownership of and responsibility for the programme • work to attract media attention for the programme

(Continued)

Table 6.1 Continued

Sports development programme aims	Social–personal change potential	Management focus
Hook programmes		
• use sport to attract at-risk or disengaged participants • integrate social programmes with sport activities to provide participants with needed skills, knowledge, and abilities	• increase social and physical skills, and educational attainment • increase ability to interact positively with adults and peers • increase confidence and self-worth • motivate participants to take responsibility for their actions • enhance sense of belonging • provide opportunities for achievement	• consider sports that are attractive to the target population • empower participants to take on key roles and responsibilities • show confidence in participants' abilities • train adult programme leaders to advise rather than command • train programme leaders in mentoring and relationship building • integrate support activities and sport activities • include informal time (and space) for adult–participant interactions • maintain focus on mission – i.e. the non-sport goals and objectives • maintain a long-term focus on outcomes • provide a safe environment for learning

References

Arnaud, L. (2002). Sport as a cultural system: Sports policies and (new) ethnicities in Lyon and Birmingham. *International Journal of Urban and Regional Research*, **26**, 571–87.

Begg, D.J., Langley, J.D., Moffitt, T., and Marshall, S.W. (1996). Sport and delinquency: An examination of the deterrence hypothesis in a longitudinal study. *British Journal of Sports Medicine*, **30**, 335–41.

Boon, C.S. and Clydesdale, F.M. (2005). A review of childhood and adolescent obesity interventions. *Critical Reviews in Food Science and Nutrition*, **45**, 511–25.

Carnegie Council (1995). *Great Transitions: Preparing Adolescents for a New Century*. New York: Carnegie Corporation.

Chalip, L. (1992). The revival of the modern Olympic Games and Pierre de Coubertin's thoughts on sport for all. *Proceedings of the 31st session of the International Olympic Academy*. Lausanned: International Olympic Committee, pp. 65–71.

Chalip, L., Thomas, D.R., and Voyle, J. (1996). Enhancing wellbeing through sport and recreation. In *Community Psychology and Social Change*, 2nd edn (D. Thomas and A. Veno, eds). Palmerston North, NZ: The Dunmore Press, pp. 126–56.

Coakley, J. (1993). Socialization and sport. In *Handbook of Research on Sport Psychology* (R.N. Singer, M. Murphey, and L.K. Tennant, eds). New York: Macmillan, pp. 571–86.

Collins, M. and Kay, T. (2003). *Sport and Social Exclusion*. London: Routledge.

Crabbe, T. (2000). A sporting chance? Using sport to tackle drug use and crime. *Drugs: Education, Prevention and Policy*, **7**, 381–91.

Davis, G. and Dawson, N. (1996). *Using Diversion to Communicate Drugs Prevention Messages to Young People: An Examination of Six Projects*. London: Home Office Paper 12.

Dishion, T., McCord, J., and Poulin, F. (1999). When interventions harm: Peer groups and problem behavior. *American Psychologist*, **54**, 755–64.

Eccles, J.S. and Gootman, J.A. (eds). (2002). *Community Programs to Promote Youth Development*. Washington, DC: National Academy Press.

Eccles, J.S., Barber, B.L., Stone, M., and Hunt, J. (2003). Extracurricular activities and adolescent development. *Journal of Social Issues*, **59**, 865–89.

Eitle, T.M. and Eitle, D.J. (2002). Just don't do it: High school sports participation and young female adult sexual behavior. *Sociology of Sport Journal*, **19**, 403–18.

Eitle, D., Turner, J., and Eitle, T.M. (2003). The deterrence hypothesis reexamined: Sports participation and substance use among young adults. *Journal of Drug Issues*, **22**, 193–222.

Fleisher, S.J. and Avelar, C. (1995). Evaluation of a judo/community organization program to treat predelinquent Hispanic immigrant early adolescents. *Hispanic Journal of Behavioral Sciences*, **17**, 237–49.

Gaunt, R., Sindic, D., and Leyens, J.-P. (2005). Intergroup relations in soccer finals: People's forecasts of the duration of emotional reactions of in-group and out-group soccer fans. *Journal of Social Psychology*, **145**, 117–26.

Geoff, N. (2004). Crime and punishment in sports development. *Leisure Studies*, **23**, 177–95.

Gray, P. and Seddon, T. (2005). Prevention work with children disaffected from school. Findings from the evaluation of two innovative community-based projects. *Health Education*, **105**(1), 62–72.

Grove, S.J. and Dodder, R.A. (1982). Constructing measures to assess perceptions of sport functions: An exploratory investigation. *International Journal of Sport Psychology*, **13**, 96–106.

Hartmann, D. (2001). Notes on midnight basketball and the cultural politics of recreation, race, and at-risk urban youth. *Journal of Sport & Social Issues*, **25**, 339–71.

Hartmann, D. (2003). Theorizing sport as social intervention: A view from the grassroots. *Quest*, **55**, 118–40.

Hartmann, D. and Depro, B. (2006). Rethinking sports-based community crime prevention. A preliminary analysis of the relationship between midnight basketball and urban crime rates. *Journal of Sport & Social Issues*, **30**, 180–96.

Heffner, J.L., Ogles, B.M., Gold, E. et al. (2003). Nutrition and eating in female college athletes: A survey of coaches. *Eating Disorders*, **11**, 209–21.

Hellison, D. and Walsh, D. (2002). Responsibility-based youth programs evaluation: Investigating the investigations. *Quest*, **54**, 292–307.

Hellison, D., Martinek, T.J., and Cutforth, N.J. (1996). Beyond violence prevention in inner-city physical activity programs. *Peace and Conflict: Journal of Peace Psychology*, **2**, 321–37.

Hill, B. and Green, B.C. (2008). Give the bench the boot! Using manning theory to design youth sport programs. *Journal of Sport Management*, **22**(2), 184–204.

Holt, R. (1989). *Sport and the British*. Oxford: Oxford University Press.

Howell, J.C. (ed.). (1995). *Guide for Implementing the Comprehensive Strategy for Serious, Violent and Chronic Juvenile Offenders*. Washington, DC: U.S. Department of Justice, Office of Juvenile Justice and Delinquency Prevention.

Jacob, B.A. and Lefgren, L. (2003). Are idle hands the devil's workshop? Incapacitation, concentration, and juvenile crime. *American Economic Review*, **9**, 1560–77.

Kiesner, J., Cadinu, M., Poulin, F., and Bucci, M. (2002). Group identification in early adolescence: Its relation with peer adjustment and its moderator effect on peer influence. *Child Development*, **73**, 196–209.

Kleiber, D.A. and Roberts, G.A. (1981). The effects of sport experience in the development of social character: An exploratory investigation. *Journal of Sport Psychology*, **2**, 114–22.

Kohn, A. (1986). *No Contest: The Case Against Competition*. Boston: Houghton Mifflin.

Labour Party (1997). *Labour's Sporting Nationa*. London: The Labour Party.

Larson, R. (2000). Toward a psychology of positive youth development. *American Psychologist*, **55**(1), 170–83.

Lauer, R.H. (1982).*Perspectives on Social Change*. Boston: Allyn and Bacon.

Lee, H. (2007). The effects of school racial and ethnic composition on academic achievement during adolescence. *Journal of Negro Education*, **76**, 154–72.

Long, J. and Sanderson, I. (2001). The social benefits of sport: Where's the proof? In *Sport in the City: The Role of Sport in Economic and Social Regeneration* (C. Gratton and I.P. Henry, eds). London: Routledge, pp. 187–203.

Loxley, C., Curtin, L., and Brown, R. (2002). Summer splash schemes 2000: Findings from six case studies. *Crime Reduction Research Series* (paper 12). London: Home Office.

MacAloon, J.J. (1981). *This Great Symbol: Pierre de Coubertin and the Origins of the Modern Olympic Games*. Chicago: University of Chicago Press.

Mahoney, J.L., Eccles, J.S., and Larson, R.W. (2004). Processes of adjustment in organized out-of-school activities: Opportunities and risks. *New Directions for Youth Development*, **101**, 115–44.

Martens, M.P., Dams-O'Connor, K., and Beck, N.C. (2006). A systematic review of college student-athlete drinking: Prevalence rates, sport-related factors, and interventions. *Journal of Substance Abuse Treatment*, **31**, 305–16.

McCormack, J. and Chalip, L. (1988). Sport as socialization: A critique of methodological premises. *The Social Science Journal*, **25**(1), 83–92.

McPherson, B.D., Curtis, J.E., and Loy, J.W. (1989). *The Social Significance of Sport: An Introduction to the Sociology of Sport*. Champaign, IL: Human Kinetics.

Morris, L., Sallybanks, J., Willis, K., and Makkai, T. (2003). Sport, physical activity and antisocial behaviour in youth.*Trends and Issues in Crime and Criminal Justice, April*. Canberra: Australian Institute of Criminology (accessed 12 November 2007 from www.aic.gov.au/publications/tandi/tandi249.html).

Newton, M., Sandberg, J., and Watson, D.L. (2001). Utilizing adventure education within the model of moral action. *Quest*, **53**, 483–94.

Nichols, G. (2004). Crime and punishment and sports development. *Leisure Studies*, **23**, 177–95.

Nichols, G. and Crow, I. (2004). Measuring the impact of crime reduction interventions involving sports activities for young people. *The Howard Journal*, **43**, 267–83.

Penman, K.A., Hastad, D.N., and Cords, W.L. (1974). Success of the authoritarian coach. *Journal of Social Psychology*, **92**, 155–6.

Petitpas, A.J., Van Raalte, J.L., Cornelius, A.E., and Presbrey, J. (2004). A life-skills development program for high school student-athletes. *Journal of Primary Prevention*, **24**, 325–34.

Pitter, R. and Andrews, D.L. (1997). Serving America's underserved youth: Reflections in an emerging social problems industry. *Quest*, **49**, 85–99.

Poinsett, A. (1996).*The Role of Sports in Youth Development*. New York: Carnegie Corporation.

Sandford, R.A., Armour, K.M., and Warmington, P.C. (2006). Re-engaging disaffected youth through physical activity programmes. *British Educational Research Journal*, **32**, 251–71.

Scanlan, T.K., Carpenter, P.J., Lobel, M., and Simons, J.P. (1993). Sources of enjoyment for youth sport athletes. *Pediatric Exercise Science*, **5**, 275–85.

Schultz, L.E., Crompton, J.L., and Witt, P.A. (1995). A national profile of the status of public recreation services for at-risk children and youth. *Journal of Park and Recreation Administration*, **13**(3), 1–25.

Semyonov, M. and Farbstein, M. (1989). Ecology of sports violence: The case of Israeli soccer. *Sociology of Sport Journal*, **6**, 50–9.

Siedentop, D. (1994). *Sport Education: Quality PE Through Positive Sport Experiences*. Champaign, IL: Human Kinetics.

Smith, A. and Waddington, I. (2004). Using 'sport in the community schemes' to tackle crime and drug use among young people: Some policy issues and problems. *European Physical Education Review*, **10**, 279–98.

Sport England (2002). *Positive Futures: A Review of Impact and Good Practice*. London: Sport England.

Spreitzer, E. and Snyder, E.E. (1975). The psychosocial functions of sport as perceived by the general population. *International Review for the Sociology of Sport*, **10**, 87–95.

Stevenson, H.C. (2002). Wrestling with destiny: The cultural socialization of anger and healing in African American males. *Journal of Psychology and Christianity*, **21**, 357–64.

Theodoulides, A. and Armour, K.M. (2001). Personal, social and moral development through team games: Some critical questions. *European Physical Education Review*, **7**(1), 5–23.

Thurman, Q.C., Giacomazzi, A.L., Reisig, M.D., and Mueller, D.G. (2001). Community-based gang prevention and intervention: An evaluation of the neutral zone.*Crime & Delinquency*, **42**, 279–95.

United Nations (n.d.). *Achieving the Objectives of the United Nations Through Sport*. Geneva: United Nations.

United Nations (2004). Our mandate. What does sport have to do with the UN? Retrieved on 20 November 2007 from http://www.un.org/themes/sport/intro.htm.

Ville de Lyon (1991). *DSQ Jean Mermoz: Charte d'objectifs*. Lyon, FR: Author.

Visek, A. and Watson, J. (2005). Ice hockey players' legitimacy of aggression and professionalization of attitudes. *Sport Psychologist*, **19**, 178–93.

Watson, G.G. (1977). Games, socialization and parental values: Social class differences in parental evaluation of little league baseball. *International Review for the Sociology of Sport*, **12**, 117–48.

Wilson, J. (1994).*Playing by the Rules: Sport, Society and the State*. Detroit, MI: Wayne State University Press.

Wilson, B. and White, P. (2001). Tolerance rules: Identity, resistance, and negotiation in an inner city recreation/drop-in center. *Journal of Sport & Social Issues*, **25**(1), 73–103.

Witt, P.A. and Crompton, J.L. (eds). (1996). *Recreation Programs that Work for At-Risk Youth: The Challenge of Shaping the Future*. State College, PA: Venture Publishing.

Witt, P.A. and Crompton, J.L. (1997). The protective factors framework: A key to programming for benefits and evaluating results. *Journal of Park and Recreation Administration*, **15**(3), 1–18.

CHAPTER 7

Mega Sporting Events and Sports Development

Milena M. Parent

Major sporting events "should link in to the wider development of sport"
(UK Sport, 1999, p. 6)

Introduction

Single and multi-sport events of all natures are multiplying, an increasing number of cities and countries want to host such events, and sponsorship is on the rise both in terms of the number of corporations wanting to be involved as well as the dollar amounts associated with sponsoring an event. These statements are especially true for mega sporting events. Such events are traditionally defined as events designated as being a 'must-see' event able to attract worldwide publicity; they should have over one million participants (e.g. athletes, volunteers, spectators, television viewers) and capital costs over $500 million (Getz, 2005).

Examples of mega sporting events typically presented are the Olympic Games and the World Cup (football/soccer). However, there are other, lesser-known examples of mega sporting events that can also fit the definition such as the Commonwealth Games, the Pan American Games, the Asian Games, the *Jeux de la Francophonie*, and some world championships like the IAAF's (athletics) and FINA's (aquatic) world championships.

One of the reasons for the increased popularity of mega sporting events is the supposed legacies the events can bring to the host region. These legacies are thought to change or impact the host region arguably for the better. Ritchie (1984) described six types of impacts that an event may have on a host region, which are not always positive (cf. Lenskyj, 1996; Whitson and Horne, 2006; Whitson and Macintosh, 1993, 1996):

- Economic (expenditures);
- Tourism/commercial (awareness, reputation);

- Physical (facilities, environment);
- Socio-cultural (regional traditions);
- Psychological (local pride); and
- Political (political propaganda, image).

Brown and Massey's (2001) literature review revealed that research on major sporting event impacts has focused on: sports participation and development, social impact, legacies, urban regeneration, tourism, and economic impact. The authors noted that these topics are interrelated. In fact, it can be argued that all these aspects are part of the legacy of a sporting event, a legacy which can be geared towards individuals (e.g. sports participation) or the community (e.g. economic impact). Brown and Massey (2001) argued that these varying levels of legacy are distinct and therefore involve different processes. However, they are not mutually exclusive; they can impact each other.

This chapter focuses on one aspect of legacy, sports development. As will be seen, sports development brings about different types of changes, at different levels, which can impact either the individual, or the community, or both. This chapter examines sports development as a social change. However, such an approach is not equivalent to community development; the emphasis is still on sport – or more precisely, mega sporting events – as a catalyst for social change.

Key concepts necessary for this chapter will first be briefly described. This will be followed by the core of the chapter, namely, the presentation of the three types of change relating to sports development and resulting from the bidding and hosting of mega sporting events. The chapter will conclude with a summary and some recommendations for sport managers.

Key Concepts

Before examining the impact of mega sporting events on sports development, it is important to define a few concepts and situate the chapter within the broader sport management field. First, this chapter uses an organization theory perspective to the research. Second, the concepts of sports development and change are briefly introduced as they are also dealt with in other chapters.

Organization Theory

This chapter uses an organization theory approach to mega sporting events and sports development. Organization theory has its roots within sociology (Clegg et al., 1996; Hinings and Greenwood, 2002). That is, sociologists began using organizations as "mini" versions of society; what happened in an organization was reflected in society and vice versa since organizations have an impact on society and society has an impact on organizations. From there, the field of organization theory was born.

The goal of organization theorists is to examine what happens within organizations to make them more effective and efficient. The focus is on the process within organizations: how they are structured, what their environment is, what they do, how they change, who holds power, who makes decisions, how decisions are made, what types of decisions are made, etc. (Parent, 2006; Pugh & Hickson, 2007). While organization theorists look at organizations, they can do so at different levels. The 'traditional' approach is to examine organizations as their own unit of analysis. However, organizations can also be studied at a more micro level, the people within organizations, or at a more macro level, the population of organizations or environment as a whole.

Thus, using an organization theory approach allows us to examine what sports development looks like within one type of organization, mega-event organizing committees, but at different levels. In other words, what types of changes within and surrounding an organizing committee and its host region are related to sports development?

Approaches to Sports Development

The firm, PriceWaterhouseCoopers (2005), prepared a social, economic, and environmental impact study report for the 2012 London Olympic Games. In their report, they suggested that sustainable social development included three accounts: (1) people, skills, and employment; (2) sporting and cultural legacy; and (3) public health. This categorization would indicate that sports development stemming from mega sporting events is only one sub-component of social development. However, as will be seen below, the first two accounts are part of sports development stemming from mega sporting events and they are related to PriceWaterhouseCoopers' broader social, economic, and environmental impacts – especially when considering infrastructure.

Mega sporting events are typically an *indigenous development* initiative (Mintzberg, 2006). A group of people in a community (often elites with political and/or business backgrounds) will come together to propose bidding for a mega sporting event because they want to do something for others in their community (a 'bottom-up' approach). However, this group will need the assistance of the government/state to support the bid and hosting activities, thus inscribing the event within *planned development*. This 'top-down' approach is usually necessary to obtain new infrastructure for the event (e.g. facilities, roads). Nevertheless, these approaches to development (indigenous and planned) are moderated by a third approach, *global development*, which is also found in the bid and hosting of a mega sporting event. Global trends, economically speaking, impact the form an event will take. Currently, a capitalist view dominates, which is why sponsorship is encouraged so that the state does not have to pay for the whole event (cf. Mintzberg, 2006).

Change

Taking an organization theory approach to examining the impact of mega sporting events on sports development involves defining change in a broad sense. Change can be radical or convergent, evolutionary or revolutionary

(Greenwood and Hinings, 1996). Radical change is seen when an actor (individual, group, organization, community, etc.) moves away from an established direction or objective, whereas convergent change is seen when the actor fine-tunes an established direction or objective. For example, the city of Sheffield exhibited radical change when it wanted to change its image from the 'city of steel' to the 'city of sport' (cf. Henry, 1999). In turn, change also varies according to its pace: evolutionary change is slow and gradual, whereas revolutionary change is swift and occurs everywhere (e.g. all departments of an organization or the whole city) simultaneously. For example, most organizing committees of mega events will experience revolutionary change within the year before the event takes place (e.g. the number of paid and volunteer staff increases exponentially over the last year from a few hundred to thousands).

There is also a growing literature on social change within organization theory. As Biese et al. (2007) explained, corporations can be agents of social change, just as individuals can. Corporations are influenced by individual, interpersonal, institutional, and environmental dynamics which will shape social change. Aguilera et al. (2007) added that corporations are increasingly pressured to undertake corporate social responsibility initiatives so as to put forth positive social change. Sports development is one example of positive social change; however, as you will see, it can also be an example of negative social change.

Types of Sports Development Changes

Getting a mega sporting event in your area usually comes with a lot of construction. That's what most people think of as the development resulting from a mega sporting event – well, that and seeing your government spend a lot of money that you think should go to 'better' pursuits such as healthcare or education. Mega sporting events have come under much criticism for issues such as low-income housing destruction, high construction costs resulting in venues never being used – the proverbial 'white elephants' – and generally high costs of hosting such events, costs more often than not born by local and national governments (see Lenskyj, 1996, 2000). For example, the Japanese government spent so much money on preparing the 1998 Nagano Olympic Games that each Japanese person (whether adult or child) was reportedly indebted to the tune of US$10 000.

Increasingly, however, organizing committees of mega sporting events are listening to such criticism and are addressing them. In fact, they are going beyond the traditional issues and truly focusing on legacies, notably on various aspects of sports development. The 2002 Manchester Commonwealth Games, the 2010 Vancouver-Whistler Winter Olympic Games, and the 2012 London Summer Olympic Games have truly led the way in preparing for sports development from the bid stage of the event. The 2002 Manchester Commonwealth Games even created a website dedicated to sports development (www.sportdevelopment.org.uk).

The increasing pressure by various stakeholders (Freeman, 1984) for bid and organizing committees of mega sporting events to exert positive social change means that there is no reason to believe that the sports development trend as a legacy will not continue with future Olympic Games, and even with other mega sporting events.

But what exactly constitutes sports development stemming from mega sporting events?

There are three types of changes brought about by mega events which are related to sports development: individual (i.e. related to volunteers, athletes, coaches, officials, etc.), infrastructure (i.e. related to facilities, equipment, etc.), and policy/planning (i.e. by governments and National Sport Organizations or NSOs). Each is described below and includes both positive and negative aspects. Examples are also provided and stem from a variety of events.

Individual-Based Changes

Athletes, coaches, officials and volunteers benefit from preparation pro-grammes, competitions, programming and facility legacies.... Social benefits range from unique work experiences, including training and youth participa-tion, to volunteer promotion and increased emphasis on fitness and health (UK Sport, 1999, p. 3).

Individual-based changes related to sports development in mega sporting events refer to, as the name indicates, the individuals which are associated with, have an impact on, or are affected by the actions of the organizing committee of a mega sporting event, whether these individuals be internal members of the organizing committee (e.g. volunteers and paid staff) or exter-nal stakeholders such as residents, community groups, athletes, coaches, and officials (see Freeman, 1984; Parent, 2005; Parent and Foreman, 2007; Parent and Séguin, 2007).

Working for a mega sporting event – whether as a volunteer or as a paid staff person – is not an easy task. Just read books by people who have bid for and/or run these events – such as Frank King and the 1988 Calgary Winter Olympic Games (King, 1991), Rod McGeoch and the bid for the 2000 Sydney Summer Olympic Games (McGeoch, 1994), Richard Yarbrough and the 1996 Atlanta Summer Olympic Games (Yarbrough, 2000), and Mitt Romney and the 2002 Salt Lake City Winter Olympic Games (Romney, 2004) – and you will see.

But, working for a mega sporting event allows you to gain valuable knowl-edge. This knowledge may be technical in nature (i.e. related to the sport(s) showcased at the event). For example, if you wish to learn about the inner technical workings of hosting a football event like the World Cup, then volunteering for the event's sport division will give you a glimpse of these inner workings. The knowledge may also be non-technical in nature. For example, you may wish to learn about international politics – mega sporting events are a great setting to do this if you volunteer in the protocol division of the organizing committee.

At a broader level, organizing committees are starting to think of another type of knowledge, one that is academically based but available to all. More precisely, the 1984 Los Angeles Olympic Games' Amateur Athletic Foundation (www.aafla.org) has an academic articles and information database accessible to all internet users, as does the 2002 Manchester Commonwealth Games' sport development organization (www.sportdevelopment.org.uk). This public information is useful to all who are interested in mega sporting events as the articles within the databases cover a wide range of topics. Nevertheless, empirical, theoretically-strong research on how to manage major sporting events is still relatively new; in fact, case study 7.1 illustrates that in the not to distant past (in 2001) very little information was available.

However, it is not only volunteers who benefit from working for an event. As for other industries, employees can (and should) develop skills in this job. Since most mega events are structured according to function (e.g. sport, operations, media/public relations, finance, information technology (IT), and corporate and/or government relations), they are great settings to build your skills in a short, pre-defined time period, within a specific area of interest to you. As well, there are a variety of paths to follow once an event is over, as case study 7.1 exemplifies.

One notable impact of working in sport, and especially in mega sporting events, is related to the close-knit nature of the environment. It can be very difficult to get your foot in the proverbial door of these events (notably the Olympic Games) if you do not know someone on the inside. To get into an Olympic Games, you often have to work yourself up the events ladder – this is the same as any other organization, where you wouldn't start as the president of a company but would work yourself up the corporate ladder. By working (either as a volunteer or as an employee) for smaller events – or local events where you have more chances of getting in – you build a network of contacts, which can become very useful in the future. People who have been 'bitten by the events bug' will often move from one event to the next. For example, Roger Jackson had worked for the 1988 Calgary Olympic Games and then was asked to be a consultant for the 1999 Winnipeg Pan American Games. He, along with two other consultants world-renowned for their technical expertise and knowledge – built by way of working for events and thus gaining that knowledge and skill – were then recruited to consult and work for the 2010 Vancouver-Whistler Olympic Games bid and organizing committees. As these individuals have moved up the organizing committee and events ladders (one of the consultants is an executive vice-president for the 2010 Olympic Games), they can hire – and will search for – people they have worked with in the past as they know the skills, knowledge, team working capabilities, etc., of these people.

Probably the most obvious positive impact of a mega sporting event on sports development is the impact on the development of athletes, coaches, and officials. Smaller or more regional sporting events – such as national championships, world championships, the Pan American Games, the Commonwealth Games, the Asian Games, the Mediterranean Games, or the *Jeux de la Francophonie* – will have a greater impact on the development of athletes as these events are stepping stones towards 'the big show' (i.e. the Olympic Games or the World Cup). However, most coaches and officials must be trained to either coach or judge/referee at increasingly higher competitive levels (i.e. regional to national to international to continental to Olympic/ World Cup events). For example, the 2001 *Jeux de la Francophonie* held in Ottawa-Gatineau, Canada had a women's coaching programme where women coaches from African countries part of the Francophonie (the French equivalent to the Commonwealth) came to Ottawa to learn advanced coaching techniques. Likewise, the International Skating Union holds training sessions at their world championships and at the Olympic Games for officials who want to judge at the international or Olympic levels – officials are not eligible to judge at such events until they have been trained to do so.

While there are many positive sports development impacts, there are also potentially negative impacts. More precisely, the leaders of the organizing committee and the representatives of the various stakeholder groups (e.g. local/national sport organizations, local/federal government) are chosen because of their past experiences in and knowledge of mega sporting events – in other words, they have done this before to some degree. Reliance on these individuals is essential for the organizing committee as they are usually volunteers – thus no money is spent on salaries for these individuals – and their expertise/knowledge allows the organizing committee to be more efficient and effective (i.e. make fewer mistakes while reaching their goals). Being a top volunteer for a mega sporting event, like the president of the organizing committee, is very demanding, a full-time job in and of itself. Yet the individual who is President is often a volunteer and therefore has a regular (paid) full-time job. Likewise, the NSO's representative has their regular full-time job with the NSO and then does probably as much work for the organizing committee.

The amount of work required to host a mega sporting event increases exponentially until you find yourself working 20-hour days for three weeks straight during the event. Many individuals experience burnout by the end of the event. It is therefore common to see top volunteers and other experienced individuals say 'this is the big one, after that, no more' and retire after the event, thereby causing a loss in knowledge and a gap in experienced individuals for the next event to be hosted in the area or country. By losing these individuals – including top athletes, coaches, or officials – sports development can be significantly hindered for the host region/country. In fact, you often hear teams and sport federations say that the year following an Olympic Games or World Cup is a re-building year, where the 'next generation' of athletes replaces the retiring, experienced athletes and begins gaining experience for the next Olympic Games or World Cup. Thus, sports development resulting from a mega sporting event may sometimes have greater positive impacts in other countries as these countries did not experience the burnout and loss of key individuals/knowledge, only the gaining for experience for the next event.

The previous individual-based changes associated with sports development are related to individual and interpersonal dynamics of social change (see Bies et al., 2007). As large as a mega sporting event (and its organizing committee) can be, it will invariably impact the individuals directly and indirectly associated with the event, whether positively or negatively. Since individuals must work together and with external stakeholders to host the event and manage its ensuing legacy, interrelationships are essential for effectively and efficiently coordinating efforts (Chelladurai, 2005; Parent, 2005). These efforts are therefore indigenous in nature (i.e. indigenous development, see Mintzberg, 2006) as they must come from the individuals themselves, but they are also

Table 7.1 Positive and negative changes related to sports development in mega sporting events.

Type of change	Individual	Infrastructure	Policy/planning
Positive impacts	Volunteer/staff knowledge, skill development Networking and other social benefits Athletes, coaches, and officials' development	Increased (facility and equipment) capacity	Creation of policies and strategic plans by governments and NSOs Trickle-down effect for future events
Negative impacts	Burnout post-event and resulting loss of knowledge in sport system Post-event bust (retirement) Other countries benefiting more from such development programs than host country	Displacement of low-income individuals White elephant	Governments' and NSOs' short attention span Funding diversion post-event
Change dynamics	Individual and interpersonal	Institutional and environmental	Institutional and environmental
Development type	Indigenous and global	Indigenous, planned, and global	Planned and global

influenced by the existing state of global development (Mintzberg, 2006). More precisely, we are currently seeing greater movement of workers between countries, especially for those with highly technical skills, which can assist in creating efficient and effective coordinating systems for mega sporting events. For example, Cathy Priestner Allinger followed her 1976 Olympic silver medal in speed skating with roles as a coach, administrator, volunteer and television broadcaster, which helped her gain a variety of knowledge, skills and networks related to sports and event management. She then became managing Director of Sport for the 2002 Salt Lake City Winter Olympic Games followed by Managing Director of Games Operations for the 2006 Turin Winter Olympic Games. Her success in these positions allowed her to become the Executive Vice-President – Sport, Paralympic Games and Venue Management for the 2010 Vancouver-Whistler Olympic Games.

Table 7.1 provides a summary of the individual-based positive and negative sports development impacts from mega sporting events, as well as the social change dynamics and the development type.

Infrastructure-Based Changes

One of the most visible changes, which a mega sporting event can bring, is related to the local infrastructure through new or renovated facilities and equipment. Many mega sporting event bids are in fact built upon what they can bring to the local region. For example, Sydney's bid for the 2000 Olympic Games was built around the revitalization of Homebush Bay, and

Beijing's bid for the 2008 Olympic Games was built around a full slate of new, state-of-the-art facilities.

One key goal for both the 2010 Vancouver-Whistler and the 2012 London Olympic Games is to provide a legacy to the region and country. Part of this legacy will be in the form of economic returns (or at least hopes to be) and part of the legacy will be in kind, especially facilities and equipment. This equipment, including such things as balls and nets, can be distributed to local amateur sports clubs in need of new equipment. It is amazing what a set of new balls and goal posts can do for a youth football team. This sports development-related legacy is probably the most consistent and assured form across all types of (sanctioned) international sporting events – all sporting events which are sanctioned by the international federation must meet the highest standards and this typically involves new equipment. So, even second- or third-tier international sporting events like the FINA World Aquatics Championships or the Commonwealth Games will contribute to some form of sports development by means of new equipment.

As Whitson and Macintosh (1993) and Whitson and Horne (2006) discussed, local politicians and businessmen are the typical applicants for a mega sporting event bid in order to re-route federal funding to the local region for new infrastructure, which can include sports facilities, roads, and new transportation means (e.g. airport, metros, or light rail/bullet train systems).

It is important to note that (new) sports facilities are critical as they are argued to be the base of sports development. More precisely, infrastructure is a limiting factor in sports development. There are only so many diving boards available for divers, so many spaces on an ice surface for figure skaters, so many football (soccer to North Americans) fields for teams to play on, so many ski hills for skiers, and so on. By increasing the number of these diving boards, ice surfaces, football fields, and ski hills, it is believed there will be a higher number of participants in the various sports because of the increased maximum capacity. At least, that is what many governments, such as the Canadian government, believe when they create their national sport policies and programmes. In fact, one of the four pillars of the Canadian sport policy is increased capacity, a major part of which is infrastructure.

However, these facilities must be built somewhere. When a region obtains a mega sporting event, construction and housing costs inevitably rise. In a bid to keep costs to a manageable level, organizing committees find less desirable locations, which are typically downtown but in low-income or rundown areas or on the outskirts of the city – a less appealing alternative as most international federations put a premium on bids where the event sites are in close proximity, not two hours away from the athletes' village. While the construction of new facilities in rundown areas of a city may 'beautify' the city, it also causes displacement of low-income residents, who then have a very hard time finding affordable housing (which is often on the outskirts of the city or in another town).

Activists aware of this potential issue can, if they become well organized, have a significant (negative) impact on a local bid for an event, as was the case for Toronto, Canada's bid for the 2000 Summer Olympic Games. The activist group, Bread Not Circuses Coalition, was opposed to Toronto's plans to revitalize the port area, which was a low-income area. The group's vocal opposition painted a negative image of the city and negatively impacted the bid – it was given to Sydney, Australia. See Lenskyj's (2000) book for more information on this topic.

Another negative impact related to infrastructure is that the infrastructure will likely become a so-called white elephant. What is a white elephant? Essentially, big empty facilities due to a lack of usage and/or high maintenance costs. As case study 7.2 demonstrates, the 1976 Montreal Summer Olympic Games became a victim of the white elephant syndrome. But they are not the only ones. The main stadium in Athens built for the 2004 Summer Olympic Games is falling into disrepair for lack of use and high maintenance costs. Also, Whitson and Horne (2006) discussed how the facilities of the 1998 Nagano Olympic Games and the 2002 Japan (and Korea) World Cup are being poorly used in Japan. If they are being used, it is not for sports development (i.e. youth programmes, amateur sports clubs/teams/organizations, the general public's use) but for professional sports, concerts/shows, and one-off events.

Infrastructure-based sports development associated changes fit with Mintzberg's (2006) indigenous and planned development approaches. More precisely, local businesspeople may want to help build their community to see new facilities and infrastructure (i.e. indigenous) but politicians are needed to approve the bid plans and make them fit with the region's existing infrastructure plans. However, infrastructure specifics are also partly determined by the existing global development trends, such as what the latest public expectations are (e.g., disability access, environmentally-friendly buildings, wireless internet capability, etc.), what the latest technology available is, and what the current global economic situation is (i.e. good economic situation = spending favourable for new infrastructure; bad economic situation = unlikely spending on new infrastructure; capitalist or private funding versus state funding and direction; etc.).

Infrastructure-based sports development changes are mainly impacted by institutional or regulative dynamics (e.g., the laws and policies of the land, the technical requirements of the international federations involved, and the wishes of the politicians and regulatory agencies in place) (see Marquis et al., 2007) and environmental dynamics (see Bies et al., 2007):

- Local, national, and global economic situation;
- Feelings of the various stakeholders (e.g., international sport federations, general public, sponsors, governments) in terms of the current use of infrastructure built for previous editions of an event so as to avoid the white elephants;
- Natural environment considerations (i.e. being environmentally friendly); and
- Socio-cultural, demographic dynamics (e.g., is the population ageing, is it mainly low-income, what are the residents' general and physical activity spending habits, etc.).

Table 7.1 provides a summary of the infrastructure-based positive and negative sports development impacts from mega sporting events, as well as the social change dynamics and the development type.

Policy/Planning-Based Changes

For people to use their new-found skills, for youth to be able to use equipment given to them through the legacy of a mega sporting event, policies and programmes must be put into place. This is typically done by local/municipal, regional/state and federal governments, and/or by NSOs. Ideally, NSOs bid for mega sporting events when it is strategic, i.e. they've planned for it; there is a fit between their goals and the hosting of the mega sporting event (Parent & Séguin, 2007). At the same time, governments and NSOs hopefully learn from their experiences with the mega sporting events in which they are involved, and use that knowledge and the opportunities brought about by the hosting of a mega sporting events (notably the possible increase in participation in the sport(s) showcased) to further sports development through the creation of policies and strategic plans. As the UK Sport's major events policy noted, "Sport organisations also benefit from increased exposure and influence and experience increased participation in their sport" (UK Sport, 1999, p. 3). For example, many countries and NSOs create various sports development and performance programmes when they find out they will host an Olympic Games. Likewise, governments will often create or modify their sport and/or event hosting policy not long after a mega sporting event was hosted on their soil.

For example, the United Kingdom focused its major policy efforts on sports development starting with its 1999 major events policy, which was followed by the hosting of the 2002 Manchester Commonwealth Games. A national framework for England was created in 2004 (Sport England, 2004). At the same time, sports development became a cornerstone of the 2012 London Olympic Games. Sustaining the legacies brought about by the 2002 Manchester Commonwealth Games and the 2012 Olympic Games (notably related to the sports development) has been on the minds of organizers and policy makers (i.e. governments and NSOs) since 2001 – thus well before 2012 – with reports such as those by Brown and Massey (2001), Coalter (2002), PriceWaterhouseCoopers (2005), and Sport England (2005).

With these various policies, programmes, and reports, the aim is typically to assist sports development in one form or another (e.g. increased grassroots participation, increased infrastructure and coaching capacity, and/or increased high performance sports). One incarnation of the resulting sports development is the creation of long-term athlete development models (see, for example, Balyi and Hamilton, 2004). Another incarnation is the gearing up for future mega sporting events. More precisely, knowledge and experience gained during one mega sporting event, as well as the policies and programmes created as a consequence of this knowledge/experience, 'trickle down' to the next mega sporting event hosted in the country so as to (i) not make the same mistakes as the previous event; and (ii) to build upon or bring the (in this case) sports development efforts to the next level, to keep the momentum going, so to speak. Thus, what the government and NSOs learned from the 2002 Manchester Commonwealth Games can be applied to the 2012 London Olympic Games.

While governments and NSOs are well-intentioned in the beginning and start creating programmes to promote sports and to increase sports participation/development when they obtain the right to host a mega sporting event, they often find themselves putting these plans on the shelf as their time and effort is re-directed to actually hosting the event. Governments are known for commissioning reports on 'hot topics' (e.g. the environment, poverty, healthcare, sport) only to shelve these reports (not put the plans into action) as their attention has been diverted to the next hot topic. This diversion can be unintentional; it is hard to plan 5, 7, 10, 12, or 20 years in advance as there will be changes in government, changes in global economic trends, environmental catastrophes, wars, etc., which all impact government policies and funding. Since NSOs are often dependent on government funding, these diversions also impact their plans.

One issue you should ponder is the complex network of stakeholders involved in creating and successfully implementing sports development policies and programs. There are governments (municipal, regional, and federal), sport organizations (municipal, regional, and national), sponsors, residents (for their support for and participation in sports development initiatives), coaches, officials/judges, and medical staff (i.e. massage and athletic therapists, psychologists, nutritionists, trainers, etc.) to consider. These individuals and groups cannot operate without proper equipment, facilities, and funding. As well, these individuals and groups each have their own policies, priorities, needs and wants. With public funding being decreased, individuals and organizations are forming coalitions so as to be in a stronger position in relation to influencing mega sporting events' legacy choices in favour of sports development. For example, on 23 May 2007, 70 participants from 37 different Canadian public, private, and non-profit organizations came together under the banner of the Public Policy Forum to discuss ways to promote sport and physical activity (i.e. sports development) in Canada with the opportunities presented by the hosting of the 2010 Vancouver-Whistler Olympic Games (Côté et al., 2007). The next steps will be to build, manage and sustain the various linkages needed to foster sports development in Canada. Case study 7.3 provides an overview of the evolution of sports development initiatives in relation to mega sporting events in Canada.

Policy/planning-based sports development changes are related to institutional and environmental dynamics (see Bies et al., 2007). These include (Marquis et al., 2007):

- Cultural cognitive dynamics: local, regional, national frames of references, ideologies (i.e. to what extent is sports development important to the local populace?);

- Social normative dynamics: linkages between public, non-profit, and for-profit organizations (e.g., are there government-NSO links, are there policy coalitions, is the for-profit sector willing to participate?);

- Regulative dynamics: the laws and policies of the land, sports development technical requirements of the international federations involved, and the wishes of the politicians and regulatory agencies in place.

Thus, Policy/planning-based sports development changes are planned development by their nature, with some global development as sports development policies and planning initiatives will partly be determined by the success/failure of past local and international mega sporting events and by the general global situation (cf. Mintzberg, 2006).

Table 7.1 provides a summary of the policy/planning-based positive and negative sports development impacts from mega sporting events, as well as the social change dynamics and the development type.

Mega-Sporting Events and Sports Development Managers

The purpose of this chapter was to describe sports development as social change within the context of mega sporting events. As we have seen, there are three main types of changes, each having positive and negative impacts:

1. Individual-based changes:
   (a) Positive impacts: volunteer/staff knowledge and skill development, networking and other social benefits, athletes/coaches/officials' development
   (b) Negative impacts: burnout post-event and resulting loss of knowledge in sport system, post-event bust, other countries benefiting more than host country
2. Infrastructure-based changes:
   (a) Positive impacts: increased capacity in terms of equipment and facilities
   (b) Negative impacts: displacement of low-income individuals, white elephant
3. Policy/planning-based changes:
   (a) Positive impacts: creation of policies and strategic plans by governments and NSOs, trickle-down effect for future events
   (b) Negative impacts: government/NSO short attention span and funding diversion post-event

By their very nature, these sports development-related changes are evolutionary in nature, they take time to accomplish. Mega sporting event sports development changes are influenced by individual, interpersonal, institutional, and environmental dynamics, and they can be indigenous, planned, and/or global development.

Given this information, what should sports development managers know? First, managers need to look at all three types of changes and strike a balance between expectations and what can realistically be done in order to avoid (as much as possible) the negative impacts, as well as ensuring that all three types are considered for true sports development at multiple levels. Of note, policy/

planning-based changes should incorporate individual- and infrastructure-based changes to be effective.

Second, it is important to remember that planning and implementing sports development-related changes needs to be done from the bid stage of an event, and even before a bid is prepared – as in the case of the 2012 London Olympic Games – and then consistently followed through upon for a truly lasting impact.

Third, both formal and informal policies and programmes can be created for sports development. While governments tend to formalize everything (if it isn't formalized, they probably won't do anything about it), this can cause unnecessary bureaucracy thereby pulling funding, effort, and time away from the actual sports development. Sometimes, a more informal approach – as in the case of Québec's B2010 group (see case study 7.3) – is more effective.

Fourth, sports development stemming from mega sporting events will most likely include volunteers in some capacity or another, especially since most sport programmes, as well as mega sporting events, are run largely by volunteers. It is therefore essential to consider their needs and wants (e.g. volunteer motivations are different than paid employees), to recruit and train them properly, to motivate them throughout, and to reward them (see Brown and Massey, 2001; Chelladurai, 1999).

Fifth, as mega sporting events are extremely complex enterprises, it is essential to properly coordinate the efforts of all key stakeholders involved, especially if you must prepare sports development-related changes during the bid stage, have both formal and informal policies and programs, and focus on volunteers to assist in the delivery of the event and sports development initiatives.

Finally, and perhaps most importantly, the sports development programs and policies related to mega sporting events should be based out of experience within the country, in other countries, and be assisted by sound research. NSO and local club managers, as well as policy makers, are encouraged to go to academic and professional conferences, to build contacts in other organizations and fields (Slack, 2007), to create a network of interested individuals and organizations (as the Public Policy Forum did in Canada) so that a concerted effort is made for effective and efficient sports development resulting from the bidding, preparation, and hosting of mega sporting events. These networking efforts should be made the moment interest is expressed to bid for a mega sporting event. The leading organization (typically the NSO or government holding the right to bid for the mega sporting event) should co-opt various individuals and organizations at all levels to build a network of actors interested in sports development initiatives stemming from the mega sporting event. Plans resulting from this network can then be incorporated into the bid plan, which will only serve to strengthen the bid, especially in the case of Olympic Games and the World Cup. However, it is important that a firm and formal commitment is made by all interested parties (e.g., multi-party agreement or MPA) to see the plans through to execution, regardless of the success of the bid–the hardest part is often creating the linkages and initiating the plans, so the mega sporting event is, in essence, only the catalyst for the efforts.

Questions

1. Describe the different types of sports development changes brought about by mega sporting events?

2. Who (in terms of individuals and organizations) is usually involved in sports development initiatives stemming from mega sporting events? Who should be involved?

3. Compare the following foundations of mega sporting events in terms of their impact on sports development:
   (a) the 1984 Los Angeles Summer Olympic Games' Amateur Athletic Foundation (http://www.aafla.org/index.html)
   (b) the 1988 Calgary Winter Olympic Games' Calgary Olympic Development Association (http://www.canadaolympicpark.ca/CODA/index.html)
   (c) the 2002 Manchester Commonwealth Games' sportdevelopment.org.uk (http://www.sportdevelopment.org.uk/index.html)

4. Determine what existing foundations have been able to undertake in terms of sports development related to mega sporting events (see question 3) and then critically analyze what the 2010 Vancouver-Whistler Winter Olympic Games (http://www.2010legaciesnow.com/content/home.asp), the 2012 London Summer Olympic Games (http://www.alastinglegacy.co.uk/), and the current Olympic Games bids are planning to do in terms of sports development.

5. Compare different tiers of sporting events   (i.e. regional, national, international, and mega) for their impact on sports development. Do smaller or larger sporting events have a greater impact on sports development, why?

6. Read case study 7.3. Compare the Canadian experience with another country's (e.g., the U.K., Australia, or China)?

7. Given that there are sports development opportunities when hosting a mega sporting event, do you believe that the state (government) should assist in the financing of the event or should the event be fully financed through private means? Why or why not?

8. What ought to be sport event researchers' role in fostering sports development stemming from mega sporting events? What should the sport event manager's role be?

References

Aguilera, R.V., Rupp, D.E., Williams, C.A., and Ganapathi, J. (2007). Putting the S back in corporate social responsibility: A multilevel theory of social change in organizations. *Academy of Management Review*, **32**(3), 836–63.

Balyi, I. and Hamilton, A. (2004). Long-term athlete development: Trainability in childhood and adolescence. *Windows of Opportunity, Optimal Trainability*. Victoria, Canada: National Coaching Institute British Columbia & Advanced Training and Performance Ltd.

Bies, R.J., Bartunek, J.M., Fort, T.L., and Zald, M.N. (2007). Corporations as social change agents: Individual, interpersonal, institutional, and environmental dynamics. *Academy Management Review*, **32**(3), 788–93.

Brown, A. and Massey, J. (2001). *Literature Review: The Impact of Major Sporting Events* (Report). Manchester, England: Manchester Institute for Popular Culture, Manchester Metropolitan University.

Chelladurai, P. (1999). *Human Resource Management in Sport and Recreation*. Champaign, IL: Human Kinetics.

Chelladurai, P. (2005). *Managing Organizations for Sport and Physical Activity* (2nd ed.). Scottsdale, AZ: Holcomb Hathaway, Publishers.

Clegg, S., Hardy, C., and Nord, W. R. (eds.) (1996). *Handbook of Organization Studies*. Thousand Oaks, CA: Sage.

Coalter, F. (2002). *Sport and Community Development: A manual* (No. 86). Edinburg, Scotland: sportscotland.

Côté, A., Elliott, J., and Leblanc, M. (2007). Making connections and broadening horizons. *The place of sport and physical activity in Canada: Exploring the potential for a broader contribution*. Ottawa, Canada: Public Policy Forum.

Freeman, R.E. (1984). *Strategic Management: A Stakeholder Approach*. Boston, MA: Pitman.

Getz, D. (2005). *Event Management & Event Tourism* (2nd ed.). Elmsford, NY: Cognizant Communication Corp.

Greenwood, R. and Hinings, C.R. (1996). Understanding radical organizational change: Bringing together the old and the new institutionalism. *Academy of Management Review*, **21**(4), 1022–54.

Henry, I.P. (1999). Globalisation and the governance of leisure: The roles of the nation-state, the European Union and the city in leisure policy in Britain. *Sport and Leisure*, **22**, 355–79.

Hinings, C.R. and Greenwood, R. (2002). Disconnects and consequences in organization theory. *Administrative Science Quarterly*, **47**, 411–21.

King, F.W. (1991). *It's how you play the game: The inside story of the Calgary Olympics*. Calgary, Canada: Script: the writers' group, Inc.

Lenskyj, H.J. (1996). When winners are losers: Toronto and Sydney bids for the summer Olympics. *Journal of Sport & Social Issues*, **20**(4), 392–410.

Lenskyj, H.J. (2000). *Inside the Olympic industry: Power, politics and activism*. Albany, NY: State University of New York Press.

Marquis, C. Glynn, M.A., and Davis, G.F. (2007). Community isomorphism and corporate social action. *Academy Management Review*, **32**(3), 925–45.

McGeoch, R. (1994). *The Bid: How Australia won the 2000 Games*. Port Melbourne, Australia: William Heinemann Australia.

Mintzberg, H. (2006). *Developing Leaders? Developing Countries? Development in Practice*, **16**(1), 4–14.

Parent, M.M. (2005). *Large-scale Sporting Events: Organizing Committees and Stakeholders*. Unpublished doctoral thesis, University of Alberta, Edmonton, Alberta, Canada.

Parent, M.M. (2006). Organization theory in sport management. In *Management du Sport: Actualités de la recherche et perspectives* (P. Bouchet & C. Pigeassou (eds.), (pp. 211–25). Clapiers, France: AFRAPS.

Parent, M.M. and Foreman, P.O. (2007). Organizational image and identity management in large-scale sporting events. *Journal of Sport Management*, **21**(1), 15–40.

Parent, M.M. and Séguin, B. (2007). Factors that led to the drowning of a world championship organizing committee: A stakeholder approach. *European Sport Management Quarterly*, **7**(2), 187–212.

PriceWaterhouseCoopers. (2005). *Olympic Games Impact Study: Final report*. London, UK: PriceWaterhouseCoopers LLP.

Pugh, D.S. and Hickson, D.J. (2007). *Writers on Organizations* (6th ed.). Thousand Oaks, CA: SAGE Publications.

Ritchie, J.R.B. (1984). Assessing the impact of hallmark events: Conceptual and research issues. *Journal of Travel Research*, **23**(1), 2–11.

Romney, M. (2004). *Turnaround: Crisis, Leadership, and the Olympic Games*. Washington, DC: Regnery Publishing, Inc.

Slack, T. (2007, June 8). *Evolution of the Academic Field of Sport Management, Current Trends, and Future Directions*. Paper presented at the 2nd World Congress in Sport Management, Sparta, Greece.

Sport England. (2004). *The Framework for Sport in England*. London, England: Sport England.

Sport England. (2005). *Sport Playing It's Part: The Contribution of Sport to Community Priorities and The improvement Agenda*. London, UK: Sport England.

UK Sport. (1999). *Major Events – A UK Policy. A 'BLUEPRINT' for Success*. London, UK: UK Sport.

Whitson, D. and Horne, J. (2006). Underestimating costs and overestimating benefits? Comparing outcomes of sports mega-events in Canada and Japan. *The Sociological Review*, **54**(s2), 71–89.

Whitson, D. and Macintosh, D. (1993). Becoming a world-class city: Hallmark events and sport franchises in the growth strategies of Western Canadian cities. *Sociology of Sport Journal*, **10**(3), 221–40.

Whitson, D. and Macintosh, D. (1996). The global circus: International sport, tourism, and the marketing of cities. *Journal of Sport and Social Issues*, **20**(3), 278–95.

Yarbrough, C.R. (2000). *And They Call Them Games: An Inside View of the 1996 Olympics*. Macon, GA: Mercer University Press.

CHAPTER 8

Youth Culture and Sports Development

Laura Hills

Introduction

This chapter explores the relationships between young people's identities and sporting cultures and considers the implications for managing sports development. Often, sports development planning is situated in relation to the agenda of a particular agency or organisation. This chapter focuses on the relationship between young people's interests and identities and the aims of sports development as a process of social and individual change. An exploration of key concepts from youth culture and sport sociology including identity, agency, resistance, and power are used to explore youth sport contexts. In addition, the interworking of gender, class, ethnicity, and sexuality is explored in relation to how young people experience sport and define themselves. Conceptualising young people's identities and sports participation as intricately linked to broader social and cultural institutions, discourses, and practices underpins the discussion.

Current British government policies, as indeed those of other governments (Slack and Parent, 2007), link sports participation to a range of positive outcomes relating to youth development, including physical health, psychological well-being, crime reduction, reduction of truancy and disaffection, academic achievement, social inclusion, and social responsibility (Sport England, 2006; World Health Organisation, 2003; Youth Matters, 2006). In addition, youth-centred policymakers and agencies have highlighted the potential of sport to assist in the fulfilment of their goals for the development and empowerment of young people. Increasingly, agencies in the voluntary and community sector are adopting sport as a method for delivering youth work objectives from raising self-esteem to increasing social cohesion (Positive Futures, 2006; Sport England, 2006; Youth Matters, 2006). For example, the Youth Green Paper (Youth Matters, 2006) specifically addresses the need for Local Authorities to provide young people with access to sporting activities as part of the planning for youth services. Similarly, the Education and Inspections Act 2006 requires Local Authorities to provide positive activities for young people and recommends access to two hours per week of sporting activity as well as recreational, cultural, and sporting experiences. Underpinning these policies is a belief that sports participation represents a positive activity for young people that enhances their development, brings about social and personal change, and in turn, contributes to the overall well-being of society.

The strength of the relationship between young people's development and sport experiences has roots in both the youth work sector and the development of sporting programmes for young people in schools and through clubs. Early youth-centred organisations such as the YMCA and the Boy Scouts featured sports activities within their programmes. In addition, schools offered sports for young people as one way of developing desirable qualities around health, leadership, teamwork, and character. The conceptualisation of sport as one way of instilling desirable traits in young people rests in part on an understanding of sport as a component in the process of socialisation, which is akin to a process of change.

Views of young people's experiences that are founded on consensus perspectives tend to focus on the ways that they are socialised into the norms and values of society. From this perspective, sport functions as one of many social institutions designed to teach young people values and skills that will lead them to become contributing members of society. Current British government policies about sport in the community often reflect this functional aspect of sport as contributing to the broader social good. While the understanding of sport as an influential institution that may be of central importance to young people's development remains, there have been many challenges to consensus perspectives both in relation to young people's development and with respect to sporting practices. For example, it seems apparent that young people do not simply absorb and assimilate social norms and values nor do they adopt ascribed social identities. The processes of young people's interpretation, negotiation, and construction of experience and identity in relation to broader social influences are integral to understanding development. The focus on shared values and norms can also prove misleading and may serve to minimise the impact of differences between individuals, the presence of inequalities, the agency of young people, and the processes of social change.

A key issue in delivering inclusive, sustainable programmes is the potential to engage with young people in the context of their social worlds and with respect to their needs, aspirations, and concerns (Hellison, D., Cutforth, N., Kallusky, J., Martinek, T., Parker, M., and Stiehl, J., 2000). Coakley (2002) has highlighted the importance of considering the impact of youth sport on broader communities and on wider social problems. And Lawson (2005) suggests that there is a need to consider empowerment as collective and social rather than simply as an individual goal. This suggests that managers need to place their consideration of potential individual positive outcomes associated with sports participation within the social context in which they are working (Donnelly and Coakley, 2002). In addition, it highlights the need to develop strategies that allow for collaboration with young people. The needs and goals of policymakers, coaches, youth workers, and teachers, therefore, must be balanced with attention to the perceptions and experiences of young people. A critical approach to understanding sporting environments as both reflecting and shaping broader social issues and practices underpins the creation of more inclusive programmes.

With respect to these issues, academics have urged critical reflection on the link between programme planning and expected outcomes. As Lawson (2005) cautions, 'If you want SEPE [sport, exercise, and physical education] professionals and their programs and practices to empower people and contribute to community development, you'll have to design them accordingly' (p. 158). For example, if a manager wishes to provide an inclusive programme that addresses issues of inequality, the programme must be designed in a particular way with specific forms of recruitment strategies. This requires sensitivity to community needs and a strategy for insuring that equitable processes and practices are in place. Sporting practices cannot be assumed to serve as a pro-social mechanism for youth development and, therefore, there is a need for critical analysis of all phases of programme planning, processes, and practices. This chapter explores insights from research on youth culture and sports in order to identify potential issues that may assist in the development and delivery of youth sport. This is in part founded on exploring contemporary understandings of youth as well as the complex ways that young people negotiate their identities in relation to sporting practices and broader social norms and values. Developing meaningful, inclusive, and sustainable sports programmes is integrally tied to the experiences and perceptions of young people and the relationships between youth, sport, culture, and identity.

Understanding Youth Culture

Youth can be defined as a socially constructed component of the lifespan positioned between childhood and adulthood. This definition emphasises understanding youth as having social and cultural components as well as biological aspects. The concept of youth culture was initially developed in light of social changes occurring in the 1950s and refers to the way in which people within the age span of youth 'develop distinct patterns of life, and give expressive form to their social and material life experiences' (Muggleton, 2005, p. 206; Hall and Jefferson, 1976). Defining features of youth culture from its inception involved social phenomena such as music, clothing, hair styles, films, and magazines. The meaning of youth has changed since the 1950s to encompass a longer and less clearly defined age bracket. The complexities of modern society have meant that it is more challenging for young people to define themselves and their plans for adult life. According to Furlong and Cartmel (1997), young people face new challenges and opportunities characterised by the weakening of traditional ties between family, school, and work. They also suggest that the appearance of greater opportunities and choices has made continuing social inequalities more difficult to detect and address. Young people tend to view themselves primarily as individuals rather than as part of particular groups. 'With traditional social divisions having become obscure, subjective risks stem from the perceived lack of collective traditions and security' (p. 9).One of the defining features of youth in contemporary times is this increasing individualisation (McCulloch et al., 2006).

Early conceptualisations of youth culture tended to focus on young people as a 'problem' group within society. Subsequently, the concept of subculture, which refers to groups within broader cultures that maintain some type of distinctive behaviours, values, and goals, was initially associated with delinquent or deviant youth (Muggleton, 2005). As Blackman (2005) writes, 'one interesting aspect of subcultures are the way in which they contrast with the dominant norms and values of society' (p. 2). Apparently alienated and rebellious youths who were labelled as deviant by society emerged as the focus of early work by the Chicago school in the USA. Becker's (1973) *Outsiders* provided an ethnographic account of drug use from young people's perspectives. The Chicago school moved understandings of deviance away from psychological frameworks to look at the ways that deviance made sense in relation to the norms, opportunities, and experiences of participants (Bennett and Kahn-Harris, 2004).

Work on youth subcultures in the UK was closely associated with research by the Centre for Contemporary Culture in Birmingham (CCCS). Although there has been some rethinking of their early work, the Centre provided frameworks that underpin much subsequent research on youth cultures and subcultures most notably through the influential collection *Resistance Through Ritual: Youth Subcultures in Postwar Britain*. Work by members of the CCCS emphasised class as a key aspect of youth culture and the societal labelling of some youth subcultures as deviant or delinquent (Hall and Jefferson, 1976; Epstein, 1998).

Young people's resistance, therefore, was conceptualised in part as resistance to dominant, hegemonic culture. However, much of the CCCS work questioned the efficacy of the resistant practices engaged in by young people (Epstein, 1998; Muggleston, 2005). For example, in *Learning to Labour*, Willis (1977) identified the ways that working class adolescent male culture adopted an anti-school stance, rejected middle-class culture, and espoused values of toughness, masculinity, and the workplace. The boys' resistance to hegemonic practices ultimately re-inscribed and reinforced their working class positioning. This perspective on subcultures suggested that while on the surface young people's practices appeared to challenge the imposition of dominant values, their activities ultimately proved to be 'imaginary solutions that failed to address economic imbalances or the prevailing social order' (Muggleston, p. 209). Key ideas emerging from the CCCS consist of the centrality of class in youth culture, the analysis of resistance, the tension between mediated youth cultures and young people's experiences, and the potential gap between youth subcultural values and dominant norms.

Critics of the CCCS have questioned the importance of class over and above other aspects of social identity, have challenged the usefulness of conceptualising subcultures as cohesive groups with shared identities situated in opposition to the mainstream culture, and have contended that a focus on spectacular youth cultures has ignored more typical adolescent experiences. Contemporary work has conceptualised youth culture as 'more fleeting, transitional and organised around individual lifestyle and consumption choices' (Shildrick, 2006, p. 63). This is perhaps most evident in recent work on dance and club cultures that demonstrates the diverse identifications of many young people and the potential for memberships in different groups. In addition, contemporary youth cultures are thought to incorporate more diverse groupings of young people of differing gender, sexuality, race, and class (Shildrick, 2006). Bennett and Kahn-Harris (2004) suggest that Maffesoli's concept of neo-tribes is a useful way to describe contemporary youth cultures which appear more fragmented, fluid, and arbitrary. Individuals may move between groups that temporarily come together to listen to music, relax, and socialise. Young people appear to have more choices and may have membership in various groups and experiment with adopting and changing styles.

Thornton (1995), extending Bourdieu's concept of capital (discussed below), has proposed that young people develop their own markers of status that relate to particular features of subcultures, which she labels subcultural capital or 'hipness'. For young people, subcultural capital may relate to awareness of current slang, listening to the right music, and wearing appropriate clothing. The development of capital within subcultures may partially be in response to or resistant to expressions of capital in dominant cultures. In contrast to Bourdieu (1979), Thornton suggests that subcultural capital is less identified with class-based preferences as it operates outside of official institutions such as the education system. Although Thorton's work has been challenged by postsubcultural theorists as conceptualising subcultures as having identifiable boundaries, her work helps to conceive of ways that young people act as active and creative agents. Subcultural and postsubcultural researchers have sought to try to gain understandings of youth culture from the perspectives of young people and have subsequently tended to employ qualitative methods and draw on a range of theoretical perspectives to explore young people's fluid and even fragmented forms of culture.

While postsubcultural thinking has helped to challenge conceptualisations of monolithic subcultural identities and to provide more inclusive definitions of youth culture, there is a danger of ignoring ongoing considerations of the relationships between inequality and identity. Muggleston (2005) suggests that this is 'especially important within the contested contexts of multiculturalism' (p. 216). Young people's social identities continue to influence how they define themselves, how they identify their desires and aspirations, and how they can acquire and utilise various forms of capital within society. For example, McCulloch et al. (2006) demonstrate the continuing influence of class on young people's subcultural choices. In their study, young people who labelled themselves as Chavs had a particular affiliation with their class background. Assumptions of individual choice can minimise understandings of the ways that social and cultural practices and discourses around gender, class, ethnicity, and sexuality can perpetuate inequalities and limit opportunities for some. Cultures remain sites of struggle and the meaning and impact of social identities can be challenged, resisted, and transformed as well as re-inscribed.

One of the most productive ways of exploring the relationship between subjectivity and social structures is evidenced in the work of Bourdieu (1979, 1980; Bourdieu and Wacquant, 1992). His concepts have been applied to the contexts of sport and education and can help illuminate the ways that social influences impact individual choices, tastes, and aspirations. Although cultural studies academics have widely used Bourdieu's work, it is important to recognise that he did not consider his work to be consonant with those perspectives (McRobbie, 2005). Bourdieu (1977) explores the ways that individuals influence and are influenced by social and cultural discourses and practices. He defines the concept of 'habitus' as 'systems of durable, transposable dispositions' that structure action and thought (p. 72). Habitus develops through experience, early socialisation, engagement with social structures, and shapes how individuals understand their social world. The habitus is developed in conjunction with an individual's social context and subsequently has a tendency to reinforce the social order. The concept of habitus helps to explain how males and females may develop socially prescribed behaviours and attitudes consistent with traditional understandings of gender.

Bourdieu's concepts of social and cultural capital have been widely used in relation to sports involvement. Connolly (1998) outlines Bourdieu's concept of capital as the:

> Range of scarce goods and resources which lie at the heart of social relations. The struggles over such resources provide the main dynamic through which social stratification and change can be understood....Acquisition of one or more of these types of capital enables individuals to gain power and status within society. (p. 20)

Cultural capital refers to knowledge that confers social status. This is typically acquired through upbringing and education while social capital involves the ability of an individual to draw on connections and to be involved in desirable social networks. Bourdieu suggests that an individual's social class may determine their taste for a particular sport. For example, playing golf is associated with a particular form of dress and etiquette that can be linked to the middle class. Individuals who have the appropriate cultural (and economic) capital may be able to be members of clubs where they may further develop their social capital through social networks and opportunities for developing business associations. There is, however, no direct correspondence between class and taste and the potential for change occurs between groups and over time. For example, Skeggs (1997) found that working class women adopted traditional middle class conceptualisations of the body, exercise, health, and appearance.

Bourdieu's concepts can also be used to explore the relationships between social structures and subjectivity within youth sport. For example, Light and Kirk (2000) demonstrate how a particular form of masculinity developed through the 'habitus' of High School rugby. Their findings revealed that appropriate male behaviour was embodied through physical force and intimidation. Social discourses, coaching practices, and peer relations reinforced this narrow conceptualisation of male physicality. While Bourdieu's work has been criticised by some as being over-deterministic, other theorists have recognised the potential for agency and resistance while still appreciating the influence of broader social structures and norms. Adam's chapter in this book discusses in greater detail the capacity of sport to develop social capital.

Youth Sport Cultures

Young people participate in a range of sporting activities in different contexts ranging from formal organised sport to informal self-directed activities. Young people may be training for elite level competition such as professional football careers or Olympic level competition, others are more likely to be involved in informal after school neighbourhood games, and some choose not to engage in sporting activities at all. Many young people have experienced physical education in schools and some have access to clubs, leisure centres, parks, and swimming pools. Young people experience their identities in complex ways that shape their sporting choices. Some young people may avoid identification with more mainstream sporting opportunities while others may choose to create their own sporting spaces and cultures.

Research on youth from the CCCS and their successors has paid little attention to youth sports. This may be because sport cultures have been more closely associated with dominant discourses and practices that are associated with mainstream institutions. Young people who participate in organised sport are, therefore, not seen as creating or engaging in resistant practices or adopting alternative styles or identities (Hughson et al., 2005; Wheaton, 2004). The concept of resistance has been central to understanding youth cultural practices (Epstein, 1998). Youth subcultures are not only about developing a specific group identity, they are also about rejecting hegemonic adult culture and practice (Epstein, 1998). In addition, mainstream sport is often organised and controlled by adults, which further minimises the elements of resistance and rebellion in relation to dominant cultures that is associated with subcultural organisation and practice. The role of adult leaders in managing youth sport remains a crucial element in balancing elements of freedom and control. There remains relatively little work that specifically links youth culture and sport participation in traditional sports, although more recent studies of lifestyle or alternative sports have utilised post/subcultural perspectives to explore these social worlds (Rinehart and Sydnor, 2003; Wheaton, 2004).

Traditional sporting cultures have often been viewed as embodying desirable social norms and values relating to leadership, discipline, teamwork, health, hard work, and competition. From this perspective, young people are thought to learn how to manage winning and losing and develop into responsible, contributing citizens. A number of positive outcomes have been associated with sports participation, although, as stated previously, there is still limited specific evidence about the processes through which sport can contribute to young people's development. As discussed previously, the more traditional view of the socialisation into and through sport processes emphasises the contribution of sport to society and shared social values. This view of sports involvement has been challenged in three key ways: (1) identifying the presence of negative aspects of sports involvement and sporting values; (2) highlighting inequalities around gender, ethnicity, class, religion, and dis/ability that have been associated with sporting cultures; and (3) acknowledging the agency that young people utilise to construct and shape their sport experiences and identities.

A range of academics have expressed the need for caution in making assumptions about the positive characteristics of participation in youth sport (Coakley, 2002; Ewing et al., 2002; Long and Sanderson, 2001). Fraser-Thomas et al. (2005) write that youth sport programmes are becoming 'increasingly expensive, competitive, and elitist' (p. 20). Young people's sports cultures have been associated with an overemphasis on competition and winning, emotional stresses, unhealthy practices relating to injury, doping, violence, eating disorders, and restricted opportunities for development in other areas of life (Eitzen, 1999; Gatz et al., 2002).

Research which has explored negative aspects of mainstream youth sports cultures has tended to focus on the ways that these contexts can reinforce hegemonic relations of power in society. Fine (1987) employed an interpretive, ethnographic approach to explore the sporting culture of little league baseball in the USA. He found that the prevailing culture of the young male players in the study embraced sexism, violence, and a hyper-competitive ethos which was either reinforced or ignored by the coaches. In addition, Benedict (1997) has explored the ways that male intercollegiate athletes' sporting cultures may reinforce sexist beliefs and behaviours.

One of the most influential theoretical perspectives on deviant behaviours in traditional sporting contexts was developed by Hughes and Coakley (1991). Their concept of positive deviance is employed to demonstrate how athletes and coaches who become immersed in the values and norms of traditional sporting contexts (the sports ethic) may actually be more susceptible to engaging in undesirable ways. The sports ethic involves the following four characteristics relating to being an athlete: sacrifice for The Game; seeking distinction; taking risks and challenging limits (Hughes and Coakley, 1991). Hughes and Coakley demonstrate how adopting these norms may lead athletes to engage in behaviours such as taking performance-enhancing drugs in order to increase their chances of success in sport. This concept has helped to challenge ideas about the inherent good of sports involvement and provided a basis for evaluating and re-visioning sports provision.

A further strand of research focusing on young people's sports experience is situated within the context of alternative or extreme sports. Not all young people are attracted to traditional sports environments and this may relate to their perceptions of their own identity as well as the perceived characteristics of the sports environment. Studies focusing on alternative and extreme sports have more consistently employed perspectives used to study youth sub/cultures and have explored the ways that young people interpret their activities as resistance and as contrasting with the norms and values of mainstream, organised sporting environments (Borden, 2001; Rinehart and Sydnor, 2003; Wheaton, 2004). These norms and values may include an emphasis on authenticity, creativity, self-organisation, engagement with the environment, and risk.

The boundaries between mainstream and alternative sports are often blurred. There have been a number of studies that have demonstrated how alternative and extreme sport cultures which are wrestling with new ways of constructing sports environments are heavily influenced by prevailing social structures, discourse and practices. Thornton (2004) discusses the *Ultimate ethos* of 'spirit of the game' which emphasises co-operation, trust, and sociability between teams. Competitions in Ultimate are self-officiated and decisions are arrived at through consensus. Part of the way Ultimate players represent themselves is through their dis-identifications with the norms of mainstream sport. Thornton, however, found that although participants were struggling to construct a new and egalitarian sporting culture there was evidence that they, in fact, did not really depart from or transform dominant norms and values. In addition, the entrance of snowboarding into the Olympics indicates the possibility of alternative sports to be co-opted into elite, competitive, mainstream cultures. Snowboarders competed for medals, wore uniforms, attained sponsors, and endorsed commercial products. Their alternative roots, however, were also apparent in the baggy style of uniform that appeared less sleek and efficient than the apparel of other winter sports competitors such as skiers, and the headphones and play lists that indicated they were listening to music while competing.

It is also important to consider the possibility of mainstream sports to operate as spaces where some young people can successfully negotiate identities, raise aspirations, and exercise self-determination. For example, women's participation in sport has challenged and even transformed limiting conceptualisations of women's physicality. Building up understandings of the complexity of sport environments and the meanings participants construct in relation to sporting discourses and practices can yield new insights into the potentialities of sport experience in contemporary life.

A key factor in work on youth culture is the recognition and appreciation of young people as active agents. Research on subcultures and alternative sports has demonstrated the desire that many young people have to challenge social norms and create their own spaces and practices for engaging in sport (Borden, 2001; Rinehart and Sydnor, 2003; Wheaton, 2004). This suggests that adult sports leaders need to consider ways to allow young people to be involved in decision-making and to develop a sense of ownership with respect to their sporting choices.

Depending on the nature of the programme, this may involve providing facilities and resources for young people to develop their own programmes in addition to more adult-centred, traditional sport settings. Within any setting, however, young people will benefit from having input. Wilson and White (2003) explore the ways that young people who were 'provided' with freedom and responsibility in a drop in recreation centre 'colonised the social space', negotiated with adult leaders, and developed their own 'unofficial' peer culture that maintained 'order and relative peace' (p. 171). In contrast, Clarke (2003) discusses the failure of a youth sport programme that did not take account of a range of perceived barriers that could have been addressed through consultation in the planning stages of the programme. Long and Sanderson (2001) also assert that self-determination and control over resources are two key elements of successful sports development programmes. Control over resources represents a particular challenge to providers, but, as Long and Sanderson state, it can ameliorate the sense of top-down delivery to community groups.

Weller (2006) draws on the concept of social capital to discuss ways that adults can work with young people to facilitate their ability to create and develop sporting opportunities that prioritise young people's sense of ownership and sense of community involvement. She documents the case of teenagers deploying social and cultural capital developed through family connections and social networks in order to raise money to maintain and improve a local skate park as well as to raise awareness through a related website. Her findings highlight the possibilities for youth workers, sports development managers, parents, and schools to encourage, support, and assist in young people's capacity to make use of social capital. Weller also addresses the importance of developing projects designed to engage young people in ways that emphasise the sharing of resources, knowledge, and networks.

With respect to young people, sociologists have explored the routes through which young people become involved in sport and the experiences that occur within sporting contexts. More recently, the ways that young people influence and exercise agency within sport environments has become a topic of interest (Donnelly and Coakley, 2002; Weller, 2006). Getting young people involved and committed to youth sports programmes may involve attention to the ways in which young people interact with each other within particular sporting spaces and communities. The role of space in sports development is explored in more detail in Chapter 9. Within the context of sports development programmes, understanding the impact of social institutions, discourses, and practices on individual choices and the development of particular norms and values can be balanced with attention to the processes of negotiation, change, and resistance that also occur.

Addressing Youth Identity and Inequality Through Sport

Youth sports cultures continue to be locations where young people negotiate and construct their social identities. As Sarup (1996) observes, there has been a shift in ways of thinking about identity and the self. In contrast to the idea that people have a coherent, fixed identity, 'the more recent view is that identity is fabricated, constructed, in process' (p. 14). Engagement with sport is one of the processes through which young people's identities come into being. A classic study by Coakley and White (1992) suggests that young people's activity choices relate to the way they view themselves and their relation to the social world. A key component of this is young people's perceptions of social identities and the subsequent impact on sporting choices. Gender, race, ethnicity, and class represent key social identities where struggles between structure and agency occur. These identities can have great influence as they are ascribed and demarcated within social structures. However, the notion of ascription may be misleading as it is essential to be aware of the different ways that members of particular social groups adapt, resist, negotiate, and embody available social identities.

Feminist and Neo-Marxist perspectives, among others, have been employed to demonstrate the ways that sporting institutions and practices support traditional hegemonic power relations and to illustrate the tendency of sports organisations to reinforce the status quo. Many of the practices that occur in sport may be viewed as commonsense rather than as inequitable or problematic. For example, it may seem normal for physical educators to provide boys and girls with a different curriculum. So activities such as cricket, football, and rugby may be perceived as more suitable for boys, while netball, hockey, and gymnastics may be associated with girls. These types of binary gender-based practices tend to reinforce particular understandings of masculinity and femininity and often accentuate differences between boys and girls. They may also mask the reality that many girls and boys enjoy participating in sports that may not be historically associated with their gender. It is important to be able to identify and reflect on ways that social identities can influence participation choices and experiences and the possible ways that young people's opportunities may be limited through the perpetuation of social stereotypes. Thomson (2007) suggests that it is critical for young people to be able to discuss the ramifications of these pre-formed identities and the underlying power struggles and inequalities publicly.

Social identities are often addressed in isolation in order to illuminate particular issues or challenges and as a basis for social change; however, individuals embody a range of intersecting identities. Collins (1999) employs intersectionality as an analytical framework that takes into account the complex interplay between and among social categories:

> The logic of intersectionality references two types of relationships: the interconnectedness of ideas and the social structures in which they occur and the intersecting hierarchies of gender, race, economic class, sexuality, and ethnicity. (p. 263)

Identity can be conceptualised as interwoven threads in cloth. It is possible to identify and discuss particular threads but these threads are always part of a larger, more complex pattern. In addition, young people may interpret and experience particular identities in differing ways. Members of particular social groups will not have homogenous, readily identifiable characteristics. This suggests that there is a need to look at how young people think of and define themselves. The rest of this section discusses some of the ways that social identities may influence young people's involvement in sports. However, it is important to balance broader understandings of identity with the specific ways that particular groups of young people may interpret and act on their beliefs.

The perceived problematic relationship between physical activity and femininity has been identified as a key area of influence on girls' interpretations of their attitudes towards involvement in sports and a site of negotiation about ideas of embodied subjectivity. Physicality within the context of sport or physical activity has traditionally been associated with masculinity (Hall, 1996; Hargreaves, 1994). Within this framework, sporting success and ideal sporting bodies have been portrayed as reinforcing notions of hegemonic masculinity and perpetuating traditional gendered power relations (Connell, 1987; Hall, 1996; Messner, 1988). Some researchers have suggested that girls may, therefore, find it difficult to reconcile involvement in sports with the social and culture demands of femininity. Cockburn and Clarke (2002) found that it was difficult for girls to be able to combine an enthusiasm for sports with the demands of heterosexual femininity.

Girls and women are, however, increasingly participating in sports and identifying with their sporting interests and skills. Understanding girls' experiences, therefore, requires an appreciation of the increasingly complex relationships between physicality, femininity, and physical activity (McDermott, 1996). Jeanes' (2005) work on girls involved in football illustrates the complex negotiations that girls may undergo in relation to reconciling their sporting interests with cultural interpretations of femininity. She found that girls who played football recognised the presence of social stereotypes relating to characteristics of femininity but felt comfortable as female footballers. Girls who are less experienced or confident, however, may find challenging perceived barriers and initiating involvement in sports more threatening. A study by Hills (2006) found that some girls hid their sporting interests from their peers or withdrew from participation due to concerns that their friends would disapprove or that they would fail to present an appropriate form of femininity. The influence of peer and other social networks combines with cultural constructs of femininity to impact girls' decisions. These issues are explored in more detail in the case study for this chapter. Understanding the influence of gender and other social identities on participation, therefore, requires a holistic approach that can untangle and address the complex factors that underpin activity choices.

It is clear that boys have more opportunities to participate in sports and may also find sports participation consistent with social understandings of masculinity. This can create difficulties for males who do not wish to participate in mainstream sports, who are not skilled, who have limited resources, or who do not feel comfortable with the demands of heterosexual masculinity. Connolly (1998) demonstrated the ostracising of males in primary school who did not conform to the dictates of heterosexual masculinity. Gay males may also find sporting environments to be threatening spaces. Price and Parker (2003) studied the experiences of gay male rugby players. Many of them stated that school was difficult, 'There was an awful lot of homophobia at school... I remember distinctly my Under-15 Rugby coach calling me a "poof" 'cos I put in a bad tackle....That cut quite deeply at the time' (p. 114). Post-school sport experiences varied between friendly banter and hostile homophobia and led to the formation of an out gay male team characterised by a safe, friendly environment.

Young people's experiences of gender also intersect with their negotiations with their ethnic backgrounds. A study by Spracklen (2001) demonstrates the ways that some males may be excluded from particular sporting domains. He suggests that a fictive identity of a northern rugby league player has been constructed within society. This fictive identity is part of an imagined 'white' community of rugby league players. This imagined identity fails to include or conceptualise players from other ethnicities. This represents a potent form of exclusion as it leaves little space for others to challenge or change this imagined space. Spracklen argues that 'for rugby league to be a powerful tool in developing Asian and black cultural identities in England, there has to be a significant shift of power to give Asian and Black people control over the symbolic boundaries' (p. 79).

Sporting practices may have particular meanings for young people who are members of certain ethnic groups. Werbner (2007) discusses how the experience of cricket for British Pakistani young men is saturated with communal identifications and meanings related to gender, ethnicity, and generation. 'For it is in the field of sport that young British Pakistanis express their love of both cricket and the home country, along with their sense of alienation and disaffection from British society...' (p. 312). These young men negotiated hybrid identities that influenced their sporting practices and identifications. The young men in her study had to negotiate with older males in the community in order to create changes in their cricket organisation which were at first perceived as a threat to adult authority. The self-organisation and determination of the young cricketers facilitated their ability to resist established practices and to create new traditions within their community. The space for young people's agency plays a role in their capacity to take ownership of and engage in meaningful activities.

Sports programmes designed to recruit and include particular ethnic groups require sensitivity to the needs and issues of particular groups. For example, Lowrey and Kay (2005) explored practices of inclusion in relation to the development of a programme designed to link sports participation with education goals for Bangledeshi girls. Strategies for ensuring sensitivity to community interests and beliefs formed a crucial aspect of facilitating participation in the programme. This included having a community insider involved in recruiting and delivering the activities and ongoing consultation with the families involved in order to gain their support for the programme. Awareness of the needs of particular social groups plays a key role in developing successful, inclusive programmes; however, this differs from making assumptions about the needs and interests of groups. Dwyer (1998) cautions against assumptions about what particular identities mean to young people. She writes, 'There are many different understandings of what it means to be a young British Muslim woman' (p. 51). She suggests that new ethnic identities are negotiated and constructed as individuals engage with, resist, and make sense of their social worlds.

Social class represents a potent form of exclusion in sports (Collins, 2003). Collins and Butler (2003) have provided evidence that sports programmes continue to be exclusive as young people from middle class and affluent backgrounds have much greater opportunities to participate in sport than their working-class counterparts. In addition, social class has been shown to influence perceptions of the desirability of particular sports for particular groups. Andrews et al. (2003) demonstrate how football (soccer) in the USA is coded as emblematic of middle class, white, suburban culture supporting normalised hegemonic values and lifestyles that contrast with imagined urban chaos and stereotypical black working class sporting interests.

In the UK, however, football has historical associations with working class cultures, interests, and tastes, while sports such as rugby union and cricket have been associated with middle class Englishness. Carrington and MacDonald (2001) illustrate how the institutions and practices associated with cricket are based around ideas representing traditional white middle class values and norms and may subsequently serve to exclude Black and Asian players. They detected the presence of some overt racism but primarily practices of exclusion were more hidden and embedded in cultural practices and discourses. There is also evidence that changes in the associations of cricket and Englishness are transforming: 'Many communities can lay claim to cricket being their game too, thus challenging and fragmenting any official notion of there being only one legitimate and authoritative way of playing, watching and consuming cricket' (p. 51).

These changing patterns of involvement have also been identified by Furlong and Cartmel (1997) who assert that one of the ways that youth culture is changing is through the blurring of class and gender divisions that is in part due to increased leisure time, changing peer relations and norms, and expanding opportunities to engage in a broader range of activities. Sports are one place where dominant understandings of identity are being altered, resisted, reconfigured, and reinforced. Understanding the complexity of young people's dis/identifications with sport cultures plays a key role in creating attractive, inclusive, and meaningful sport experiences and opportunities.

Many sports organisations have acknowledged the influence of social categories and adopted equal opportunities policies and anti-discriminatory practices. Hylton and Totten (2001) have identified the increased number of policies and initiatives that have developed in response to identified inequities. Researchers have developed a good understanding of the types of material barriers and constraints that may face different groups in relation to participation. However, as discussed above, there remains a need to explore more subtle forms of exclusion that occur in relation to gender, race, ethnicity, and class. This includes gaining understandings of the ways that sports cultures reproduce, as well as challenge, sexist, racist, and ablest understandings of differing social groups. Simple structural understandings of these social identities are insufficient to explain how they influence youth sport participation in practice (Collinson et al., 2005). The case study associated with this chapter presents an example of how ethnographic methods have been employed to try to gain in-depth information about the ways that identities influence girls' involvement in sports.

Changing Cultures and Identities: Implications for Sports Development Managers

There is still much work to be done in relation to understanding the processes and practices that will most effectively lead to young people's development and facilitate their involvement in sports. The social and management aspects of sport play a key role in how young people choose and experience sports programmes. Sports development programmes are clearly embedded within society and can, therefore, be conceived of as saturated with the social imprint of diverse groups and the concomitant elements of cohesion, conflict, inclusion, and exclusion. Sports environments and programmes that are delivered are necessarily imbued with gendered, raced, and classed associations and meanings. Trying to understand how inequities may be institutionalised, experienced, and practiced in both overt and more subtle, taken for granted practices is a complex process that incorporates and moves beyond an awareness of equal opportunities policies – although this is an important task for a manager – to more considered reflection on the social meanings that become constructed in sport contexts. Sports managers will, therefore, need to develop knowledge of equity policies and initiatives and be willing to reflect on and evaluate their own beliefs and practices. This may be facilitated through consultation with others and by incorporating evaluation procedures that provide qualitative information about equality and inclusion on the ground.

Young people may hold assumptions about sports involvement that are based on stereotypes, traditions, and practices that could serve to shape, facilitate, or limit their engagement in particular activities. In order to gain a sense of the influence of social 'structures' on young people's experience, it will be useful to provide opportunities to discuss potential constraints to participation. For example, girls may benefit from discussing the link between gender and sports participation, the impact of peer relations, and increasing opportunities to enjoy involvement in a wide range of activities. Young people may gain more understanding in how social identities can constrain their engagement in activities and how they challenge perceived limitations. This is part of developing strategies that will assure young people that they will be socially and emotionally safe if they try activities that are new or unfamiliar or that have particular social and cultural associations. Subsequently, sports managers will need to evidence sensitivity and empathy towards young people's perceptions of the barriers and difficulties that impact their involvement in and enjoyment of sports.

In addition, young people may need to reflect on the ways that their perceptions of gender, race, ethnicity, class, and sexuality influence their behaviour and their treatment of other people. Sport development managers have to appreciate that they are involved in the processes of facilitating social and personal change. This entails understanding, influencing, and possibly changing youth culture and identity. Managers need to be prepared to raise awareness and educate young people about how inequalities work and to employ strategies for effectively intervening when sexist, racist, and homophobic behaviours occur. As demonstrated, sports development activities often imply a reconstruction of identity. Skills in negotiation and group facilitation as well as commitment to inclusion and equality are key components of challenging disempowering, exclusive, and inequitable practices that may be part of some youth cultures.

Finally, the importance of allowing the possibility for young people to develop a sense of self-determination within sporting environments has been shown to be crucial for the development of successful programmes. Whenever possible, young people can be involved from the beginning and their input may be used to help to generate ideas about the operation of the programme. Planning programmes designed to empower young people necessitates practices that will provide them with opportunities to engage in associated activities and develop relevant qualities. Empowering practices include developing young people's capabilities, sharing power and resources, developing opportunities for collaboration, and providing opportunities for civic engagement (Lawson, 2005). Managers can foster young people's valuing of inclusive practices and can help them to acquire relevant knowledge and skill in negotiating power relations, distributing resources, and balancing needs of differing group members, developing social networks, and contributing to their community. While adult leaders have particular responsibilities related to the intentions and running of the programmes on offer, exploring ways that young people can utilise and develop their own forms of capital can help to create programmes that will facilitate their sustained involvement, aspirations, and agency.

References

Andrews, D.L., Pitter, R., Zwick, D., and Ambrose, D. (2003). Soccer, race, and suburban space. In *Sporting Dystopias* (T.C. Wilcox, D.L. Andrews, R. Pitter, and R.L. Irwin, eds). Albany, NY: State University of New York Press, pp. 197–220.

Becker, H.S. (1973). *Outsiders: Studies in the Sociology of Deviance.* New York: Free Press.

Benedict, J. (1997). *Public Heroes, Private Felons: Athletes and Crimes against Women.* Boston, MA: Northeastern University Press.

Bennett, A. and Kahn-Harris, K. (2004). *After Subculture: Critical Studies in Contemporary Youth Culture.* New York Palgrave Macmillan.

Blackman, S. (2005). Youth subcultural theory: A critical engagement with the concept, its origins and politics, from the Chicago school to postmodernism. *Journal of Youth Studies*, **8**(1), 1–20.

Borden, I. (2001). *Skateboarding, Space and the City: Architecture and the Body.* Oxford: Berg.

Bourdieu, P. (1977). *Outline of a Theory of Practice.* Cambridge: Cambridge University Press.

Bourdieu, P. (1979). *Distinction: A Social Critique of the Judgement of Taste.* London: Routledge.

Bourdieu, P. (1980). *The Logic of Practice.* Stanford, CA: Stanford University Press.

Bourdieu, P. and Wacquant, L. (1992). *An Invitation to Reflexive Sociology.* Cambridge: Polity Press.

Carrington, B. and MacDonald, I. (2001). Whose game is it anyway?: Racism in local league cricket. In *Race, Sport and British Society* (B. Carrington and I. Macdonald, eds). London: Routledge, pp. 49–69.

Clarke, M.A. (2003). Researching youth sport programmes in a metropolitan setting: Essentials of, barriers to, and policy for achieving a comprehensive programme. In *Sporting Dystopias* (T.C. Wilcox, D.L. Andrews, R. Pitter, and R.L. Irwin, eds). Albany, NY: State University of New York Press, pp. 179–95.

Coakley, J. (2002). Using sport to control deviance and violence among youths: Let's be critical and cautious. In *Paradoxes of Youth and Sport* (M. Gatz, M.A. Messner, and S.J. Ball-Rokeach, eds). New York: SUNY, pp. 13–47.

Coakley, J. and White, A. (1992). Making decisions: Gender and sport participation among british adolescents. *Sociology of Sport Journal*, **9**, 20–35.

Cockburn, C. and Clarke, G. (2002). 'Everybody's looking at you!': Girls' negotiations of the 'femininity deficit' that occurs in physical education. *Women's Studies International Forum*, **25**(6), 651–65.

Collins, P.H. (1999). Moving beyond gender: Intersectionality and scientific knowledge. In *Revisioning Gender* (M.M. Ferree, J. Lorber, and B.B. Hess, eds). London: Sage, pp. 261–84.

Collins, M. (2003).*Sport and Social Exclusion.* London: Routledge.

Collins, M. and Butler, J. (2003). Social exclusion from high-performance sport: Are all talented young sports people being given an equal opportunity of reaching the Olympic podium? *Journal of Sport & Social Issues*, **27**(4), 420–42.

Collinson, J.A., Fleming, S., Hockey, J., and Pitchford, A. (2005). Evaluating sports-based inclusion projects. In *Evaluating Sport and Active Leisure for Young People* (K. Hylton, J. Long, and A. Flintoff, eds). Leisure Studies Association, pp. 45–59.

Connell, R.W. (1987). *Gender and Power.* Stanford, CA: Stanford University Press.

Connolly, P. (1998). *Racism, Gender Identities and Young Children: Social Relations in a Multi-Ethnic Inner-city Primary School.* London: Routledge.

Donnelly, P. and Coakley, J. (2002). *The Role of Recreation in Promoting Social Inclusion.* The Laidlaw Foundation.

Dwyer, C. (1998). Contested identities: Challenging dominant representations of young British Muslim women. In *Cool Places: Geographies of Youth Culture* (T. Skelton and G.Valentine, eds). London: Routledge, pp. 50–65.

Eitzen, D.S. (1999). *Fair and Foul: Beyond the Myths and Paradoxes of Sport*. Lanham, MD: Rowman & Littlefield.

Epstein, J.S. (ed.) (1998). *Youth Culture: Identity in a Postmodern World [Introduction]*. Oxford: Blackwell.

Ewing, M.E., Gano-overway, L.A., Branta, C.F., and Seefeldt, V.D. (2002). The role of sports in youth development. In *Paradoxes of Youth and Sport* (M. Gatz, M.A. Messner, and S.J. Ball-Rokeach, eds). Albany, NY: SUNY, pp. 31–47.

Fine, G.A. (1987). *With the Boys: Little League Baseball and Preadolescent Sport*. Chicago: University of Chicago Press.

Fraser-Thomas, J.L., Cote, J., and Deakin, J. (2005). Youth sport programmes: An avenue to foster positive youth development. *Physical Education and Sport Pedagogy*, **10**, 19–40.

Furlong, A. and Cartmel, F. (1997). *Young People and Social Change*. Berkshire: Open University Press.

Gatz, M., Messner, M.A., and Ball-Rokeach, S.J. (eds). (2002). *Paradoxes of Youth and Sport*. Albany, NY: SUNY.

Hall, M.A. (1996). *Feminism and Sporting Bodies: Essays on Theory and Practice*. Champaigne: Human Kinetics.

Hall, S. and Jefferson, T. (1976). *Resistance Through Rituals: Youth Subcultures in Postwar Britain*. Hutchinson (for) the Centre for Contemporary Cultural Studies, Birmingham: University of Birmingham.

Hargreaves, J. (1994). *Sporting Females: Critical Issues in the History and Sociology of Women's Sports*. London: Routledge.

Hellison, D., Cutforth, N., Kallusky, J., Martinek, T., Parker, M., and Stiehl, J. (2000). *Youth Development and Physical Activity: Linking Universities and Communities*. Champaign, IL: Human Kinetics.

Hills, L. (2006). Playing the field(s): An exploration of change, conformity and conflict in girls' understandings of gendered physicality in physical education. *Gender and Education*, **18**(5), 539–56.

Hughes, R. and Coakley, J. (1991). Positive deviance among athletes: The implications of overconformity to the sports ethic. *Sociology of Sport Journal*, **8**(4), 307–25.

Hughson, J., Inglis, D., and Free, M. (2005). *The Uses of Sport: A Critical Study*. London: Routledge.

Hylton, K. and Totten, M. (2001). Developing 'Sport for All?': Addressing inequality in sport. In *Sports Development: Policy, Process and Practice* (K. Hylton, P. Bramham, D. Jackson, and M. Nesti, eds). London: Routledge, pp. 37–65.

Jeanes, R. (2005). Girls, football participation and gender identity. In *Sport, Active Leisure and Youth Cultures* (P. Bramham and J. Caudwell, eds). Eastbourne: Leisure Studies Association, pp. 75–96.

Lawson, H. (2005). Empowering people, facilitating community development, and contributing to sustainable development: The social work of sport, exercise, and physical education programs. *Sport, Education and Society*, **10**(1), 135–60.

Light, R. and Kirk, D. (2000). High school rugby, the body and the reproduction of hegemonic masculinity. *Sport, Education and Society*, **5**(2), 163–76.

Long, J. and Sanderson, I. (2001). The social benefits of sport: Where's the proof? In *Sport in the City: The Role of Sport in Economic and Social Regeneration* (C. Gratton and I.P. Henry, eds). London: Routledge, pp. 187–203.

Lowrey, J. and Kay, T. (2005). Doing sport, doing inclusion: An analysis of provider and participant perceptions of targeted sport provision for young muslims. In *Youth, Sport and Active Leisure: Theory, Policy and Participation* (A. Flintoff, J. Long, and K. Hylton, eds). Eastbourne: Leisure Studies Association, pp. 73–90.

McCulloch, K., Stewart, A., and Lovegreen, N. (2006). 'We just hang out together': Youth cultures and social class. *Journal of Youth Studies*, **9**(5), 539–56.

McDermott, L. (1996). Toward a feminist understanding of physicality within the context of women's physically activity and sporting lives. *Sociology of Sport Journal*, **13**, 20–30.

McRobbie, A. (2005). *The Uses of Cultural Studies*. London: Sage.

Messner, M. (1988). Sports and male domination: The female athlete as contested ideological terrain. *Sociology of Sport Journal*, **5**, 197–211.

Muggleton, D. (2005). From classlessness to clubculture: A genealogy of post-war British youth cultural analysis. *Young*, **13**(2), 205–19.

Positive Futures (2006). *Positive Futures Impact Report: End of Season Review*. Home Office.

Price, M. and Parker, A. (2003). Sport, sexuality and the gender order: Amateur rugby union, gay men, and social exclusion. *Sociology of Sport Journal*, **20**(2), 108–26.

Rinehart, R.E. and Sydnor, S. (2003). *To the Extreme: Alternative Sports, Inside and Out*. New York: State University of New York Press.

Sarup, M. (1996). *Identity, Culture and the Postmodern World*. Edinburgh: Edinburgh University Press.

Shildrick, T. (2006). Youth culture, subculture and the importance of neighbourhood. *Young*, **14**(1), 61–74.

Skeggs, B. (1997). *Formations of Class and Gender*. London: Sage.

Slack, T. and Parent, M. (2007). *International Perspectives on the Management of Sport*. Oxford: Butterworth-Heinemann.

Sport England (2006). *Sport Playing it's Part: The Contribution of Sport to Meeting the Needs of Young People*. London: Sport England.

Spracklen, K. (2001). 'Black pearl, black diamonds': Exploring racial identities in rugby league. In *Race, Sport and British Society* (B. Carrington and I. Macdonald, eds). Routledge, pp. 70–82.

Thomson, R. (2007). Belonging. In *Understanding Youth: Perspectives, Identities and Practices* (M. Kehily, ed.) London: Sage, pp. 147–80.

Thornton, S. (1995). *Club Cultures: Music, Media and Subcultural Capital*. Cambridge: Polity Press.

Thornton, A. (2004). 'Anyone can play this game': Ultimate frisbee, identity and difference. In *Understanding Lifestyle Sports: Consumption, Identity and Difference* (B. Wheaton, ed.) London: Routledge, pp. 175–96.

Weller, S. (2006). Skateboarding alone? Making social capital discourse relevant to teenagers' lives. *Journal of Youth Studies*, **9**(5), 557–74.

Werbner, P. (2007). Fun spaces: On identity and social empowerment among British Pakistanis. In *The Sport Studies Reader* (A. Tomlinson, ed.) London: Routledge, pp. 309–36.

Wheaton, B. (ed.). (2004). *Understanding Lifestyle Sports: Consumption, Identity and Difference*. London: Routledge.

Willis, P. (1977). *Learning to Labour: How Working Class Kids Get Working Class Jobs*. Farnborough, Hants: HantsSaxon Press.

Wilson, B. and White, P. (2003). Urban sanctuary: Youth culture in a recreation drop in centre. In *Sporting Dystopias* (T.C. Wilcox, D.L. Andrews, R. Pitter, and R.L. Irwin, eds). New York: SUNY, pp. 153–78.

World Health Organisation (2003). *Annual Global Move for Health Initiative*. WHO document production services.

Youth Matters. The Youth Green Paper, 2006. Norwich: HM Government.

CHAPTER 9

Geographies of Sports Development: The Role of Space and Place

Emma Wainwright and Nicola Ansell

Introduction

Sports geography or the geography of sports is often regarded as the study of spatial variations in the pursuit of various sports and the impact that sporting activities have on the landscape (Johnston, 2000a). John Bale (2003, p. 2), the most prolific writer on sports geography, has chastised geographers for neglecting the study of sport arguing, 'sport – like geography – is a spatial science' and warrants much greater interest and further research (see also Bale and Vertinsky, 2004). However, sports geography remains quite narrowly conceived with an especially strong focus on changing patterns of sporting activities (Johnston, 2000a).

However, thinking about the geography or the multiple geographies of sports development can counter some of these shortfalls, and broaden our understanding of both sports development and sports geography. Essentially, sports development is an encounter between people and place that takes place in and through space. In its pitch to host the 2014 Commonwealth Games, Glasgow has titled its bid document 'People, Place, Passion', emphasising the centrality of this encounter and the fundamental role of geography. As Louise Martin, Chair of the Commonwealth Games Council for Scotland explained, 'the title reflects the context for the Games – a diverse and welcoming population, an amazing city and country and an extraordinary passion for sport and the Games' (http://www.cgcs.org.uk/News).

Space and the spatial are understood by geographers in a number of different ways. Spaces of sports development may be absolute, material and concrete but can also be metaphorical and imaginative. Thus sports development is used to shape space and give meaning to place. This latter interpretation of space and the spatial differs markedly from a more empiricist view of space as enabling sports development to be situated and marked out, with patterns of location waiting to be recognised and mapped. Through this chapter we reinforce the notion of sports development as a *process* that takes place through space involving negotiations over the meaning of place and who belongs in it.

As stipulated in the introductory chapter, the discourse of modern development has emphasised temporal change through notions of enlightenment and progress. Moreover, this temporality has been prioritised over any sense of the spatial and spatial change. As geographers have argued pervasively, social science has privileged time over space, constructing them as binary opposites, with time seen as a source of change, movement and history, and space marginalised and viewed as static. However, Massey (2005) among others has argued that, on the contrary, space is inherently dynamic. This conceptualisation is essential in thinking through sports development, not just as a temporal process but as a thoroughly spatial one as well. It is this spatial dimension that is too often lacking and hinders a fuller understanding of sports development.

This chapter begins by outlining what geographers mean by the terms space and place and how they are used here. It then goes on to place sports development within a wider discourse of urban development and regeneration. Intended to ameliorate the negative consequences of urban decline, regeneration programmes are increasingly using some form of sports development to rejuvenate and support vulnerable communities and localities and to create uniqueness and identity. By exploring a number of examples, the processes and outcomes of regeneration through sports development will be probed. In so doing, the chapter will highlight the power struggles over the meaning of place and inclusion that these processes can create for insiders (people who live there) and outsiders (people who visit). In particular, it will stress the differential involvement and impact sports development can have in different areas and upon different groups. Further, the chapter will explore the role of sports development in place-(re)making in both a material context (through structural and environmental change) and an imaginary sense (of place marketing and promotion).

Throughout, a number of examples and case studies are used which work through different scales and articulate a range of activity spaces, from the local impacts of stadia to the hosting of a global sporting event. As large-scale sporting developments bring into sharp focus local and global geographies of sports development and their tensions, the chapter's main case study, referred to throughout, is that of the 1992 Barcelona Olympic Games and its legacy. By probing sports development through a spatial dimension, the chapter stresses the complex considerations that need to be addressed by sports development managers in relation to different groups and at different spatial scales. Sports development is a means by which socio-spatial relations are produced, maintained and resisted.

The Importance of Space and Place

Space and place are central themes in geographical thinking. Despite this, they remain difficult to define and have been used in differing ways and through varied perspectives through the history of Geography as a discipline. However, before articulating their relevance and purchase on sports development, these terms need to be explored and explained.

Space is often considered the 'fundamental' of human geography (Thrift, 2003) and the production of geographical knowledge is anchored in claims to know space in particular ways. Historically, notions of space have focused on 'locating' events, places and phenomena on the earth's surface and representing these in maps (Gregory, 2000). Philosophical debates about space have been dominated by the dichotomy of absolute space and relational space. The former sees space as a container: clearly distinct, real and objective (Mayhew and Penny, 1992). Hence absolute space focuses on the characteristics of things in terms of their concentration and dispersion and it is this notion of the spatial that is closely linked to the processes and history of map-making and the concern for precise measurement of locational relationships (Goodall, 1987). In contrast, relative or relational space is perceptual and socially produced and focuses on the characteristics of places (Goodall, 1987).

Using these notions of space, some geographers consider the production of material, concrete spaces, while others are concerned with the production of imagined and symbolic spaces. Importantly, geographers emphasise the recursive relationship between the two: space is continually created and constructed through social relations just as social relations are constructed through and by space. Thus space is dynamic – it is always in the process of being made and given meaning. In this chapter, then, it is this notion of relational space that we use to explore the construction and contestation of material, social and imagined spaces of sports development.

Place is a commonly used term in the everyday vernacular but its meaning can become obscured. Agnew (1987) has argued that place consists of three elements: location – a point in space with specific relations to other points in space; locale – the broader context (both built and social) for social relations; and sense of place – subjective feelings associated with place. Until recently, these three perspectives were framed by a 'mosaic' metaphor that implied places were singular, discrete and unique (Castree, 2003). However, an increasingly globalised world has challenged geographers to think differently about these understandings of place:

> The globalisation of production, trade, finance, politics and culture, themselves facilitated by remarkable advances in transport and telecommunications, has made the world a 'global village'.
>
> (Castree, 2003, p. 166)

Thus, for some writers, globalisation has signalled the end of place (see Castells, 1996). However, rather than making the notion of place invalid, most geographers argue that globalisation requires a redefinition of what place means. Places in the contemporary world are clearly no longer separate but connected by an intricate web of flows and processes that stretch across the globe. Thus we need to have a 'global sense of the local' (Massey, 1994, p. 51), with global forces having variable local effects and globalisation coincident with new forms of place differentiation.

The importance of globalising forces in understanding and challenging notions of place and identifying places underlines the significance of scale. Scale refers to one or more levels of representation, experience and organisation of geographical events and processes (Johnston, 2000b). In this chapter in discussing the role of space and place, we will explore how sports developments are shaped by both local and global forces and produce local and global outcomes. The local and global are intricately caught up with one another, causing geographers to discuss the 'glocalisation' (Swyngedouw, 1989) of place and identity.

Sports Development and Urban Regeneration

Many major cities in Europe and North America developed through the rise of industrial capital from the mid-nineteenth century onwards. However, this process of industrial development began to subside in the closing decades of the twentieth century with many cities as a consequence experiencing severe economic and social problems. Places that were once economically and socially 'active' were being transformed into 'places of loss', characterised by an abandoned industrial landscape (Degen, 2001). To mitigate the effects of this deindustrialisation and ameliorate the negative consequences of urban decline, regeneration initiatives have been pursued (Hall, 2006) by both public and private interests. Though these initiatives vary widely, they all share one or more of the following goals: improvements to the physical environment, improvements to the quality of life of certain populations, improvements to the social welfare of certain populations and the enhancement of the economic prospects of certain populations (Hall, 2006). As Hall argues, regeneration projects have changed over time from a concern primarily with living conditions to include social, economic and environmental goals. The latter having become especially important as environmental sustainability has risen up the political agenda since the 1992 UN Earth Summit in Rio de Janeiro and the international adoption of Agenda 21. Significantly, the International Olympic Committee was the first international sports governing body to implement the Rio recommendations and developed its own 'Agenda 21' policies which since have been used as a blueprint in sports development policies of many international and national sports governing bodies (IOC, 1992).

Increasingly, sporting developments of varying size and scope are being used to spearhead regeneration through the use of public–private partnerships. Events like the Olympics and World Cup are the oft-cited 'mega-events' linked to regeneration processes and outcomes, rated mainly for their post-event 'legacy' (as discussed in Chapter 7). But, on a smaller scale, sports stadia have grown in importance as a tool of urban regeneration. This has been a notable trend in the UK in recent years where a number of cities have developed policy founded on the ability of sporting events and stadia to stimulate economic and physical regeneration (see Gratton and Henry, 2001 for a good review). By focusing on a number of different events and developments, we reflect here on the geographical impact they can have on urban spaces and local residents.

In terms of prestige, international media exposure and potential for regenerating an area, the 'mega-event' of the Olympics is the most highly sought after (Hall, 2006). The 1992 Barcelona Games are often held up as the ultimate example of a successful Games, enabling the city to redefine and redevelop itself, with clear geographical outcomes. Hailed as 'the most successful global model for post-industrial urban regeneration based on its urban design' (Degen, 2004, p. 131), the Olympics were used as a catalyst for physically and symbolically reconfiguring the city of Barcelona. Since then, sporting mega-events have been used by cities to improve infrastructure, regenerate run-down urban areas, promote economic growth and enhance place-image.

While it can be argued that this has been successfully achieved in Barcelona, however, other Olympic cities have fared less well.

In the early 1980s the urgency to regenerate Barcelona was economic, as the city found itself struggling with massive industrial closures and very high unemployment. As the city council argued, the major programmes necessary to stage the Olympics would have a vital social as well as economic purpose, namely, to upgrade deprived districts and extend and improve public space and facilities (Marshall, 1996). The various infrastructural improvements vital to hosting a global sporting event were seen as having important social gains and contributing to long-term economic regeneration. Hence construction for the Olympics started a process of radically reordering and reassembling Barcelona's geography and spatially transforming the city (Garcia and Degen, 2006).

The Barcelona example demonstrates the inherent local/global nexus central to the hosting of the Olympic Games. Barcelona used the Games – its global dimensions, platform and players – to embark on a peculiarly local programme of redevelopment and urban enhancement, aimed at improving the lives of its residents. As Degen (2004, p. 134) puts it, 'cities rework and situate globalisation', with the Olympic Games providing a springboard for Barcelona to become a member of the 'global city' circuit. However, reminders of Barcelona's industrial past remain on the landscape (see Figure 9.1) and in

Figure 9.1   Traces of Barcelona's industrial past.
Source: E. Wainwright (2005)

amongst the Olympic Village. Here it is useful to view the urban landscape as a palimpsest. Historically, a palimpsest referred to a writing tablet that could be used and reused. However, the tablet could never be entirely made clean and hence traces of former writings would build up. In the same way, urban landscapes are never completely erased of their prior uses and meanings (Crang, 1998). These marks on the landscape serve as important reminders of what the city was once like and, crucially, just how far it has come and how much change has taken place.

While the 1992 Games 'refashioned Barcelona as a tourist paradise' and is considered a 'good' games, the hosting of the 2004 Games in Athens has fared less well (*Guardian*, 10 July 2005). Athens, pre-Olympics, found itself in a similar economic and social position to Barcelona. Similarly, the Athens Games were used to regenerate particularly deprived areas of the city by locating facilities in them. However, according to Howden (2005), there is little evidence that they have had any significant impact upon the city's urban problems. Indeed, the Athens Games have been widely reported to have left a scar on the city. Costing over £8 billion to stage, much of the sporting infrastructure (only 8 out of 21 Olympic facilities are being used) has stood empty since the closing ceremony with the nickname 'the herd of white elephants' unsympathetically attributed to the empty stadia and other venues.

In London, the 2012 Olympics are being used to regenerate an area east of the city centred on Stratford and the Lower Lea Valley. The Games' organisers have been very explicit about the need for regeneration, and regeneration objectives formed a central plank of London's bid. However, for the bid to succeed, this area of East London had to be constructed as in *need* and want of transformation through the hosting of the Olympics. According to the London Organising Committee of the Olympic Games' website, the main Olympic site is in dire need of regeneration with the Olympics able to unlock the potential that has so far gone untapped:

> The area in and around the Olympic Park is a site of huge potential. It has a young, diverse community but is also home to significant areas of deprivation.

> Much of the site itself is contaminated, derelict and abandoned. The waterways in the area have suffered from years of neglect: water quality is poor, river walls are in a bad condition and the landscape is scarred with abandoned shopping trolleys and other rubbish strewn along the river channels. (http://www.london-2012.co.uk/Urban-regeneration)

Without doubt, the area has been suffering from various environmental and social problems and has, in contrast to other areas of London, 'lost out' in terms of economic growth and development. However, this example demonstrates that 'urban problems do not present themselves to policy-makers; rather they are defined in various ways' (Hall, 2006, p. 60). 'Problems' and a 'problem area' need to be identified and defined to legitimise regeneration interventions.

The Lower Lea Valley area will now be transformed into the Olympic Park which will hold the Olympic Village, housing athletes and the main venues including the Olympic Stadium, Velodrome and BMX Circuit, plus the Fencing, Hockey, Handball and Basketball arenas, all of which will be accessible by the new Olympic Park Loop Road. After the Games, the Park will be transformed into 'the largest urban park created in Europe for more than 150 years', with over 9000 new homes, many aimed at key workers (such as nurses and teachers) and shops, restaurants and cafes for the local community. It is hoped the Games will spearhead long-term economic renewal; it is anticipated that thousands of new jobs will be created in the Park alone, many of them from the conversion of the International Broadcast Centre/Main Press Centre (see http://www.london2012.com/plans/). A range of transport improvements serving the Park are already underway, including an extension to the Docklands Light Railway, increased capacity on the Jubilee Line and the upgrade of Stratford Regional Station. Hence, this extensive construction will see the area's geography considerably reworked. This change is aimed at giving the area an entirely new image. However, the change is not welcomed by and does not welcome everyone (as discussed below).

Through the example of the Olympics, we see how a global event has very local consequences on space and place. A city's spatial transformation involves a complex network of global and local forces reshaping the city's environment. In the same way as global mega-sporting events, stadium construction in many cities is the result of more than a desire to improve sporting facilities for both participants and spectators. North American cities have a tradition of competing strongly with each other for inward investment and the sports industry, especially the big football and baseball leagues, is particularly big business (Thornley, 2002). As a consequence, local states are intricately involved in the development of stadia as a means of attracting big players and businesses to their region. For example, the Dodger Stadium in Los Angeles was used to draw attention to the city's transition from a regional centre to a national metropolis (Lipsitz, 1984). Furthermore, the construction of the Superdrome in New Orleans and the Skydrome in Toronto set the stage for tourist-based growth in the cities' downtown areas (Bale, 2003), generating economic growth in their localities through their national and global reach. Stadia can become tourist attractions in their own right – notable for their design, for example, the Munich Olympic Stadium, or for the reputation of their team such as the Nou Camp Stadium in Barcelona. However, whilst there is an extensive literature on the role and impact of sports stadia in the development process in North America, corresponding awareness and interest in the UK has only emerged over the past decade. Here we draw on examples where stadia are used as stand alone developments or as part of a wider scheme of sporting activity.

Wembley stadium in West London is one example where sports development is being closely tied to wider regeneration objectives. Wembley is the UK's national stadium and has recently gone through demolition and rebuilding. This extensive process, pushed forward by Wembley National Stadium Limited, Brent Council and Quintain Estates and Development plc, has been worked through a discourse of 'prosperity for all', with especial emphasis placed on the benefits to the local area and the role of local residents. This is in contrast to other stadium developments which are often criticised for not involving local communities. For example, the construction of Vancouver's BC Place Stadium neglected existing residents and even led to the displacement of some 'locals' (Lee, 2002). To counter such concerns, the Wembley consortium webpage suggests

> The benefits of having the national stadium at Wembley are far reaching for Wembley, Brent and indeed the Capital as a whole. The Stadium is being used to stimulate the regeneration of its surrounding area and Brent Council, as well as Wembley National Limited, are determined to maximise the positive impact of the new Wembley Stadium on the local area. (http://www.wembleystadium.com/brilliantfuture/localcommunity/regneration.htm)

In addition to the stadium itself, the development process is to include new homes, leisure facilities, shops, bars, restaurants, offices and public space. Thus, though undoubtedly a national building with global reach, the new Wembley intends to be positioned within a local arena of regeneration. The website promotes this inclusivity with a section dedicated to the needs and interests of the local community, making Wembley 'a place where people are proud to live and eager to visit' (http://www.wembleystadium.com/about/localcommunity/introduction.htm). However, Thornley (2002) notes that local people tend not to use stadia and the economic impacts of stadium construction on the immediate area are often limited. It then remains to be seen how successful the rebuilding of Wembley stadium is in delivering its promised wider benefits to the local community.

Another example of stadium development is the Millennium Stadium in Cardiff which came about in tandem with the Welsh Rugby Union's bid to host the 1999 Rugby World Cup, supported by Cardiff County Council. The city has viewed sport and related infrastructure as important drivers of growth and urban regeneration and a 'good bet' in a post-industrial world (Jones, 2002). A new stadium on the site of the old was deemed necessary to host the event which, in the longer term, could provide conference and event facilities. It was constructed between 1996 and 1999 in the heart of Cardiff's commercial district. Unlike Wembley, the city centre location did not suffer from problems of deprivation and did not require regenerating, though it inevitably saw changes to its physical landscape. In addition to the 'physically dominating stadium' (Jones, 2001a), infrastructural improvements included the development of the bus and train station, pedestrian improvements to the city centre and redevelopment of the river walk area.

Kidd (1995) suggests that benefits following stadium development may accrue unevenly across different sections of a city – often benefiting the already affluent. He also notes that stadia can act as a means of privatising urban public space and reasserting commercial control over a landscape formerly the preserve of minority or less well-of groups (see also Fainstein and Fainstein, 1986). The Millennium Stadium is a good example of how local areas can take on new meaning and lead to the disruption and destruction of previous amenities. The construction of the stadium led to the demolition of the Empire Road Pool, a participatory sporting facility available at low cost to local residents, which was replaced by relatively expensive retail and food outlets and a health club (Jones, 2001b).

The process of completing the stadium on time has had repercussions on local residents in other ways too, most notably in the form of road closures, dust and construction noise. Another consequence of the hosting of the Rugby World Cup was the creation of a temporary 'red light district' in which prostitution would be tolerated for the duration of the event. This was intended to minimise the negative effects of prostitution incurring into residential areas (see Jones, 2001a for further details) during such 'mega-events'. Hence the Millennium Stadium and the hosting of the Rugby World Cup were not uniformly positive in their impacts on the urban environment. To be effective, '[stadium] development needs to be integrated into a local regeneration strategy' (Thornley, 2002, p. 816) that considers the full range of effects on urban communities.

Place Meaning and Sports Development

Besides the physical transformations stressed so far, sports development and its use as a tool of urban regeneration is also an effective and important means of changing place meaning and promoting place. In this section we shift focus to consider the role of sports developments in transforming and promoting certain kinds of images of place. For example, the Millennium Stadium development was used to promote newly devolved power in Wales – a 'politically vibrant Wales, willing to take its place on the world stage' (Jones, 2002, p. 822). And Beijing is using the Olympics 'to transform itself into a fitting capital for a 21st century superpower' which, for the ruling Communist Party, 'is also an important re-branding exercise' (http://news.-bbc.co.uk/1/low/world/asia-pacific/6164330.stm). As sports developments of varying size, scale and purpose transform the material geography of an area, so can they be used to transform the meanings of place. This section links to some of the issues discussed in Part Two of the book on the vision of sports development and draws on examples of the role of sports development in changing place meaning and promoting an often very carefully controlled place image.

Since the mid-1980s, a central pillar of urban regeneration programmes has been the deliberate manipulation and promotion of place images (Hall, 2006). It is now the rule, rather than the exception, to find an urban area engaged in vigorous place promotion. In the US, place promotion or place marketing has become a multi-billion dollar industry as public relations experts rebrand, package, advertise and sell cities (Holcomb, 1993). Understandably, this process of place promotion has been used most rigorously and persuasively in areas affected by deindustrialisation and deprivation. Place promotion can work in two ways. First, it can operate *within*, to promote a certain image to its residents. For example, in Barcelona, it has been argued that the Olympics contributed to a 'collective imaginary of democratic Barcelona for its citizens' (Balibrea, 2001, p. 199). Second, it can have an external function, promoting *outwards* to potential visitors and investors and creating a tourist location. As Jones (2001a, p. 241) remarks, this is increasingly apparent:

> many cities that, hitherto, have not possessed a defined and globally acknowledged tourism product have attempted to take a 'short cut;' towards global recognition through the production of events which garner a global audience.

Thus place promotion works through an economic logic – of luring inward investment from industry, tourists and shoppers, and a social logic – of convincing local people that they are 'important cogs in a successful community'. (Philo and Kearns, 1993, p. 3)

'Geography of spectacle' is a term attached to heavily imagineered and marketed events, including the Olympic Games and other sporting occasions which are often global in reach (Ley, 2000). They are linked closely to the attendant national and global television audience that is seen as significant to the long-term fortunes of any city and, despite a universal language of promotion and marketing, extol the supposedly 'unique' qualities of 'unique' places (Philo and Kearns, 1993). According to Gratton et al. (2006), in order to maximise place marketing, event organisers should work closely with broadcasters and other media to ensure the effective showcasing of key local attractions as the backdrop to event coverage.

Turning attention to Barcelona again, the 'seductive Barcelona of the 1990s' (Balibrea, 2001, p. 188) was primarily based on a particular hegemonic construction of the city through image:

> Along with the creation of the new Barcelona in bricks and mortar came a sponsored city promotion of Barcelona-as-concept, a seductive cocktail of architecture, imagination, tradition, style, nightlife and primary colours.
> (Time Out Guide, 2002, p. 25)

The new and regenerated buildings, infrastructure and open spaces were imbued with symbolic meaning that emphasised culture and independence and represented the stark transformation from a run-down industrial metropolis to one of Europe's most desirable tourist venues (Degen, 2004).

Besides Barcelona as a tourist destination, Olympic and related developments were directed at changing the image of the city for its residents. Borne out of the city's history and politics, the Barcelona Games were effective in generating a strong sense of local patriotism, a sense of involvement and ownership:

> The Olympic Games generated a civil fraternity, materially embodied and reinforced in every architectural and urban project, which was perceived as required by the event.
> (Balibrea, 2001, p. 198)

This collective imaginary of the city and its Olympics is probably best exemplified in the way the city's inhabitants volunteered to participate in the

Games' infrastructure. Very much as Philo and Kearns (1993) have suggested, this indicates that locals are vital components in a flourishing city. However, as Garcia and Degen (2006, p. 30) warn, as time has passed, this creation of a very place-specific identity has been criticised for being merely a 'marketing exercise for the outside market', potentially leaving residents behind and feeling excluded (discussed further below).

Whilst Barcelona has focussed on the uniqueness of its geography and place identity, in contrast, the marketing for the 2012 Olympics in London appears to be 'placeless' and has been criticised for abolishing its geography (Jack, 2007). When London hosted the Olympics in 1948, the advertising combined the Olympic rings, Big Ben and an ancient statue of a Greek discus thrower; a clear and strong marker of both place and sporting endeavour. However, the 2012 logo, revealed in June 2007, has met with a furore from both the popular media and 'Londoners'. For many, criticism stems from the sidelining of the city in favour of a 'placeless' presentation of a sporting event. But, organisers have argued that they are purposely playing to a global field and that the Olympics is not about one city. As the BBC explained:

> The objective in resisting an iconic image was to emphasise that while the Games is hosted in London, it is not just for London, but also for the UK and for the world. (http://news.bbc.co.uk/1/hi/magazine/6719805.stm)

However, the backlash has continued with Wolff Olins, the agency responsible for the 2012 logo, accused of being the 'enemy of the local' and 'eroding our already diminished sense of belonging' (Jack, 2007). Clearly, *place* promotion through sports development does matter, especially developments that are global in reach.

Sports Development, Belongings and Exclusions

In the post-industrial city, spaces of sports development and consumption hold important symbolic value: 'of the supposed unity of a class-divided and racially segregated city. Professional sports activities and events like the Los Angeles Olympic Games perform a similar [unifying] function in an otherwise fragmented society' (Harvey, 1989, p. 271). Hence, as stipulated above, sports developments often herald a sense of 'local patriotism' and a collective desire to rise to the occasion (Balibrea, 2001). However, as highlighted in the case study of Barcelona, this notion of coming together and inclusion often masks a reality of exclusions and segregation, with sporting developments including, benefiting and being used by specific social groups.

At this juncture the concepts of 'sense of place' and 'socio-spatial exclusion' are insightful. Sense of place refers to how people feel and think about places and is used by many geographers to emphasise that places are significant because they are the focus of personal feelings (Rose, 1995), as highlighted through discussions of the London 2012 logo. Sense of place is important because it is linked closely to identity and how we make sense of ourselves and our lives. Social exclusion, a term that has increasingly been adopted by politicians, refers to a 'situation in which certain members of society are, or become, separated from much that comprises the normal "round" of living and working within that society' (Philo, 2000, p. 751). While it is often conceptualised in strictly social terms, it has a clear spatial dimension and hence more accurately should be termed socio-spatial exclusion:

> excluded individuals will tend to slip outside, or even become unwelcome visitors within, those spaces which come to be regarded as the 'loci' of mainstream social life.
>
> (Philo, 2000, p. 751)

Here, we look at exclusions and belongings in relation to sports development processes, venues, wider geographies and concomitant image.

Writing about the BC Place Stadium project in Vancouver, Lee (2002) notes that despite being well received by the business community, the Provincial Government failed to take into consideration opposing views to the development. In particular, local residents' associations argued against the government engaging in stadium financing as, they felt, money could be better spent on affordable housing and other amenities. A central concern for many locals was that the development would result in increased house prices, which in turn would have an exclusionary impact on them. This is a fear that materialised in post-Olympics Barcelona (Marshall, 1996) and is echoed by local residents in East London in anticipation of the effects of the London Olympics:

> After the Olympics the property mob will move in. You'll get a lot of people with money here and it will never be the same again. I want to keep it like this.
>
> (cited in *The Guardian*, 21 June 2006)

Hence local residents can be wary that sporting developments – of various size – can change the meaning of place, have an exclusionary impact on them in terms of being marginalised and not having their voices heard in the planning process and then, very often, being the group least likely to be advantaged by any subsequent economic prosperity.

Preparation for the London Olympics in 2012 has seen the possession of a huge site in Stratford with the 'necessary' relocation of 208 businesses, 425 residents, 35 traveller families and 64 allotment holders (*The Guardian*, 24 July 2007). This process of relocation or eviction has been met with vocal and visible resistance within the local community (see Figure 9.2). According to the political commentator, George Monbiot (2007), since the 1988 Olympics in Seoul, more than 2 million people worldwide have been driven from their homes to make way for the Olympics. One group that has been evicted from the London 2012 site are the Travellers from Clays Lane in Newham (see also Barkham, 2007). This follows the purging of similar groups for the Sydney and Barcelona Games. In an open letter to *The Guardian* newspaper (29 September 2007), Tracie Giles, on behalf of the travellers, described the delays in their relocation and expressed her belief that they are considered 'easy prey' given that they do not live in 'bricks and mortar'. Such examples show that exclusion can involve a process of physical removal and the creation of spatial boundaries whereby incursion into sites of sports development are prohibited. At the time of writing,

Figure 9.2 Resistance to the 2012 London Olympics in the Lower Lea Valley.
Source: E. Wainwright (2006)

this is evidenced by an 11-mile blue fence that marks off the 2012 Olympic site – leading commentators to ponder whether this is a necessary security measure or more a symbol of the Games' divisiveness (Beckett, 2007).

A sense of belonging or exclusion is, to a large extent, based on place-image. As remarked on above, the Barcelona Olympics effectively galvanised its local population to feel a part of the Games and take pride in their city. Image is thus not only about signification and symbolisation but can have very real material consequences for certain groups. Though Barcelona was considered to have achieved an inclusive Games, certain parts of the city, most notably the Ramblas and waterfront were 'morally cleansed' of their 'less desirable' users. Similarly, Manchester's city centre was 'cleansed' of prostitution during the 2002 Commonwealth Games (Degen, 2001, 2004). This process represents a purification of space with deviant behaviours and bodies excluded from the polished image of place and its material spaces.

There are mounting concerns in Barcelona that the creation of the city as a globally recognised brand, precipitated by the Olympic Games, has become more interested in the tourist's and the world's gaze, rather than the lives of its own residents, and that economic concerns are beginning to overpower local needs (Degen, 2004). Tensions have developed over who has access to the city and whom the city is for, with locals beginning to voice concerns about the negative effects the increasing number of visitors has on their daily lives. And in 2005 a debate emerged in the local press over whether the city should restrict incoming tourists (Garcia and Degen, 2006).

The actual sites of sporting activity can also exclude. In his appraisal of the impacts of the Millennium Stadium in Cardiff, Jones (2001a) found that while the local population welcomed the stadium, attendance costs placed it out of the reach of many. Exclusion can further operate through hegemonic constructions of sporting spectators and participants, along the lines of class, race, gender and sexuality. At the start of the millennium in the UK, only 40% of members of ethnic minority groups participated in sport compared with 46% of the general population. Moreover, only 19% of Bangladeshi women took part in sport (Sport England, 2001). As Vertinsky (2004, p. 9) argues, it is necessary to explore the power relations which work to include and exclude:

> Different sporting places can be distinguished from each other through the operation of the relations of power that construct boundaries around them, creating spaces with certain meanings in which some relationships are facilitated, other discouraged.

In relation to sexuality, through research into women's footballing subculture in England, Caudwell (2007) has explored how lesbian-identified sports teams provide a challenge to the heterosexing of sport by resisting heteronormative meanings of sport space and sporting identities. Focusing on spectators, Muller (2007) has probed how heternormativity is naturalised within arena spaces of basketball in the USA, suggesting that teams and marketing personnel distance themselves from their lesbian fan-base and consumers. Instead, Muller argues, they prefer to reproduce a 'safe' heteronormative space and image, creating a sense of not belonging and being 'out of place' among a large cohort of their fan base.

At a broader level, Sport England is working to tackle social exclusion through promoting access to sport and encouraging more people of all ages, abilities and backgrounds to participate. Part of this process is ensuring there are enough suitable sporting venues – whether pools, halls, courts or pitches – to enable local sporting participation (Sport England, 2001). Hence sporting development is as much about the micro-geographies of these smaller venues and participation as national stadia and mega-events. One scheme, Sport Action Zones (SAZ), is based in some of England's most deprived communities and is aimed at increasing participation in sport and physical activity among hard-to-reach groups. In the SAZ in Liverpool, for example, recent research has showed the effectiveness of this scheme: overall regular participation in sport and physical activity went up by 5% from 60% to 65%, and notably, among the most socio-economically deprived groups it increased by 10% from 43% to 53% (Sport England, 2006). Hence sports developments can have a positive impact in including people in sporting activity in and through their local area.

Space, Place, Meaning and Sports Development Managers

By taking a geographical perspective and working through various substantive issues and empirical case studies, this chapter has highlighted a number of issues of interest and concern to the management of sports development. First and foremost there is a need to balance the 'global pressures and local effects' (Thornley, 2002, p. 818). Sports development is likely to be increasingly used as a tool of regeneration, as cities compete for prominence and investment on a global stage. By attracting inward investment, it is expected that exclusion and deprivation may be combated, although this is not a guaranteed outcome. There are expectations concerning the short-term impacts as well as the longer-term legacy, although not all outcomes can be foreseen. There are differential effects on different groups and at different scales: a balance is needed, for instance, between the needs of local residents and those of a tourist population, although where this balance lies is a subjective judgement.

The spatial impacts of sports developments are both material and symbolic. Development works best when all groups among the local population, including those generally excluded, are included through the planning and building process and when they can themselves benefit, materially or otherwise, from the final sporting venue. Sports development can also be used in remaking place images, but is not all-powerful in its capacity to do so. The meanings of space and place are not fixed but dynamic and open to resistance and contestation. Thus successful sports development needs to construct place images that are inclusive. When successfully implemented, sports developments can evoke both national and local pride, and, as a consequence, criticism of sport-based development policy is sometimes labelled as unambitious or disloyal (Schimmel, 1995). Jones makes the salient point that in such an atmosphere, 'a full understanding of the ways in which the [development] . . . impacts upon the host economy, and the extent of those impacts, can be compromised' (Jones, 2002, p. 821). Furthermore, images and attitudes may change over time, particularly if a development is perceived to be transformed from a public to a private space, and those who once saw themselves as part of the project cease to feel any ownership or belonging. Thornley (2002, p. 814) notes that 'there is often popular support for a stadium if it is part of an Olympic or similar bid where national or city pride plays a part. However when transferred to a private club people's reaction often change to one of opposition'.

This chapter has stressed the importance of thinking about sports development not only in temporal terms but also in terms of the spatial, by highlighting the central and dynamic role of space. Space and place are not simply inert blank canvases to be built upon and developed, but are instead made and remade through the development process. As an encounter between people and place, sports developments can interrupt and dislodge prevailing, and engender and promote new, meanings of place.

From this, there are a number of clear lessons for sports development managers to heed:

1. The sports development process must be inclusive and managers must consult widely within the local community:
   (a) Managers need to include all local businesses and local social groups – even the most disadvantaged and hard-to-reach – early on in the planning process.
   (b) In depth and wide-reaching community consultations could effectively mitigate frictions and conflicting interests within the local area.

2. Sports development managers must be sensitive to the impact development has on the physical environment and use of space, and in changing place meaning:
    (a) Managers must consider not only potential tourism and inward investment but whether local residents benefit from the changes to their area.
    (b) Any community consultation should gauge people's perceptions of the local area – its meaning and importance – to fully realise the impact of development.
3. The short and long-term legacy of development and its impact on place and population need to be fully explored and, where possible, worked into a broader programme of regeneration that has material benefits for existing communities.

References

Agnew, J. (1987). *Place and Politics*. Boston: Allen and Unwin.

Bale, J. (2003). *Sports Geography*, (2nd edn). London: Routledge.

Bale, J. and Vertinsky, P. (2004). Introduction. In *Sites of Sport: Space, Place, Experience* (P. Vertinsky and J. Bale, eds). London: Routledge, pp. 1–7.

Balibrea, M. (2001). Urbanism, culture and the post-industrial city: Challenging the 'Barcelona model'. *Journal of Spanish Cultural Studies*, **2**(2), 187–210.

Barkham, P. (2007). On the move again. *The Guardian*, 19 October.

BBC news (2006). Beijing building the Olympic dream. 20 November, http://news.bbc.co.uk/1/low/world/asia-pacific/6164330.stm (accessed 4 October 2007.

BBC news (2007). 'Oh no' logo. 5 June, http://news.bbc.co.uk/1/hi/magazine/6719805.stm (accessed 4 October 2007).

Beckett, A. (2007). Cordon blue. *The Guardian*, 21 September.

Castells, M. (1996). *The Rise of the Network Society*. Oxford: Blackwells.

Castree, N. (2003). Place: Connections and boundaries in an independent world. In *Key Concepts in Geography* (S. Holloway, S. Rice, and G. Valentine, eds). London: Sage, pp. 165–86.

Caudwell, J. (2007). Queering the field? The complexities of sexuality within a lesbian-identified football team in England. *Gender, Place and Culture*, **14**(2), 183–96.

Commonwealth Games Council for Scotland (n.d.). People, place, passion'. Glasgow 2014 makes its pitch for the commonwealth games, http://www.cgcs.org.uk/News (accessed 8 October 2007).

Crang, M. (1998). *Cultural Geography*. London: Routledge.

Degen, M. (2001). Sensed appearances: Sensing the 'performance of place'. *Space and Culture*, **11/12**, 52–69.

Degen, M. (2004). Barcelona's games: The Olympics, urban design and global tourism. In *Tourism Mobilities: Places to Play, Places in Play* (M. Shuller and J. Urry, eds). London: Routledge, pp. 131–42.

Fainstein, N. and Fainstein, S. (1986). Economic change, national policy and the system of cities. In *Restructuring the City: The Political Economy of Urban Redevelopment* (S. Fainstein, N. Fainstein, R. Childs-Hill, and D. Judd, eds). New York: Longman.

Garcia, M. and Degen, M. (2006). *Barcelona – The Breakdown of a Virtuous Model?* Paper presented at XVI ISA World Congress of Sociology, Durban.

Giles, T. (2007). The Olympics have made our lives hell. *The Guardian*, 29 September.

Goodall, B. (1987). *Penguin Dictionary of Human Geography*. London: Penguin.

Gratton, C. and Henry, I. (2001). *Sport in the City: The Role of Sport in Economic and Social Regeneration*. London: Routledge.

Gratton, C., Shibli, S., and Coleman, R. (2006). The economic impact of major sports events: A review of ten events in the UK. In *Sports Mega-Events* (J. Horne and W. Manzenreiter, eds). London: Blackwell.

Gregory, D. (2000). Human geography and space. In *The Dictionary of Human Geography* (R. Johnston, D. Gregory, G. Pratt, and M. Watts, eds). Oxford: Blackwell, pp. 767–72.

The Guardian (2005). Glorious take-off – or downward spiral? 10 July.

The Guardian (2006). Olympic evictees go without a struggle, 21 June.

The Guardian (2007). Demolition of 2012 site to begin, 24 July.

Hall, T. (2006). *Urban Geography*, (3rd edn). London: Routledge.

Harvey, D. (1989). *The Urban Experience*. Oxford: Blackwell.

Holcomb, B. (1993). Revisioning place: De- and re-constructing the image of the industrial city. In *Selling Places: The City as Cultural Capital, Past and Present* (G. Kearns and C. Philo, eds). Oxford: Pergamon.

Howden, D. (2005). Wanted: A home for the 'herd of white elephants' left by the Athens Olympics, *Independent*, 1 April.

International Olympic Committee (1992). *Olympic Movement's Agenda 21: Sport for Sustainable Development*. IOC.

Jack, I. (2007). The 'edgy' 2012 logo has abolished Olympian grace and geography. *The Guardian*, 9 June.

Johnston, R. (2000a). Geography of sport. In *The Dictionary of Human Geography* (R. Johnston, D. Gregory, G. Pratt, and M. Watts, eds). Oxford: Blackwell, p. 783.

Johnston, R. (2000b). Scale. In *The Dictionary of Human Geography* (R. Johnston, D. Gregory, G. Pratt and M. Watts, eds). Oxford: Blackwell, pp. 724–7.

Jones, C. (2001a). Mega-events and the host-region impacts: Determining the true worth of the 1999 Rugby World Cup. *International Journal of Tourism Research*, **3**, 241–51.

Jones, C. (2001b). A level playing field? Sports stadium infrastructure and urban development in the UK. *Environment and Planning A*, **33**(5), 845–61.

Jones, C. (2002). The stadium and economic development: Cardiff and the Millennium Stadium. *European Planning Studies*, **10**(7), 819–29.

Kidd, B. (1995). Toronto's skydrome: The world's greatest entertainment centre. In *The Stadium and the City* (J. Bale and O. Moen, eds). Keele: Keele University Press, pp. 175–95.

Lee, P. (2002). The economic and social justification for publicly financed stadia: The case of Vancouver's BC Place stadium. *European Planning Studies*, **10**(7), 861–73.

Ley, D. (2000). Geography of spectacle. In *The Dictionary of Human Geography* (R. Johnston, D. Gregory, G. Pratt, and M. Watts, eds). Oxford: Blackwell, p. 782.

Lipsitz, G. (1984). Sports stadia and urban development: A tale of three cities. *Journal of Sport and Social Issues*, **8**, 1–18.

London 2012 Olympic and Paralympic Games (n.d.). Olympic Park, http://www.london-2012.co.uk/Urban-regeneration/ (accessed 5 October 2007).

London 2012 Olympic and Paralympic Games (n.d.). Our plans, http://www.london2012.com/plans/ (accessed 5 October 2007).

Marshall, T. (1996). Barcelona – fast forward? City entrepreneurialism in the 1980s and 1990s. *European Planning Studies*, **4**(2), 147–65.

Massey, D. (1994). *Space, Place and Gender*. Oxford: Polity Press.

Massey, D. (2005). *For Space*. London: Sage.

Mayhew, S. and Penny, A. (1992). *The Concise Oxford Dictionary of Geography*. Oxford: Oxford University Press.

Monbiot, G. (2007). London is getting into the Olympic spirit – by kicking out the Games. *The Guardian*, 12 June.

Muller, T. (2007). Liberty for all contested spaces of women's basketball. *Gender, Place and Culture*, **14**(2), 197–213.

Philo, C. (2000). Exclusion. In *The Dictionary of Human Geography* (R. Johnston, D. Gregory, G. Pratt, and M. Watts, eds). Oxford: Blackwell, pp. 751–2.

Philo, C. and Kearns, G. (1993). Culture, history, capital: A critical introduction to the selling of places. In *Selling Places: The City as Cultural Capital, Past and Present* (G. Kearns and C. Philo, eds). Oxford: Pergamon, pp. 1–33.

Rose, G. (1995). Place and identity: A sense of place. In *A Place in the World?* (D. Massey and P. Jess, eds). Milton Keynes: Open University, pp. 87–132.

Schimmel, K. (1995). Growth politics, urban development and sports stadium construction in the USA: A case study. In *The Stadium and the City* (J. Bale and O. Moen, eds). Keele: Keele University Press, pp. 111–56.

Sport England (2001). *Sport England Annual Report 2000–2001*. Sport England.

Sport England (2006). *Sport Action Zones: The Key to Transforming Community Participation*. Sport England.

Swyngedouw, E. (1989). The heart of place. *Geografisak Annaler*, **B71**, 31–42.

Thornley, A. (2002). Urban regeneration and sports stadia. *European Planning Studies*, **10**(7), 813–18.

Thrift, N. (2003). Space: The fundamental stuff of geography. In *Key Concepts in Geography* (S. Holloway, S. Rice, and G. Valentine, eds). London: Sage, pp. 95–108.

Time Out Guide (2002). *Barcelona*. London: Penguin.

Vertinsky, P. (2004). Locating a 'sense of place': Space, place and gender in the gymnasium. In *Sites of Sport: Space, Place, Experience* (P. Vertinsky and J. Bale, eds). London: Routledge, pp. 8–24.

Wembley Stadium (n.d.). Introduction, http://www.wembleystadium.com/about/localcommunity/introduction.htm (accessed 1 October 2007).

Wembley Stadium (n.d.). Regeneration of Wembley. http://www.wembleystadium.com/brilliantfuture/localcommunity/regneration.htm (accessed 1 October 2007).

PART FOUR

Sports Development Delivery

CHAPTER 10

Building Organisational and Management Capacity for the Delivery of Sports Development

Andy Adams

Introduction

This chapter sets out to examine the delivery of sport development, within a UK context, with specific reference to the notion of organisational capacity as a structural condition that has been engineered, from national to local level, to incorporate a number of partner sporting and non-sporting agencies under the steerage of the Department of Culture, Media and Sport (DCMS). Indeed capacity building has become a common refrain in the language of sports (policy) development in the UK (DCMS/Strategy Unit, 2000, 2002; Carter, 2005; Sport England, 2007a) and if it is to have any significant discursive value must necessarily form part of the interrogation of the practice of sports development. It is in this context that the national level focus on capacity building as set out in *Game Plan* (DCMS, 2002), which amounted to the upskilling and training of sports professionals and volunteers, the drafting in of expertise and the general professionalising of key systems, needs careful interpretation as much for the intended outcomes but also for the immanent outcomes (see Chapter 1 in this volume).

Whilst this chapter focuses on the UK context, the issue of capacity building is a generic sports development and sports development policy issue that has currency within broader European and international contexts. To this end capacity building can obviously be interpreted at different levels depending on particular and unique constellations of ideological, politically economic and cultural conditions that coalesce within different nation states. In this respect, the need to interrogate capacity building, address the attendant and concomitant issues thrown up by such an analysis and reflect on practical policies that emerge for sports development becomes an international as much as it is national issue.

A Policy Framework for Capacity Building

The current UK policy framework implicitly acknowledges the nature of government steerage, indicating a more intimate relationship between political leadership and its operative elements than the 'arms length' one of previous administrations (Oakley and Green, 2001); it also reveals a less adversarial relationship between the state, private business and the voluntary sector (Pierre and Peters, 2000). The upshot is that the state has become located within a legitimating interventionist ideology where 'steering' tacitly acknowledges the legitimate role of the state as a set of political institutions that '...are the only actors who can define goals and make priorities on behalf of the polity' (Pierre and Peters, 2000, p. 56). Arguably, New Labour's interventionist intentions rotate around a neoliberal axis which has enabled consecutive prime ministers to not only look towards the reinvigoration of civil society, but also to put individualism and choice at the heart of the relevant steerage. For former Prime Minister Blair 'The Third Way recognises the limits of government in the social sphere but also the need for government...enabling government strengthens civil society rather than weakens it' (Blair, 1998, p. 14). For New Labour's second term in office steerage became further enmeshed in Blair's desire to ensure 'coherence' around commitments to strengthen communities to guarantee 'civic renewal' (Lister, 2004, p. 163). As Gordon Brown, before taking up office, had signalled that the Third Way was '...not so much about what the state can do for you, but about what the state can enable you to do for yourself' (Brown, 1994, p. 25).

The above framework also reminds us that structure and agency are reflexively conditioned, such that whilst the state is entwined within a legitimating ideology that permits and encourages intervention it is the state itself that has acted as actor to reflexively enable the conditions within which its actions have validity. In this sense an actor may be identified as '...an entity that, in principle, has the means of formulating and acting upon decisions' (Sibeon, 1999, p. 141); this position knowingly excludes non-reflexive action from 'agency' (an issue developed further by Hoggett, 2001 in his examination of agency and social policy). In asserting the above definition it is worth noting that actors can be construed of as individuals, small groups, committees, voluntary organisations, pressure groups, government departments and the like. Social structure, however, presents a set of social conditions within which actors operate, and that have an element of continuity but are not unchange-able. For Lewis (2000) social conditions present themselves as a pre-structured context which influences '...the actions that people choose to take' (p. 258). Furthermore Giddens (1993) has noted that structure can constrain or facilitate actors in achieving their objectives, depending of course on the circumstances of the structure and the nature of the actors.

The state in this respect is a valid actor, which provides the conditions for the exercising of its own agency. Whilst this is something of an over-simplification and treats the notion of the state as a somewhat reified entity, the point is that state involvement in sport development practices in the UK has become legitimised by and subject to wider social policy practices. In particular, the incorporation of social capital theory into the architecture of social policy development has provided an appropriate infrastructure for building the organisational capacity of sports development. In the first instance it facilitates the establishment of a platform upon which 'civic renewal...active citizenship, [and] strengthened communities' (Blunkett, 2003, p. 38) can be both developed and extolled. Second, it has enabled notions of community and community development to become New Labour's 'central collective abstraction' discursively linking the concept across wide areas of policy which has itself been deduced from a wider constellation of Third Way politics and communitarian social engineering (Levitas, 2000). Third, as a consequence of the privileging of voluntary associationalism as the desired form of civil society, the incorporation of social capital theory has served to focus attention onto sports volunteering and voluntary sports clubs as sites for both sport development and community development outcomes to be met. This is prescient given that (a) sports volunteering is the single largest area of volunteering in the UK (Taylor et al., 2003) and (b) sports volunteers have become subject to the need for 'better capacity building...to ensure that both the quality and quantity are maintained' (DCMS, 2002, p. 166).

The focus on the organisational capacity building of sports development must also be seen in the context of pressures to modernise. In particular the distillation of New Labour's version of social democracy has resulted in an ongoing desire to modernise and be modernised which in turn has facilitated such policy areas as individual liberty, the enhancement of citizenship and accountability. Within what has been referred to as 'the governance approach' (Stoker, 1998), New Labour's managerialism has focused attention onto performance, competence as well as core values as a result the two overarching policy agendas of modernisation and community development have consistently been at the forefront of many cross-cutting agendas (Driver and Martell, 1998). Furthermore, New Labour's exhortation of community as both agent and target of modernisation, together with an acceptance of the need for civic renewal has given rise to a political potency and level of reification that in relation to community empowerment would have hitherto been extremely unlikely (Levitas, 2000).

The key questions to which this chapter now turns are what is capacity building and why is it important for sport development? What is civil society and why is it important to develop our understanding of the capacity building enterprise for sports development? What is social capital and what is the relationship between this concept, civil society and the need or desire to build organisational and management capacity for sports development? These are multifaceted questions which represent an amalgam of consequential and non-sequential issues and coordinates and to provide answers may render contextual explanations necessarily broader than a reader of sports text might imagine. Although given the development orientation of this volume, the ensuing discussion of the questions outlined necessarily looks to the broader sports development milieu as one that is indivisible from broader societal themes of economics, culture and politics. These issues are brought in to more sharp relief within the accompanying case study that examines the impact of capacity building for voluntary sports clubs in England. The next section begins with a brief exposition of modernisation as an overarching political and policy agenda and then turns to the concept of capacity building itself. Next the chapter considers civil society insofar that processes of networking and relationship building are crucial to the notion of capacity building vis-à-vis the voluntary sector. After that the chapter addresses social capital as both a theoretical device and explanatory tool that not only underpins the capacity building enterprise of sports development, but is implicated as a key architectural device to the development of social policy under New Labour.

Modernisation Agenda and Sports Development

The modernisation agenda of New Labour is much more than a reaction to long years of electoral isolation, Thatcherism and policy reviews that picked over ideological positions and responses to a range of challenges (Driver and Martell, 1998, 2002; Finlayson, 2003; Hefferman, 2000). Indeed reflecting further on the notion of structure-agency elaborated previously modernisation can be thought of as being both a process and an outcome in that it both provides the conditions for action (by actors) as well as being the result of that action (of actors). Consequently modernisation can, at a conceptual level, be interpreted as a means of structuring and organising thoughts and actions (Levitas, 1998). In the context of modernity – which requires the constant examination and alteration of social practices in the light of incoming information about those practices – those thoughts and actions are structured reflexively. In other words, the outcome is the pursuance of the constant revision of social activity in the light of new knowledge and the collection of statistical information about populations and commerce by governments in order to facilitate planning and marketing (Giddens, 1991).

Finlayson (2003, pp. 67–8) refines this idea arguing that in this context modernisation has three aspects: its rhetorical function; its concrete reference and its deployment as a strategy of governance. Rhetorically modernisation persuades and motivates, it unifies through coherence and naturalises the notion of progress; concretely, modernised things are 'lean, flexible, efficient' and utilise relevant technology to advance; and in terms of governance it diagnoses problems and establishes solutions in the management of public services. To be sure the popularity for progressive politics, as evidenced by New Labour's electoral success, has, as claimed by Ruth Lister, a certain 'inevitability' to it given the foundations of the modernisation discourse '...that brooks no opposition, for who wants to appear as old-fashioned and backward looking?' (Lister, 2000, p. 8). Politically modernisation has ensured that New Labour have been able to operate according to third way principles, which Fairclough (2006) has argued have a pervasive meaning of 'not only but also' (rights and responsibilities) and establish a '...team' a 'community' of some sort to be the body that both experiences and undertakes modernisation' (Finlayson, 2003, p. 96). For the sports development community, modernisation has not only been instrumental in establishing a coherent delivery framework (Sport England, 2007a) but has also ensured that formalisation and professionalisation have become fundamentally interwoven into the fabric of contemporary sports development (Houlihan and White, 2002). Throughout all levels of sport current practices are consistently reviewed, and as the modernisation agenda (as process) has developed, targets, performance indicators, service agreements as well as policy statements and government commissioned reports and surveys have become the norm. Furthermore sports organisations at all levels have been encouraged to work in partnership within and outside of their traditional boundaries in order that they can become modernised (as an outcome).

Modernisation is thus a key aspect to interpreting the how and why of building capacity for development within sports organisations, indeed an interesting distinction may be drawn between building capacity *for* sport development and building capacity *of* sports development. This chapter highlights New Labour's invocation of community as its default metaphor involving particularised views of social capital and civil society as guiding concepts that locate active citizenship and civic renewal as the key determinants driving the capacity building of sports development. It is on the capacity *of* sports development that the chapter focuses and not just on managerial aspects such as the nature of core management competencies and skills at various levels, but also examining voluntary grass roots sport and its role as a means to reactivate, motivate and stimulate greater civic participation through citizen involvement.

What is Capacity Building and Why is It Important for Sport Development

The mixed economy of welfare which encourages partnerships, which have been and still are a 'holy grail' (Atkinson, 2000) for New Labour is fundamentally indicative of the move from government to governance (Rhodes, 2000). A corollary of this move has been the reinvigoration of New Labour's commitment to welfarist principles, epitomised by sports development being viewed primarily in social policy terms. This reflects the 'core policy paradigms' of New Labour, namely, pragmatism, community and third way politics (Houlihan and White, 2002), which not only defines New Labour but also tailors particular policy strands that invigorate particular policy networks. In this respect liberal individualism is at the heart of third way governments and can readily be detected in the notion of well-being through individual choice, which results in a 'new culture' of self-reliance that is itself based in 'personal development and relationships' (Jordan, 2006, p. 130). The outcome being that core issues such as modernisation, the mixed economy of welfare and social inclusion have become wrapped up in the promulgation of social capital through a reinvigorated civil society. The resulting policy context has therefore offered a particular challenge to reconnect citizens to each other and to their particular communities, primarily via civil society and the importance attached to civil society organisations, but more specifically through the voluntary associationalism of the many sports clubs across the UK.

Interestingly, Saward (2003) regards these sorts of challenges as part of the inevitable complexity involved in moving from a focus on social infrastructure development (roads, schools, hospitals, etc.) to processes occurring within the structure. For many such as Giddens (1996) these are the necessary politics of lifestyle, which Stoker (2006) has termed 'soft wiring' of society and has suggested that local government, in part as a result of being modernised itself, has moved towards a model of multi-level governance (Stoker, 2004). The basis of which has been to provide a framework that has enabled local government to work through Local Strategic Partnerships with a range of partners and organisations in achieving specific outcomes, which have arguably sought to include a degree of empowerment for the particular communities concerned (Corry and Stoker, 2002; Lowndes and Wilson, 2001; Maloney et al. 2000; Stoker, 2004). There has subsequently been an acknowledgement of the inevitable complexity and technical difficultly involved within this systemic development, which '...requires a different form of organisation and accountability in light of these "soft wiring" challenges' (Stoker, 2006, p. 174). Indeed top-down decision making is insufficient in the globalised post-modern era, and arguably this framework of relatively autonomous decision makers forming policy is shaped by the logics associated with the compulsory and obligatory attachment of the machinery of accountability and sustainability.

In light of the framework suggested above, Sport England (2007b), together with a number of other government agencies, has felt the need to publish a series of documents under the title of *Sport Playing its Part*. This campaign not only announces the importance of addressing the claims of social capital theory in increasing the capacity of 'sport' to make a social impact, but also highlights the technical difficulty implicit in the complex nature of using sport for wider social outcomes. In the campaign Sport England states that 'Sport can enrich peoples quality of life, raise self esteem . . . It also has a much larger part to play in building stronger, safer communities, strengthening the economy and developing the skills of local people, meeting the needs of children and improving everyone's health' (Sport England, 2007b). This, seemingly necessary restatement of the value of sport from Sport England not only locates sport as a functional institution with a key role to play in addressing many of the social and economic challenges faced by government, but is also as much about the drive for evidence-based policy, with which to sustain pragmatic policy making (Sport England – Active People Survey, 2007c). It is also Sports England's desire to prove that despite reorganisation (DCMS, 2002; Carter, 2005) it is the still the lead body for community sports development in England.

It is in this context that the language associated with the concept of capacity building has developed. For Collins and Kay (2003) it is essentially a bottom-up process that whilst relying on skilled workers allows development to be at the pace of local groups. Moreover, capacity building in sports development is fundamentally about sustaining capacity in the civic arena and to that extent is concerned with '...giving citizens the opportunity to engage with each other rather than directly with a public authority' (Stoker, 2006, p. 194). This language has become common since the publication of *A Sporting Future for All* in 2000 and *Game Plan* in 2002 and is reflective of third way politics and policies that assert a corporatist conditionality within a framework of civic renewal. Integral to development theory for a number of years (Eade, 1997; Eade and Sayer, 2006), the ultimate aim of capacity building is arguably empowerment which is vital '...if development is to be sustainable and centred in people' (Eade, 1997, p. 1). See the voluntary sports club case study for a more applied and nuanced interpretation of this notion of 'empowerment'.

Given the functionalist nature of New Labour's policy making (Prideaux, 2005), the adherence to communitarian values of empowerment, reciprocity and trust as well as maintaining a neo-liberal economic stance, the need to increase capacity within those sports organisations that provide the major vehicle for sports participation, is both pragmatic and coherent. Indeed those sports organisations that facilitate community empowerment are those that are controlled and organised locally and consequently enable individuals to develop local networks of reciprocal engagement. These organisations are namely the plethora of voluntary sports organisations and clubs that exist across the UK, and it is their mutual aid ethos (Bishop and Hogget, 1986) and reliance on governance structures (Stoker, 2004) that sits at the heart of their ability to empower participants and community alike. Arguably capacity building represents a logical extension of community development via 'soft wiring' which requires not only new governance arrangements between different partners who are implicitly involved in social capital creation, but also the idealising and rationalising of civil society. Furthermore, it is the governmental sponsoring of voluntary associations and volunteering in particular, since the establishment of a British *Compact* in 1998 (Home Office, 1998) that provides much of the practical purchase for the current discussion of capacity building and social capital theory.

This is particularly the case given that within civil society, social capital creation would seem to be increasingly identified in a discursive relationship with voluntary associational activity. The importance of which was demonstrated by Taylor et al. (2003) in the report *Sports Volunteering in England,* which not only identified that 26% of all voluntary activity in the UK occurred in sport and physical activity, but also estimated that the total number of volunteers in sport was over 5.8 million (14.8% of the population) who donated 1.2 billion hours a year. Of key importance to this discursive relationship concerning sports development, social capital and policy making has been the traditional and general philosophical view that has tended to regard sport as 'self-evidently a good thing' (Rowe, 2005). In this sense participation in sport, and particularly participation occurring within a voluntary sports club or organisation, reflects the virtuous and moral status that has tended to surround sport in England since its emergence from almost a century of public school-dominated amateur values (Holt, 1989; Polley, 1998). Moreover the 'values' of sport, derived as they are from public school athleticism roots, have been frequently cited as being conducive to creating both the well-rounded individual who learns to play by the rules, doesn't cheat, wins with grace and loses with honour and suppresses individualism for the sake of the team, as well as in the collectively organised sense of a voluntary sports club (VSC), facilitating social cohesion across any number of social divisions. The strength of this claim lies in the very 'interests, principles and meanings' created by sport and which 'do not exist if there is no sport' (Allison, 1998, p. 710). In essence, the case is made for the particular contribution that 'sport' can make to civil society, beyond the established value of the voluntary association itself, particularly when participated in within a sports club environment. For Dyreson, commenting on the American experience, these values collectively and cumulatively may be referred to as 'cultural power', which amounts to the identification of sport (for Americans at least) as being 'the most important tool for making social capital' (Dyreson, 2001, p. 24).

What is Civil Society? (Social Capital and Capacity Building)

The recurring theme of civil society is critical to the development of sport in Britain not least because most organised sport in Britain is participated in freely (that is voluntary) and tends to be set within an associational setting within a wider sporting structure (sport clubs affiliated to a governing body). Further-more the British 'tradition' of 'arms length' contact between the state and sport (Green and Houlihan, 2006) has come under consistent and persistent pressure from New Labour's utilitarian and evidence-based policy making (Driver and Martell, 2002; Hefferman, 2000). The consequence for sport (a key part of civil society) can be witnessed in former Prime Minister Tony Blair's introduction to *Game Plan* where he stated that 'Sport is a powerful and often under-used tool that can help Government to achieve a number of ambitious goals. We have to ensure that we are well equipped to do that' (DCMS/SU, 2002, p. 5). In the context of the current examination of capacity building for the delivery of sports development, it is perhaps the last sentence of Blair's statement that is most illuminating. For not only is sports develop-ment now a political tool that is to be used for other non-sport interventions but that sports development must have the capacity to fulfil this expanded role that government has envisaged. Moreover the emphasis given by New Labour to developing capacity within civil society, the focus on sports development and the enhanced view of voluntary sports associations in achieving the former is therefore a consequence of the 'summative' concept of social capital, which necessitates both an active citizenry and 'community' development (Coalter, 2007).

Before highlighting further the conceptual roots of civil society it is worth noting three contextual points. First, that there is general agreement amongst writers that civil society is a 'revived concept' (Allison, 1998; De Hart and Dekker, 1999), but not a consensus on the concept of civil society itself. Second, that there is a limited conceptual consensus concerning its common-est contemporary application which tends to revolve around the functioning and operation of the modern democratic state (Gellner, 1994). Third, that conceptually civil society has been theorised beyond western democratic inter-pretations to account for its presence or absence in totalitarian regimes (Fine, 1997; Tempest, 1997). The focus of this brief exploration of civil society concerns the realm in which individuals can organise themselves into groups and associations and participate in 'uncoerced human association' (Walzer, 1995) or 'voluntary activity' (Deakin, 2001). Subsequently forming voluntary associations and organisations '...that do not form part of the state machin-ery, whose core does not lie in the individual sphere of the formal economy, and which are open to voluntary membership' (De Hart and Dekker, 1999, p. 75). The corollary of this definition is, as Diamond suggests, that, 'Civil society is an intermediary entity, standing between the private sphere and the state' (Diamond, 1994, p. 7). In this guise associational life, whether social, cultural or political, whether of the self-help or charitable variety, has as its defining feature a volunteerism that implicitly rejects interference and pressure from others. Thus, the notion of civil society has both spatial and operational dimensions that centre on institutions as diverse and as basic as the family and religion to the great assortment of voluntary associations and in particular voluntary sports organisations that are found in many societies where citizen action is employed in improving their communities and societies. Almond and Verba (1963), Diamond (1994), Gellner (1994), Putnam (1993, 2000) and Fukuyama (1999, 2000) argue to varying degrees that the voluntary activity within civil society is the wellspring for the civic virtue that is a fundamental aspect of a democratic and pluralistic society. Indeed Gellner's (1994) statement 'no civil society, no democracy' succinctly encapsulates the almost universal notion of civil society as a protective sphere constraining state interference.

What is Social Capital?

Following on from the above account of civil society as an underpinning contextual framework for capacity building, it is apparent that in order to develop our understanding of capacity building from a development perspective to a sports development perspective we need to consider the more nuanced concept of social capital. Historically, social capital stems from the writings of Alexis de Tocqueville who observed that Americans had a distinct propensity to gather to form voluntary associations (Farr, 2004), which he viewed as particularly important, as it was the formation of groups of all shapes and sizes that acted to reverse much of the potential for excessive individualism that modern democracies could promote (De Tocqueville, 2003). De Tocqueville referred to this phenomenon as the 'art of association' and notwithstanding other notable authors/approaches, the importance of De Tocqueville's work lies in his attribution of voluntary associationalism as the key building block of social capital. For sports development, which is fundamentally predicated on the notion of participation in a group (preferably) of one's own choosing (i.e. a voluntary group). The implication is that sports participation is likely to be within civil society and that increasing organisational capacity for the delivery of sports development necessarily implicates voluntary sports participation as a key mechanism in the process. The outcome of which is itself an exercise in social capital creation, which within our concept of civil society suggests a whole range of important social functions can be associated with one's voluntary activity.

Numerous commentators have analysed and defined the concept of social capital and other than some general agreement that 'networks matter' there is little agreement as to how the constituent parts of social capital are both organised and organising in relation to particular outcomes (Blackshaw and Long, 2005; Farr, 2004; Fine, 1997; Field, 2003; Portes, 1998; Edwards and Foley, 1997). Social capital, like many other social science concepts is thus a contested term, and in order to utilise the explanatory power of social capital in relation to the building of the organisational capacity necessary to deliver sports development, it is necessary to briefly outline the three main tributaries that social capital theory flows along.

The dominant theory of social capital stemming from the work of Robert Putnam (1993, 1995, 2000) follows in the De Tocqueville tradition and is academically and ontologically located within the realms of political science. As such the concern of much of Putnam's work has been to establish macro or system wide accounts of the maintenance of the democratic political system using a particular orientation to social capital that Lewandowski (2006) has referred to as the 'democratic strain' of this theory. Putnam (1996) has established 'networks, norms and trust' as the primary ingredients of social capital, later defining it as referring '...to connections among individuals – social networks and the norms of reciprocity that arise from them' (Putnam, 2000, p. 19). In essence then for Putnam social capital is created by trust and reciprocity, which are viewed as part of the social norms that arise from social networks. The main assertion of the democratic strain is thus that normative social networks are fundamentally intertwined both with and within the abundance of associational life that exists outside of both the state and private sectors. Furthermore a predisposition to engage in voluntary associationalism is assumed to be an indicator of the strength of the civic core of any given society. Both implicitly and explicitly voluntary associational activity is implicated as the prime means of community development and connectedness necessary to provide the trust, reciprocity, norms and values that enable the enduring maintenance of western democratic values and systems. It is perhaps to this end why Putnam chose the metaphorical image of the solitary bowler to represent the apparent decline in organised regular associational activity in *Bowling Alone* (2000). Although Putnam's vivid imagery has served as a springboard for an acknowledgement of the role that voluntary sport organisations can make to social cohesion and has reinvigorated policy networks and communities associated with sports development, it is within this Tocquevillean orientation to establish causal links between sports development and wider democratic political ideals that a notable emphasis has been placed on the normative quality of sport and particularly in its use to combat social exclusion (Collins and Kay, 2003).

A different approach to understanding the role of social capital is offered by Coleman (1988, 1994) who has developed an intellectual framework that combines the concerns of sociology with Becker's (1964) economic rationale. Coleman was concerned to develop an explanation for human action rather than just provide explanations that clarified the conditions and influences under which certain human action could be interpreted. Thus this second social capital thesis proposed an economic generator of human action, and can be referred to as a 'rational strain' (Lewandowski, 2006) that '...sees the actor as having goals independently arrived at, as acting independently and as wholly self-interested. Its principal virtue lies in having a principle of action, that of maximising utility' (Coleman, 1988, p. 95). For Coleman (1990) then, social capital is a functional resource strategically pursued by individuals within a given social structure, so that connections between and among individuals have a functional utility. In this respect social capital is no more than physical or human capital in being a functional resource necessary to reach one's particular ends. In short the term 'capital' is appropriate because in similar fashion to economic capital, social capital is the store or 'bank' of connections, links or 'bridges' which an individual can use to maximise their interests by achieving those things difficult, if not impossible, to attain in the absence of such resources.

Despite a grounding in methodological individualism, by employing the notion of 'closure' – where individuals know or are known to each other – Coleman argues that this type of network acts as a way of sanctioning behaviour via normative processes thus reducing potential expenditure costs in the operation of a network. Importantly whilst there is the implicit normative development of trust, there is also the more explicit establishment of obligation which ensures that relations between different individuals and institutions are mutually reinforcing thus ensuring reciprocity. For Coleman sport associations can provide locations for the provision of public goods, but need the presence of a prescriptive norm. In a group or associational situation the necessary norm would facilitate and reinforce particular behaviours, specifically the norm would need to ensure the forgoing of self-interest for the interests of the shared group or association. In the instance of a specific sport and a specific VSC the sort of norm identified above equates to a 'subculture' which instills in participants a propensity to act in accordance with the particular norms and values of the sport and the club (Bishop and Hogget, 1986). For Bishop and Hoggett the notion of a 'subculture' emerges from the group dynamic and can '…be seen to occupy an intermediate position, existing in the space between the individual or club engaged in a leisure activity and the wider social order' (Bishop and Hogget, 1986, p. 43). Similarly Horton-Smith's suggestion, in the context of grass roots associations, of a 'group ideology' that equates to '…the values and beliefs that support the goals, existence, virtues structure and activities of a given set of people' (2000, p. 63), is indicative of the social processes that surround sports participation and especially participation in a specific sport through a VSC. Indeed Smith and Waddington (2004) have suggested that club subculture or ideology is just one of a number of components that makes up the institutional capital of a VSC.

Bourdieu provides the third distinct approach to the interpretation of how social capital can operate and can be referred to as the 'critical strain' (Lewandowski, 2006). Bourdieu's version of social capital is located within his project to understand 'social practice' and social reproduction and has been referred to as a particularly socialised account of the phenomenon (Jenkins, 1992; Lane, 2000). Bourdieu defines social capital as '…the sum of the resources, actual or virtual, that accrue to an individual or a group by virtue of possessing a durable network of more or less institutionalised relationships of mutual acquaintance and recognition' (Bourdieu and Wacquant, 1992, p. 119).

For Bourdieu social capital is tied up with other forms of capital notably cultural capital and symbolic capital and thus constitutes a very human property that is essentially generated and bounded by the relations and relationships that humans form with one another over time. Bourdieu employs the concept of 'habitus' as the key instrument to explain an individual's background in interpreting human behaviour. A habitus is an 'embodied internalised schema' (Jarvie and Maguire, 1994) that functions as the structuring structure for the production and reproduction of human action and amounts to a shared set of durable dispositions, perceptive schemes and ingrained orientations (Lewandowski, 2006). The upshot for Bourdieu is that one's habitus is status conferring and one's social connections allow one's social capital to be operationalised facilitating the opening up of opportunities that otherwise would not have been possible. Thus in Bourdieu's scheme, social capital is used to benefit either an individual or a group and as such does not provide for the public benefit per se, but rather is linked to how particular agents use social capital to exploit the other forms of capital in their possession. It is therefore not the individual utility maximisation (of rational choice theory) that constructs the social and economic worlds inhabited by individuals, rather it is their differential access to capital that is the key driving and determining force (Foley and Edwards, 1999).

Furthermore in relation to associations, Bourdieu refers to associations as 'social groups' (1987). He argues that social groups are not voluntary cooperative enterprises, but rather coalesce on the basis of 'non-voluntary predispositions' and as such social capital becomes a shared marker or 'credit' (Bourdieu, 1997). Thus in the Bourdieun take on social capital, power is inescapably linked to the notion of having and using social capital, a quite different approach to the more benign approaches to social capital discussed thus far. Power is exercised by individuals operating to reproduce their social position, and social capital functions in a transmutative fashion to reinforce ones symbolic and hence cultural capital. This corresponds with Bourdieu's concern for the reflective status that cultural capital confers on those who possess and are knowledgeable about this form of capital. Table 10.1 summarises the main approaches to social capital and their implications for sports organisations' capacity building.

Having identified the three major theorists/positions in the field of social capital it should become obvious why the 'democratic' strain has become the most dominant for the analysis of social phenomenon. First, it is politically expedient and chimes with the political direction of 'third way' governments; second, it centralises and raises the importance of the 'organisational capacity of communities' and suggests that social exclusion is best addressed by examining the social processes and relationships that serve to marginalise and alienate individuals from mainstream society (Coalter, 2007); third, it is functional in that associations or civil society are seen as outcome focused and consequently can be viewed as 'we' phenomena (Tuomela, 1995), which have a normative impact on people's ability and potential to trust, be trustworthy and exhibit reciprocity in social relations; fourth, it empowers community and is an antidote to the less palatable notion of people acting as individual atoms acting in self-gratifying ways to achieve their own ends or being 'merely stratifyingly habituated group members' (Lewandowski, 2006). Finally, the remedy of the democratic strain of social capital to social ills is placed squarely on voluntary associationalism (Putnam, 2000). This is convenient in that within democratic societies in the main voluntary associations, which implicitly accede to deep-rooted western democratic notions of liberalism and

Table 10.1 Social capital theory implications for sport organisations capacity building.

Theoretical approach	Main claims	Implications for sport organisations capacity building
Democratic strain (Putnam)	From political science and pluralist in intention. Emphasis that networks and connections matter – individuals create community via their normative capacity as social facts. Attempts to reconcile individualism and collective action. Makes an assumption that normatively, trust and reciprocity are created or arise from social networks. Civil society is idealised and voluntary associationalism is identified as both indicator and creator of social capital	Voluntary sports associations and the volunteering occurring within them are privileged as the place and means to establish an active citizenry and a civic culture. Form part of communitarian approach to policy making whereby the creation of social networks underpins social connectedness. Voluntary associations are 'encouraged' to expand their capacity in order to be able to fulfil functions ascribed to civil society by government, in particular promoting a vision of a normalised and centralised community. Standardisation, linked to modernisation becomes a necessary aspect of managing this aspect of civil society
Rational strain (Coleman)	From economic sociology, employs methodological individualism to account for rather than explain human action. Concerned with the functional resources individuals might posses as aggregations of rational individuals where choice is governed by utility principle. Collective action is possible where norms act to reduce expenditure costs, value is thus utilitarian	Sport organisations (SO) capacity building is dependant on individual strategic value of participation – in this sense norms determine the extent of collective action. Closure in SOs whilst enabling collective action, may also be exclusive and potentially divisive. Viewed as a benefit accruing to individuals from being part of an organisation. It is difficult to see how norms might be maintained or sustained over long periods of time
Critical strain (Bourdieu)	From sociology and anthropology – social capital is a 'credit' shared among a group where it reinforces distinction and exclusion. Structurally dominant – all human action related to background 'habitus'. Social groups are neo-Marxist classes in that membership is determined by factors residing outside of an individual's framework of choice. It is a highly group specific, context dependent socially stratifying resource	Increasing capacity likely to cause dissonance within and amongst SOs. Capacity building is likely to bring greater numbers of individuals together who share similar predispositions and as such may create greater division within society. Any potential public goods are likely to be subsumed by increases in 'club' goods. Within SOs individuals may find other means to express particular aspects of power relationships through forms of social distinction

freedom already exist thus enabling these societies to heal themselves. To this end the case study addresses and discusses some of these issues as they relate to voluntary sports clubs in particular as potential agents for social engineering. Despite the wide spread political take-up of Putnamism, particularly in Anglophone countries, to attempt any brief critique here would be fruitless as there already exists a vast array of critical literature on the ideas put forward by Putnam and the reader shall be pointed in the direction of those.

Social Capital, Modernisation and the Organisational Capacity for the Delivery of Sports Development

The relationship between sport and social capital is ambivalent, equivocal and inconclusive with notable authors such as Collins and Kay (2003), Weed et al. (2005) and Coalter (2007) pointing to the lack of available evidence regarding the ability of sport organisations to create social capital. To be sure the important point to bear in mind is that social capital has become an essential and explicit part of the architecture of governmental social policy (Performance and Innovation Unit, 2002). A social policy which at its most basic has established (Putnamian) social capital theory as the foundation for the identification of community as a site of action and voluntary associations (within those communities) as the key mechanism by which individuals can communally act together. It is in this context that capacity building for sports development needs to be considered. That is as a response to the processes of modernisation that have, through the reification of community and the idealisation of civil society, standardised and centralised both volunteerism and volunteering. Figure 10.1 outlines the spatial relationships between the key elements involved in capacity building for sports development; it indicates the nature of outcomes and outputs involved in sets of complex and convoluted relationships although it is important to note that the figure is not intended to identify causality flows per se.

Much has been made of the obvious or 'self-evident' value of sport, which in itself speaks of moral and functionalist interpretations of sport, but moreover has been used to elicit normative characteristics that extend beyond the scope of particular sports. In this sense sport (voluntary organisations) can provide common interests, a common location and a spatial embeddedness which policy makers have sought to capitalise on for building capacity via social capital creation strategies. For Marian Taylor, policy makers have tended to make the assumption '. . . that common location or interests bring with them social and moral cohesion, a sense of security, and mutual trust. But they [the policy makers] also tend to go a step further and assume that norms will be turned into action; that is, that communities can be turned into agency, with people caring for each other, getting involved in collective enterprises and activities and acting together to change their circumstances' (Taylor, 2003, p. 38).

The result has been to not only implicate social capital theory within the whole notion of individual and collective action, but more particularly to identify sport as a suitable vehicle from which community cohesion can

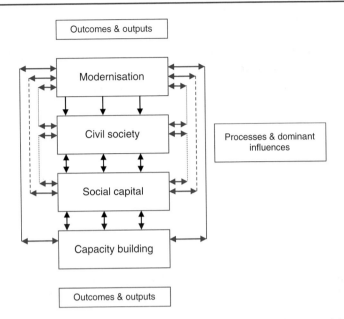

Figure 10.1 The relationship between modernisation, civil society, social capital and capacity building.

Dotted lines: Indicate the two-way relationship that exists between civil society and modernisation and between civil society and social capital. Civil society is the location for the 'democratic' version of social capital to be created and exercised and is also privileged by the modernisation process. The clear move towards governance structures empowers as closer relationships between the public and service providers develop.

Dashed lines: Modernisation has implicated social capital as the key tool in social and civic renewal; reflexively modernisation is affected by the potential power of social capital to create further opportunities for engagement by increasing capacity within voluntary associations. If the democratic strain of social capital develops then greater civic engagement creates new and further demands for accountability and transparency.

Solid lines: In order for social capital to be created, capacity in organisations needs to be established, in NGBs, for example, the conditions are set through modernisation that facilitate networks, communication and an outward focus through the need to work both in and though partnerships.

Black arrows: Indicate the notional direction of potential outcomes/outputs. An output of modernisation, for example, being the need to work and exercise influence in partnership with other agencies/organisations. An output from capacity building is the increased emphasis on the volunteer workforce via VSCs in particular to expand; an outcome may be seen in the increased expectation on behalf of volunteers to be professionalised, thus professionalisation of VSCs is an outcome of the drive to increase capacity within those sports clubs.

spring. In this way the building of organisational capacity necessary for governance strategies to work is both a moral and purposive outcome. In the first instance the raft of community orientated programmes established from 1997 onwards – New Deal for Communities (1998), Education Action Zones (2000), Health Action Zones (1998), Home Zones (2001) and Sports Action

Zones (2001) (Frazer, 2002; Imrie and Raco, 2003) – are testimony to the importance attached to reciprocity, social solidarity and civic responsiveness within an idealised notion of community that is at the heart of New Labour policy (Levitas, 2000). They also raise some questions as to the long term sustainability of what Hodgson (2004) has referred to as 'manufactured civil society'. Manufactured civil society refers to the formation and funding of community level groups through some type of state initiative that seek to impart moralistic values that lead to the production of 'rounded' individuals. This manufacturing process may impinge on more traditional 'organic' perceptions of how sports development occurs and may impact on the mutual aid ethos, identified by Bishop and Hogget (1986) as central to a leisure/sports club. For sports development the upshot of this wider governmental approach has been to see sport as a suitable vehicle for developing some of the organisational capacity necessary for communities to be able to develop resulting in '...a broad shift from developing sport in communities to developing communities through sport' (Coalter, 2007, p. 39). Essentially in this context the concern with building the organisational capacity for the delivery of sports development is fundamentally premised on the notion of creating social capital. That is to say that under the steerage of the DCMS (2000, 2001, 2002) sports development has taken on many of the concerns of social policy (particularly that of social exclusion) by employing social capital as the key mechanism for incorporating, integrating and empowering individuals within their communities. Given this scenario, at the heart of capacity building debate is the value that sports development can have in relation to community level activity and in particular the regeneration of civic society with an emphasis on the active citizen involved in civic participation. Indeed voluntary sports club participation is active citizenship at its most obvious and in the context of the above discussion of social capital has become the prime venue and mechanism for increasing the capacity of sports development. The question of the extent to which grass roots sport is prone to a charge of state manufacturing together with the subsequent development issues associated with this engineering process are not discussed further in this chapter. Suffice to acknowledge that they raise some important research questions that will need to be addressed in the near future.

Capacity Building for Delivering Sports Development: Lessons for Managers

It is clear that sports development in the last 10 years has been subject to a vision that whilst encompassing the goals of pragmatic politics that involves important aspects of modernisation, accountability and individual liberty has crucially been centred on civic renewal. This itself has coalesced around the potential of the democratic strain of social capital within a wider voluntary associationalism perceived to be at the heart of civil society (Levitas, 2000). From sports development vision to sports development practice the building of organisational capacity for the delivery of sports development has become enmeshed and enshrined in government managerialism (Pierre and Peters, 2000) as structural forces have dominated the management of sports development resources. No longer is sports development a discrete service or process in England where sports development professionals can reside detachedly within their own enclaves (if ever they could) (Houlihan, 2001), but is part of a multi-level governance approach where cross-cutting in relation to issue-based policy formulation is the dominant paradigm (Stoker, 2006).

The reinvigoration of civil society and recourse to social capital theory as a key foundation concept has enabled mass participation sport to be incorporated within a community focused and community building ethos that can be seen to be part of the government's wider strategic objectives. This tactical restructuring of the sports development infrastructure is evidenced in the first instance by the division of the sports council in 1997 into the four national sport organisations along with UKSport as the elite sport arm for principally the Olympic sports. Latterly, New Labour has further reinforced these structural conditions, first via the restructuring and repositioning of Sport England so that the organisation is more focused on its core business of enabling and investing in community sport (DCMS/S U, 2002). More recently four of the (five) recommendations made by Carter (2005) – the introduction of robust measurement and monitoring systems; the promotion of the benefits of sport and physical activity; the improvement of local delivery; and the development of a single access point and brand for sport – are all indicative of a greater organisational and management capacity within sports development to accept the challenges of social 'soft wiring' (Stoker, 2006) by increasing the capacity of civil society organisations through the imposition a particularised interpretation of social capital. For New Labour the Putnam version of social capital has become the touchstone in its approach to building capacity within communities as well as establishing the idea of community as a political tool. This has often resulted in policies towards sports development, which create and sustain social capital and hence build capacity for service provision within a particular (geographic) community, being no more than intermediate policies as a means to achieve improvements in wider aspects of social or welfare policy such as in individual health, educational attainment and crime reduction. The upshot for sports development is that sports ends in themselves have become superseded by broader community aims, and within the context of New Labour's managerialist paradigm. The exhortation of community as both agent and target of modernisation has not only met with an acceptance of the need for civic renewal, but has presaged a rise to a political potency and level of reification of community empowerment that foreshadows the potentiality to build the necessary capacity to develop (Levitas, 1998, 2000).

For those concerned with the management of sports development, which if one accepts as concerned with a process (Hylton and Bramham, 2008) involving a whole range of diverse actors and agencies, there has been a recognition that the skills and values and approaches 'traditionally' associated with promoting sporting opportunities have had to both change and become modernised in themselves. Central to these concerns are the multi-level governance structures that modernisation processes have enabled to become entrenched thus ensuring that the engagement of citizens, largely through social capital creation, has become paramount to the building of that capacity for the delivery of sports development.

Within these multi-agency decision-making structures the lessons for sports development managers are multifaceted: first, an appreciation of the political context for sports development is invaluable; despite a reliance of governance approaches which presuppose a bottom-up interpretation of network and relationship development, top-down structuring structures are critical to the shape and direction of sports development processes (Maloney et al., 2000); second, despite much research concerning the value of sport or the contribution that sport can make, sports development managers should question the validity of some sport forms and question the impact that some programmes can make as often presumed outcomes are based on the notion of sports as 'self evidently a good thing' (Rowe, 2005); third, managers should question the validity of utilitarian approaches to sport which predicate capacity building towards prescribed outcomes from government or other agencies. Again this issue is critical in relation to maintaining stability and continuity within grass roots sports development and has been described as providing '...a very precarious balance between using clubs as part of national policy initiatives, and disillusioning current and potential volunteers in such clubs. Any initiatives that seek to use clubs as agents of sports participation policy must therefore be sensitive to the needs of volunteers' (Weed et al., 2005, p. 42); finally, managers need to be aware that capacity building brings a whole set of extant pressures to bear on the voluntary sports sector and sports volunteers themselves (Nichols et al., 2005), pressures that should alert policy makers and practitioners to the creeping professionalisation and formalisation of grass roots sport, which Horch has aphoristically described as the 'self-destroying processes of sport clubs' (1998).

New Labour's return to community rather than society (Levitas, 2000) has boosted the concept of social capital as a means and method to understanding a more detailed analysis of structures and functions of community. The importance of volunteerism to New Labour has been shown to be integral to wider policies where social capital creation has become the foundation for its communitarian vision. To this extent, and as the attending case study highlights, voluntary sports clubs represent a significant and important aspect of civil society that have the potential to create forms of social capital, empower individuals as well as building capacity for a socially and morally expanded interpretation of sports development.

Social capital like many other social science concepts turns out to be a contested term and therefore it is important to point out that as New Labour have largely accepted the Putnam model of social capital. The analysis of capacity building for the delivery of sports development has necessarily evaluated outcomes and outputs within the intended policy context. Whilst it is reasonable to accept a Putnamian conception of social capital as central to interpreting capacity building enterprises within sports development practices, it is also necessary to use the tools advocated by the critical strain (Bourdieu) and rational strain (Coleman) (Lewandowski, 2006) to produce knowledge that is both critical and analytical. This chapter has only offered limited critical analysis of the impact of the dominance of the democratic strain of social capital upon the policy contexts of sports development in the UK. And although this has allowed for a more nuanced understanding of the social processes implicit to any capacity building exercise centred on voluntary sector organisations, it suggests that there are still many questions to be answered. Arguably visions of sports development now largely reside outside of sport itself, and instead can be found in a community orientated structure where the potential for capacity building is linked to visions of the good society. Sports development practices must therefore negotiate the emerging issues and tensions that may play out here, particularly those that concern structure and agency and the role of the voluntary sector in sports development.

References

Allison, L. (1998). Sport and civil society. *Political Studies*, **46**, 709–26.

Almond, G. and Verba, S. (1963). *The Civic Culture*. Princeton: Princeton University Press.

Atkinson, R. (2000). Combating social exclusion in Europe: The new urban policy challenge. *Urban Studies*, **37**(5–6), 1037–55.

Becker, G.S. (1964). *Human Capital: A Theoretical and Empirical Analysis*. New York: National Bureau of Economic Research.

Bishop, J. and Hogget, P. (1986). *Organising Around Enthusiasms: Mutual Aid in Leisure*. London: Comedia.

Blackshaw, T. and Long, J. (2005). What's the big idea? A critical exploration of the concept of social capital and its incorporation into leisure policy discourse. *Leisure Studies*, **24**(3), 239–258.

Blair, T. (1998). *The Third Way: New Politics for the New Century*. London: Fabian Society.

Blunkett, D. (2003). Active citizens, strong communities – Progressing civic renewal. *The Home Secretary's Scarman Lecture*, 11 December 2003. London: Home Office.

Bourdieu, P. (1987). What makes a social class? On the theoretical and practical existence of groups. *Berkley Journal of Sociology*, **32**, 1–16.

Bourdieu, P. (1997). The forms of capital. In *Education: Culture, Economy, Society* (A. Halsey, H. Lauder, H. Brown et al., eds). Oxford: Oxford University Press.

Bourdieu, P. and Wacquant, L. (1992). *An Invitation to Reflexive Sociology*. Chicago: University of Chicago Press.

Brown, G. (1994). *Fair is Efficient – A Socialist Agenda for Fairness*. London: Fabian Society.

Carter, P. (2005). *Review of National Sport Effort and Resources*. London: Sport England.

Coalter, F. (2007). Sports clubs, social capital and social regeneration: 'Ill-defined interventions with hard to follow outcomes'. *Sport in Society*, **10**(4), 537–59.

Coleman, J.S. (1988). Social capital in the creation of human capital. *American Journal of Sociology*, **94**(Supplement), S95–120.

Coleman, J.S. (1990). *Equality and Achievement in Education*. Boulder: Westview Press.

Coleman, J.S. (1994). *Foundations of Social Theory*. Cambridge, MA: Belknap Press.

Collins, M. and Kay, T. (2003). *Sport and Social Exclusion*. London: Routledge.

Corry, D. and Stoker, G. (2002). *New Localism: Refashioning the Centre-Local Relationship*. London: The New Local Government Network.

Deakin, N. (2001). *In Search of Civil Society*. Basingstoke, Palgrave.

De Hart, J. and Dekker, P. (1999). Civic engagement and volunteering in the Netherlands: A 'Putnamian' analysis. In *Social Capital and European Democracy* (J.W. Van Deth, M. Maraffis, K. Newton et al., eds). London: Routledge.

Department for Culture Media and Sport (2000). *A Sporting Future for All*. London: DCMS.

Department for Culture Media and Sport (2001). *The Governments Plan for Sport*. London: DCMS.

Department for Culture Media and Sport/Strategy Unit (2002). *Game Plan: A Strategy for Delivering the Government's Sport and Physical Activity Objectives*. London: DCMS.

De Tocqueville, A. (2003). *Democracy in America and Two Essays on America* (Translated by Gerald, E. Bevan). London: Penguin.

Diamond, L. (1994). Toward democratic consolidation. *Journal of Democracy*, **5**(3), 4–17.

Driver, S. and Martell, L. (1998). *New Labour: Politics after Thatcher*. Cambridge: Polity Press.

Driver, S. and Martell, K. (2002). Blair's Britain, Cambridge: Polity.

Dyreson, M. (2001). Maybe it's better to bowl alone: Sport, community and democracy in American thought. *Culture, Sport and Society*, **4**(1), 19–30.

Eade, D. (1997). *Capacity Building*. Oxford: Oxfam.

Eade, D. and Sayer, J. (2006). *Development and the Private Sector: Consuming Interests*. Bloomfield, CT: Kumarian Press.

Edwards, B. F. and Foley, M. (1998). "Civil Society and Social Capital beyond Putnam." *The American Behavioural Scientist*, **42**(1), 124–134.

Fairclough, N. (2006). Tony Blair and the language of politics. *Open Democracy*, downloaded 2 May 2007 (available at http://www.opendemocracy.net/articles/ViewPopUpArticle.jsp?id=3&articleId=4205).

Farr, J. (2004). Social capital: A conceptual history. *Political Theory*, **32**(1), 6–33.

Field, J. (2003). Social Capital, London: Routledge.

Fine, R. (1997). Civil society theory, enlightenment and critique. In *Civil Society: Democratic Perspectives* (R. Fine and S. Rai, eds). London: Frank Cass.

Finlayson, A. (2003). *Making Sense of New Labour*. London: Lawrence and Wishart.

Foley, M. and Edwards, B. (1999). Is it time to disinvest in social capital? *Journal of Public Policy*, **19**(2), 141–73.

Frazer, E. (2002). Local social relations: Public, club and common goods. In *Reclaiming Community* (V. Nash, ed.). London: IPPR.

Fukuyama, F. (1999). *The Great Disruption: Human Nature and the Reconstitution of Social Order*. London: Profile Books.

Fukuyama, F. (2000). *Social Capital and Civil Society*. IMF Working Paper, International Monetary Fund, April 2000.

Gellner, E. (1994). *Conditions of Liberty Civil Society and Its Rivals*. London: Hamish Hamilton.

Giddens, A. (1990). *Modernity and Self Identity, Self and Society in the Late Modern Age*. Cambridge: Polity Press.

Giddens, A. (1993). *New Rules of Sociological Method* (2nd edn). Cambridge: Polity Press.

Giddens, A. (1996). In defence of sociology essays, interpretations and rejoinders. Cambridge: Polity.

Green, M. and Houlihan, B. (2006). Governmentality, modernization and the 'disciplining' of national sporting organizations: Athletics in Australia and the United Kingdom. *Sociology of Sport Journal*, **23**(1), 47–71.

Hefferman, R. (2000). *New Labour and Thatcherism: Political Change in Britain*. Basingstoke: Palgrave.

Hodgson, L. (2004). Manufactured civil society: Counting the cost. *Critical Social policy*, **24**(2), 139–64.

Hoggett, P. (2001). Agency, Rationality and Social Policy, *Journal of Social Policy*, **30**(1), 37–56, Cambridge: Cambridge University Press.

Holt, R. (1989). *Sport and the British: A Modern History*. Oxford: Oxford University Press.

Home Office (1998). *Compact: Getting it Right Together Cm4100*. London: The Stationery Office.

Horch, H.D. (1998). Self-destroying processes of sports clubs in Germany. *European Journal for Sport Management*, **5**(1), 46–58.

Horton-Smith, D. (2000). *Grassroots Associations*. Thousand Oaks: Sage.

Houlihan, B. (2001). Citizenship, civil society and the sport and recreation professions. *Managing Leisure*, **6**(1), 1–12.

Houlihan, B. and White, A. (2002). *The Politics of Sport Development: Development of Sport or Development Through Sport*. London: Routledge.

Hylton, K. and Bramham, P. (eds). (2008). *Sports Development: Policy, Process and Practice* (2nd edn). London: Routledge.

Imrie, R. and Raco, M. (2003). Community and the changing nature of urban policy. Urban renaissance? In *New Labour, Community and Urban Policy* (R. Imrie and M. Raco, eds). Bristol: Policy Press.

Jarvie, G. and Maguire, J. (1994). *Sport and Leisure in Social Thought*. London: Routledge.

Jenkins, R. (1992). *Pierre Bourdieu*. London: Routledge.

Jordan, B. (2006). *Social Policy for the Twenty-First Century*. Cambridge: Polity Press.

Kendall, J. (2000). The Mainstreaming of the Third Sector into Public Policy in England in the Late 1990's: Whys and Wherefores. *LSE Civil Society Working Paper 2*. London: LSE.

Labour Party. (1997). *Building the Future Together*. London: The Labour Party

Lane, J.F. (2000). *Pierre Bourdieu: A Critical Introduction*. London: Pluto Press.

Levitas, R. (1998). *The Inclusive Society? Social Exclusion and New Labour*. Basingstoke: MacMillan Press.

Levitas, R. (2000). Community, Utopia and new labour. *Local Economy*, **15**(3), 188–97.

Lewandowski, J. (2006). Capitalising sociability; rethinking the theory of social capital. In *Assessing Social Capital: Concepts Policy and Practice* (R. Edwards, J. Franklin, and J. Holland, eds). Newcastle: Cambridge Scholars Publishing.

Lewis, P.A. (2000). Realism, causality and the problem of social structure. *Journal for the Theory of Social Behaviour*, **30**(3), 249–68.

Lister, R. (2000). To Rio via the third way: New labour's 'welfare' reform agenda. *Renewal: A Journal of Labour Politics*, **8**(4), 1–14.

Lister, R. (2004). The third way's social investment state. In *Welfare State Change: Towards a Third Way* (J. Lewis and R. Surrender, eds). Oxford: Oxford Univesity Press.

Lowndes, V. and Wilson, D. (2001). Social capital and local government: Exploring the institutional design variable. *Political Studies*, **49**(4), 629–47.

Maloney, W., Smith, G., and Stoker, G. (2000). Social capital and urban governance: Adding a more contextualised 'top-down' perspective. *Political Studies*, **48**, 802–20.

Nichols, G., Taylor, P., and James, M. et al. (2005). Pressures on the UK sports sector. *Voluntas*, **16**(1), 33–50.

Oakley, B. and Green, M. (2001). Still playing the game at arm's length? The selective re-investment in British sport 1995–2000. *Managing Leisure*, **6**, 74–94.

Performance and Innovation Unit (2002). *Social Capital: A Discussion Paper*. London: Cabinet Office.

Pierre, J. and Peters, B.G. (2000). *Governance, Politics and the State*. Basingstoke: Macmillan.

Polley, M. (1998). *Moving the Goalposts: A History of Sport and Society Since 1945*. London: Routledge.

Portes, A. (1998). "Social capital: its origins and applications in modern sociology." *Annual Review of Sociology*, **24**, 1–24.

Prideaux, S. (2005). *Not So New Labour: A Sociological Critique of New Labour's Policy and Practice*. Bristol: Policy Press.

Putnam, R.D. (1993). *Making Democracy Work: Civic Traditions in Modern Italy*. Princeton: Princeton University Press.

Putnam, R. (1995). Tuning in, tuning out: The strange disappearance of social capital in America. Political Science and Politics. The 1995 Ithiel de Sola Pool Lecture, 664–83.

Putnam, R.D. (1996). The strange disappearance of civic America. *The American Prospect*.

Putnam, R.D. (2000). *Bowling Alone: The Collapse and Revival of American Community*. New York: Simon & Schuster.

Rhodes, R.A.W. (2000). Transforming British government. *Volume 1: Changing Institutions*. Basingstoke: Macmillan/ESRC.

Rowe, N. (2005). Keynote paper: How many people participate in sport? The politics, practice and realities of measurement – The English experience. International Association for Sports Information, Beijing Sport University.

Saward, M. (2003). *Democracy*. Cambridge: Polity Press.

Sibeon, R. (1999). Agency, structure and social chance as cross-disciplinary concepts. *Politics*, **19**(3), 139–44.

Smith, A. and Waddington, I. (2004). Using 'sport in the community schemes' to tackle crime and drug use among young people: Some policy issues and problems. *European Physical Education Review*, **10**(3), 279–98.

Sport England (2007a). Sport England policy statement. The delivery system for sport in England. London: Sport England.

Sport England (2007b). Sport playing its part. Retrieved on 21 August 2007 from http://www.sportengland.org/index/get_resources/sport_playing_its_part.htm.

Sport England (2007c). Active people survey. Retrieved on 21 August 2007 from http://www.sportengland.org/index/get_resources/research/active_people.htm.

Stoker, G. (1998). Governance as theory: Five propositions. *International Social Sciences Journal*, **155**(1), 17–28.

Stoker, G. (2004). *Transforming Local Governance*. Basingstoke: Palgrave.

Stoker, G. (2006). *Why Politics Matters: Making Democracy Work*. Basingstoke: Palgrave.

Taylor, M. (2003). *Public Policy in the Community*. Basingstoke: Palgrave.

Taylor, P., Nichols, G., Holmes, K., James, M., Gratton, C., Garret, R., Kokolakadikis, T., Mulder, C. and King, L. (2003). *Sports Volunteering in England 2002*. London: Sport England.

Tempest, C. (1997). Myths from Eastern Europe and the legend of the West. In *Civil Society: Democratic Perspectives* (R. Fine and S. Rai, eds). London: Frank Cass.

Tuomela, R. (1995). *The Importance of Us: A Philosophical Study of Basic Social Notions*. Stanford: Stanford University Press.

Walzer, M. (1995). The civil society argument. In *Theorising Citizenship* (R. Beiner, ed.). Albany: State University of New York Press.

Weed, M., Robinson, L., Downward, P., Green, M., Henry, I., Houlihan, B. and Argent, E. (2005). *Academic Review of the Role of Voluntary Sports Clubs: Final Report*. Loughborough: Institute of Sport and Leisure Policy.

CHAPTER 11

Networks and Partnerships in Sports Development

Barrie Houlihan and Iain Lindsey

Power, Politics and Partnerships

Over the last twenty years or so a variety of organisational arrangements have been utilised for the delivery of sports development with the most common being either the establishment of time-limited, stand alone units which generally employed staff on fixed term contracts or the adoption of more traditional hierarchical forms of delivery which typified many sports development units in the UK's larger cities. However, which ever organisational form was dominant there was always a necessity for a substantial degree of collaboration across departmental boundaries in local authorities and with external bodies. The emergence of more formal partnership working can therefore be seen, to an extent at least, as a development of existing delivery practices which were given substantial additional momentum from the Labour government elected in 1997. The purpose of this chapter is to examine the practice and impact of networks and partnerships on sports development. The chapter begins with a review of the issues that are raised by the increasing adoption of partnerships and includes concerns relating to the distribution of power and the achievement of effective accountability. A brief discussion of the emergence of partnership working in sports development is followed by a more detailed examination of three examples of contemporary partnerships: School Sport Partnerships; County Sport Partnerships; and New Opportunities for PE and Sport Programme Partnerships. The chapter concludes with a review of the issues that are raised by the three cases and by partnership working more generally.

Since the early 1980s the concept of partnership working has become firmly embedded in the culture of British sub-national government. According to Rhodes (1994, 1996, 1999; see also Kooiman, 1993) partnerships illustrate a new form of governance, a self-organising institutional network, the result of, and further contributing to, the 'hollowing out' of the traditional state. One explanation for the rise in the use of partnerships is the failure of the traditional welfare state services (professionally based, bureaucratically structured and state delivered) to have an impact on the 'wicked problems' (Rittel and Webber, 1973) facing society which included the persistent social marginalisation, low educational attainment and low employability of some sections of society and also, regarding sport, the continuing difficulty in raising levels of participation among particular social groups. While the Thatcher governments sought a solution to the perceived failure of the traditional welfare state in marketisation and privatisation, New Labour, despite endorsing much of the Thatcherite analysis, also looked for solutions in new ways of governing. 'Joined-up' government was part of the Labour government's response to the way in which problems cut across established functional divisions of government and across levels of government (Clarke et al., 2000; Gewirtz, 2002). Low participation levels in sport, for example, were the partial concern of public bodies (sports councils, schools and local authorities), not-for-profit bodies (governing bodies of sport) and different levels of government (DCMS and the four home country sports councils at the national level, regional offices of Sport England, county councils or unitary authorities and district councils). Partnership working was thus seen as a way of overcoming bureaucratic inertia in policy planning and coordination and, perhaps more importantly, facilitating implementation of policy through direct engagement with agencies closest to the service user and the general public. It was hoped that partnership working would lead to better problem analysis and more effective policy development due to the opportunity to pool expertise across professional boundaries and through closer engagement with the public. In addition, partnerships would, it was argued, result in more effective implementation due to the closer involvement of organisations representing service users in policy formulation. Partnerships were therefore seen as flexible, innovative and adaptive and part of the solution to the problems of 'overloaded' and under-performing government.

The optimism surrounding partnership working was, to an extent, borne out by a number of studies which claimed that multi-professional partnerships could be fruitful (see for example, Griffiths, 2000; Milbourne et al., 2003). McQuaid (2000) identifies three main justifications for promoting partnerships: first, increased pool of resources (such as expertise and administrative capacity); second, improved effectiveness and efficiency; and third, enhanced legitimacy through the involvement of a broader range of stakeholders. For Mackintosh (1993) partnerships are justified if they enlarge the available budget, add value through the more effective utilisation of resources or if they benefit from the synergy that the bringing together of a relatively diverse group can generate. Although the list of perceived advantages is impressive the list of potential disadvantages is often longer. Goss (2001) points to the unwieldy nature of many partnerships, the tendency for partnerships to drift away from their initial objectives or to lack clear objectives in the first place. McQuaid also points to the potential for partnerships to be dominated by cliques, to lack consensus on objectives and to be expensive to manage, while Huxham and Vangen (1996, 2005) highlight the problems in overcoming differences in culture and working practices between partners, the difficulty of building trust and the fine balance in many partnerships between the creation of collaborative advantage and the creation of collaborative inertia.

Pierre (2000) and Bache and Flinders (2004) draw particular attention to the consequences of increased partnership working for the democratic control of public services. At an ideological level the concept of partnership, with its implications of shared power, access to decision-making and co-ownership of policy, is, like its parent concept 'modernisation', part normative insofar as it prescribes particular practices and part rhetorical discourse more concerned with persuasion and motivation. Like modernisation, partnership 'is an "up" word, that makes things sound exciting, progressive and positive' (Finlayson, 2003, p. 63): partnerships are presented to civil society as self-evidently positive and benign. However, behind the normative and rhetorical flourishes are substantive issues of power. As McDonald observes while some examples of partnerships may indeed 'offer progressive forms of governance' others 'may be ideological fig leaves for dominant powers' reproducing and reinforcing existing power relations within policy sectors and within communities (2005, p. 579; see also Lowndes, 2001; Milbourne, 2002; Skelcher et al., 2005; Yandell 1999). Indeed partnerships are best seen as the product of existing power relations rather than as necessarily a democratic counter-weight to the privileged position that some organisations and interests hold in the UK sport policy field. We should consequently be alert to the possibility that partnerships are a means of legitimising and diverting attention away from embedded power inequalities: the membership structure of partnerships often offers the illusion of equality in decision-making which masks a substantive inequality in influence.

Emergence of Partnership Working in Sports Development

The early partnerships in the sport policy area, such as the national demonstration programme (NDP), were pragmatic responses to particular projects or circumstances rather than a valued outcome in their own right. The national demonstration programme was launched in 1984 and was concerned to promote participation in line with the 1982 strategy, *Sport in the Community: The Next Ten Years* (Sports Council, 1982). The 15 projects that comprised the NDP relied heavily on partnership working for their success. Some projects sought to develop sports participation through outreach work (e.g. women in rural areas in conjunction with the Women's Institute), some were directed at particular problems (e.g. health and exercise promotion in Liverpool in conjunction with the regional health authority), while others were dependent on cooperation with schools (e.g. the Active Lifestyles Project in Coventry schools). As well as helping to raise the profile of sports development among a range of partners, especially local authorities, the NDP also provided invaluable experience of the potential of partnership working and an awareness of some of the challenges.

The review of the demonstration projects conducted by the Sports Council was generally positive regarding their impact on participation, but highlighted the problems of managing the wide range of partners necessary for project implementation and the challenge of reconciling sports development objectives with those of non-sport partner bodies. One problem was the failure of many partners to ensure that the sports development objectives of the partnership were recognised and supported within the core activities of each partner organisation. The sport development objectives of the partnership were often marginalised or even undermined by the core activities of the other partner organisations. The Council noted that, on occasion, projects drifted from their initial objectives with ' "non-sporting" objectives being allocated a higher priority' (Sports Council, 1991, p. 31). These problems were most evident when working with health authorities and the probation service where sport and sports development were unfamiliar activities. The Council showed a clear recognition of the problems of working with non-sports organisations and stated that 'If we in the sports world wish to use other organisations as a resource to further our own objectives, we must fully understand the aims and objectives of our new partners' (Sports Council, 1991, p. 31). Yet this view of sport and health or the probation service as equal partners is undermined by an assessment, perhaps more realistic, of the relationship in which the Council noted that 'to get the maximum benefits from the partnerships, sports development objectives must try to fit-in with the objectives of the partner organisation and not vice versa' (1991, p. 31). Indeed it took some time even for other sports-related organisations, such as local authorities, to 'see sports development, partnership initiatives, and target group promotions as a fundamental part of *their* role' (emphasis added) (1991, p. 32). The report also noted, with regard to national governing bodies of sport, a 'marked change in the attitudes of all our traditional sporting partners in the intervening five years' (1991, p. 41). However, it should be emphasised that the embrace of partnership working was less the result of the success of the NDP and more the consequence of pump-priming funding from government and a growing degree of conditionality of funding.

The negotiations required within the NDP projects in order to reach a workable consensus on objectives and procedures highlighted one enduring problem of partnerships. A further problem arose from the instability of the financial and policy environment within which partnerships had to operate. All too often the initial interest stimulated by partnership subsided once the period, usually three years, of project funding ended. The short term nature of funding for partnerships was frequently compounded by the instability of policy objectives which were often dictated by the dominant social problems of the day. Indeed the Sports Council report noted the tendency for policy drift from 'an original concentration on target groups towards projects which are addressing contemporary issues' (1991, p. 1).

Fifteen years after the national demonstration programme the Active Sports project provided a second major opportunity to test the partnership model. The Active Sports project, to be funded for five years from 1999, was an attempt to bridge the gap between participation and excellence. In the terminology of the sport development continuum it was located at the performance stage. With the increasing bifurcation between participation and excellence, the English Sports Council recognised the divide that was opening between participation programmes and the increasingly specialised World Class programmes and consequently designed Active Sports to bridge the gap and provide performance pathways for young people. The programme aimed to bring together local authorities and governing bodies from nine sports to work in 45 local partnerships covering the whole of England. Local sports clubs working with schools were at the heart of the delivery of the programme, which was intended to provide access to coaching, clubs and competitive opportunities for young people.

The review of the Active Sports programme in 2003 found, *inter alia*, that the more successful Active Sports partnerships were those where there was prior experience of partnership working; early involvement of local authorities; clarity of roles and responsibilities among partners; committed advocates; and effective communication systems (KKP, 2005). The future form of Active Sports is in some doubt and it may be the case that they are subsumed within individual whole sport plans that NGBs are being encouraged to prepare and within the development plans being developed by County Sport Partnerships.

Examples of Contemporary Partnerships in Sport Development

School Sport Partnerships

In April 2000 the Government announced, in *A Sporting Future for All* (DCMS, 2000), its intention to establish 600 School Sport Coordinators in England in communities of greatest need and linked to the network of specialist sports colleges. Later renamed School Sport Partnerships (SSPs) they were introduced across the country in phases and by 2007 all schools in England were members of a SSP. Each Partnership was led by a full-time Partnership Development Manager who was usually located at a local specialist sports college and was accountable, in part, to a local steering (management) group comprising a wide range of partnership members (most frequently, secondary and primary school head teachers, the Director of Specialism and the local authority sports development unit: less frequently, local sports clubs, the LEA and local community organisations). A typical SSP would include between four and eight secondary schools each of which would have the services of a School Sport Coordinator (SSCo) usually employed for two or two and a half days per week. The SSCo would, in turn, be responsible for between four to six primary schools each of which would have a nominated Link Teacher. Of the four policy outcomes identified for the SSP programme three require developing partnerships with actors outside the education system. The outcomes concerned with increasing participation amongst school age children, improving standards of performance by children across a range of sports and increasing the numbers of qualified and active coaches, leaders and officials in secondary schools, local primary schools and local sports clubs/facilities all require networking with a range of partners including local clubs, regional NGBs and local authorities.

The SSP programme has been subject to a number of evaluations most notably by the Institute of Youth Sport on behalf of the Department for Children, Schools and Families and by Ofsted (Office for Standards in Education). Although the Ofsted reports understandably focus on the impact of SSPs on curriculum PE and the quality of out-of-school hours sports programmes, they have made some reference to the operation of the wider partnership. In Ofsted's third report (Ofsted, 2006) it was noted that not only had SSPs helped to 'improve the quality of provision in physical education and school sport, particularly in primary schools', it also commented that the 'schools had developed strong links with local sports clubs and sports coaches in the community, giving pupils many more opportunities to play sport outside school' (Ofsted, 2006, p. 3).

In the 2006 Institute of Youth Sport study of the impact of SSPs, on which the remainder of this section is based, it was reported that SSPs 'continue to establish themselves as important elements in the infrastructure of sports opportunities for young people. Most Partnerships already have close and complementary relationships with sports colleges, local authority sports development departments, and the recently formed County Sport Partnerships' (IYS 2006, p. 13). In terms of evaluating the operation of SSPs as partnerships, it is necessary to distinguish between the school network and the wider network that includes clubs and local authorities. The former is, in many respects, an internal network or partnership as each member (school) has a paid representative of the SSP within their organisation which implies a degree of formal acknowledgement and acceptance of SSP outcomes. The strongest partnership links are between secondary schools (via the SSCo) and their cluster of primary schools. In general the relationship is perceived as being mutually beneficial insofar as primary schools, who often do not have a specialist PE teacher, receive training from the Coordinator while the secondary school receives new entrants to year seven who have a higher standard of sports skills. However, equally important are the perceived benefits to the secondary school that are not associated with the outcomes of the SSP. Of particular importance is that secondary schools, who are often in intense competition with each other for primary pupils, see the work of their Coordinator as a way of promoting and marketing the school to primary pupils (and their parents). This same observation also partly explains why cooperation between secondary schools within SSPs is much weaker. Whereas there is no market competition between secondary and primary schools, there is frequently fierce competition between secondary schools for new pupils which is often a disincentive to cooperate (see also Flintoff, 2003). In addition, a number of secondary schools consider that they have little to gain from active involvement in the SSP as they have good facilities and sufficient qualified PE staff and fear that they might lose by allowing pupils from other secondary schools access to their resources.

Straddling the inner partnership of schools and the wider partnership with clubs and other community organisations is the relationship between the SSP and the sports college. Not only is it usual for the sports college to host the SSP, but it is also common for the Director of Specialism (the manager of sports college activities) to be the line manager of the Partnership Development Manager. In most cases the relationship is close and positive for both partners. The major benefit for the SSP is that sports colleges usually have already established a network of links with sports clubs which the Partnership can access. In addition, the sports colleges tend to have good sports facilities which can be used for SSP activities. A less positive aspect of the close relationship is that it is sometimes difficult for SSPs to establish a public identity distinct from the college. One strategy for establishing the distinctiveness of the SSP would be through a strong and broad-based steering group. Unfortunately, very few SSP have effective steering groups and often where they do exist their membership is skewed heavily in favour of public sector organisations (local authorities and schools). Moreover, in many SSPs the steering group has been subsumed within the management group of the sports college. Given that the issues that concern the sports college are more narrowly focused on education and curriculum topics the integration of the SSP steering group with that for the sports college makes it even less likely that local sports clubs, disability associations and youth organisations will feel that they are equal partners and have a contribution to make to the strategic development of the SSP.

As regards the relationship with the wider network a key relationship is with the local authority sports development unit which is often both close and mutually beneficial, with local authority sports development officers (SDOs) providing specialist sports development expertise, helping to link schools with clubs and allowing access to municipal facilities. However, in a relatively small minority of Partnerships the relationship is less fruitful with the local authority seeing the SSP as a competitor in the out-of-school hours market for young sports participants. The website provides a case study in which SSPs had both productive and challenging relationships with different sections of the same local authority.

The involvement of clubs and national governing bodies (NGBs) in the Partnership is more variable due mainly to the uneven distribution of clubs across the country. In general, sports clubs are less common in the less affluent areas and sports clubs with capital resources (i.e. their own grounds and changing facilities) are more common in the traditionally middle class sports, such as rugby union, hockey and cricket. An additional issue is the different objectives pursued by clubs and schools in relation to young people. Schools emphasise inclusiveness in sport and the whole-school and wider community benefits of out-of-school hours participation whereas many clubs are concerned with success in competition (and often pay only lip service to the government's social objectives in order to obtain grant aid). Consequently, some clubs want to be selective rather than inclusive with regard to the young people that they accept as members. Furthermore, there is a significant capacity problem for many sports and clubs. While a medium sized city may have 50 or more football clubs it might only have one athletics club. Not only can young footballers be spread over a number of clubs, but football is also a sport where group training is the norm. By contrast, not only are young athletes seeking membership of the same club they will be spread across a number of very different disciplines which have a tradition of individual coaching. Consequently, even where athletics clubs have a commitment to SSP outcomes they are more likely than team sports to lack coaching capacity.

County Sport Partnerships

County Sports Partnerships (CSPs) are a network of agencies aiming to provide a delivery system for sport and were a direct response to the criticisms of fragmentation and initiative overload expressed in Game Plan (DCMS/Strategy Unit, 2002). By early 2007 49 CSPs were in place across the country often hosted by local authorities. The intended characteristics of CSPs included the maintenance of a focus on children and young people; a commitment to equity; sports development driven through NGB plans; attention to local need; a focus on investing in people; and, significantly, a high level of independence such that the 'core partnership team' is impartial in order to broker progress. The two core functions of CSPs are to contribute to the delivery of the government's target of a one percentage point increase in participation up to 2020 by 'developing more community sports opportunities for young people by supporting the delivery of the PESSCL (Physical Education School Sport and Club Links) strategy [and by] helping developing more opportunities for hard to reach groups and those not already engaged in community sport' (http://www.sportengland.org/index/get_resources/county_sports_partnerships.htm). The three priority areas for CSP action, namely, pathways for young people, club development and workforce development, all involve extensive networking with other agencies. Creating pathways for young people involves close cooperation with schools, local authorities and sports clubs, while club development and workforce development requires close and sustained work with a range of local clubs and schools. In practice the work on club and workforce development needs to precede the construction of pathways for young people and it is not surprising that in many CSPs the two over-riding immediate priorities are first to encourage and support local clubs in their pursuit of Clubmark (this is the Sport England quality accreditation for clubs with junior sections. It is an accreditation, available across all sports, for clubs that comply with minimum operating standards in areas including child protection, sports equity and ethics and programming of activities) or equivalent accreditation, and second to recruit, train and retain volunteers.

The key relationship for the CSPs is that with SSPs and also indirectly with the Youth Sport Trust. In the words of one CSP manager the role of CSPs is 'to line up behind SSPs' and provide support, especially with regard to fostering school-club links (personal communication, 31 August 2007). Not only does the CSP seek to develop school–club links to help construct the sports pathway for young people, but it also finds placements with clubs for junior sports leaders. Given that support for PESSCL is specified as a 'core function' it would be surprising if this set of relationships was not strong and positively evaluated. By contrast the relationship between CSPs and local authority sports development units is more varied and generally problematic. On the one hand there are those local authorities, often larger cities and more populous counties, which have well-established sports development teams who are often sceptical about the added value that the CSP can bring. On the other hand there are a large number of, often small rural authorities, who have no sports development units and consequently no partner to be brought into the CSP network. Where links have been forged between CSPs and local authorities there is occasionally tension due to the refocusing of local authority objectives since 1997. Following the election of the Labour government, local authorities were strongly encouraged to integrate sports development activity into the council strategy to tackle the series of cross-cutting issues (such as community safety, life-long education and social inclusion) which came to dominate the public sector agenda. Consequently, there is a degree of incompatibility between CSP and local authority objectives with the former focused on increasing participation while the latter are primarily concerned to deliver personal and community development, albeit through sport. The final key network actors are the NGBs who, according to one CSP manager, tend to have adopted a 'wait and see' attitude due to a belief that NGBs were 'let down' by Sport England by the 'abandonment of Active Sports' (personal communication, 31 August 2007).

Although it is still early in the life of CSPs, the initial evidence suggests that Partnerships have been reasonably successful in encouraging representation from a wide cross-section of actors although there was a tendency for public sector partners and NGBs of the larger sports to be relatively over-represented. Evidence is also scant in relation to the effectiveness of CSPs in achieving their core objectives. However, a recent evaluation of the role of CSPs in the delivery of the Step into Sport programme, which is a national programme intended to introduce more young people to voluntary work in sport, reported positively on the contribution of CSPs. Not surprisingly the most important partners in developing young volunteers were the SSPs, who had access to the potential volunteers, and the clubs of the larger sports, who were more likely to have the capacity to accommodate volunteers. Of particular importance was that the NGBs that were active in the CSP with regard to volunteers were those that had experience of involvement in previous partnership programmes such as Active Sports. However, by far the most substantial problem facing CSPs was the relative scarcity of clubs in some areas. As was noted in the report 'the geographical distance between sports clubs with volunteering opportunities and the residential location of young people [militated] against the full realisation of the Step into Sport project' (IYS 2005, p. vi). The report also drew attention to the fact that some partners might be willing, but might not be suitable due to a lack of capacity (e.g. a lack of a range of volunteering opportunities) while others, which have the capacity, might be unwilling to modify or adapt existing structures and programmes to accommodate young volunteers.

A second, more general, evaluation of the impact of CSPs reinforced the assessment by the IYS insofar as it concluded that 'CSPs have made a demonstrable difference to the delivery of sport in some key areas' (KKP, 2005, p. 14). However, the generally positive assessment of the impact of Partnerships was tempered by a series of observations about the constraints on the operation of Partnerships. For example, the report observed that 'the credibility of CSPs is, in part, subject to sustaining development activity initiated by Active Sports' (KKP, 2005, p. 18). The second observation related to the location of the Partnership and the impact that location has on perceptions of independence. 'Hosting arrangements appear to have a significant effect on the extent to which CSP partners are perceived as equal' (KKP, 2005, p. 20). In other words, the hosting organisation, often a local authority, was frequently perceived as having excessive influence on CSP policy. Finally, there was often confusion about what constituted 'the partnership' with it being noted that 'in a significant number of cases, the "core team" [i.e. the full-time staff of the CSP] is seen by partners as "the partnership" rather than an equal partner [with others such as NGBs, local authorities, etc]'.

The early work of CSPs in club and workforce development is clearly aimed at creating the pathways for young people in sport and links closely with the objectives of the PESSCL strategy and the government's concern to increase participation levels among young people. However, in recent years there have been some signs of a tension emerging between the current core priorities of the CSPs programme and Sport England's increasing concern to raise participation levels among the post-16 age group. Sport England's Public Service Agreement with the government sets the target of a three percentage point increase in post-16 participation between 2005 and 2008. One consequence of the PSA target is that Sport England is putting pressure on CSPs to refocus some of their effort away from supporting the delivery of PESSCL and towards the post-16 age group illustrating the tendency for partnership objectives to change over time. One consequence of the current tension in the objectives set for CSPs is that it makes potential partners wary of becoming too deeply involved in the partnership and reluctant to commit resources. According to one CSP manager a number of NGB actors were irritated by the apparent demise of Active Sports and are now unsure of the future direction of CSPs (personal communication 7 September 2007).

The New Opportunities for Physical Education and Sport (NOPES) Programme

In 2001, the Big Lottery Fund (formerly the New Opportunities Fund) allocated £750.75 million to the NOPES programme which was to build and refurbish indoor and outdoor sports facilities for school and community use. In line with government priorities, the Big Lottery Fund placed a strong emphasis on partnership working within all their programmes and especially within the NOPES programme.

In the NOPES programme, every local authority with responsibility for education in the United Kingdom was given a provisional allocation of funding for projects in their area. The scale of allocated funding was based on population and deprivation factors. In order to apply for, and access, this allocated funding local authorities were required to develop partnerships between a range of agencies.

As they were ultimately responsible for their allocation of NOPES funding, the education department in local authorities automatically had a key position in the local partnerships. The Big Lottery Fund also suggested that these local partnerships should include a range of local and non-local agencies. Through seminars and programme guidance notes, the Big Lottery Fund suggested potential partner organisations which included NGBs, Sport England and the Youth Sport Trust as well as more local agencies such as representatives of local authority leisure departments and Primary Care Trusts.

The Fund expected these local partnerships in each local authority area to discuss and make decisions on schools and other facilities to benefit from the allocation of NOPES funding. Subsequently, the partnership groups were expected to make further strategic decisions on, for example, any major changes to their portfolio of NOPES projects as well as undertake operational tasks in the application, design and construction of NOPES projects. The role of these partnerships after the construction of projects was unclear in formal and informal guidance from the New Opportunities Fund.

Although partnerships were also expected to be developed at individual NOPES projects, this section will focus on the partnerships developed for the NOPES programme at local authority level.

General Types of Partnership in the NOPES Programme

Drawing on data from the national evaluation of the NOPES programme, Lindsey (2006) provided an analysis of different types of local authority-level partnership developed for the NOPES programme. Table 11.1 gives a broad overview of the three types of partnerships found in the 11 case studies that were included in the national evaluation.

'Local Authority Community' partnerships comprised a small number of members who often had substantial prior experience of working together. These members were drawn solely from local authority departments and, in particular, those departments responsible for education (including individuals responsible for PE and school sport) and leisure (commonly sports development staff).

In Type 2 partnerships there was a core group of key members who often had a history of working together. These core groups were similar to the local authority communities. The core group of members were responsible for driving the initial development of the NOPES portfolio in their area. Beyond the core group, wider networks were developed to involve representatives of other organisations. These wider networks were used to include individuals with particular expertise or to undertake scrutiny of the decisions made by the core group.

Type 3 'inter-organisational networks' partnerships included a diverse range of personnel who represented a variety of different agencies. In areas where this type of partnership existed, there were large differences in the degree to which partnership members had worked together previously.

Table 11.1 Type of NOPES partnerships.

Type 1 Local authority community	Type 2 Wide network/tight core	Type 3 Inter-organisational network
Small group from local authority departments only	Wider network including members from inside and out with the local authority	Wide network with variety of organisations represented
Members had previous experience of working together	Strong integration between core group of local authority personnel	Differing levels of previous interaction between members
	Core group drove the development of the NOPES programme	Responsibility for NOPES equally distributed between members

In the analysis of these partnerships Lindsey (2006) found that, with few exceptions, each partnership type was linked to a particular home country. Local authority communities were identified in two case studies in Scotland as well as an anomalous case study from London. The partnerships which comprised a wide network with a tight core were found exclusively in England and Wales. Inter-organisational networks were only present in case studies located in Northern Ireland. In explaining this pattern, Lindsey (2006, p. 176) commented that 'more than anything [the country specific nature of partnerships] reflects the different context of local government in the four home countries'.

Different policy processes, particularly in the selection of NOPES projects, were found in each of the different types of partnerships. In local authority communities, top-down decisions on the projects to be funded were based solely on the knowledge and expertise of members of the partnership. There was a balance between top-down decision making and bottom-up applications from schools in the method of project selection in those partnerships that had a wide network with a tight core. Finally, where there were inter-organisational networks an entirely bottom-up process was enacted whereby bids from schools and other organisations were objectively assessed by members of the partnership group using detailed assessment criteria. For Lindsey (2006), this analysis demonstrated a clear link between the type of NOPES partnership and the policy processes that were enacted within it.

Subsequently, after the initial selection of projects, there was not such a clear link between the types and the roles of NOPES partnerships. In some case studies that formed part of the national evaluation, the NOPES programme was regarded purely as a capital programme and as a result partnerships ceased to operate when construction of NOPES facilities was completed. In other case studies, there was a more proactive approach by partnerships to supporting individual NOPES projects after they opened and often individuals employed by the partnership to manage the whole NOPES portfolio had a key role in doing so.

Examples of NOPES Partnerships

Beyond the general features described above, individual NOPES partnerships display some distinct characteristics and performed slightly different roles in the programme as illustrated by the following examples. Both examples, referred to here as Midcity and Northtown respectively, are unitary authorities in medium to large English cities.

The membership of NOPES partnerships in Midcity and Northtown were very similar. Local authority officials from the education department with responsibility for PE and school-based sport and from leisure departments with responsibility for sports development were key members of both partnerships. Other members were drawn from within and outwith the local authority and included individuals whose roles encompassed capital facility planning and maintenance as well as other agencies with an interest in PE, school and community sport. While all members of the partnership in Northtown had clearly defined roles, in Midcity it was suggested that some members were included merely to fulfil Big Lottery Fund criteria.

Despite similarities in membership, the form of NOPES partnerships differed significantly in Northtown and Midcity. Although there were changes over time (a facet identified on other programmes by Lowndes and Skelcher, 1998), the NOPES partnership in Northtown was characterised by its highly formalised structure. This reflected a similar level of formalisation in partnerships within the sport block of the Local Strategic Partnership in which many of the members of the NOPES partnership were involved. Conversely, in Midcity, the core of the NOPES partnership was based on the strong, largely informal working relationship between the local authority's Head of Sport (from the Regeneration & Culture Department) and the PE and Sport Strategic Manager (from the Education Department). Despite their strong relationship, there were higher level tensions between these two officers' respective departments and there appeared to be a high level of self-interest in partnerships that they were involved in.

There were strong similarities in the processes to select NOPES projects and the role of NOPES partnerships in these processes in both case studies. In both cases, the partnerships developed strong initial visions for the NOPES programme in their locality. Therefore, although all schools in the local authority areas were invited to suggest projects, core members within the NOPES partnerships collectively had the greatest input into the selection process. Projects were chosen based upon the expertise of these members and their knowledge of the wider strategic context in the case study area. The wider NOPES partnerships in both case studies provided a level of accountability and scrutiny to the choice of NOPES projects.

After the initial selection of projects, Portfolio Managers were appointed in both case studies and their different roles are again of interest. In Midcity, the Portfolio Manager was an existing officer based within the local County Sport Partnership that covered three local authorities. The extended remit of this officer meant that his role in the NOPES programme was limited to overseeing the processes of application, design and construction at individual NOPES projects on behalf of the NOPES partnership. Conversely, the full-time Portfolio Manager in Northtown had a greater role in supporting collaborative working within the NOPES partnership itself and developing links between the NOPES partnership and individual projects.

There were significant differences in the role of NOPES partnerships in Midcity and Northtown after NOPES facilities opened. In Midcity, the degree of involvement of partnership group members after NOPES facilities opened depended on the extent to which they matched or conflicted with wider strategic interests. For example, the Sport Services section (that was led by the Head of Sport) managed one school-based NOPES facility as it was in an area with no other local authority-managed sport facilities. At another NOPES project, school staff believed that there were tensions as a result of unnecessary interventions by staff from the Sports Services section. Other schools that had NOPES projects were largely left to develop them in isolation and, often, were in competition with local authority sports facilities to attract community users. Alternatively, in Northtown, partnership structures were developed to support every individual NOPES project after the new facilities opened. Furthermore, the NOPES Portfolio Manager and a team of external leisure consultants not only provided support to NOPES projects, but also enabled a level of coordination across different NOPES projects.

Managing Partnerships in the Delivery of Sports Development

The typology outlined in Table 11.1 indicates the variety of forms that partnerships can take and illustrates the vagueness of the concept of partnership. This conceptual imprecision notwithstanding it is also clear that there are many examples of fruitful collaboration between organisations. In many cases, as illustrated in the previous section, the partnership is arguably more than the sum of its parts. However, the fundamental question to be considered is how would we know whether partnerships are a more effective tool of service provision than the alternatives? For example, it is undoubtedly the case that SSPs have increased the range of sports opportunities for young people, improved the experience of sport for primary pupils and, over the life of the programme, raised participation rates. However, some improvement in all these indicators should have been expected simply because of the scale of new resources being injected into the schools involved. The question is what additional value did partnerships add to the outputs and outcomes of the programme? Indeed the three types of partnerships reviewed above provide plenty of examples of conventional top-down bureaucratic management. This is not to argue against the use of partnerships even if the primary basis for their use is the lack of capacity within the conventional machinery of government, but rather to suggest a degree of caution in ascribing too much significance to the partnership form.

This caveat notwithstanding it is useful to identify the factors that appear to make for successful partnerships. Of particular importance is the presence of an organisational actor that can fulfil a leadership role in a specific partnership. In the website case study, the lack of an organisation actor providing a strategic lead for sport in the local authority area inhibited the development of a coordinated sporting system that encompassed all potential partners. Similarly, as John (2001), Greenaway et al. (2007) and Walker et al. (2007) have argued in relation to partnerships in other policy areas it is often the energy, ability and commitment of the partnership manager that enables the potential of a partnership to be realised. However, leadership of partnerships may require a different set of skills from those traditionally identified as being required within organisational hierarchies. The example of SSPs demonstrates the important role, initially at least, of the sports college Director of Specialism in enabling links to be formed between different agencies including schools and sports clubs. Within the NOPES partnership in Northtown, a similar role was undertaken by the Portfolio Manager. In this vein, both Sullivan and Skelcher (2002) and Ranade and Hudson (2003) identify the leadership role taken by 'boundary spanners' within partnerships and describe some of the characteristics of such individuals.

A second common issue identified in the three types of partnership discussed in this chapter concerns the clarity and stability of partnership objectives. The examples presented suggest that this issue is relevant at two levels. First, the stability of objectives set for particular partnerships is important. For example, the drift in objectives found in the CSP programme nationally is a possible explanation for the slow pace at which some are becoming embedded in the local sports development strategy. Secondly, within partnerships there needs to be space to negotiate a shared sense of purpose and common objectives. Once more the examples of the NOPES partnerships in Midcity and Northtown provide examples of the successful creation of a local vision for the programme within the wider objectives set nationally for the programme by the Big Lottery Fund. In the broader partnership literature, Huxham and Vangen (2005) identify the importance of developing of shared objectives although they also suggest that this is not always a quick or easy process.

An important barrier to realising the potential of partnerships is often the general congestion in the policy area and the need to compete with other agencies and partnerships for similar policy space. For example, local authority sports development units, County Sports Partnerships, SSPs and Specialist Sports Colleges are among the range of partnerships and organisations aiming to increase the participation levels of young people. In the Metcity case study (on the website), partnership working was inhibited by the variety of organisations, all with slightly different agendas and ethos, involved in sports development in the local area. The risk is that the establishment of a cluster of delivery mechanisms results not in synergy and the development of specialist expertise, but in confusion, competition and congestion. A second concern, and one discussed in the introduction, is that the concept of partnership implies a degree of equity between members that often masks a substantial imbalance in power: the rhetoric of horizontal interdependency and goal consensus hides the reality of hierarchy. There is still far too little examination of power in partnerships because, as Klijn and Skelcher note, 'of the powerful underlying assumptions of cooperation, mutuality and consensus between actors' (2007, p. 602). While much partnership working in the area of sport can be seen as benign, there is much evidence of local authority sports development units and particularly sports clubs adopting partnership outcomes with a degree of reluctance. A third general concern is the blurring of lines of accountability. It is often unclear to whom and by what means partnerships are accountable. Far from re-energising local democracy (John, 2001) partnerships may 'obfuscate and undermine ...democracy' (Greenaway et al., 2007, p. 718). Most striking is the fact that very often the last group to whom a partnership is accountable is its partners.

References

Bache, I. and Flinders, M. (2004). Multi-level governance in British politics. In *Multi-level Governance* (I. Bache and M. Flinders eds). Buckingham: Open University Press.

Clarke, J., Gewirtz, S. and MacLaughlin, E. (2000). Reinventing the welfare state. In *New Managerialism* (J. Clarke, S. Gewirtz and E. MacLaughlin ed.). London: Sage.

Department of CultureMedia and Sport (2000). *A Sporting Future for All*. London: DCMS.

Department of Culture Media and Sport/Strategy Unit (2002). *Game Plan: A Strategy for Delivering the Government's Sport and Physical Activity Objectives*. London: DCMS/Strategy Unit.

Finlayson, A. (2003). The meaning of modernisation. *Soundings*, **23**(1), 62–83.

Flintoff, A. (2003). The school sport coordinator programme: Changing the role of the PE teacher?, sport. *Education and Society*, **8**(2), 231–50.

Gewirtz, S. (2002). *The Managerial School: Post-welfarism and Social Justice in Education*. London: Routledge.

Goss, S. (2001). *Making Local Governance Work: Networks, Relationships and the Management of Change*. Basingstoke: Palgrave.

Greenaway, J., Salter, B. and Hart, S. (2007). How policy networks can damage democratic health: a case study in the government of governance. *Public Administration*, **85**(3), 717–38.

Griffiths, M. (2000). Collaboration and partnership in question: Knowledge, politics and practice. *Journal of Education Policy*, **15**(4), 383–95.

Huxham, C. and Vangen, S. (1996). What makes partnerships work? In *Public-Private Partnerships: Theory and Practice in International Perspective* (S. Osbourne ed.). London: Routledge.

Huxham, C. and Vangen, S. (2005). *Managing to Collaborate: The Theory and Practice of Collaborative Advantage*. Abingdon: Routledge.

Institute of Youth Sport (IYS) (2005). Step into sport. *County Sport Partnerships: An Evaluation of Work to Facilitate High Quality Volunteering Placements for Young Volunteers at Sports Clubs*. Loughborough University: IYS.

Institute of Youth Sport (IYS) (2006). *School Sport Partnerships. Annual Monitoring and Evaluation Report for 2006*. Loughborough University: IYS.

John, P. (2001). *Local Governance in Western Europe*. London: Sage.

Klijn, E.-H. and Skelcher, C. (2007). Democracy and governance networks: Compatible or not. *Public Administration*, **85**(3), 587–608.

Knight, Kavanagh and Page (2005). *Active Sports/CSP Impact Study Year 3: Final Report*, Bury: KKP.

Kooiman, J. (Ed.) (1993) *Modern governance*. Sage: London.

Lindsey, I. (2006). Local partnerships in the United Kingdom for the new opportunities for PE and sport initiative: A policy network analysis. *European Sports Management Quarterly*, **6**(2), 167–84.

Lowndes, V. (2001). Rescuing Aunt Sally: Taking institutional theory seriously in urban politics. *Urban Studies*, **38**(11), 1953–71.

Lowndes, V. and Skelcher, C. (1998). The dynamics of multi-organisational partnerships: An analysis of changing modes of governance. *Public Administration*, **76**(2), 313–33.

Mackintosh, M. (1993). Partnerships: Issues of policy and negotiation. *Local Economy*, **7**(3), 210–24.

McDonald, I. (2005). Theorising partnerships: Governance, communicative action and sport policy. *Journal of Social Policy*, **34**(4), 579–600.

McQuaid, R. (2000). The theory of partnerships. In *Public-Private Partnerships: Theory and Practice in International Perspective* (S. Osbourne ed.). London: Routledge. Milbourne, L. (2002). Unspoken exclusion: Experiences of continued marginalisation from education among 'hard to reach' groups of adults and children. *British Journal of Sociology of Education*, **23**(2), 287–305.

Milbourne, L., Macrae, S. and Maguire, M. (2003). Collaborative solutions or new policy problems: Exploring multi-agency partnerships in education and health work. *Journal of Education Policy*, **18**(1), 19–35.

OFSTED (2006). *School Sport Partnerships: A Survey of Good Practice*. London: Ofsted.

Pierre, J. (2000). *Debating Governance: Authority, Steering and Democracy*. Buckingham: Open University Press.

Ranade, W. and Hudson, B. (2003). Conceptual issues in inter-agency collaboration. *Local Government Studies*, **29**(3), 32–50.

Rhodes, R.A.W. (1994). The hollowing out of the state. *The Political Quarterly*, **13**(8), 138–51.

Rhodes, R.A.W. (1996). The new governance: Governing without government. *Political Studies*, **44**(4), 652–7.

Rhodes, R.A.W. (1999). *Forward, Control and Power in Central-Local Relations* (G. Stoker ed.). Aldershot: Ashgate.

Rittel, H. and Webber, M. (1973). Dilemmas in a general theory of planning. *Policy Sciences*, **4**, 155–69.

Skelcher, C., Mathur, N. and Smith, M. (2005). The public governance of collaborative spaces: Discourse, design and democracy. *Public Administration*, **83**(3), 573–96.

Sports Council (1982). *Sport in the Community: The Next Ten Years*. London: Sports Council.

Sports Council (1991). *National Demonstration Projects: Major Issues and Lessons for Sports Development*. London: Sports Council.

Sullivan, H. and Skelcher, C. (2002). *Working Across Boundaries: Collaboration in Public Services*. Palgrave Macmillan: Basingstoke.

Walker, R., O'Toole, L. and Meier, K. (2007). It's where you are that matters: The networking behaviour of English local government officers. *Public Administration*, **85**(3), 739–56.

Yandell, J. (1999). Obstructing the highway: Resisting EAZs in hackney. *Education and Social Justice*, **2**, 13–17.

CHAPTER 12

Funding of Sport Development

Ian Jones

Introduction

This chapter explores the funding of sport development activities, focusing particularly on the issues related to the actual processes by which funding is gained and the key concerns affecting both funding bodies and those seeking funding. The main focus of the chapter is to examine some of the issues related with funding sport development within a complex and dynamic environment, with a focus upon public sector involvement in the broad aim of increasing participation. The funding network for sport is extremely complex, and within the constraints of a single chapter, it is simply not possible to address all of the appropriate sources and mechanisms via which money is channelled into sport. Neither is the intention of the chapter to simply list those sources of funding available, as this detail is available elsewhere (see, for example, http://www.sportengland.org/index/get_funding.htm). There will obviously be some omissions that are worthy of debate beyond that available here, for example, the massive unpaid contribution of the vast number of volunteers who contribute to sport (see, for example, Nichols et al., 2004). Instead, the chapter will focus upon some of the key funding sources and examine some of the issues associated with the use of these sources in funding sport development. The provision of such funding in itself does not lead to positive outcomes, such as increased participation, and some of the concerns surrounding the associated resource issues of using such funding will also be discussed. Whether the focus of sport development is on equity, or equality, 'many SDO's and deliverers of sport development programmes more prosaically have identified a lack of funding as the major obstacle to achieving equality of opportunity' (Jackson and Nesti, 2001, p. 151). Public sector funding of sport has faced, and will continue to face, a variety of challenges and the National Lottery is only a partial answer. As Jackson and Nesti (2001, pp. 156–7) suggest, 'if there is to be a realistic chance of Sport England's strategy achieving its objectives, the mission of More People, More Places, More Medals is implicitly underpinned by another catchline of More Money'.

Such financial support will always be finite, however, and thus the means by which such funding is provided is important not only to which schemes receive funding, but also those which do not. Thus the structure of the chapter will be first to examine the general context of sport funding. A brief examination of the funding for elite sport will be provided. The focus then turns to the funding related to increasing participation in sport, with an emphasis upon the processes associated with Sport England and National Lottery funding. The role of performance indicators and critical success factors will be discussed. The chapter will conclude with a brief discussion of the inherent risks of funding sport development initiatives.

The Sports Development Funding Context

Sport and physical activity is delivered through four sectors: local government, educational establishments, the voluntary sector and the private sector. The overall responsibility for sport policy however, which guides funding, lies with Central Government. The majority of funding for sport in the UK is channelled through Local Government. Although budgets for the provision of sport have increased in recent years, increases have been below inflation, and thus there has been a gradual real-terms decrease in the funding for the public sector and subsequently an increasing reliance on lottery funding. This has taken place in a context that has begun to value economic efficiency above social criteria (Henry and Theodoraki, 2002). The five Sports Councils have a key role in the distribution of both government and lottery funding which form the link between government and sports organisations, clubs and bodies, operating at 'arms length' from government, although accountable to key stakeholders, such as Central Government and the general public. UK Sport focuses on high-performance sport, whereas the other four Sports Councils (Sport England, sportscotland, the Sports Council for Wales and the Sports Council for Northern Ireland) have a much broader remit.

A key driver influencing the ethos underlying the funding of sport is the Game Plan document (DCMS, 2002), which identified a number of issues concerned with participation in sport and physical activity within the UK. These issues included both the quantity and quality of participation being below a desired level, with high levels of drop out and lower levels of participation amongst women, lower socio-economic groups, ethnic minorities and the disabled. Whilst successful in some sports, success in key sports was limited. The funding of sport was identified as fragmented and potentially unsustainable given the decline in National Lottery sales and increasing pressures on Local Authority budgets.

Within this context, four key objectives were outlined in the Game Plan document. These were

1. Grassroots participation: the need for a wide range of initiatives, with a focus on economically disadvantaged groups, in particular the young, women, disabled and the elderly. Such initiatives were needed to remove structural barriers to participation such as failures in appropriate provision.

2. High-performance sport: A need for prioritisation of which sports were to be funded at the highest level; better development of talented sportsmen

and women with funding streams and service delivery more focused on customer needs.

3. Mega sporting events: the need for a more cautious approach to hosting major sporting events. A set process for government involvement, including a clear assessment of the benefits was required. Obviously the award of the 2012 Olympic Games to London has, to all intents and purposes, meant that this objective became outdated and in need of significant modification.

4. Delivery: organisational reform and determining exactly what is effective before any further increase to investment in sport is made by the central government. A reduction in bureaucracy and increased partnership working between public, private and voluntary sectors towards a common goal.

The Funding of High Performance Sport

Whilst the focus of the chapter is upon funding of schemes designed to increase participation, equality and equity within sport, it is useful to briefly examine the funding of elite sport. Elite Sport Development has been a 'key policy concern' since the mid-1990s (Green, 2004) and is currently the responsibility of UK Sport, who receive funding from the Department of Culture, Media and Sport (DCMS) to address three strategic priorities, those of World Class Success, Worldwide Impact and World Class Standards. To achieve these, eight 'Primary Activities' have been agreed between DCMS and UK Sport, these being (DCMS, 2005):
World Class Success:

1. Support athletes to succeed in world class events.

2. Develop skilled people to support UK world class athletes.

3. Drive the development of a world class high performance system for the UK.

   Worldwide Impact:

1. Establish the UK as an authoritative and leading player in world class sport.

2. Develop an international development assistance programme in and through sport.

3. Develop a sports-focused strategy for staging major international events across the UK.

World Class Standards:

1. Lead a world class anti-doping programme for the UK.

2. Work with athletes and others to promote the highest standards of conduct in sport.

The funding received from the DCMS is allocated through UK Sport largely through National Governing Bodies, but with some funding used to attract major sporting events to the UK. Additional funding is available through the National Lottery to support schemes such as the World Class Development Programme, The World Class Talent Programme and the World Class Events Programme.UK Sport adopt a 'no compromise' strategy whereby funding is provided to those sports that are capable of winning medals and funding is not awarded to or removed from those NGBs failing to meet such criteria. Criteria are assessed through factors such as results at the previous Olympic Games, the sport's overall track record in significant competition, its projected medal capability at major events and mastery of the 'athlete pipeline' from talent identification to successful performer. Hence, sports that have shown success such as cycling, sailing and rowing have received increased funding compared to sports such as athletics and gymnastics. Funding is focused more on fewer numbers, hence spending more per potential medal on fewer people. Essentially this scheme works on the basis of funding by performance, rewarding those sports that can demonstrate success whilst penalising those which are unsuccessful.

Funding Participation in Sport

Whilst the focus on elite sport will undoubtedly benefit the broader population, for example, in terms of the sense of communites developed through events such as the Olympic Games (Chalip, 2006), there is still a need to increase participation amongst those for whom any form of competitive sport is normally out of reach and even participation in any form of physical activity is rare. The benefits of participation in sport and physical activity have been widely documented. Both Lawson (2005) and Collins (2003) summarise the social and economic benefits of participation, such as personal (for example, those concerned with health), social (such as the strengthening of families), economic, environmental and national. Thus the desirability to encourage participation seems unarguable. The Game Plan review, however, identified the relative weaknesses in terms of participation within the UK and the need to ensure that funding was available to deal with some of the issues of non-participation. Sports Councils also have a key role to play here, and it is their role in the funding of sport development that will be explored within the remainder of the chapter, with an emphasis upon the role of Sport England in the delivery of funds to support participation in sport and physical activity.

In 2003, following the publication of Game Plan, Sport England changed and simplified the way its funding was allocated, replacing the 75 existing funding programmes with two investment streams – national and community. National Investment Funding is prioritised towards 31 key sports. There are 10 English priority sports, 10 UK/GB priority sports and 11 English development/world class sports. Funding is only available through this scheme to those key sports, their National Governing Bodies and partners with appropriate expertise, for example, in coaching, equity or volunteering. Each governing body is accountable for delivering the targets in its strategic plans in order to receive – and continue receiving – National Investment Funding. The sports involved are shown in Table 12.1.

Table 12.1   National investment sports.

English priority sports	2005/6 funding totals (£)	In principle four-year funding totals (£)
Badminton	4 231 595	16 012 215
Cricket	6 415 803	18 368 448
Football	22 731 275	57 816 559
Golf	2 070 000	9 332 500
Hockey	3 567 259	11 136 477
Netball	4 137 048	13 546 477
Rugby League	3 240 557	11 546 373
Rugby Union	6 319 443	17 300 201
Squash	1 646 000	7 397 500
Tennis	5 507 021	16 480 767
UK/GB priority sports.		
Athletics	3 138 572	n/a
Canoeing	2 150 555	7 988 055
Cycling	3 525 555	13 413 055
Equestrian	1 035 000	4 035 000
Gymnastics	2 758 055	8 505 555
Judo	1 962 332	7 235 163
Rowing	3 532 222	13 419 722
Sailing	2 630 000	11 482 500
Swimming	5 492 775	17 873 116
Triathlon	876 000	3 504 000
English development/world class sports.		
Angling	185 000	740 000
Baseball	300 000	1 200 000
Basketball	1 999 566	5 062 010
Boxing	958 400	4 271 100
Bowls		
Karate	250 000	n/a
Lacrosse	287 333	1 127 333
Movement and Dance	106 500	400 500
Mountaineering	170 000	680 000
Orienteering	420 000	1 545 000
Rounders/Softball	100 000	400 000
Table Tennis	1 735 472	5 989 972
Volleyball	417 917	1 467 917
Water Skiing	175 000	700 000

Source: Sport England

Non-lottery funding is also available directly from the Treasury, channelled through the DCMS by the Sports Match scheme. Essentially this provides match funding with commercial partners to promote both capital and revenue-based schemes. The total funding (£3.6m p.a.) is relatively small, with grants ranging from £500 for small-scale school-based projects to larger projects to a maximum of £50 000. The key criteria for Sport Match funding are the securement of match funding, the likelihood that funding will lead to increased participation or performance at grass roots, the focus on priority groups and the requirement for the Sport Match scheme to receive adequate promotion (up to 10% of the grant is generally for the purposes of publicity).

How is Funding Allocated?

The Community Investment Fund (CIF) is the funding available for sports organisations that do not meet the criteria for National Investment Funding and is open to all interested parties through an open application process. CIF funding is managed at a regional level by the nine regional Sports Boards (RSBs) established to bring together key regional sports stakeholders, including regional agencies, local authorities, the voluntary and the private sectors as part of a wider 'delivery system' that focuses down from the national (Sport England) to the regional (RSBs) to the county-wide (County Sport Partnerships) and community (Community Sport Networks). The delivery system allows – in principle at least – a seamless link between national policy and local needs and priorities.

There is, as part of this process, a strong link between the regional plan produced by each board, detailing the key priorities within that particular region, and the subsequent evaluation of applications for funding, in that clear evidence needs to be presented that any schemes that apply for funding need to assist in meeting the stated priorities. As well as a requirement to meet regional priorities, the issue of partnership funding is important. The principles of partnership funding are clearly laid out by Sport England:

1. Leverage Target – within each of the Regional Sports Boards investment portfolios, a minimum of £2 partnership funding should be attracted for every £1 of Sport England grant invested.

2. Applicant Contribution – All applicants for funding must contribute to a proportion of the project costs either from their own or from other partners' resources. The applicant organisation should have some of its own funding to put towards the project, normally a minimum of 10% of the total cost, depending on affordability.

3. Cash and In-Kind – Partnership funding can be in the form of cash and/or in-kind. 'In kind' contributions take the form of goods and services provided free of charge where they would otherwise have to be paid for. Such a contribution could also be land provided free of charge by a genuine third party. The value of the contributions 'in kind' should be identified separately from the project costs and separately from financial partnership funding.

4. Other Sport England Funding – the only funding that can be considered as a contribution towards achieving the partnership funding 'leverage target' is funding that has NOT originated from Sport England.

5. Confirmation of Partnership Funding – All partnership funding needs to be confirmed before the start of the project and must be realistically achievable. Sport England does not accept speculative bids or future income as eligible partnership funding.

The two criteria that are essential and need to be carefully assessed by the applicant before any formal application is made are those of

1. The degree of fit between the application and the objectives of the Regional Sports Board;

2. Evidence of agreed partnership support.

Without these, any application for funding will almost certainly be unsuccessful. The type of projects meeting these criteria may be further assessed in terms of other criteria laid down by either Sport England or the Regional Sports Board; for example, Sport England identifies a number of additional criteria that need to be fulfilled for successful funding applications. These include

■ Priority to applications that are located in wards listed in the top 20% of the Index of Multiple Deprivation and which also focus on specific Sport England target groups (such as women and girls, the over 45s, young people, persons with disabilities and BME groups).

■ Contribution to the aspiration of increasing participation in the South East by 1% per annum, whilst addressing the particular issues raised in the South East Plan for Sport.

■ Demonstration of links to coaching and volunteering initiatives and reference to National Governing Bodies and Local Authority Sports Strategies and other strategies relevant to that particular project.

■ Large requests for a single grant award over £400000 and projects requesting less than £50000 for capital and £30000 for revenue are unlikely to be funded.

■ Revenue projects will normally receive a maximum of three years phased funding and must be supported by a robust business plan that includes provision for sustainability. All projects should demonstrate how sustainability has been addressed both from a project development and business-planning viewpoint as well as an environmental impact.

■ Applications will be considered from community organisations or charities and not-for-profit trusts that are properly constituted in accordance with Sport England guidance. Applications will also be considered from Local Authorities and other statutory agencies providing there is robust evidence of partnership working and they are able to demonstrate the fund is not replacing statutory funding.

■ All applicants must demonstrate they have a developed an active child protection policy in place and this applies also to any other clubs/ organisations/coaches anticipated or likely to use the facility being funded.

■ Applicants will be encouraged to work towards achieving good practice accreditation such as Clubmark, Quest and Investors in People.

■ All projects must be innovative in their approach including, for example, multi-purpose use or multi-activity and produce solutions that increase participation among all sections of society, in particular reaching those who don't normally take part.

■ It is unlikely that projects with football as the primary activity will be considered. Applications for football will be directed to the Football Foundation.

(*Source*: http://www.sportengland.org/community_investment_fund_regional_ criteria.pdf).

The types of activities that will not receive funding are clearly outlined, for example:

■ Projects intended primarily for private gain;

■ Grant awards that contribute directly to a company's distributable profits;

■ Endowments;

■ Funds to build up a reserve or surplus;

■ Retrospective or duplicate funding;

■ Loan repayments;

■ Activities that primarily promote religious belief;

■ Purchase of leaseholds of less than 21 years;

■ Minor works, renewals, repairs or maintenance including resurfacing. Work that is necessary as a result of past neglect and insufficient maintenance;

■ Replacement facilities without robust evidence to prove significant improvement or upgrading;

■ Floodlighting for natural pitches;

■ Outdoor Swimming Pools;

■ Vehicles or leasing of vehicles including team mini-buses, vans etc.;

■ Personal equipment (including sports equipment) and fixed or loose equipment not part of a wider capital build;

- Maintenance equipment, fixed or loose equipment or office equipment not essential and integral to the equipping of the facility or for use by a new post-holder;

- Continuation of existing activity, funding for existing posts and on-going running costs.

(*Source*: http://www.sportengland.org/community_investment_fund_regional_criteria.pdf).

The Funding Process

Applications for funding are assessed using a three-stage process (Table 12.2). Stage one is an enquiry stage whereby applications are vetted. The possible outcomes are those of 'encourage' or 'discourage'. Those receiving a 'discourage' will not be able to proceed, those receiving an 'encourage' are able to progress to stage two and three. Sport England have outlined a series of questions that applicants need to address before applying for stage one. These are

1. Can you clearly explain why your project is needed?

2. Can your project clearly deliver against local and regional priorities?

3. Have you considered alternatives to fund this project? If not, can you explain why these options have not been explored?

4. Can you set out the project's objectives and its planned outcomes?

5. Will you be able to measure progress using the appropriate key performance indicators (KPIs), show how the project is achieving its aims and demonstrate when targets have been met?

6. Have you considered how your project fits with the published investment priorities of the Regional Sports Board and how you will make the best possible case against them?

7. Can you provide an accurate cost breakdown for your project?

Table 12.2 Sport England eight stage Funding Process.

Stage 1		Stage 2			Stage 3		
Milestone 1	Milestone 2	Milestone 3	Milestone 4	Milestone 5	Milestone 6	Milestone 7	Milestone 8
Pre-application	Stage 1 submission	Ratification – eligibility and essential documentation	Project development	Stage 2 submission	Post-award processes and support	Reporting and compliance	Learning zone

Source: https://secure.sportengland.org/milestones/index.html

8. Sport England aims to achieve £2 for every £1 of its investment. Can you clearly demonstrate that you have or can secure at least 65% of the cost of your project?

9. Given the fierce competition for Sport England funds, have you considered a contingency plan should your application be unsuccessful?

10. Have you carried out an assessment of all possible risks associated with the project and the steps you would take if they arise?

11. Have you read the Regional Investment Strategy and can you clearly articulate and demonstrate the benefits, costs, need and risk for your project?

12. Have you identified and spoken to partners who can support the development and delivery of your project and who you intend to work with? These could include the National (or County) Governing Body for each sport involved, the County Sports Partnership, your local council, the local education authority, schools etc.

13. Have you sought and taken advice from knowledgeable sources (including your partners/consultees)?

14. Have you looked at, and acted upon, the Pre-Application Guidance Notes and Templates downloadable from the Sport England website?

15. Have you drawn up an outline a project implementation plan that identifies all the actions, resources and timescales involved, so that at least some tasks could be carried out concurrently?

16. Have you thoroughly considered how your project will increase participation year on year, how your project will keep achieving this and how you will demonstrate this – as this is the primary focus of our funding?

17. Have you identified and planned for how your project will continue post Sport England funding?. All projects must demonstrate that the outcomes will be sustainable post Sport England award funding.

18. And finally, are you sure you are eligible to apply for funding? Critically, can you confirm that: (a) you do not impose any unreasonable restrictions on membership or access to sport for all? (b) you have not already entered into a prior commitment to undertake the project?

(*Source*: http:// www.sportengland.org/4_are_you_ready_to_apply.pdf).

Monitoring and Evaluation of Funded Schemes

Since the introduction of Best Value, performance indicators have gained precedence within the management of sport. No longer does the funding process end with the delivery of funds to the sport organisation, but subsequent performance has to be assessed and managed. Essentially, performance management is about the need to enhance performance, as well as developing a shared understanding of what needs to be achieved, between the funding body and recipient of funding. There are two associated terms that are used, these being performance indicators (PIs) and performance targets. Robinson (2004) highlights the reasons why performance management exists. First, there is a need to demonstrate that public money has been spent appropriately and efficiently. It could be argued that this is especially pertinent given that contribution to the National Lottery is voluntary and concern over the use of lottery funding could have impacts upon future public expenditure. Secondly, performance management allows the management of stakeholder expectations, through clearly defined targets and measurement of performance against these targets. Thirdly, performance managers allow those responsible to manage their sport provision to achieve these results. Finally, performance management allows individual performances to be managed to assist with meeting the overall goals set.

Performance indicators become especially pertinent to funded schemes. All schemes funded by Sport England are required to report every quarter using between one and five key performance indicators (KPIs). The number and type of KPIs required will depend on the nature of the project, but will include evaluation of areas such as:

- Participants/active members – information about the characteristics of those taking part in the activity. If the scheme is run as a membership scheme, details of active members can be provided. If not, then registration or booking forms will need to be used.

- Throughput – this is a measure of how much activity is taking place. If the event is open to all, with no membership or registration, a means will need to be found to identify actual numbers participating, broken down into sub-groups, for example, in terms of male and female participants.

- Coaching – if the activity involves coaches, then data will need to be collected on the number of coaches, gender breakdown, coach qualifications, status in terms of paid/unpaid and coaching hours delivered as part of the scheme.

- Volunteers – if the scheme involves volunteers other than those involved in purely a coaching capacity, then data will need to be collected on the total number of volunteers, broken down by gender and the total number of volunteer activities involved.

Performance indicators become a useful tool not only once funding has been secured, but also as a means by which to clarify the actual nature of the activity for which funding is sought. Rather than viewing KPIs as simply a bureaucratic hindrance to be dealt with once the scheme is in operation, those seeking funding can use them to develop their application beforehand. An evaluation of the likely PIs can often clarify a number of issues before the application for funding takes place, for example, in terms of clarifying the exact purpose of the funding. If the funding is to increase participation, for example, the likely PIs of by how much participation should increase, by which groups and to which of the region's priorities does this increase relate to, then the application may become more focused and relevant.

Using PIs is not always straightforward, however. As Robinson (2004) notes, there are a number of potential pitfalls that need to be addressed. Perhaps the main issue is that they generally provide quantitative data that provides a measure of performance – for example, identifying an increase (or otherwise) in the number of volunteers involved in an activity – but fails to address the issue of *why*. Their use can be made more valuable, however, by using certain key principles (Audit Commission 2000 cited in Robinson, 2004):

- KPIs should only focus on relevant information. Information should be deemed relevant in terms of whether it can help explain or manage performance.

- KPIs should be hierarchical. If the priority is on increasing participation, then this KPI must take precedence over KPIs on coaching or volunteers, for example.

- KPIs should be used. If the funded scheme is not meeting targets, then action needs to be taken, such as reviewing the delivery of the sporting opportunity or providing feedback to those staffing the opportunity.

- They should be used in association with targets. These targets should be challenging and set standards of service.

- Those delivering the programmes should see their value. If staff are delivering sport development events and are required to collect PI data, then they need to be aware of its value, rather than viewing its collection as detracting from the activity itself.

It could also be argued that some of the key targets cannot be easily addressed by PIs. The impact upon social capital or crime reduction, for example, are not easily measurable. The quality of experience is equally difficult to address. More qualitative measures that could address some of these issues are, however, simply beyond the capability of most funded schemes.

Critical Success Factors in Sports Development Funding

Performance indicators provide a useful goal by which to assess the progress of funded projects; however, it is important to identify and address the factors that may impact upon success in achieving targets. The sporting environment is rapidly changing and there are a huge number of factors that impact upon performance of funded initiatives. Rather than try to examine all of the factors that will have an effect, it is only feasible to focus upon those which are key to success, the critical success factors (CSFs). Critical success factors are 'those resources, skills and attributes...that are essential to deliver success' (Lynch, 2006, p. 92). In the field of sport development, these will generally be factors that are valued by the actual or potential users. By focusing upon the CSFs, it is suggested that the chances of achieving targets will be maximised. On the other hand, if certain CSFs are not achieved, then success is unlikely. Badminton England's vision, for example, is to ensure that England becomes the world's No.1 nation in Badminton, by general consent and evidence of winning medals, that there continues to be increased participation and interest in the game and that Badminton England has sound corporate governance and is considered fit for purpose. To achieve this, a number of CSFs have been identified. Some of these can be outlined as follows:

- Establish badminton as a major part of sport and health programmes in schools and further education, based on new initiatives to be introduced in 2006.

- Work in partnership with key agencies to ensure easy access to the game for everyone and provide opportunities to retain all participants in the game as appropriate.

- Invest in programmes and adaptations of the sport to reflect the specific needs of participants e.g. disability or disaffected young people.

- Achieve the Intermediate and Advanced level of the Safeguarding Children in Sport Standards by 2008.

- Achieve the Intermediate and Advanced level of the Equality Standards by 2008.

- Ensure that all coaches, volunteers, officials and staff working with, or around, young people are in receipt of a satisfactory Criminal Records Bureau (CRB) check.

- Establish a Child Protection training programme and ensure attendance of all Club and County Welfare Officers by 2008.

- Publish an annual Coach Education programme designed to recruit and develop the best coaches where they are most needed.

- Ensure significant input from the National Coaching Team into the design and delivery of our Coach Education Programme.

- Establish a mechanism that measures how active coaches are – active defined by coaching a minimum of one hour per week.

- Continue to develop the Academy Schools programme with the aim of having a minimum of one Academy in every School Sports Partnership in England by 2010.

- Take a 'Bottom Up' approach to the competitive structure ensuring that from local to national level, the system joins up.

- Set up a team of appropriately trained tournament organisers able to deliver the competition programme.

- Develop a Club Assessment system enabling clubs and BADMINTON England to clearly identify areas of strength and improvement.

- Identify and develop a network of Performance Centres which demonstrate they have the infrastructure to recruit and retain members as well as develop a base of talented young players.

- Focus a larger percentage of regional resources on those clubs that provide a 'badminton payback' – clubs which are committed to achieving accreditation and where investment will make a significant difference to the sport.

- Establish a streamlined Strategic Management Team (SMT) who are accountable to deliver success.

- Develop a Commercial Strategy with clear and measurable objectives and one that is financially supported.

(*Source*: Badminton England, 2006).

An assessment of all likely CSFs needs to be made by any organisation of body seeking funding and also be considered by those responsible for allocating funding. The key factors can be classed under three areas (Ohmae, 1983) which, although not sport specific, are useful to address the issues that may lead to a funded scheme being successful. These areas are first those concerned with the customers/potential customers. For schemes that focus upon increased participation, this will be largely focused upon those who do not participate, and will address such factors as overcoming the barriers and constraints faced by such individuals or identifying specific needs and desires of the target group(s). Secondly, the competition needs to be explored. Competition is used here to refer to competing non-sporting/physical activities, for example, sedentary activities. Finally, those factors related to the capacity of the sporting club, organisation or body to actually deliver in terms of meeting targets need to be examined. This will focus on administrative staff, coaches and volunteers and their skills and motivations to deliver the plan.

Whilst an acknowledgement of CSFs by both the body applying for funding and the funding body is desirable, it is also important to recognise that they do have their limitations, and that successfully addressing each CSF will not necessarily result in the success of any funded scheme. First, simply identifying the relevant CSFs is difficult. The CSFs in one particular context may not apply to another, or those applying for funding simply may not have the skills or experience to identify which will be important to their objectives. It may also be difficult to identify how such factors affect the success of an initiative. Finally, some CSFs may only become apparent once an initiative has started, and thus some contingency funding should always be included within any application or award.

Managing the Funding of Sports Development

The comprehensive nature of the application process has a number of functions, including not only transparency, objectivity, but also the reduction – or apparent reduction – in the chances of funding risky or inappropriate projects.

In reality, however, the very nature of funding for sport development will always involve some form of risk, despite the application procedure and the effective identification of CSFs. Given the reliance upon publicly funded (through the National Lottery) grants, accountability is an important aspect. Yet the very nature of funding sport development means that there are inherent risks. Leat (2005) provides a useful outline of the key issues. Two key challenges exist. First, that of making the application process as secure as possible to allow fair decisions that minimise the risk of failure, whilst keeping the process accessible to those bodies which may need funding most, such as disadvantaged groups. Secondly, the need to increase stakeholder understanding of the funding process so that an awareness of the inherent risks is developed. Risk will always be an issue as:

- Funding decisions are made on the basis of what may be achieved, rather than on completed activities.

- Those making funding decisions will often be faced with large numbers of applications from applicants with which they have had little prior experience or knowledge.

- Funding is often made for new, innovative or untried schemes.

- Applicants will generally choose to present only that information which supports their requirements.

Once acknowledgement of risk exists, however, Leat (2005) suggests a redefinition of risk away from potential to harm, towards a conceptualisation in terms of risk as potential. This allows increased experimentation, innovation and accessibility. Schemes should certainly not be rejected solely on the basis that they may be risky.

The funding of sport development is a complex and fragmented issue, with a number of key stakeholders. This chapter has largely focused upon the funding offered through the sports councils, with particular reference to Sport England to demonstrate some of the complexities inherent within the process of securing funding. Two key issues emerge for those managing this aspect of sport development. First, the need to relate funding applications to the priorities of the funding body is crucial. This will, to some extent, exclude many sport organisations from securing funding; however, resources are limited and this has to be seen as a necessary part of allocation of that which is available. Secondly, the use of such funding needs to be carefully assessed by all parties. The question of ensuring that the funding achieves its purpose can be – to some extent at least – addressed by the use of CSFs, and the identification of such CSFs by both those seeking funding and those offering funding. A final point to be aware of is that the funding environment is a complex and dynamic one. Many of the key issues discussed within the chapter will develop over time, and this needs to be taken into account through the willingness to adopt emergent and flexible approaches to funding sport and physical activity. As Collins (2003) notes, any changes in key personnel – whether in government or other agency – often result in changes to processes, and the need to maintain an illusion of currency often results in change being made regularly.

References

Badminton England. (2006). *100 Point Plan: A Decade of Delivery*. National Badminton Centre: Milton Keynes.

Chalip, L. (2006). Towards social leverage of sport events. *Journal of Sport & Tourism*, **11**(2), 109–27.

Collins, M. (2003). *Sport and Social Exclusion*. London: Routledge.

DCMS (2002). *Game Plan: A Strategy for Delivering Government's Sport and Physical Activity Objectives*. London: DCMS/Strategy Unit.

DCMS (2005). *DCMS – UK Sport Funding Agreement: 2005/6–2007/8*. Department of Culture, Media and Sport.

Green, M. (2004). Changing policy priorities for sport in England: The emergence of elite sport development as a key policy concern. *Leisure Studies*, **23**(4), 365–85.

Henry, I. and Theodoraki, E. (2002). Management, organisation and theory in the governance of sport. In *Handbook of Sport Studies* (J. Coakley and E. Dunning, eds). London: Sage.

Jackson, D. and Nesti, M. (2001). Resources for sport. In *Sports Development: Policy, Process, and Practice* (K. Hylton, P. Bramham, D. Jackson, and M. Nesti, eds). London: Routledge, pp. 149–70.

Lawson, H. (2005). Empowering people, facilitating community development, and contributing to sustainable development: The social work of sport, exercise, and physical education programs. *Sport, Education, Society*, **10**(1), 135–60.

Leat, D. (2005). *Discussion Paper on Risk and Good Grant Making*. Big Lottery Fund Research 17.

Lynch, R. (2006). *Corporate Strategy*. Harlow: FT Prentice Hall.

Nichols, G., Taylor, P., James, M. et al. (2004). Voluntary activity in UK sport. *Voluntary Action*, 6(2), 31–54.

Ohmae, K. (1983). *The Mind of the Strategist*. Harmondsworth: Penguin.

Robinson, L. (2004). *Managing Public Sport and Leisure Services*. London: Routledge.

CHAPTER 13

Accounting for Sports Development

Cora Burnett

Introduction

The sport development discourse reflects on the construction of a social process of change that is emerging, contested and challenged. Not only are academics faced with the challenge of developing a body of knowledge as evidence base for a wide variety of programmes, but the needs and foci of role players requiring monitoring and evaluation results are equally diverse.

In addressing this rather daunting and complex task, this chapter will first explore the varied manifestations of sport within a development framework and reflect on both phenomena (sport and development) as these diverse paradigms find a synthesized expression in development work (UNICEF, 2006). The role of stakeholders is discussed in terms of the reciprocal agency and shared ownership that is required for sustained development (Coalter, 2006; Lawson, 2005). A bottom-up approach is advocated with clear guidelines on how co-ownership could be negotiated and could function for monitoring, evaluation and impact assessments of sport development programmes and interventions (Burnett, 2006; Cunningham and Beneforti, 2005).

The provision of an evidence base posed unique challenges as diverse theoretical frameworks inform a comprehensive body of knowledge, ranging from studies in the economic sciences (e.g. economic impact), medical sciences (e.g. physical health), humanities (e.g. psychological impact) and social sciences (e.g. social impact). The evidence is scrutinized relating to the diverse theoretical frameworks, research designs, methodologies, nature and analysis of data in relation to the contents and contexts of development work. A practical tool for managing, monitoring, evaluation and impact assessments that may enhance comparative research and implementation of sport development is suggested.

Development and Sport

To meaningfully write about development and sport is to unpack the phenomena as they find expression in a myriad of contexts, complex relationships and varied manifestations. At the core of the most basic assumption, the concept of 'development' poses some form of deliverance of 'positive change' over time. The projected or assessable change is most often associated with the notion of progress within normative conceptual frameworks of the state, market and/or science (Girginov, in this volume, Vanden Auweele et al., 2006). The 'social rewards' reported in the case study of the Australia-Africa Active Community Clubs' initiative on the book website demonstrate change inherent in the programme design and envisaged outcomes. Despite the inherent assumption that 'progress', whether induced or spontaneous, is associated with positive outcomes, the premise of the beneficiaries remains a contentious issue. In this sense, the 'positive' economic outcomes of Beijing as host city of the 2008 Summer Olympic Games will also have a prize tag for the displaced as victims of 'progress', very much in the same vein as such events may leave environmental scars (Sage, 1999).

In recognition of cost-benefit consequences of development projects, earlier social impact assessment studies sought to determine the viability of such ventures by projecting the human and environmental costs and sought to help individuals, groups, communities and organizations to understand the ideological, social, cultural and economic impacts of proposed change (Barrow, 2000). The benefits often addressed political agendas of powerful role players who provided the vision, resources and direct development practices to bring about a desirable state of being to the 'underdeveloped'. This is evidenced in global processes of diffusion and imperialism whereby developing countries (being within the process of development) are the recipients (Giddens, 2000). Social change is the result of development practices of which sport serves as a 'deliverable' framed within a developmental approach.

The development and diffusion of modern sport and the normative framework of development embedded in the social world of sport add to the complexity of sport and development as interrelated social constructs (Jarvie and Maguire, 1994). Within a development continuum, movement phenomena exist in varied formalized and institutionalized versions of play, physical activity, games and sport (Mangan, 2002). On the one side of the continuum, modern, elite and competitive sport poses notions of diffusion and development inherent in imperialist, capitalist and industrial-complex visions and practices, juxtaposed to sport and physical activity as means to reach humanitarian development objectives (Maguire, 2006).

In an attempt to capture these diverse paradigms, scholars and agencies differentiated semantically between 'sport development' ('sport plus model') and 'sport for development' (plus sport model) (UNICEF, 2006). The former model focuses on sport-based activities involving the promotion of sport and positive experiences of play *plus* additional developmental, personal and societal benefits. Issues such as nation-building, elite sport development and mass sport participation may be categorized under this approach (Cingiene and Laskiene, 2004), whereas 'sport for/in development' (plus sport model) emphasizes sport as a tool to achieve development-based outcomes such as the development of HIV/AIDS awareness, and promoting 'active citizenship' through volunteering (UNICEF, 2006). Such developments are reported in the case study of the Australia-Africa 2006 Active Community Clubs' Initiative.

The social work of sport has been placed on the world stage as a relatively cheap, pleasurable and novel anecdote for the many ills of society, hence the recognition of the 'social problem industry' (Pitter and Andrews, 1997). Sport captivated the imagination of main agents striving to find solutions and actively address risk behaviours such as drug abuse, delinquency (Diana, 2000; Nichols, 2004), inclusion of vulnerable populations (e.g. women, the aged, at-risk youth and the poor) (Burnett, 2004; Farrell et al., 1996) and the prevention of diseases of endemic proportions such as malaria and HIV/AIDS (Uwakwe, 2001).

The Millennium Development Goals (MDG), international conferences, declarations, recognition of 2005 as the International Year of Sport and Physical Education (United Nations, 2005) made a case for the potential value of sport in addressing development matters at global level. At lower levels, 'Sport for Peace' projects utilize sport as an inclusive, human, social practice to improve community life, citizenship (meso-level) and quality of life for individuals (micro-level). Sugden (2006) reports on the Football for Peace (F4P) project that addresses the issue of peaceful co-existence, acceptance, tolerance and national identity confirmation between Jewish and Arab children from the towns and villages of the Galilee region. Such ethnographic accounts offer insights in the process of peace-building and change within a given socio-historical and political context. Programmes focusing on quality of life, community regeneration and health-related outcomes reflect the process of change in the spheres, and may differ significantly from the delivery of tangible product-related evidence in terms of resources and elite athlete development (Hemana, 2007; Pedlar, 1996).

Local sports programmes, clubs and community centres are viewed as instrumental in the social construction of citizenship (Glover, 2004), whereas sport events and collective leisure pursuits represent focal practices that may create shared meaning. The provision of local sports facilities may become revitalization tools in generating employment opportunities and providing some image benefits (Chapin, 1999). Clarity on whose needs are primarily addressed and how locals react to development forms part of the reflective management approach, as developing agents may experience challenges concerning compatibility of goals and acceptance of co-ownership. Shuttleworth and Wan-Ka (1998) reported on different normative structures of Western sport that celebrate individualistic elitist capitalist values and the local collective and family norms of Chinese youth in general in Hong Kong. Such dissonance may derail or influence outcomes of development initiatives and programmes.

Reciprocal Agency for Sustainable Development

Major stakeholders involved in the designing, managing implementation and striving for successful and sustainable service delivery of sport and recreation programmes, include international organizations (e.g. UNICEF, WHO, FIFA, the IOC and transnational companies such as Nike), government agencies (e.g. Sport England, the Australian Sports Commission, state-level organizations and sports federations), NGOs operating at all levels, research and tertiary institutions and consultancies. The names of programmes often address the core deliverable of a programme such 'Right to Play' (Canada), 'Active Community Clubs' (Australia, see associated case study on the book website), 'Kick Aids Out' (Africa) and 'Millennium Volunteers' (UK) (Eley and Kirk, 2002; United Nations, 2003). Key international role players have initiated several declarations, international forums and networking such as the Next Step Conferences since 2005 to forge global partnerships for utilizing sport as a means of promoting development and peace (Vanden Auweele et al., 2006).

Influential agents such as the UN are using sport-related activities in UN peacekeeping missions worldwide as an integral part of nation-building and peace keeping, aimed at promoting dialogue between groups in conflict and fostering goodwill within local communities (United Nations, 2006). Teaming up with a powerful sports organization like FIFA provides the forum to advocate the message of peace, create an awareness of sports' potential humanitarian role and fund programmes. On unveiling the emblem for the first World Cup in Africa, Kofi Annan, Secretary-General of the UN tapped into the 'universal language of football' in his advocacy for peace by saying: 'We use it to heal emotional wounds of war among young people in refugee camps, and in countries recovering from armed conflict. We use it to try to bridge ethnic, social, cultural and religious divides. We use it to promote teamwork and fair play. We use it to empower girls. We use it in our work to reach the Millennium Development Goals' (United Nations, 2006, p. 1).

Forging partnerships with strategic partners at international, regional and national levels represents an emerging system of global sports development governance with increased capacity. Collaboration at that level is mutually beneficial to identify and engage in advocacy, resource allocation and service delivery, yet increased capacity at the decision-makers level does not guarantee effective implementation and community-level uptake. Sports development managers and agents who do not involve the 'community-in-development' may expect rejection, as top-down, product-driven interventions are often met with resistance. Claimed trusteeship by public stakeholders (political power), commercial partners (financial capital) and voluntary agents (self-motivation) would require legitimacy for their development work from the recipients (Vanden Auweele et al., 2006).

Development work is inevitably value-laden with the development of outcomes by the trustees and main stakeholders to serve their development interests. Political objectives may, however, be tempered by multi-stakeholder engagement and the facilitation of local agency. Coalter et al. (2000) advocate an outreach or bottom-up approach where sport programmes address wider personal and social development issues. This ties in with a 'whole-of-community approach' where programmes are adapted to be culturally appropriate, needs-based and controlled by the community for sustainability, identification of success and change-related manifestations (Burnett, 2006; Cooperative Research Centre for Aboriginal and Tropical Health, 2002). Reciprocal agency represented within two quite diverse sources, seems to be the key element for community-development projects as it is the practitioners and implementers who need to be consulted about community interests where the process of

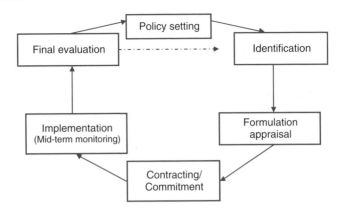

Figure 13.1 The project cycle.

engagement in sport and recreation requires praxis rather than a product delivery only (Pedlar, 1996). Bridging ties of social inter-dependence thus need to be forged at different levels of service delivery and implementation, as sport programmes are social systems with their own internal dynamics, embedded in a wider social fabric (Kirk and MacPhail, 2003).

The interconnectedness of 'decision-makers' and 'decision-takers' is clearly set out in the project management tools of the *Toolkit Sport for Development* (United Nations, 2005). In the project cycle, the meaningful collaboration of strategic planners and implementers is continued and linked to functional engagement during all the different phases (Figure 13.1).

The collaboration during the 'identification phase' entails the gathering of baseline data for a situation analysis, followed by more detailed planning and the development of objectively verifiable indicators in addition to the 'sources of verification' of how, where and what information should be obtained to inform success indicators and to select and refine potential outcomes. The completed plan and process indicators ensure a basis for management, monitoring and evaluation (Wright et al., 1998). Implementers are best positioned and act as community-based strategic partners who should be recruited for the implementation of a project. Based on evaluation results, implementers should also have a say in policy development so as to ensure cultural and context sensitivity essential for identification of good practices and recommendations (United Nations, 2005).

Enabling all stakeholders to meaningfully contribute to the implementation, needs-based service delivery, sustainability and success of programmes or interventions require more than mere contractual agreements of intended collaboration (Ife, 1999). Placing the 'delivery' and 'uptake' in a relation of synthesis rather than juxtaposed implicates the building of capacity that is empowerment-oriented. Gore (1993) critiques the claim to the empowerment of people served by professionals who often do little to consult and involve the people they claim to empower. Conceptually, empowerment is evidenced by: (a) the redistribution of power; (b) access to one or more kinds of resources; and (c) collaboration based on voluntary relations and equal partners where the target group (system) is an integrative part of the action system (Lawson, 2005).

Empowerment cannot be bestowed upon a person. Interventions should thus allow for self-determination and self-directions in conceiving, pursuing and achieving 'own goals' (Gahin and Paterson, 2001; Pedlar, 1996). Collaboration and empowerment become crucial in most sport-related development projects that aim to facilitate human and social development (forging of social relationships and networks) as core outcomes (Balatti and Falk, 2002). Decision makers' foci, the nature, scope and resources of a programme to a large extent determine the indicators ('input' – such as training; 'process' – such as delivery; and 'output' – such as impact).

Indicator Development for Monitoring, Evaluation and Impact Assessment

Essential in the process of design and planning are the development of good quality indicators that are SMART (Specific, Measurable, Achievable, Relevant and Time-bound) (Coalter, 2006) and SPICED (Subjective, Participatory, Interpretable and Communicatable, Cross-checked and Compared, Empowering, Diverse and Desegregated) (United Nations, 2005). The complex reality and socio-political, economic and dynamics of other systems at local level may affect scientific designs for data collection and interpretation, but within the conceptual framework of development even anecdotal evidence becomes critical data because of the value of the source. It also implicates that representatives at the 'receiving end' of a development initiative should be empowered and educated to fulfil a meaningful role. Cunningham and Beneforti (2005) stress the importance of community engagement in defining relevant indicators for programme implementation, monitoring and assessment.

The lack of robust evidence of sport-related development projects relate to the multifaceted and complex phenomena of sport, recreation, physical activity and the myriad foci of development projects which are implemented in very different contexts and grounded in different conceptual frameworks (Carnduff, 2001). Broad, ambitious and unclear outcomes such as 'improve the quality of life', 'reduce crime and drug abuse', 'increase social cohesion' without clear identification and supportive evidence complicate the measurability and interpretation of such confounding variables.

Vague or product-only outcomes and little analysis of long-term impacts translate into a lack of evidence. Considering the main goals of an intervention or programme, process and outcome indicators inform results and recommendations as evidenced by various 'indicator studies' (Balatti and Falk, 2002; Gahin and Paterson, 2001). Comprehensive bands and fields of indicators tap into various theoretical paradigms, applied theory and research evidence. Such clusters identified by Balatti and Falk (2002) represent categories of health (physical, psychological and mental well-being), human capital identified by education and learning, employment and quality of working life, command over goods and services, time and leisure, physical environment, personal safety and social environment with links to network formation, trust, community regeneration and social capital. Programme viability and sustainability, participation and outcome indicators are proposed by Cunningham and Beneforti (2005) who reflect community-specific outcomes developed through consultation.

Gahin and Paterson (2001) distinguish mainly between social and economic indicators where the former are considered to fall in a grey area that complicates their 'effect and effectiveness'. Health and social outcomes are relatively long term and should thus be broken down in achievable process variables or outcomes to be assessed over time, considering the timeframe and maturity of a project. Economic models and indicators seek information on the costs and benefits of proposed projects for multi-year and/or multi-context analysis and comparison (Kanters et al., 2001).

The function of indicators is to indicate task areas for policy budgeting, monitor progress, produce evaluation data and measure the quality of processes leading to an outcome which can include direct and indirect measures. It also serves to determine change over time against set targets or benchmarks. In the field of sport and recreation, they may be utilized to explore the relationship between physical activity and various health outcomes. Scholars mainly recommend the development of process and outcome indicators that are informed by a credible evaluation framework and sensitive to the culture when measuring change over time. Some may 'fit' into an experimental-control design according to the type, focus and scope of the intervention (Burnett, 2006). However, the accurate identification and the isolation of a cause–effect relationship between contributing variables and intervention outcomes remain a challenge for the research community. It is further complicated by issues of context and the lack of control in real life settings where indicators and evidence can hardly capture the complexities and interrelatedness of health and social outcomes (Cooperative Research Centre for Aboriginal and Tropical Health, 2002).

Accounting for the Value of Sport

Practitioners and academics are increasingly faced with the need to demonstrate that their work is based on a sound evidence base to inform research designs, monitoring, evaluation, impact studies and providing some substantiation of 'good practice' models. Frameworks are thus provided for integrating critical reviews of research evidence with contextual and practical considerations relevant for implementation and scientific discourse. The question often asked by developers, politicians or funding agencies is 'What value do we get for our money?' The value of sport substantiated by scientific literature is also prevalent for decision-makers and researchers to make informed decisions for their different endeavours. The classification developed by Sport England (2007) on the 'value of sport' is utilized for the discussion.

The generation of empirical and comparative data in *economic impact assessments* mostly relates to macro- or meso-level studies whereby the direct and/or indirect economic impact of sport events, facilities, teams or related commercialized sport is projected or assessed within different phases of its occurrence (e.g. before, during or after events) (Madden and Crowe, 2004). In the systematic analysis of the economic impact on a range of factors, including the gross state product, multiplier analysis is utilized within a cost-benefit framework (Crompton, 1995). Multidisciplinary approaches and empirical data reflect the income-generating capacity and economic returns of host cities for comparable events (Gratton et al., 2000), teams (Crompton, 1995) and facilities (Chapin, 1999), in addition to estimates of spectator attendance, visitor expenditure, tourism (including local income retained and lodging industry revenue) as well as job creation (Dermody et al., 2003). Similar research paradigms and methodologies allow for inter-venue and event comparisons, considering the types of venues and events in term of timing, duration and scale. It is within the non-economic benefits such as claims to community regeneration of such physical resources where an evidence base is less substantial (Chapin, 1999).

Another economic denominator concerns the cost factor of disease prevention. Findings seem to favour the adult population of over 45 years of age (Nicholl et al., 2004), despite statistical support of the overall health benefits of physically active youth and a wide range of *physical health* benefits. These benefits include improved health relating to cardiovascular, musculoskeletal, metabolic, endocrine, immune systems and the control or reduction on health markers (e.g. weight control, Type 2 diabetes and reduced risk of ischemic stroke) (Biddle et al., 2004). National health surveys attempted to quantify the positive value of sports participation and an active lifestyle in support of the existing body of medical and epidemiological literature (Farrell and Shields, 2004). Healthy active lifestyles of youth translate into positive health choices (responsible sexual behaviour, alcohol consumption, non-smoking and a balance diet), despite evidence of a higher frequency of sports-related injuries, binge drinking and overtraining of serious athletes (Miller et al., 2000).

Experimental research paradigms, control and statistical analysis generate acclaimed 'scientific evidence', but are not clear in terms of validity measures of self-reported health, dosage prescription, long-term health benefits and behaviour relating to risk-inducing and risk-reducing dimensions of different types of physical activity and the related health consequences. The effect of the advocacy role of sport in health campaigns (Cavill and Bauman, 2004) and education for the prevention and control of disease such and HIV/AIDS (Uwakwe, 2001) is more complex. Contributing factors to this state of affairs include a wide range of variables that simultaneously impact on the behaviour that a causal relationship between activity, health education and disease manifestations is difficult to trace. The need for longitudinal studies in real life settings may provide more clear-cut evidence. Another challenge seems to be the interrelatedness of physical and psychological benefits ascribed to physical activity.

Scientific evidence exists for the contribution of different types of physical activity of sufficient duration and intensity towards the improvement of general aspects of *psychological well-being*. Such evidence substantiates claims of positive changes in anxiety, stress management, mood, body image, physical and global self-worth and self-esteem, although the functional relationship and interactive dynamics (between the physical and psychological) often obscure causal relationships (Fox, 2000). Different mechanisms are affected by types and the regularity of activities and programmes which enable participants to develop such attributes through health-related fitness regimes or programmes designed and implemented to elicit such benefits (Kirsten et al., 2003).

Meta-analytical evidence, the standardization of research instruments and scales may deliver the comparable evidence within specified psychological parameters (Allen, 2005). Experimental designs and focused interventions indicate positive correlations between healthy self-perceptions and resilience, as well as on subscales of personal appearance, social, athletic and scholastic competence among at-risk youth (Wright et al., 1998). Statistical evidence does not provide comprehensive insight into the complex experience of active participation as qualitative data is required for that purpose.

Considering human development aspects, it seems that research evidence is the strongest for physical and psychological health in individualized measurements that utilize experimental designs, standardized research instruments with relatively high levels of internal validity and control. The collection of participation data, health clinic attendances and access to health-related programmes and services may serve as supportive indirect measures at the aggregate community level. The long-term effect, transferability and extrapolation of research evidence are however questionable. Statistical regression models and useful scales produced evidence on the development of personal competencies and social motivational orientations through sport participations informed by behavioural research approaches (Allen, 2005).

Motivational studies also provide insights into the relationship between childhood and adolescent *participation*, and possible projections of life-long participation against the background of contextual and cultural constraints. There is conclusive evidence that early exposure to varied physical activities that allows for a choice according to the interest, competency and level of maturity significantly contributes to a prolonged active lifestyle, although projections for life-long participation necessitate longitudinal, rather than retrospective methodology. It also seems that significant others such as parents, teachers and coaches primarily influence children's socialization in sport and physical activity, rather than sport stars or distant role models who are dissimilar to role learners (Payne et al., 2003).

Methodological limitations, diverse theoretical models and contextual influences limit comparative research data to support convincing arguments in favour of sport participation. Different content and delivery issues may positively or negatively affect continued participation. Participation alone will not necessarily produce desired outcomes and programme design, implementation and the focus of delivery and resultant experiences should be aligned to facilitate envisaged impacts.

Pro-social behaviour and altruistic orientations are fostered, which may affect aspects of group cohesion and increased cooperative behaviour within social institutions (Langbein and Bess, 2002). Case-study analysis provided ethnographic evidence of the development of pro-social values within a team context according to an expected code of conduct (Burnett, 2006). The development of pro-social behaviour and/or *changes in anti-social behaviour* such as criminal offending, substance abuse and inclusive participation practices may indirectly reflect on aspects of individual and social development contributed to a particular intervention. However, evidence obtained through logistic regression models of sport and physical activity programmes to combat crime and anti-social behaviour among at-risk populations does not emphatically support the deterrence hypothesis (Begg et al., 1996). Reductions in recorded crimes and the analysis of the relationship between a programme, such as Midnight Basketball on a national scale, show sport participation as one of many factors that could have contributed to the decrease in certain crime rates, yet lack clear conceptual frameworks and cause–effect measures (Diana, 2000; Hartmann and Brooks, 2006).

Evidence of positive changes that may indirectly impact on the reduction of anti-social behaviour relates to positive changes in the self-concept (Farrell et al., 1996). Nichols (2004) explored the links between sport participation as diversion and parallel increases in some psychological aspects and positive experiences as inherent value of sport participation, yet could not provide significant support for crime reduction related to a specific intervention.

Anthropological frameworks and qualitative data from self-reported accounts, in addition to observational evidence of the reduction of deviant behaviour, need to be further explored through case-study analysis and the triangulation of methods. It is speculated that a causal relationship between intervention outcomes and crime reduction will be better substantiated if there are complete focus on the latter as outcome (Coalter et al., 2000). It can thus be concluded that evidence obtained from multidimensional programmes may show some indication of the reduction in criminal behaviour, but may also be ascribed to the simultaneous influences of psycho-social and other influences.

Evidence of the contribution of active participation in sport and physical activity towards the expression of the *social self*, development of leadership and positive peer relations are supported by research evidence from controlled experimental designs (Dobosz and Beaty, 1999). Within a broad theory of change, framework and real and perceived barriers affecting practices of *social inclusion* of minority ethnic groups provided issue-related evidence. It also relates to positive social learning experiences, social network formation and development transitions in the formation of athletic and global self-identities (Heere and James, 2007; Smith, 2003). In accordance to interventions focusing on issues of equity and inclusion, quantifiable measurements and participation patterns seem to provide a framework for the context and description of stratification and social behaviour of different target groups earmarked for inclusion (e.g. women, girls, at-risk youth or people with disabilities). A synthesis of theoretical approaches, quantitative and qualitative data, interpretation of content and context may represent less scientific rigor, but will go further to capture the complex reality.

Social development within a communitarian framework focuses on civic engagement where issues of collective ownership, obligations and the collaboration of stakeholders within sport fraternities made valuable contributions towards forging a communitarian philosophy and network formation (Jarvie, 2003). Tapping into theoretical frameworks of capital theory hypothesis, network theory and social capital as conceptualized by scholars such as Bourdieu, Coleman and Putnam (see Chapter 10 for an extensive discussion), the formation of supportive networks and development of bonding (intra-group) and bridging (inter-group) ties provide evidence in various studies of the development of trusting relations and cohesive clustering (Arai and Pedlar, 2003; Burnett, 2006). The included case study on the book website of the Australia-Africa 2006 Active Community Clubs' Initiative provides 'evidence' on network development in a rural community in the Eastern Cape Province of South Africa. Evidence for the development of civic virtue and 'active citizenship' are also intertwined with other social benefits evident in the impact of the Millennium Volunteers programme in which 1.5 million young people participated in the UK in 1996 (Eley and Kirk, 2002). Access to operational networks (social capital) and the building of tolerance and acceptance as part of peace-building interventions are difficult to quantify, whereas qualitative data contributes to the understanding of context, processes and issues relating to the use of sport for conflict resolution (Sugden, 2006). Interrelated and multi-directive programme outcomes, the focus on process and unclear cause–effect relationships result in 'anecdotal evidence'. The lack of triangulation (multi-source and multi-method), absence of longitudinal data and implementation of pre-post comparative data analysis and the lack of control over external variables further contribute to 'grey areas' of data interpretation. The relatively short time span of interventions, effect size, high staff turnover, limited funding, lack of control over contextual issues, ethical considerations (not to have an experimental-control design as the latter might not gain access to the intervention), diverse conceptual frameworks and methodologies complicate the extracting of academically sound and practice-based evidence.

Accounting for sports development goes further than mere building a case based on the best scientific evidence available. Advocates of the cause may benefit greatly by learning about *good practices* and success stories to inform effective management, capacity building, context-sensitive intervention designs, indicators development and research. The sport development discourse is constructed as a social process of change with emerging and changing relationships at the operational level. Within the national and commercial context, reciprocal agency is required between the trustees, practitioners and recipients. The triangulated partnership between those who design and deliver development programmes and the recipients thereof constitutes the contextual dynamics that can be translated into desirable practices from which lessons can be learnt. The evidence base could be abstracted in generating applied knowledge as meta-language to inform the academic discourse and as directive for development practices.

The lack of evidence is mostly contributed to the absence of comprehensive and coherent scientific literature to guide monitoring and evaluation of sport-based programmes. As an emerging field of inquiry, scholarly work in the field of monitoring, evaluation and impact assessment should be produced to address the production, comparison and scrutiny of evidence (Balitti and Falk, 2000; Burnett, 2006). In so doing, the value of sport and physical activity may find academic support and meaningfully inform policy formation, programme design and management for, of and in development. Within the domain of management *for* development, managers require core skills required for policy development, design, development of instruments and management of inter-organizational collaboration. For management *in* development change management translatable in psycho-social components, communication and resource management are apparent. At the practice-level, management *of* development relates to operational management, planning, capacity building, empowerment and the monitoring and evaluation of interventions (Girginov, 2008).

Advocating a developmental, conceptual and managerial framework for monitoring and evaluation (Coalter, 2006), the development of an instrument for measuring programme effectiveness (Weese, 1997) and S•DIAT (Sport-in-Development Impact Assessment Tool) are some of the recent contributions that may have value for research and practices in a variety of contexts. As co-designer of the S•DIAT, a brief overview of this tool may demonstrate its potential application for development work.

A Tool for Sport-in-Development Assessment

The conceptual framework for the development of the S•DIAT tapped into merging paradigms and a multi-disciplinary synthesis of an empirically grounded knowledge base of variable- and accounted-centred methodologies within the field of Social Impact Assessment and sports-related texts (Burnett and Uys, 2000).

Two national sport development projects and several studies of the Australia-Africa Community Clubs Initiative (Burnett, 2001) facilitated extensive local consultation for indicator development and the refinement of the Tool to 'measure' sport-related impact (on a grading scale from 'negative' to 'very high') in different contexts and at different levels (from micro-, to meso- and macro-level) (Burnett and Hollander, 2006). Two main indicator bands were developed, namely (i) programme management and delivery; and (ii) human and community development. For both bands, 25 indicators were developed based on 13 corresponding indicator fields to serve as a 'menu' for future selection, adaptation and refinement (Burnett and Hollander, 2006).

Reciprocal agency was ensured by adopting a PART model (Participatory Action Research Training). Local fieldworkers and implementers were trained and capacitated to assist in collecting and interpreting data, as well as prioitizing and determining indicators and benchmarks. In turn, they were assisted to use the findings for strategic planning and proposal development.

A developmental approach suggests that regular monitoring should run in conjunction with impact which is also scheduled to take place during different phases of programme development. This will allow for a pre-post assessment and tracing of change according to process indicators established during the pre-impact phase (Figure 13.2).

Assessment can thus be done at different phases of programme development, as it is premised on a pre-post design which allows for a cyclic process of monitoring and assessment. A time-line design allowed for comparison of baseline (established through a pre-impact study) to benchmark data (established through a post-impact study). Findings can be translated into strengths and weaknesses for strategic planning and for the formulation of new benchmarks and outcomes (Figure 13.3).

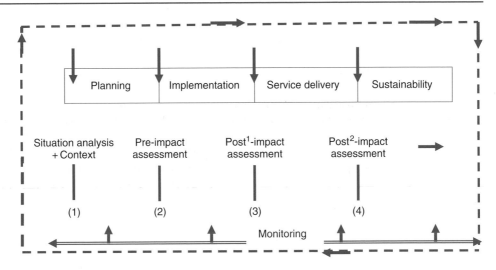

Figure 13.2 The sport development programme cycle.

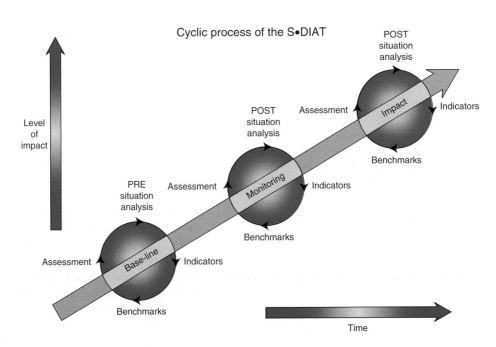

Figure 13.3 Process of the S•DIAT.

To enhance the internal validity and reliability of the research, different groups of research participants and methods were used. These included structured interviews with main stakeholders and questionnaires (programme-related experiences, an HIV/AIDS and self-esteem questionnaire), focus groups and case studies. Purposive sampling of stakeholders, representatives of house-holds, community leaders, presenters or coaches and administrators was followed by randomized sampling of participants according to gender, age and the type of activity.

The integration of management and monitoring, as well as impact assessment according to process indicators necessitated the publication of results for local and academic consumption (Burnett, 2006). The S•DIAT may assist agencies to implement monitoring and evaluation in a development framework by empowering all to ensure optimal service delivery and impact through shared vision and ownership.

Conclusion

The complexity of sport-in-development as a multifaceted phenomenon provides layers of construction and deconstruction – who should be accountable, to whom, for what, when and how? The multi-disciplinary nature, diverse and value-laden discourses pose unique challenges to agents, implementers and scholars. It is a field that represents an emerging body of applied knowledge and implications for articulation between local and global agency and practice. Key measurement issues for managers relate to programme management and delivery with reference to planning, documentation and policies, as well as access to main resources in terms of information, physical, financial and human resources. For policy development and facilitating development initiatives, managers should be able to draw on the results of human and social development indicators (for monitoring) and results (impact assessment) to adjust programme design, indicator development and practices. Monitoring, evaluation and impact assessments that drew on a meta-language for research, strategic, participative management and collaborative implementation may give impetus to an already evolving sport development discourse within a developmental framework.

References

Allen, J.B. (2005). Measuring social motivational orientations in sport: An examination of the construct validity of the SMOSS. *International Journal of Sport & Exercise Psychology*, **3**(2), 147–61.

Arai, S. and Pedlar, A. (2003). Moving beyond individualism in leisure theory: a critical analysis of concepts of community and social engagement. *Leisure Studies*, July, **22**, 185–202.

Balatti, J. and Falk, I. (2002). Socio-economic contributions of adult learning to community: A social capital perspective. *Adult Education Quarterly*, **52**(4), 281–98.

Barrow, C.J. (2000). *Social Impact Assessment. An Introduction*. New York, NY: Oxford University Press.

Begg, D.J., Langley, J.D., Moffitt, T., and Marshall, S.W. (1996). Sport and delinquency: An examination of the deterrence hypothesis in a longitudinal study. *British Journal of Sports Medicine*, **30**, 335–41.

Biddle, S.J.H., Gorley, T., and Stensel, D.J. (2004). Health-enhancing physical activity and sedentary behaviour in children and adolescents. *Journal of Sport Sciences*, **22**, 679–701.

Burnett, C. (2001). Social impact assessment and sports development. Social spin-offs of the Australia – South Africa junior sport programme. *International Review for the Sociology of Sport*, **36**(1), 41–58.

Burnett, C. (2004). *The status of SA Women in Sport & Recreation 1994 to 2004*. Pretoria: South African Sports Commission.

Burnett, C. (2006). Building social capital through an 'Active Community Club'. *International Review or the Sociology of Sport*, **41**(3–4), 283–94.

Burnett, C. and Hollander, W. (2006). *S•DIAT. Manual for Implementers*. Johannesburg: University of Johannesburg.

Burnett, C. and Uys, T. (2000). Sport development impact assessment: Towards a rationale and tool. *S.A. Journal for Research in Sport, Physical Education and Recreation*, **22**(1), 27–40.

Carnduff, S. (2001). *Sport and Recreation for Indigenous Youth in the Northern Territory: Scoping Research Priorities for Health and Social Outcomes*. Darwin: Cooperative Research Centre for Aboriginal and Tropical Health and the Australian Sports Commission.

Cavill, N. and Bauman, A. (2004). Changing the way people think about health-enhancing physical activity: Do mass media campaigns have a role? *Journal of Sports Sciences*, **22**(8), 771–90.

Chapin, T.S. (1999). *Urban Revitalization Tools: Assessing the Impacts of Sports Stadia at the Micro-Area Level*. Eugene, OR: Microform Publications, University of Oregon.

Cingiene, V. and Laskiene, S. (2004). A revitalized dream: Basketball and national identity in Lithuania. *International Journal of the History of Sport*, **21**(5), 762–79.

Coalter, F. (2006). Sport-in-development: Process evaluation and organizational development. In *Sports and Development* (Y. Vanden Auweele, C. Malcolm, and B. Meulders, eds). Leuven: LannooCampus, pp. 149–63.

Coalter, F., Allison, M., and Taylor, J. (2000). *The Role of Sport in Regenerating Deprived Urban Areas*. Edinburgh: The Scottish Executive Central Research Unit.

Cooperative Research Centre for Aboriginal and Tropical Health (2002). *Indigenous Sport and Recreation Indicators Project*. Unpublished report. Darwin, Northern Territory Australia: Project Reference Group Meeting.

Crompton, J.L. (1995). Economic impact analysis of sports facilities and events; eleven sources of misapplication. *Journal of Sport Management*, **9**(1), 14–35.

Cunningham, J. and Beneforti, M. (2005). Investigating indicators for measuring health and social impact of sport and recreation programs in Australian Indigenous Communities. *International Review for the Sociology of Sport*, **40**(10), 89–98.

Dermody, M.B., Taylor, S.L., and Lomanno, M.V. (2003). The impact of NFL games on lodging industry revenue. *Journal of Travel & Tourism Marketing*, **14**(1), 21–36.

Diana, A. (2000). *Youth at Play: Preventing Youth Problem Behaviour Through Sport and Recreation*. Eugene, OR: Microform Publications, University of Oregon.

Dobosz, R.P. and Beaty, L.A. (1999). The relationship between athletic participation and high school students' leadership ability. *Adolescence*, **34**(133), 215–20.

Eley, D. and Kirk, D. (2002). Developing citizenship through sport: The impact of a sport-based volunteer programme on young leaders. *Sport, Education & Society*, **7**(2), 151–66.

Farrell, L. and Shields, M.A. (2004). Playing sport and feeling healthy: Evidence from the Health Education Monitoring Study. Retrieved on 18 August from http://sss. sportengland.org/vosm/document_63.

Farrell, W.C., Johnson, J.H., Sapp, M. et al. (1996). Redirecting the lives of urban black males: An assessment of Milwaukee's midnight basketball league. *Journal of Community Practice*, **2**(4), 91–107.

Fox, K.R. (2000). The effects of exercise on self-perceptions and self-esteem. In *Physical Activity and Psychological WellBeing* (S.J.H. Biddle, K.R. Fox, and S.H. Boutcher, eds). London: Routledge, pp. 88–117.

Gahin, R. and Paterson, C. (2001). Community indicators: Past, present, and future. *National Civic Review*, **90**(4), 347–60.

Giddens, A. (2000). *Runaway World. How Globalisation is Reshaping Our Lives.* London: Profile Books.

Girginov, V. (2008). Management of sports development: Visions, processes and practices. In *Management of Sports Development* (V. Girginov, ed.). Oxford: Butterworth-Heinemann.

Glover, T.D. (2004). The 'community' center and the social construction of citizenship. *Leisure Sciences*, **26**, 63–83.

Gore, J. (1993). *The Struggle for Pedagogies: Critical and Feminist Discourses as Regimes of Truth.* London: Routledge.

Gratton, C., Dobson, N., and Shibili, S. (2000). The economic importance of major sports events: A case-study of six events. *Managing Leisure*, **5**, 17–28.

Hartmann, D. and Brooks, D. (2006). Rethinking sports-based community crime prevention. A preliminary analysis of the relation between midnight basketball and urban crime rates. *Journal of Sport and Social Issues*, **30**(2), 180–96.

Heere, B. and James, J.D. (2007). Sports teams and their communities: Examining the influence of external group identities on team identity. *Journal of Sport Management*, **21**(3), 319–37.

Hemana, C. (2007). Active after-school communities: Programme evaluation. *Active & Healthy Magazine*, **13**(4), 14.

Ife, J. (1999). *Community Development: Creative Community Alternatives – Vision, Analysis and Practice.* South Melbourne, Australia: Addison-Wesley Longman.

Jarvie, G. (2003). Communitarianism, sport and social capital. 'Neighbourly insights into Scottish Sport'. *International Review for the Sociology of Sport*, **38**(2), 139–53.

Jarvie, G. and Maguire, J.A. (1994). *Sport and Leisure in Social Thought.* London: Routledge.

Kanters, M.A., Carter, D., and Pearson, B. (2001). A community-based model for assessing the economic impact of sport and recreation services. *Journal of Park & Recreation Administration*, **19**(2), 43–61.

Kirk, D. and MacPhail, A. (2003). Social positioning and the construction of a youth sports club. *International Review for the Sociology of Sport*, **38**, 23–44.

Kirsten, L., Patriksson, G., and Fridlund, B. (2003). Parents' conceptions of the influence of participation in a sports programme on their children and adolescents with physical disabilities. *European Physical Education Review*, **9**(1), 23–41.

Langbein, L. and Bess, R. (2002). Sports in school: Source of amity or antipathy? *Social Science Quarterly*, **83**(2), 436–54.

Lawson, H.A. (2005). Empowering people, facilitating community development, and contributing to sustainable development: The social work of sport, exercise, and physical education. *Sport, Education and Society*, **10**(1), 135–60.

Madden, J. and Crowe, M. (2004). *Economic Impact of the Sydney Olympic Games.* Research and Information Paper. University of Tasmania, Office of Financial Management: NSW Treasury and The Centre for Regional Economic Analysis; 1997.

Maguire, J. (2006). Development through sports science and sports industrial complex: The case of human development in sports and exercise sciences. In *Sports and Development* (Y. Vanden Auweele, C. Malcolm, and B. Meulders, eds). Leuven: Lannoo-Campus, pp. 107–22.

Mangan, A. (ed.). (2002). Making European masculinities: Sport, Europe, gender. *The European Sports History Review*, Vol. 2. London: Frank Cass.

Miller, K.E., Sabo, D.F., Melnick, M.J. et al. (2000). *The Women's Sports Foundation Report: Health Risks and Teen Athletes.* East Meadow, New York: Women's Sports Foundation.

Nicholl, J.P., Coleman, P., and Brazier, J.E. (2004). Health and healthcare costs and the benefits of exercise. *PharmacoEconomics*, **5**(2), 109–22.

Nichols, G. (2004). Crime and punishment and sports development. *Leisure Studies*, **23**(2), 177–94.

Payne, W., Reynolds, M., Brown, S., and Fleming, A. (2003). *Sports Role Models and Their Impact on Participation in Physical Activity: A Literature Review*. Victoria: VicHealth.

Pedlar, A. (1996). Community development: What does it mean for recreation and leisure? *Journal of Applied Recreation Research*, **21**(1), 5–23.

Pitter, R. and Andrews, D.L. (1997). Serving America's underserved youth: Reflections on sport and recreation in an emerging social problems industry. *Quest*, **49**(1), 85–99.

Sage, G. (1999). Justice do it! The Nike transnational advocacy network: Organization, collective actions, and outcomes. *Sociology of Sport Journal*, **16**, 206–35.

Shuttleworth, J. and Wan-Ka, C. (1998). Youth sport education and development in Hong Kong: A conflict model social impact assessment. *Sport, Education and Society*, **3**(1), 37–58.

Smith, A.L. (2003). Peer relationships in physical activity contexts: A road less travelled in youth sport and exercise psychology research. *Psychology of Sport and Exercise*, **4**, 25–39.

Sport England (2007). Retrieved on 8 August from http://www.sportengland.org./vosm/vosm.htm.

Sugden, J. (2006). Teaching and playing sport for conflict resolution and co-existence in Israel. *International Review for the Sociology of Sport*, **41**(2), 221–48.

UNICEF (2006). *Monitoring and Evaluation of Sports-Based Programming for Development*. Workshop Report 31 January–2 February 2005. New York, NY: UNICEF.

United Nations (2003). *Sport for Development and Peace: Towards Achieving the Millennium Development Goals*. Report from the Inter-Agency Task Force on Sport for Development and Peace.

United Nations (2005). Toolkit sport for development. Retrieved on 28 April from http://draftoolkitsportfordevelopment.vankempensonsultancy.com/html.

United Nations (2006). Updates on UN sport-related activities supporting efforts to achieve the Millennium Development Goals and promote peace. Number 21. Retrieved on 17 July from www.un.org/sport2005.

Uwakwe, C.B.U. (2001). Integration HIV/AIDS education and prevention for reproductive age women in community-oriented family planning program in South-Eastern Nigeria. *Journal of the International council for Health, Physical Education, Recreation, Sport & Dance*, **37**(1), 52–5.

Vanden Auweele, Y., Malcolm, C., and Meulders, B. (eds). (2006). *Sport and Development*. Leuven: LannooCampus.

Weese, W.J. (1997). The development of an instrument to measure effectiveness to campus recreation programs. *Journal of Sport Management*, **11**, 263–74.

Wright, P., Harwell, R., and Allen, L. (1998). Programs that work. Project STRIDE: A unique summer intervention program for youth-at-risk. *Journal of Park and Recreation Administration*, **16**(1), 97–113.

CHAPTER 14

Managing Visions, Changes and Delivery in Sports Development: Summary and Prospects

Vassil Girginov

Introduction

This volume conceptualised the management of sports development as being concerned with three interrelated meanings including a vision, process of social change and delivery. As a vision (macro level), the focus of management was *for* sports development aimed at progressive and sustainable change. The main function of management was one of setting policy visions about the role of sport in society, focusing on establishing frameworks and policy instruments in the field to be promoted locally, nationally or internationally. Considered as a social change, the role of management was realised *in* the context of a sports development process. Particular importance was given to the framing of change, which always unfolds simultaneously at social, community and individual levels, and that there is a complex interplay between them. Management at this level (meso) concerned the engineering strategies for using sport to affect wider changes in society. When conceived as delivery, management became *of* sports development and was concerned with the planning and outcomes of various interventions. The practice of development at this level (micro) consisted of operations and individual associations (communities, clubs, leisure/sport centres or teams) and directly affects the daily lives of people.

The 12 contributions in this volume further unpacked the three meanings of the management of sports development and both provided support for its conceptualisation and revealed new uncharted aspects. The purpose of this concluding chapter is to re-examine the conceptualisation of the management of sports development and to suggest ideas for future research, teaching and practice.

Management *for* Sports Development as a Holistic Process

As Hylton and Bramham, Collins, Green and Beacom and Levermore demonstrated, visions of sports development do matter. This is because visions expressed through various policies, statements, strategies and programmes inform practice and push sports development workers towards particular forms of interventions and outcomes evaluation. Visions of sports development, however, are not based on a unitary logic. Some visions tend to follow a linear causal thinking which solves problems either through control of the processes that lead to the problem (e.g. provision of sport to prevent juvenile crime) or through removing the problem after it occurs (e.g. tackling obesity). A similar thinking assumes that the problem is well bounded, clearly defined and follows the cause and effect logic (cf. Hjorth and Bagheri, 2005). Coalter (2007) questioned this line of reasoning of the British government in sport as inconclusive and based on weak evidence. Other visions acknowledge the complexity of the sports development project and promote a more holistic approach. System thinking implies a holistic approach to sports development and that change in one part of the system triggers changes all over the whole. For example, Sport England (2004, p. 6) delivery plan identified a clear national objective 'to increase by 3% the number who engage in at least 30 minutes of moderate intensity level' and put in place a long-term strategy until 2020. This includes a methodology designed to translate the vision into practice and a number of capacity and infrastructure-building activities and partnerships to support the delivery process.

Under closer examination Sport England's Delivery Plan (2004) reveals a combination of assumptions and predictions which are indicative of linear and system thinking. Assumptions imply more system thinking and are about possibilities, as expressed both in the funding available and future financial allocations for sport. Predictions follow a linear logic and concern probabilities which are manifested in setting specific future scenarios, as in the case of London's ambition to get 60 670 people per annum participating more in sport between 2007 and 2009. But is it possible to sustain such a change in the number of people in sport over time and the demand it is going to place on the supply system? This is a very hard question to answer because it requires looking ahead, whereas the past is the only guide we have for constructing believable scenarios about the future. As this kind of intended development has never been attempted before we can only speculate about what might happen. This observation urges us to reconsider the nature of the sustainable sports development enterprise.

Drawing from Voss and Kemp (2005) and Bagheri and Hjorth (2007) it is proposed that sustainable sports development is neither a state of the sport system to be increased or decreased nor a static goal or target to be achieved. Sustainable sports development is an ideal and a moving target. The history of any sport organisation will testify to that as it represents an ongoing evolution of ideas, changing organisational forms and performances. Sports development visions therefore represent ideals which come from ethics and values we hold and are essentially a moral enterprise. Those values are indeed non-quantifiable so improvements in our understanding about the social and economic environment in which sports development occurs impact on the goals setting approaches and interventions we choose. The current drive for evidence-based sport policy making in the West supports this argument (Australian Sport Commission, 2005; DCMS, 2002; Sport Canada, 2002). Thus, sports development visions inevitably involve a process of social learning. This renders the management of sustainable sports development as a continuous process aimed at creating value but with an unknown end point. It also places local actors on the central stage, as any meaningful vision about change in individuals, communities and organisations produced by sport has to be derived from local symbols, knowledge and behaviours. The management for sports development, as Hylton and Bramham point out in this book, should engage with social justice as ultimate goal of any vision of development. In pursuing those visions the management for sports development should represent a form of 'thoughtful action' which accounts for underlying political issues and power processes and possesses a clear plan for action at the same time.

Various visions of sports development, as expressed in the policies of public, non-governmental, private and international agencies, create a number of tensions between individual and collective needs, grass-roots and elite level of sport, expectations and outcomes, organisational motivations and participants' culture, domestic and international development agencies and the amateur ethos of NGOs and the governmental push for more professional management. These present sports development managers with a difficult balancing act. Similar to the conceptualisation of sports development as a simultaneous process of destruction and construction, the management for sports development also involves destruction in terms of compromising its developmental orientation (construction) with an insistence on complying with specific functionalist targets and norms (destruction).

Key Processes *in* the Management of Sports Development

The second part of the book considered the management of sports development as a process of social and individual change. The contributions of Green, Parent, Hills and Wainwright and Ansell highlighted a number of key processes in the context of sports development. Six such key processes pertinent to the three levels of change, social, community and individual, and their management implications are briefly considered below.

The first process is of vision setting or getting sports development issues on the political agenda and takes place at international, national and local levels. The resultant changes occur at social, community and personal levels and involve complex negotiations and consultations between a range of actors. From a developmental point of view this process should be bottom up so the needs of those subject to development are properly addressed by various trustees. Vision setting is intrinsically linked to the second process of sports development governance which involves three main forms of social interaction. These include interferences, interplays and interventions and correspond to three modes of governance: self-governance, co-governance and hierarchical governance (Diedhiou, 2007). Interferences take place at the primary, self-help community organisations or voluntary sport clubs level of societal interaction and involve running physical activity classes, coaching, fund-raising activities (see Chapter 12 case study) and relationship building through a number of sports development programmes (Green, Chapter 6). Interplays guide interactions within the co-governance mode and include various forms of collaboration and co-operation, as in the case of county and school sport partnerships (Houlihan and Lindsey, Chapter 11) or between UK Sport and national and international partners (Beacon and Levermore, Chapter 5). Interventions represent formal types of interaction and are designed to exert a degree of control over the behaviour of sports development actors. These include formal government policies (Collins, Chapter 3; Adams, Chapter 10; Wainwright and Ansell, Chapter 9) and international developmental programmes (Beacon and Levermore, Chapter 5; Parent, Chapter 7) with well-defined objectives, rules, procedures and expected outcomes. The management of sports development will involve different sets of considerations and skills at each mode of governance.

The third process concerns the 'UNs' of sports development and involves overcoming a perception of what one is not. The management of sports development then becomes about making underdeveloped sports developed, unsuccessful sport organisations successful, underrepresented age, gender, disability or ethnic groups represented or unethical sport behaviour ethical, and the list looks almost endless. Overcoming those perceptions entails making change at social, community and personal levels. The fourth process has to do with the 'BE-commings' of sports development and involves the construction of personal identities (Hills, Chapter 8) and space and place meaning construction (Wainwright and Ansell, Chapter 9). Here sports development managers have to grapple with a range of complex issues related to gender, sex and culture and to ensure that interventions will facilitate and reinforce positive identities. Equally, as the construction of personal identities takes place within particular spaces and places managers have to project participants' personal experiences within the context of specific time. The important point is that space, place and time are mutually constructive as they bring to the fore the interplay between personal and community/social change and cannot be treated in isolation. Increasingly, sports development managers are expected to pay attention to a fifth process of leveraging the opportunities which the implementation of various global, national and local visions presents. This entails working with a range of non-sport partners in different political and financial environments (Jones, Chapter 12). Sport has been persistently employed by all kind of public, non-profit and commercial organisations to deliver a wide range of development outcomes. Managers therefore have to learn how to best leverage the funding, networking and promotional opportunities which those situations entail (Adams, Chapter 10; Green, Chapter 4). Finally, the sixth process concerns sports development as a cognitive enterprise which incorporates the previous five processes. More specifically, it involves social and personal learning and knowledge creation and management. Indeed, sports development was conceptualised as a moving target, identity and a space construction activity, a set of interactions and perceptions overcoming, all of which depend on learning. Lorentzen (2005, p. 1019) pointed out that 'the social process of learning requires a social environment which encourages knowledge sharing among individuals and groups'. This process is neatly captured by the notion of *ba* which Nonaka and Toyama (2005, p. 428) defined as 'a shared context in motion, in which knowledge is shared, created and utilized'. They asserted that 'the essence of *ba* is the contexts and the meanings that are shared and created through interactions that occur at a specific time and space, rather than a space itself' (2005, p. 428). This attitude to learning clearly presents the management of sports development as a knowledge-creating process where the new knowledge comes from the interactions between sport participants. Green (Chapter 6) vividly illustrates this point by asserting that relationship building and positive experiences are the two central factors that determine the success of sports development programmes. Managers therefore have to be very perceptive and allow learning to take place by valuing all skills that are brought to the table and encourage contributions from all participants (Frisby and Millar, 2002). Moreover, they also have to develop the skills to synthesise the new knowledge so it can be applied in practice where it becomes a source for further knowledge generation. The above six processes are responsible for turning sports development in to a specific language with meaning-generating capacity, which becomes a powerful tool in the repertoire of sports development managers.

Management *of* Sports Development as Delivery

The third part of the book examined the management of sports development as the practice of delivering a multiplicity of visions and interventions. Sports development is not to be reduced to practice and it is important to critically reflect on what has been done in the name of development by various trustees. As Adams demonstrates (Chapter 10) the focus of the management of sports development becomes creating social capital and empowering people. However, managers should question the validity of some sport forms and their capacity to deliver particular outcomes based on the notion of sport as 'self evidently a good thing'. This apparently 'self evidently good' nature of sport, as Green (Chapter 6) argued, is not given but has to be delivered and what really matters for sports development managers is the actual implementation of various programmes. Capacity building and empowerment can be highly politically charged and managers have to avoid getting into the trap of subscribing to the official political line whilst failing to address the underlying power structures and real capacity needs of those concerned.

Much of the sports development delivery is undertaken not by single agencies but by various public, private and voluntary partnerships. From a political and practical point of view, as Houlihan and Lindsey (Chapter 11) sensitise us, this raises the fundamental question of how would we know whether partnerships are a more effective tool of service provision than the alternatives? Here, theory and practice become mutually reinforcing to form what Wallace (1971) calls the 'wheel of science' where inductive and deductive approaches complement each other. This further stresses the need for practitioners and academics to work together with those they try to develop in order to successfully tackle the challenges presented by this form of delivery. The key tasks of management include assuming a leadership role in the partnership, negotiating a shared sense of purpose amongst the partners and utilising delivery mechanisms that result in synergy and curb confusion and competition. All sports development interventions require resources of some kind. The fact that sport makes significant contribution to personal and social well-being does not automatically qualifies it for funding. Increasingly funding has been provided with conditions attached for the delivery of specific outcomes (Green, Chapter 4). In this regard, as Jones (Chapter 12) points out, the management of sports development urges managers to regularly scan the environment for funding beyond the traditional sources ensured by government agencies and national and international sport governing bodies. Careful preparation and establishing the critical success factors becomes a key to greater effectiveness of sports development interventions.

The delivery of sports development will not be complete without an important management role and a set of practical skills concerned with measuring and evaluating the impact of various interventions. These are necessary both in terms of accountability to funding agencies or members and the need to answer the question 'what works and why?' As established, a management of sport with developmental orientation challenges the traditional organisational hierarchies and the notion of managers as the professionals who teach the lay people how to play. As a result, the process of sports development evaluation is also reconsidered to accommodate those new roles and relations between trustees and those being developed. As Burnett (Chapter 13) vividly demonstrates, managers have to engage in a complex process of construction and deconstruction of who should be accountable, to whom, for what, when and how? Once the answers to these questions are established, managers may then concentrate on using specific tools to monitor and evaluate the success of sports development interventions.

Towards a Definition of the Management *of* Sports Development

This book started by defining separately 'sports development' and 'management' before bringing them together in order to better make sense of an emerging academic field and profession (Chapter 1). The management of sports development possesses three interrelated aspects including *normative* (for), which reflects various ideals of development; *analytical* (of) dealing with how the specific tasks involved in different interventions have to be managed; and *process oriented* (in), which presents it not simply as a set of tasks to be performed but an ongoing set of relations. The 12 chapters helped further examine the complexities of this undertaking. Therefore, it would be appropriate at this point to synthesise the new knowledge by repeating the same exercise. Sports development concerns a process of constructing, destructing and maintaining opportunities for people to participate and excel in sport and life. Management is also a process concerned with bringing out the energy that exists naturally within people and involves inspiring and engaging individuals and communities. When those understandings of 'sports development' and 'management' are put together we arrive at a more concise definition. It suggests that the management of sports development is concerned with a process of inspiring and engaging people, while learning and creating opportunities for participation in sport and enhancing personal and social well-being. The book and the associated case studies offer a detailed discussion about the skills needed by managers to successfully perform those tasks. The management of sports development involves a dynamic interaction between visions, processes and practice in which visions are connected to a practical context whereas practice serves as a foundation for sharing experiences produced by those visions. Here ideas, identities, places and actions are mutually reinforcing.

A similar understanding of the management of sports development presents a range of opportunities and challenges for researching, teaching and working in the field. As Nonaka and Toyama (2005, p. 428) observed 'to participate in *ba* means to get involved and transcend one's own limited perspective'. Thus, we may have to reconsider the ontological and epistemological premises on which our research agenda is built. The scientific rationality and the universa-lising powers of the state and the market are no longer sufficient to explain a whole multiplicity of ontologies that organise human experience. In this regard there has been a growing realisation in the sport management commu-nity about the value of action research (Amis and Silk, 2005; Frisby et al., 2005) for generating indigenous knowledge and solutions to sport problems by involving trustees, those being developed and researchers. Due to action researchers' insider roles, they produce unique knowledge which, from a sports development point of view, is seen as an additional resource that can be drawn upon to promote action and social change.

How we teach sports development also needs re-evaluation. As demon-strated, sports development represents a rich content domain including an ever growing number of policy, professional, academic and media publications and which is not well-organised. Some of the typical features of not well-organised knowledge domains include non-uniformity of explanation across the range of issues, non-linearity of explanation and content dependency. Delivering information and transferring it into knowledge in a rich and not well-structured domain, such as sports development, inevitably leads to the loss of information and makes education harder. The traditional approach to sports development education relies on linear media, e.g. textbooks and lec-tures, is teacher-led, offers little feedback to the learner and is informational rather than developmental. The advance of new multimedia technology has transformed the relationship between teachers and learners. As the amount of information that is made available electronically is increasing all the time the notion of the teacher and sports development manager as a repository of knowledge is replaced by the concept of the teacher and manager as an expert guide. This implies introducing new forms of knowledge management in the field where knowledge is jointly created by academics, students, managers and participants. Nonaka and Takeuchi (1995, p. 59) asserted that information is a flow of messages while knowledge is created by that very flow of information, anchored in the beliefs and commitment of its holder. Conceptualising the management of sports development also as a learning process charges aca-demics and professionals working in the field with the responsibility to create epistemic hunger by nurturing communities of sports developers who are eager to inquire, learn and enhance their experiences.

In an attempt to attend to those challenges to researching, teaching and learning in sports development, this book has been complemented by a dedicated website (www.sportsdevelopmentbook.com). Here the reader will find 13 case studies for each chapter in the book as well as a range of questions pertinent to those cases designed to encourage further exploration of the material. The reader will also find the papers delivered by world class experts at the 2008 conference on *'Studying Sports Development: Researching, Teaching and Writing in the Field'* held at Brunel University. These papers were designed to stimulate further ideas for and discussions about researching and teaching in sports development. As well there are other resources including web links, policy documents and research reports and an online discussion forum. In addition, the publisher Elsevier has kindly sponsored a special annual award for the best student essay in the management of sports development. Students world wide are encouraged to submit their papers which will be assessed by an independent panel of reviewers and the best three will be awarded and published.

References

Amis, J. and Silk, M. (2005). Rupture: Promoting critical and innovative approaches to the study of sport management. *Journal of Sport Management*, **19**, 355–66.

Australian Sport Commission (2005). *Strategic Plan 2006–2009*. Canbera: ASC.

Bagheri, A. and Hjorth, P. (2007). Planning for Sustainable Development: a paradigm Shift Towards a Process-Based Approach, *Sustainable Development*, **15**, 83–96.

Coalter, F. (2007). *A Wider Social Role for Sport. Who's Keeping the Score?* London: Routledge.

Department for Culture, Media and Sport/Strategy Unit (DCMS) (2002). *Game Plan: A Strategy for Delivering Government's Sport and Physical Activity Objectives*. London: DCMS/Strategy Unit.

Diedhiou, A. (2007). Governance for development: Understanding the concept/reality linkages. *Journal of Human Development*, **8**(1), 23–38.

Frisby, W. and Millar, S. (2002). The ctualities of doing community development to promote the inclusion of low income population in local sport and recreation. *European Sport Management Quarterly*, **2**, 209–33.

Frisby, W., Colleen, R., Millar, S., and Larena, H. (2005). Putting 'participatory' into participatory forms of action research. *Journal of Sport Management*, **19**(4), 367–86.

Hjorth, P. and Bagheri, A. (2005). Navigating towards sustainable development: A system dynamics approach. *Futures*, **38**(1), 74–92.

Lorentzen, A. (2005). Strategies of learning in the process of transformation. *European Planning Studies*, **13**(7), 1013–33.

Nonaka, I. and Takeuchi, H. (1995). *The Knowledge Creating Company*. Oxford: Oxford University Press.

Nonaka, I. and Toyama, R. (2005). The theory of knowledge-creating firm: Subjectivity, objectivity and synthesis. *Industrial and Corporate Change*, **14**(3), 419–36.

Sport Canada (2002). *The Canadian Sport Policy*. Ottawa: Sport Canada.

Sport England, (2004). *The Framework for Sport in England (including Delivery Plan)*. London: Sport England.

Voss, J.P. and Kemp, R. (2005). Reflective governance for sustainable development. Incorporating feedback in social problem-solving. *Paper* for ESEE Conference, (Lisbon).

Wallace, W. (1971). *The Logic of Science in Sociology*. New York: Aldine.

Andy Adams is a senior lecturer in sports management within Southampton Business School at Southampton Solent University. Andy has presented papers dealing with voluntary sports clubs, politics and policy and has published articles on sports volunteering. He is currently completing his doctoral studies which focus on Social Capital and voluntary sports clubs.

Dr Nicola Ansell teaches human geography at Brunel University. She has published widely on social and cultural change in southern Africa and in particular the geographies of young people and development. She obtained her PhD at Keele University for research looking at gender and power relations in rural southern Africa. She is currently researching the livelihoods of AIDS-affected young people in Malawi and Lesotho.

Dr Aaron Beacom is currently Senior Lecturer and Programme Leader for the MA Applied Sport Development at the University College Plymouth, St Mark & St John. After six years in sport centre management, Aaron returned to education, teaching on a range of sport and management-related programmes. Alongside his teaching, he studied for an MA in European Politics and a PhD in Politics (University of Exeter, 2003) During this period he published two papers in the academic journal *The Sports Historian*. Since completion of this PhD he has developed his research profile in sport and politics. Most recently, delivery of papers relating to sport in international development at three international conferences was followed by the publication of a paper in *European Sport Management Quarterly* (March 2007). Aaron is co-editor of a text entitled *Sport and International Development* which is due for publication in late 2008. Aaron is a keen hill walker and swimmer – open water where possible.

Dr Peter Bramham is an experienced lecturer and researcher who has spent over 30 years in academic life in several Higher Education institutions in the UK. He has published work in conjunction with colleagues in the UK and across Europe and regularly makes conference contributions in the broad 'leisure and sport policy' area. He has served on the Leisure Studies Association (LSA)

National Executive Committee and he acted as Chair of the LSA. He was appointed as a Reader in 2004. Recent publications include 'Habits of a lifetime?: Youth, generation and lifestyles' in P. Bramham and J. Caudwell (eds) *Sport, Active Leisure and Youth Cultures* (2005), with C. Critcher, 'Devil still makes work' in J. Haworth and A.T. Veal (eds) *Work and Leisure Thirty Years On* (2005) and with K. Hylton, *Sports Development: Policy, Process and Practice* (2008).

Cora Burnett is Professor in the Department of Sport and Movement Studies at the University of Johannesburg where she is currently lecturing in the Sociology of Sport and Research Methodology. She has obtained two doctorates, one in Human Movement Studies (PhD) from the University of Stellenbosch and a DLitt et Phil from the Rand Afrikaans University in Social Anthropology. She has published and presented widely including 10 international keynotes in the last three years. Since 1997 she specialised in impact studies and has since authored or co-authored 16 research reports. In collaboration with Prof. Wim Hollander she developed the Sport-in-Development-Impact-Assessment-Tool (S•DIAT) which received the 2007 SIRC (Sport Research Intelligence Sportive) Africa Research Award. The Tool was developed over a decade, based on 70 local, national and international case studies. It is in the process of being patented and 100 implementers have been trained at grassroots level in South Africa.

Mike Collins has had a career as a human geographer, town and transport planner and then 32 years in sports research and planning, first at the Sports Council where he managed over 500 projects and was heavily involved in the Council of Europe and in planning policy. Then at Loughborough his research was in the impacts of sport in town and country, sports development, sport and social exclusion (book of that title; 2003 Routledge), and social capital. At the University of Gloucestershire in semi-retirement he is bringing together his interests in sports and in religion in new courses and research.

Dr Vassil Girginov is Reader in Sport Management/Development in the School of Sport and Education at Brunel University, West London. He has taught at the National Sports Academy in Sofia, Bulgaria, the University of Luton, England and the University of Windsor, Canada. His research interests and publications (including five books) are in the fields of sports development, comparative management, policy analysis, the Olympic movement and Eastern European sport. Vassil Girginov is currently working on two projects concerning the relationship between the culture of national sport organisation and participation in sport and the process of constructing sporting legacy in relation to the 2012 London Olympic Games.

Dr B. Christine Green is Associate Professor in the Department of Kinesiology and Health Education at The University of Texas at Austin. She holds the Judy Spence Tate Fellowship for Excellence and serves as the Director of the University of Texas Sport Development Lab. Her research focuses on sport development and the marketing of sport events. It has appeared in leading tourism, leisure and sport journals and has been funded in four countries. She is a member of the editorial board of three journals in the field and currently serves as Editor of *Sport Management Review* and an Associate Editor of the *Journal of Sport & Tourism*. Green was elected a Research Fellow of the North American Society of Sport Management in 2005.

Dr Mick Green is Lecturer in Sport and Leisure Policy and Management in the School of Sport and Exercise Sciences at Loughborough University. He has published widely on British sports policy, including elite sport development, school sport and physical education, sport for all and the 'modernisation' of British sport under a New Labour Government. He has also published research on developments in elite sport systems and policy change in different countries.

Dr Laura Hills is course leader for the BA Youth Sport Work at Brunel University. Her research and teaching centres on gender, physicality and identity in the context of youth sport and leisure cultures. Her recent publications have focused on social and embodied aspects of girls' physical education experiences and gender, class and body in mediated sport. She is currently working on a book on sports media and, as a US citizen living in the UK, sustains an interest in cross-cultural comparisons of mediated sport.

Barrie Houlihan is Professor of Sport Policy in the Institute of Sport and Leisure Policy at Loughborough University, UK. He has written widely on many aspects of sports policy including doping, sports development, the diplomatic use of sport, theorising the sport policy process and sport and young people.

Dr Kevin Hylton co-edited the first substantive text on sports development in 2001 for Routledge *Sports Development: Policy, Process and Practice*, which has now been revised for a 2nd edition (Hylton and Bramham, 2008). Kevin has been conferred as a Visiting Fellow at the University of Leeds having won a Promising Researcher Fellowship sabbatical at Leeds Met (2006/7). He is currently writing *Critical Race Theory and Sport* (Routledge). Kevin has recently been made an Associate of the Higher Education Association's Centre for Sociology, Anthropology and Politics (C-SAP). Kevin's research interests are focused upon 'race', antiracism, inclusion/exclusion and community sports development. Recent publications include Hylton, K. (2005), 'Race', Sport and Leisure: Lessons from Critical Race Theory *Leisure Studies*; Hylton, K., Long, J., and Flintoff, A. (2005) *Evaluating Sport and Active Leisure for Young People* and Hylton, K. (forthcoming 2008) *Critical Race Theory and Sport*, Routledge.

Dr Ian Jones is Associate Dean for Sport and Leisure and Acting Director of the Centre for Event and Sport Research (CESR), based in the School of Services Management at Bournemouth University. His research interests have continued to focus upon the relationships between sporting identities, participation and the concept of 'serious leisure'. His main teaching areas lie in the areas of sport sociology and research methods for sport and leisure. He is co-author of *Research Methods for Sport Studies* and co-editor of both *Leisure Cultures: Investigations in Media, Technology and Sport* and *Serious*

Leisure: Extensions and Applications. Ian is also a member of the Editorial Advisory Boards for the *Journal of Sport & Tourism* and the *Journal of Hospitality, Leisure, Sport and Tourism Education*.

Dr Roger Levermore is Lecturer in International Development at the University of Liverpool Management School. He is also a member of the Football Industry Group that focuses on the socio-economic impact of the football industry and offers an MBA programme. He teaches and researches on dimensions of international development, especially in relation to the role of sport and business in stimulating development assistance. He edited the 2004 book on sport and international relations and is co-author with Aaron of *Sport and International Development* which is due for publication in late 2008. Roger is a keen follower of Cameroon and Norwich in football.

Dr Iain Lindsey is Lecturer in Sport and Physical Activity at the University of Southampton. After undertaking a Masters Degree in Sports Development at the University of Gloucestershire, he worked for 3½ years with the Youth Sport Development Project in Dundee. This project sought to develop sport in four Social Inclusion Partnership areas of Dundee as well as utilise sport as a tool for social inclusion. Iain joined the Institute of Youth Sport at Loughborough University in 2003. He primarily worked on the large-scale national evaluation of the New Opportunities for PE and Sport programme funded by the Big Lottery Fund. Iain was also involved in other research work on the Cricket Foundation's Chance to Shine programme and on sports organisations in Zambia that utilise sport as a context to deliver education on HIV and AIDS. While at Loughborough, Iain studied part time for a PhD that examined partnership working across PE, school and community sport in local authorities.

Dr Milena M. Parent is Assistant Professor in the School of Human Kinetics at the University of Ottawa. Her research focuses on organising committees and stakeholders of major sporting events such as the Olympic Games, Pan American Games, the *Jeux de la Francophonie* and FINA World Aquatics Championships. Her areas of expertise are organisation theory and strategic management. She has published in the *Journal of Sport Management*, *European Sport Management Quarterly* and the *International Journal of Sport Finance*. Her research has been featured at various conferences, including the *North American Society for Sport Management* conference, the *Administrative Sciences Association of Canada* conference, the *Academy of Management* conference and a keynote address at the 2nd World Congress in Sport Management.

Dr Emma Wainwright teaches urban and social geography at Brunel University. She completed her first degree at the University of Aberdeen and her PhD at the University of St Andrews. She has published widely on her doctoral and subsequent research exploring the historical and social geographies of women, work and the welfare state. Running through her research interests is a focus on the social geography of cities and she is currently working on a project exploring the role of tourist guides in the construction of city knowledges, identities and landscapes.